TEXAS
Life and Health Insurance

License Exam Prep
Updated Yearly

Study Guide Includes State Law Supplement and 3 Complete Practice Tests

Previously published under ISBN 9781521120118 as *(2020 Edition) Texas Life, Accident and Health Insurance Agent License Exam Study Guide with 3 Complete Practice Exams: General Lines – Life, Accident, Health and Annuities*

Leland Chant

This edition contains the most thorough and accurate information available at printing time. Due to the dynamic nature of insurance licensing, examination content outlines constantly change, and this edition may not feature this new or revised content.

This study guide provides complete and reliable information regarding the covered subject matter. The publisher does not provide accounting, legal, or other professional services. If such assistance is required, seek the services of a competent professional.

If you find errors or incorrect information in this publication or have any questions or comments, please email us at brightideapublishers@gmail.com.

CONTENTS

INTRODUCTION

Thank you for choosing Bright Idea Publishers. You are preparing to pass the Texas Life and Health Insurance license exam using the content found in this book. We've developed our state-specific prep books based on the exam content outlines published by testing providers in each state (e.g., Pearson VUE, PSI Exams, Prometric). Leland Chant, who has over two decades of experience in the insurance industry, provides the most up-to-date information and educates test-takers in a streamlined manner Our goal is to prepare you for the exam and help you pass the test on the first attempt.

Study Pointers

- The author presents the information in each chapter based on the exam subject matter outlines provided by the state of Texas. This material covers only the information you need to learn for the exam.
- Be sure to take notes. This best practice will help you be proactive and engage in the learning process to solidify these insurance concepts.
- Create an outline or "hint" sheet. This best practice will help you complete a full review at the end of each chapter or the end of the book.
- Review the Exam Index section to identify how each chapter corresponds to the licensing exam. Test questions are associated with each chapter to help you focus your study efforts accordingly.
- If you've been studying hard and feel like you're struggling to retain information, taking a few days off can help you recharge your mind and come back to your studies with a fresh perspective.
- Keep the information fresh by studying until the day of your exam. When you cannot take the exam immediately after finishing the book, you should begin the study and review process again. It is always better to delay taking the exam than to be unprepared.
- Practice exam answers include the page number to the corresponding section of the book. This feature will help streamline the studying process!

Test Taking Pointers

- Get a whole night's sleep, and don't study right before taking the exam. This best practice will allow you to be well-rested and alert when you arrive at the testing center.
- Carefully read the test tutorial and follow the instructions. Depending on your state, test providers may divide the exam into multiple parts. In these cases, you cannot review your answers after completing the section.
- Be calm and feel at ease. Breathe deeply and remember it is just an exam. If you prepare, the correct answers will become clear if you put in the time.
- Read every question and all the answer choices carefully, but do so quickly. Try not to linger on any one question.
- If a particular question stumps you, you can mark it for review and move on to the next question. Sometimes you may answer a question later in the exam, which may jog your memory.
- Answer every question!
- Try to understand what the question is asking. Don't allow unfamiliar terms to throw you off since test builders mostly use them as examples or distracters. Read the question multiple times if necessary.
- Rule out incorrect answers. Each answer you exclude increases your chance of selecting the correct one.
- Trust your first answer. If you studied thoroughly, you know the material. Listen to your gut instinct and try not to overthink the question.
- Keywords such as NEVER, ALWAYS, EVERY, EXCEPT, ALL, or NOT may change the meaning of a question. Be sure to pay extra attention to them.
- Every question is multiple choice, and they are commonly either direct questions, incomplete sentences, or "all of the following EXCEPT."
- Remember that being a little nervous is not a bad thing. Most people perform better when they know the heat is on.
- Most importantly, RELAX! If you put in the work and if you put in the time, the results will be there.

Setting Expectations

Before taking your state exam, you must know the material and be familiar with testing procedures and the testing center environment.

Each state provides a candidate handbook or bulletin containing important information about specific testing procedures:

- Scheduling or rescheduling exams;
- Required identification;
- Arriving at the testing center; and
- Items prohibited in the testing center.

Test-takers should read the candidate handbook in preparation for their exam. This handbook is on the Texas Department of Insurance (TDI) website and their state testing provider's (Pearson VUE) website.

The Exam	• It will test your knowledge and include questions about various concepts and laws. • Test questions are designed to evaluate your basic understanding and retention of the material in this book. • Verify specific forms of identification required for your state exam by reviewing the candidate's handbook or bulletin or calling the testing center.
The Testing Center	• Be sure to arrive at least 30 minutes before your scheduled exam. • You cannot take personal items like cell phones or study materials into the testing center. Some testing centers will provide lockers. • Food, drinks, or gum are prohibited inside the testing center. • Have your identification ready when you check in at the front desk. • Adjust the seat height and computer monitor as needed to feel comfortable. • Before beginning a computer-based exam, you will have a chance to take a tutorial to help you learn how to mark and review answers. • Remain focused and do not get distracted by others around you. Other test-takers may enter and leave the room while taking your exam.
Taking the Exam	• Most testing centers will provide scratch paper and a pencil to write down challenging questions during the exam. • When you review marked questions, go over the rest of the questions to ensure you didn't overlook any familiar concepts or terms that change what the question is asking.

Exam Index

The Exam Index will help you focus your studies. All three practice tests include a breakdown of the number of questions attributed to each chapter. Concentrating your efforts will most certainly benefit you when taking the actual exam.

General Lines – Life, Accident & Health - English
InsTX-LAH05
145 Questions (130 scoreable plus 15 pretest)
Time Limit: 2 hours 30 minutes
Passing Score: 70

GENERAL KNOWLEDGE *(100 scoreable questions plus 10 pretest questions)*	% of Exam
Completing the Application, Underwriting, and Policy Delivery	9%
Types of Life Policies	12%
Life Policy Riders, Provisions, Options, and Exclusions	12%
Taxes, Retirement, and Other Insurance Concepts	6%
Field Underwriting Practices	6%
Types of Health Policies	12%
Health Policy Provisions, Clauses, and Riders	11%
Social Insurance Health Insurance Policies	5%
Other Health Insurance Concepts	4%
STATE SPECIFIC CONTENT *(30 scoreable questions plus 5 pretest questions)*	
Texas Statutes and Rules Common to Life and Health Insurance	11%
Texas Statutes and Rules Pertinent to Life Insurance Only	5%
Texas Statutes and Rules Pertinent to Accident and Health Insurance Only	5%
Texas Statutes and Rules Pertinent to Health Maintenance Organizations (HMOs)	2%

TDI (in coordination with Pearson VUE) established an exam's passing score after completing an in-depth study for each exam. Raw scores are converted to scaled scores ranging from 0 to 100. The scaled score you receive is neither the number of questions answered correctly nor the percentage of questions correctly answered. A passing score is 70. Any score below 70 demonstrates how close you came to passing. The exam score is not based on each portion separately but on each exam as a whole.

CHAPTER 1:

Completing the Application, Underwriting, and Delivering the Policy

Effective underwriting is a journey of accurately and illustratively applying potential risks to an insurer. This chapter is your guide, focusing on the producer's central role as a field underwriter. The first chapter takes you through the specific steps of the application process, from completing the application to delivering the policy. More than that, this chapter is the starting point of your learning journey into insurance concepts, paving the way for you to master the rest of the content in this book. By the end of this chapter, you will be well-versed in the following:

- Contract Law
- Completing the Application
- Underwriting
- Delivering the Policy
- USA Patriot Act and Anti-Money Laundering

Contract Law

A *contract* is an agreement between two or more parties designed to be enforceable by law. Insurance transactions have unique aspects; therefore, the general definition of contracts needs to be modified to meet specific insurance needs.

Elements of a Legal Contract

Insurance contracts are legally binding, and they all contain four essential elements:

- Agreement (Offer and Acceptance);
- Consideration;
- Competent parties; and
- Legal Purpose.

Offer and Acceptance – One party must make a definite offer, which the other party must accept in its exact terms. In the case of insurance, the applicant usually makes the *offer* when applying. *Acceptance* occurs when an insurance provider's underwriter approves the application and issues a policy.

Consideration – The binding force in any contract is known as *consideration*. Consideration occurs when each party gives something of value to the other. The consideration on the insured's part is the premium payment and the representations provided in the application. The consideration on the insurance provider's part is the promise to pay if a loss occurs.

Competent Parties – In the eyes of the law, the *parties to a contract* must be able to enter into a contract willfully. Usually, this requires that both parties be mentally competent to comprehend the contract, of legal age, and not under the influence of alcohol or drugs.

Legal Purpose – The contract must have a *legal* purpose and not be against public policy. For example, to ensure the legal purpose of a life insurance policy, it must have both insurable interest and consent. A contract or agreement that does not have a legal purpose is considered void and is not enforceable by any party.

Distinct Characteristics of an Insurance Contract

Insurance *transfers* the risk of loss from a person or business entity to an insurance provider, spreading the costs of unforeseen losses to many individuals. If an insurance apparatus does not exist, the loss expense would be absorbed solely by the person who sustained the loss.

Contract of Adhesion – One of the parties to the agreement (the insurer) drafts a *contract of adhesion*. The other party (the insured) either accepts or rejects it. Insurance companies do not write policies through contract negotiations; an insured has no input regarding its provisions. Insurers also offer contracts on a "take it or leave it" basis.

Aleatory Contract – Insurance contracts are *aleatory*. In other words, the parties to the agreement are involved in an unequal exchange of amounts or values. Premiums paid by the insured are small compared to the amount the insurance provider will pay in a loss.

Example of Life and Health Insurance – Chad purchases a life insurance policy for $50,000. His monthly premium is $50. If Chad only had the policy for two months, he would have paid only $100 in insurance premiums. If he unexpectedly dies, his beneficiary will receive $50,000. A $100 contribution on the insured's part in exchange for a $50,000 benefit from the insurance provider illustrates an aleatory contract.

Example of Property and Casualty Insurance – Karen purchases a homeowner's insurance policy for $50,000. Her monthly premium is $50. If Karen only had the policy for two months, she only paid $100 in insurance premiums. If a covered peril unexpectedly destroyed the home, Karen would receive $50,000. A $100 contribution on the insured's part in exchange for a $50,000 benefit from the insurance provider demonstrates an aleatory contract.

Unilateral Contract – In a *unilateral contract*, only one of the parties to the agreement must act according to the law. The insured makes no lawfully binding promises. Regardless, an insurance carrier must legally pay for losses covered by an in-force policy.

Conditional Contract – Before each party fulfills its obligations, a *conditional contract requires that the policy owner and insurance company* meet certain conditions to execute the agreement. For the insurer to cover a claim, the policy owner must pay the premium and provide proof of loss.

Representations and Warranties

Warranty – A *warranty* is an utterly true statement upon which the credibility of an insurance policy ultimately hinges. Breaches of a warranty are grounds for voiding the policy or a return of premium. Because of such an exact definition, statements made by applicants for life and health insurance policies, for instance, are typically not considered warranties, except when fraud occurs.

Representations and Misrepresentations – *Representations* are statements believed to be accurate and true to the best of one's knowledge; however, they are not guaranteed to be true. For insurance purposes, representations are the answers an insured provides to the questions on an insurance application.

Untrue statements on an insurance application are *misrepresentations* and can void the contract. A *material misrepresentation* is a statement that would modify the insurer's underwriting decision if discovered. Additionally, if material misrepresentations are *intentional*, they are considered fraudulent.

Completing the Application

The *application* is the building block and primary source of information the insurance company uses during the risk selection process. Although applications are not uniform and can vary from one insurance provider to another, they all contain the same essential elements.

Part 1 - General Information – *Part 1 - General Information* of the application includes general questions about the applicant, such as name, age, gender, birth date, address, marital status, occupation, and income. It will also inquire about existing policies and whether the proposed insurance will replace them. Part 1 identifies the policy type and the coverage amount and typically contains information regarding the beneficiary.

Part 2 - Medical Information – *Part 2 - Medical Information* of the application includes information regarding the proposed insured's medical history, present health condition, any medical visits in recent years, the medical status of living relatives, and the causes of death of deceased relatives. If the insurance amount is relatively small, the agent and the prospective insured will complete all the medical information, making it a nonmedical application. The insurance provider generally requires a medical exam for more significant insurance amounts.

The agent's (or producer's) responsibility is to ensure that the application is completed correctly, completely, and to the best of the applicant's knowledge. The agent must probe beyond the stated questions in the application if they have a reason to believe the applicant is concealing or misrepresenting information. Agents must also be able to help applicants who do not understand specific questions. Any inaccurate, misleading, or illegible information might delay the issuance of the policy. If the producer suspects there could be some misrepresentation, they *must notify the insurer*. Some insurance companies require that the applicant complete the application within the agent's presence. In contrast, other insurers require that the agent fill out the application to help avoid unanswered questions and mistakes.

The agent serves as the front line for an insurance provider and is referred to as a field underwriter because the agent is typically the one who has solicited the proposed insured. As a field underwriter, the agent has several essential responsibilities to fulfill during the process of underwriting and beyond, including:

- Preventing adverse selection;
- Properly soliciting prospective applicants;
- Completing the application;
- Obtaining required signatures;
- Collecting the initial premium and, if applicable, issuing the receipt; and
- Delivering the policy.

As a field underwriter, the agent is considered the most critical information source available to the insurance provider's underwriters. The agent's report provides an insurer with personal observations regarding the proposed insured. Although it is not included in the entire contract, it is a crucial part of the application process.

Required Signatures

Both the producer and the prospective insured, who is typically the applicant, must sign the application. The proposed insured and the policy owner do not have to be the same person. It can also be a business purchasing insurance for an employee. In that case, the policy owner must also sign the application. An exception to the prospective insured signing the application would be an adult, as a parent or guardian, applying for an insurance policy on a minor child.

Changes in the Application

When an application correction is required, agents can update the incorrect information and have the applicant initial the change or complete a fresh new application. An agent should never erase or use white-out to delete any information on an insurance application.

Consequences of Incomplete Applications

Before a policy can be issued, the applicant must answer each question on the application. If the insurance provider receives an incomplete application, they must return it to the applicant for completion. When an insurer issues a policy with unanswered questions, the contract is issued as if the insurance provider surrendered or waived its right to have an answer to the question. In other words, the insurance provider cannot deny coverage based on any information that the unanswered question might have included.

Collecting the Initial Premium and Issuing the Receipt

Most insurance agents will try to collect the initial premium and submit it along with the application to the insurance provider. Receiving the initial premium payment at the time of the application increases the likelihood that the applicant will accept the policy once it is issued. The agent must issue a *premium receipt* whenever the agent collects a premium. The type of receipt issued to the insured will determine when coverage becomes effective.

The most common type of receipt is a *conditional receipt*. Agents provide this receipt when the applicant turns in a prepaid application. The conditional receipt stipulates that coverage becomes effective on the application date or the date of the medical examination, whichever occurs last, provided that the applicant is insurable as a standard risk. The insurer issues the policy to the applicant per the application. This rule will not apply if the applicant declines a policy or if the policy is rated or issued with riders excluding specific coverages.

Example 1.1 – An agent or producer collects the initial premium from an applicant and provides the applicant with a conditional receipt. When the applicant dies the following day, the underwriting process will continue as though the applicant were still alive. If the insurance provider approves the coverage, the applicant's beneficiary will receive the policy's death benefit. On the other hand, if the insurance provider concludes that the applicant is not an acceptable risk and declines the coverage, the premium is refunded to the beneficiary. The insurance provider does not have to pay the death benefit.

Replacement

Replacement means terminating an existing policy or allowing it to lapse, and obtaining a new one. Producers must ensure that replacing insurance is appropriate and in the policyholder's best interest. Agents and insurers must take special underwriting measures to help policyholders make educated and informed decisions.

Underwriting

Underwriting is the process of risk selection and classification. It involves carefully analyzing many factors to conclude the insurance applicant's acceptability. In particular, underwriting is when an insurer determines whether or not an applicant is insurable and, if so, what premium to charge them.

Insurable Interest

To buy insurance, the policyholder must face the possibility of losing money or something of value in the event of a loss. This potential for loss is known as *insurable interest*. In life insurance, an insurable interest exists between the policy owner and the insured at the time of application. However, once the insurance provider has issued a life insurance policy, they must pay the policy benefit whether or not an insurable interest exists.

A valid insurable interest exists between the policy owner and the insured when the policy insures:

1. The policy owner's own life;
2. The life of a family member, such as a close blood relative or a spouse; or
3. A key employee's life, a business partner's life, or someone with a financial responsibility to the policyholder, such as the debtor to a creditor.

It is important to note that beneficiaries do not require an insurable interest. Since the beneficiary's well-being depends on the policy owner and the beneficiary's life is not insured, the beneficiary does not have to show an insurable interest when purchasing a policy.

Sources of Underwriting Information

The insurance provider must obtain the applicant's medical history and background information to select and classify an insurance risk correctly. Several sources of underwriting information are available to those who underwrite insurance policies.

Application – The individual applying for insurance must ask the insurance company for approval before issuing a policy. The *application* is one of the insurer's primary sources of underwriting information.

Agent's Report – The *agent's report* allows the agent to correspond with the underwriter and provide them with information about the applicant that might assist in the underwriting process.

Inspection Report – To supplement the information on the application, the underwriter may order an *inspection report* on the applicant from a credit agency or independent investigating firm, which covers moral and financial information. These are generic reports of the applicant's character, finances, employment, habits, and hobbies. Insurance companies that use inspection reports are subject to the rules and regulations included in the Fair Credit Reporting Act.

Fair Credit Reporting Act (FCRA) – The *Fair Credit Reporting Act (FCRA)* created procedures that consumer-reporting agencies must follow. The FCRA ensures that records are accurate, confidential, relevant, and properly used. This law also protects consumers against obsolete or inaccurate financial or personal information.

Insurance providers determine risk acceptability by checking the individual risk against several factors directly related to the risk's potential for loss. Along with these factors, an underwriter sometimes asks for additional information about a particular risk from an outside source. These reports usually fall into two categories: Consumer Reports and Investigative Consumer Reports. Someone with a legitimate business purpose can use both reports, including employment screening, underwriting, and credit transactions.

Consumer Reports include written and oral information about a consumer's character, credit, habits, or reputation collected by a reporting agency from credit reports, employment records, and other public sources.

Investigative Consumer Reports are comparable to Consumer Reports. They also provide information on the consumer's reputation, character, and habits. The main difference is that insurers obtain the data through an investigation and interviews with the consumer's friends, neighbors, and associates. In contrast to Consumer Reports, insurers cannot get an Investigative Report unless the consumer receives written notification about the report within three days of the date the consumer requested the report. Consumers must receive confirmation that they have a right to ask for additional information regarding the report. The reporting agency or insurance provider has five days to provide the consumer with the additional information.

The reporting agency and information users are subject to civil action for failure to comply with the FCRA's provisions. Any individual who intentionally and deliberately obtains information on a consumer under pretenses from a consumer reporting agency may be fined or imprisoned for up to two years.

Any person who *unwittingly* violates the FCRA is liable in the amount equal to the loss to the consumer and any reasonable attorney fees incurred during the process.

Any individual who *knowingly* violates the FCRA enough to constitute an overall pattern or business practice will be subject to a penalty of up to $2,500.

Under the FCRA, if an insurance policy is modified or declined because of information in an investigative or consumer report, the consumer must be notified and provided with the reporting agency's name and address. It is the consumer's right to know what information is in the report. Consumers have a right to know the identity of anyone who has obtained a report during the past year. When the consumer challenges any information in the report, the reporting agency must reinvestigate and amend the report if warranted. Also, when a consumer report is inaccurate and corrected, the agency must send the updated information to all parties who reported the erroneous information within the last two years.

Consumer reports cannot contain specific types of information if the bank or insurer requests a report in connection with a credit transaction of less than $150,000 or a life insurance policy. The prohibited information includes arrest records or convictions of crimes and bankruptcies over ten years old. It also includes civil suits or other negative information over seven years old. The FCRA defines a negative report as providing information about a customer's delinquencies, late payments, insolvency, or defaults.

Medical Information Bureau (MIB) – The underwriter typically requests a *Medical Information Bureau (MIB)* report and an attending physician's report. The MIB is a membership corporation owned by member insurers. It is a *nonprofit trade organization* that receives adverse medical information from insurers and maintains private medical impairment information on individuals. It is a systematic method for insurance companies to compare the information collected on a prospective insured with information already discovered by other insurance companies. The MIB can only help insurers know what areas of impairment they might need to investigate further. Insurance providers cannot refuse an applicant merely because of adverse information discovered through the MIB.

Medical Examinations – For policies with higher coverage amounts or if the application raised additional questions about the prospective insured's health, the underwriter might require the insured to undergo a medical examination. Depending on the reason for the medical examination, there are two options:

1. The insurance provider may only request a *paramedical report* that a registered nurse or a paramedic completes; and
2. The underwriter may require a medical practitioner who treated the applicant for a prior medical problem to provide an *Attending Physician's Statement (APS)*.

The insurance company may require paramedics or physicians to conduct medical examinations at the insurer's expense. Such exams are usually not necessary for health insurance, subsequently emphasizing the importance of the agent or producer when recording medical information on the application. The medical exam requirement is relatively common in life insurance underwriting. If an insurance company requests a medical exam, *the insurer is responsible* for the costs.

It is common among insurance providers to require an HIV test when an applicant applies for a large amount of coverage or any increased and additional benefits. Insurers seek to protect the insured's privacy and ensure they correctly obtain and handle test results. States have also enacted the following laws and regulations for insurance providers requiring an applicant to submit to an HIV test:

- The insurance provider must disclose the use of testing to the applicant and obtain written consent from the applicant on the approved form; and
- To ensure confidentiality, the insurance provider must establish written policies and procedures for the internal distribution of test results among its employees and producers.

Use and Disclosure of Insurance Information – Agents must provide each applicant with a written disclosure statement for a life insurance policy that includes basic information about the cost and coverage of the insurance policy. Producers must give this disclosure statement to the applicant before the insurance application is signed. Disclosure statements help the applicant make more educated and informed decisions about their insurance choice.

Insurance providers must first give the applicant or insured a written Disclosure Authorization Notice when they pursue and use information obtained from investigators. It will state the insurance provider's practice concerning collecting and using personal data. The disclosure authorization form needs to be in plain language; the head of the Department of Insurance must approve it.

HIPAA – The *Health Insurance Portability and Accountability Act (HIPAA)* is a federal law that protects private health information. HIPAA regulations protect the privacy of certain personally identifiable health information. Payment information that can identify the person or demographic data related to a physical or mental health condition is *protected health information*. Under the Privacy Rule, patients have the right to view their medical records and know who has accessed them over the previous six years. The Privacy Rule, however, permits disclosures without individual authorization to public health officials authorized by law to receive or collect the information to control or prevent injury, disease, or disability.

Risk Classification

When classifying a risk, the insurance carrier's underwriting department will examine the applicant's current physical condition, prior medical history, occupation, habits, and morals. If the applicant is deemed acceptable, the underwriter must determine the risk or *rating classification* to decide whether or not the applicant will pay a higher or lower premium. A potential insured may be rated as one of the three *standard*, *substandard*, or *preferred* classifications.

Preferred – *Preferred risks* are individuals who meet specific requirements that qualify them for lower premiums, unlike those who are a standard risk. These applicants are in peak physical condition and maintain healthy lifestyles and habits.

Standard – *Standard risks* are individuals who, according to an insurance company's underwriting standards, are entitled to insurance coverage without an extra rating or special restrictions. Standard risks are representative of the majority of people with similar lifestyles at their age. They are the average risk.

Substandard – *Substandard risks* or *high-exposure* applicants are unacceptable at standard rates because of their occupation, current physical condition, personal or family history of illness, disease, or dangerous habits. These policies are "rated" because they could be issued with the *premium rated-up*, resulting in a higher premium payment.

Declined Risks – Applicants who are not issued policies are considered *declined risks*, which are risks that the underwriting departments assess as uninsurable. Insurers can decline a risk for one of the following reasons:

- No insurable interest exists;
- The applicant is deemed medically unacceptable;
- It does not meet the definition of insurance because the potential for loss is so great; or
- Insurance is illegal or prohibited by public policy.

Stranger-Originated Life Insurance (STOLI) and Investor-Originated Life Insurance (IOLI)

Stranger-originated life insurance (STOLI) is an arrangement in which an individual with no relationship to the insured (a "stranger") purchases a life policy on the insured's life. The intention is to profit financially when the insured dies and sell the policy to an investor. In other words, STOLI can finance and purchase insurance to sell for life settlements.

STOLI *violates the principle of insurable interest*, which ensures that an individual obtaining a life insurance policy is interested in the insured's longevity rather than the insured's death. For this reason, insurance providers take an aggressive legal stance against policies they believe are involved in STOLI transactions.

Lawful life settlement contracts are not considered stranger-originated life insurance. Life settlement transactions result from existing life insurance policies. STOLI is used to initiate the purchase of a policy that would benefit an individual with no insurable interest in the insured's life at the time of policy origination.

Another name for STOLI is *investor-owned life insurance (IOLI)*. Third-party investors can initiate a transaction to transfer the policy's ownership rights to a different party with no insurable interest. The hope is to profit upon the insured's or annuitant's death.

Delivering the Policy

Once the insurance provider completes the underwriting process and issues the policy, the agent will deliver it to the insured. Although personal delivery of the insurance policy is the best way to finalize the insurance transaction, mailing the policy directly to the policyholder is also acceptable. The policy is legally delivered when the insurance provider relinquishes the policy by sending it to the owner. It is advisable, however, to obtain a signed *delivery receipt*.

Explaining the Policy and its Provisions, Riders, Exclusions, and Ratings to the Client

Personal delivery of the policy allows the agent to ensure that the insured understands all aspects of the contract. Reviewing the contract with the client involves explaining riders or provisions that may differ from expectations and describing their effect on the contract. Also, the agent should explain the rating procedure to the insured, especially if the policy is rated differently than when the applicant initially applied. The agent should also discuss any other provisions and choices that may become available to the policyholder.

Buyer's Guide – A *buyer's guide* provides prospective applicants with basic, general information about life insurance policies limited to language approved by the Department of Insurance. This document explains how a buyer should select the type and amount of insurance to purchase and how a buyer can save money by comparing the costs of similar policies. Before accepting the initial premium, insurance companies must provide a buyer's guide to all potential applicants. The policy includes a free-look period (unconditional refund provision) of at least ten days. In that instance, producers can deliver a buyer's guide with the policy.

Policy Summary – A *policy summary* is a written statement describing the elements and features of the issued policy. It includes the agent's name and address, the insurer's full name and administrative office or home office address, and the generic name of the basic policy and each rider. The summary will also include the cash value, premiums, dividends, surrender value, and death benefit figures for specific policy years. When the policy is delivered, agents must also provide the policy summary.

When Coverage Begins

When the applicant does not submit the premium with the application, the agent must collect it at policy delivery. In this situation, the policy is not yet effective until the premium is collected. The agent may also be required to obtain a *statement of good health* from the insured. The insured must sign this statement verifying that the insured has not sustained an injury or illness since the application date.

If the agent *collected the initial premium* with the application and the policy was issued as requested, the policy's coverage usually coincides with the application date if no medical exam is required. If a medical exam is required, the coverage date coincides with the exam's date.

USA Patriot Act and Anti-Money Laundering

On October 26th, 2001, the Uniting and Strengthening America by Providing Appropriate Tools Required to Intercept and Obstruct Terrorism Act, also known as the *USA Patriot Act*, was enacted. The act addresses economic, social, and global initiatives to prevent and fight terrorist activities. It allowed FinCEN (the Financial Crimes Enforcement Network) to mandate banks, broker-dealers, and other financial institutions to create new standards in *anti-money laundering (AML)*. Under these new rules, FinCEN incorporated the insurance industry into this group.

FinCEN implemented an AML Program that requires monitoring every financial transaction to accomplish the Patriot Act's goals. It reports suspicious activity to the federal government and bans corresponding accounts with foreign shell banks. A comprehensive verification procedure and customer identification are also in place. The AML program consists of the following requirements:

- Have a clear idea of internal controls, policies, and procedures based on an in-house risk assessment, including:
  - o Instituting AML programs similar to securities lenders and banks; and
  - o Filing suspicious activity reports (SARs) with Federal authorities;
- Appointing a qualified compliance officer to be responsible for implementing the AML program;
- Continual training for applicable producers, employees, and others; and
- The program must have independent testing regularly.

Suspicious Activity Reports (SARs) Rules

Any financial company subject to the AML Program is also subject to SAR rules. These companies design plans and procedures to identify activity that one would deem suspicious of terrorist financing, money laundering, and other illegal activities. Financial companies and insurance providers must report withdrawals, deposits, transfers, or other deals involving $5,000 or more. Transactions involving suspicious activity meet the following criteria:

- It has no lawful or business purpose;
- It deliberately misstates other reporting constraints;
- It uses the insurance provider or financial institution to assist in criminal activity;
- It uses fraudulent funds generated from illegal activities; or
- It disguises funds earned from other illegal activities.

The following examples are "red flags" to identify an activity deemed suspicious:

- A customer uses a fake ID or modifies a transaction after learning that they must show an ID;
- Two or more customers using similar IDs;
- A customer conducts transactions that fall just below amounts that require recordkeeping or reporting;
- Two or more customers working together to evade the Bank Secrecy Act (BSA) requirements by breaking one transaction into two or more; or
- A customer is trying to evade BSA requirements by using two or more money service business (MSB) locations or cashiers on the same day to break one transaction into smaller transactions.

Financial institutions must file relevant SAR reports with FinCEN within 30 days of discovering suspicious activity. Reporting occurs on FinCEN Form 108.

Chapter Review

This chapter broke down some of the basic principles and processes of life insurance underwriting. Let's review them:

GENERAL CONCEPTS	
Insurance	• Transfers the risk of loss from an individual to an insurance company • Based on the principle of indemnity • Based on the law of large numbers and the spreading of risk (risk pooling)
Insurable Interest	• Must exist at the time of application • Insuring one's own life, family member, or a business partner
Federal Regulations	• *Fair Credit Reporting Act* – protects consumers against circulation of obsolete or inaccurate information • USA PATRIOT Act/Anti-money Laundering and Suspicious Activity Reports Rules

INSURANCE CONTRACTS	
Elements of a Legal Contract	• *Agreement* – offer and acceptance • *Consideration* – representations and paying premiums on the part of the insured; paying claims on the part of the insurer • *Competent parties* – must be of legal age, have sound mental capacity, and not under the influence of alcohol or drugs • *Legal purpose* – must not go against public policy
Contract Characteristics	• *Adhesion* – one party prepares the contract; the other party must accept it as is • *Aleatory* – a contract involving an exchange of unequal amounts • *Conditional* – a contract where certain conditions must be met • *Unilateral* – only one of the parties to the contract is legally bound to do anything

PROCESS OF ISSUING A LIFE INSURANCE POLICY	
Underwriting	• Field Underwriting (by agent): - *Application* – must be completed correctly and signed - *Agent's report* – the agent's observations about the applicant that can assist in the underwriting process - Premiums are collected with the application, and conditional receipts are issued • Company Underwriting: - Multiple sources of information that include the application, consumer reports, and the MIB - *Risk classification* – three types of risk include standard, substandard, and preferred
Premium Determination	• Three critical factors for life insurance include mortality, interest, and expense • *Mode* – the more frequently a premium is paid by a policy owner, the higher the premium
Policy Issue and Delivery	• *Effective date of coverage* – if the premium is not paid with the application, the agent must obtain the premium and a statement of continued good health at the time of policy delivery

CHAPTER 2

Types of Life Policies

This chapter explains the major types of life insurance policies, their functions and characteristics, and who is best served by each policy type. This chapter also covers the topic of annuities, which will teach you about annuity periods, the parties to the annuity, and how to recognize different annuities. After completing the chapter, you will have learned:

- Term Life Insurance
- Traditional Whole Life Insurance
- Interest-Sensitive, Market-Sensitive, and Adjustable Life Products
- Combination Plans and Variations
- Annuities

Term Life Insurance

Consumers have access to many types of life insurance products. Although all life insurance products offer death protection, they also include unique features and benefits to serve the varying needs of insureds.

Every life insurance policy provides temporary and permanent protection regarding the length of coverage.

Term insurance, or pure life insurance, offers temporary protection since it only provides coverage for a specific time. Compared to any other form of protection, term insurance policies provide the most significant coverage for the lowest premium. There is a maximum age above which insurance providers will not renew or offer coverage.

Term insurance provides insureds with *pure death protection*:

- When the insured dies during the policy term, the policy pays the beneficiary the death benefit;
- If the policy is canceled or expires before the insured's death, there is no payment at the term's end; and
- There is no cash value or other living benefits.

Types of Term Policies

Based on *how the face amount (death benefit) changes* during the policy term, there are three types of term coverage available:

- Level Term,
- Increasing Term, and
- Decreasing Term.

Irrespective of the type of term insurance purchased, the premium is level throughout the policy term. Only the death benefit amount may fluctuate depending on the term insurance. Upon converting, selling, or renewing the term policy, the insurer calculates the premium at the insured's age when the transaction occurs, also called attained age.

It is important to note that this book does not discuss increasing term insurance since this topic is not on the state licensing exam.

Level Term – The most common form of temporary protection that policy owners may purchase is level-term insurance. The word "level" refers to the death benefit that does not change throughout the policy's life.

Level premium term provides a level premium and a level death benefit during the policy term. If the insured dies within the next ten years, a $100,000 10-year level term policy will provide a $100,000 death benefit. The premium remains level during the entire 10-year period. If the policy renews at the end of the ten years, the insurer will base the premium on the insured's attained age.

Annually Renewable Term – The purest form of term insurance is *annually renewable term (ART)* insurance. The death benefit remains level, and the policy may be guaranteed renewable yearly without proof of insurability. However, as the probability of death increases, the premium increases annually according to the attained age.

Decreasing Term – *Decreasing term* policies have a level premium and a death benefit that decreases yearly over the policy's lifespan. Decreasing term is most appropriate when the amount of needed protection is time-sensitive or decreases over time. Credit life insurance with decreasing term coverage is commonly purchased to insure a *mortgage payment or other debts* if the insured dies prematurely. The coverage amount consequently decreases as the outstanding loan balance decreases each year. A decreasing term policy is typically convertible. It is usually not renewable since the death benefit is $0 at the end of the policy term.

Return of Premium – *Return of premium (ROP)* life insurance is an increasing term insurance policy that pays the beneficiary an additional death benefit, which equals the amount of the premiums paid. Insurers will return the paid premiums if the death happens within a specified period or if the insured outlives the policy term.

ROP policies are structured to consider the low-risk factor of a term policy but at a significant increase in the premium cost, sometimes as much as 25-50% more. Traditional term policies offer a simple, low-cost death benefit for a specified term. They have no cash value or investment component. The policy expires when the term ends, and the insured is no longer covered. An ROP policy offers the pure protection of a term policy. However, when the insured remains healthy and is still alive once the term expires, the insurance provider guarantees a return of the premium. Notwithstanding, the returned premiums are not taxable since the amount returned equals the amount paid.

Example 2.1 – A healthy, 35-year-old man pays $360 annually for a $250,000, 30-year term policy. At the end of the 30 years, he has spent $10,800 in premiums, which the insurer will return if he outlives the policy term. The insurer has determined that $250 per year, or $7,500 over 30 years, will cover the actual cost of protection. The excess funds, which the insurance company invests, provide the cash for the returned premiums.

Special Features

Most term insurance contracts are renewable, convertible, or both renewable and convertible (R&C).

Renewable – The *renewable* provision lets a policy owner renew their coverage without evidence of insurability. Insurers will base the new premium for the term policy on the insured's current age. For instance, an insurer can renew a 10-year renewable term policy at the end of the ten years for a subsequent 10-year period without evidence of insurability. However, the insured must pay the premium based on their attained age. When an individual buys a 10-year term policy at age 30, they will pay a premium based on age 40 upon renewal.

Convertible – The *convertible* provision allows policy owners to convert the policy to permanent insurance without evidence of insurability. Insurance providers will base the premium on the insured's attained age at conversion.

Traditional Whole Life Insurance

Permanent life insurance is a broad term for policies that build cash value. Such policies remain effective for the insured's entire life (or until the insured reaches age 100), provided the policy owner pays the premium. Whole life insurance is considered the most common type of permanent insurance.

Whole life insurance includes a cash value (or savings element) and provides lifetime protection. Whole life policies are endowed when the insured reaches the age of 100. In other words, the cash value created by the accumulating premiums equals the face amount of the policy at age 100. Insurance carriers calculate the policy premium, assuming the policyholder will continue paying the premium until that age. Premium payments for whole life policies are generally higher than premiums for term insurance.

The essential characteristics of whole life insurance include:

- **Level Premium** – Insurers base the premium for a whole life policy on the age at policy issue; therefore, it remains the same throughout the policy period.
- **Death Benefit** – The death benefit is guaranteed and remains level for the policy's life.
- **Cash Value** – The cash value created by the accumulation of premiums will equal the face amount of the policy when the policy matures (the insured reaches age 100). At policy maturity, insurers pay cash values to the policyholder. Remember, the insured and the policyholder do not have to be the same person. The policy's cash values are credited regularly and have a guaranteed interest rate.
- **Living Benefits** – Policyholders can borrow against the cash value when the policy is effective, and the policy owner can receive the cash value when they surrender the policy. The cash value, also known as the nonforfeiture value, does not typically accumulate until the third policy year and grows tax-deferred.

Three primary forms of whole life insurance include straight life, limited-pay whole life, and single premium whole life. However, other forms and combination plans may also be available.

Ordinary Whole Life

Straight life, also called ordinary life or continuous premium whole life, is the most basic whole life policy. The policyholder pays the premium from the time the insurer issues the policy until the insured's death or the age of 100, whichever occurs first. Straight life policies will have the lowest annual premium of all whole life policies.

Limited Payment

Unlike straight life, policy owners will entirely pay up the coverage premiums of limited-pay whole life well before age 100. A typical version of limited-pay life is 20-pay life, where policy owners pay for coverage over 20 years. LP-65 (life paid-up at 65) is another version of limited-pay life. In LP-65 policies, policy owners pay for coverage by age 65. All other factors being equal, this policy has a shorter premium paying period than straight life insurance. Therefore, the annual premium will be higher. Cash value builds up faster for these limited-pay policies.

Limited-pay policies are well-suited for insureds who only want to pay premiums within a specific period. For instance, an individual might need some protection after retirement but does not want to pay premiums. A limited-pay (paid-up at 65) policy purchased during the individual's working years will accomplish that objective.

Single Premium

Single premium whole life (SPWL) provides a level death benefit until the insured reaches age 100 for a one-time, lump-sum payment. The policy is fully paid after one premium payment and generates immediate cash.

	TERM LIFE	WHOLE LIFE
Type of protection	Temporary	Permanent until age 100
Premium	Level	Level
Death benefit	• Level • Increasing • Decreasing	Level
Living benefits	Not available	• Cash values • Policy loans • Nonforfeiture values

Interest-Sensitive, Market-Sensitive and Adjustable Life Products

There are several other types of whole life insurance policies. While they all have the same fundamental characteristics, whole life policies offer unique features based on how the policy owner invests or pays the premium.

Adjustable Life

Insurance companies established *adjustable life* to provide the insured with term and permanent coverage. Adjustable life policies can take the form of either term insurance or permanent insurance. The insured generally determines the required coverage and an affordable premium amount. The insurance provider will select the appropriate type of insurance to meet the insured's needs. As the needs of the insured change, the policy owner can adjust their policy. Usually, the policy owner has the following options:

- Increase or reduce the premium or the premium-paying period;
- Increase or decrease the policy face amount; or
- Change the protection period.

The policy owner also chooses to convert from term life to whole life or vice versa. However, changing to a lower premium type of policy or increasing the death benefit will typically require proof of insurability. The insurance carrier can adjust the death benefit when policyholders convert from a whole life policy to a term policy. Under the permanent form, the policy owner can pay additional premiums above and beyond what is required to accumulate more cash value or shorten the premium-paying period.

Adjustable life policies include most of the standard features of other whole life policies. The *cash value* of adjustable life policies only develops when the paid premiums are greater than the cost of the policy.

Universal Life

The generic name of flexible premium adjustable life insurance also refers to *universal life* insurance. This reference indicates that the policy owner can increase the premium amount paid into the policy and decrease it later. Policy owners can even skip paying a premium. The policy will not lapse, provided that there is sufficient cash value to cover the monthly deductions for the insurance cost. However, the policy will expire if the cash value is insufficient to cover the premium costs.

Since the premium payment can be adjusted, the insurance providers may give the policy owner a choice to pay either of the two types of premiums:

- The *minimum premium* amount keeps the policy in force for the current year. Paying the minimum premium makes the policy perform like an annually renewable term product.
- The *target premium* is a suggested amount that policy owners should pay on a policy to keep the policy in force for the duration of its lifetime and to cover the cost of insurance protection.

Universal life policies have two components: a *cash account* and an *insurance component*. *Annually renewable term insurance* is always the insurance component of a universal life policy.

Universal life policies allow the *partial surrender*, or *partial withdrawal*, of the policy cash value. However, there may be a charge for each withdrawal. There are typically limits on how much and how often policyholders can make a withdrawal. The earned interest on the withdrawn cash value can be subject to taxation during the withdrawal, depending upon the plan. The amount of any partial surrender will lower the death benefit, as partial surrenders from universal life policies are not the same as a policy loan.

Universal life insurance offers the policy owner one of two death benefit options. *Option A* provides a level death benefit, and *Option B* provides an increasing death benefit.

The death benefit remains level under *Option A (Level Death Benefit)*. At the same time, the cash value steadily increases, consequently lowering the pure insurance with the insurance provider in the later years. Pure insurance decreases as time passes, reducing expenses and allowing for a larger cash value in the older years. The increase in the death benefit at a later point is because the policy will comply with the "statutory definition of life insurance." The IRS established this definition, which applies to all life insurance products issued after December 31st, 1984. According to this definition, a life insurance policy must maintain a specified "corridor" or gap between the death benefit and the cash value. The percentages that apply to the corridor appear in a table published by the IRS and vary based on the insured's age and the coverage amount. If this corridor is not maintained, the policy is no longer considered life insurance for tax purposes. Consequently, it loses most of the tax advantages associated with life insurance.

Under *Option B (Increasing Death Benefit)*, the death benefit gradually increases yearly by the amount of cash value that increases. At any point in time, the face amount of the policy plus the current amount of cash value will always equal the total death benefit. The pure insurance with the insurance company remains level for life, and the expenses of this option are higher than those of Option A. In this case, the cash value will be smaller in the older years.

Variable Whole Life

Variable life insurance, sometimes called variable whole life insurance, is a level, fixed premium, investment-based product. Similar to traditional forms of life insurance, these policies have a guaranteed minimum death benefit and fixed premiums. However, the cash value of the policy is not guaranteed. It fluctuates with the portfolio's performance in which the insurance provider has invested the premiums. In variable contracts, the policy owner bears the investment risk.

Because the insurer is not incurring the contract's investment risk, the contract's underlying assets cannot be kept in the insurer's general account. Insurers must hold these assets in a separate account, investing in stocks, bonds, and other securities. Any domestic insurance provider issuing variable contracts has to establish one or more separate accounts. Each account must maintain assets with a value that is at least equal to the amount held in reserves and other contract liabilities. Insurers must not commingle holdings in a separate account with assets in the general account.

Variable Universal Life

Variable universal life insurance combines universal life with variable life. Like universal life, it provides the policyholder an adjustable death benefit and flexible premiums. Like variable life, policyholders decide where to invest the cash value (net premiums) rather than the insurance carrier. Also, like variable life, the death benefit is not fixed, and the cash values are never guaranteed. The death benefit or cash value might increase or decrease over the policy's life depending on the underlying investment performance of the sub-account. However, the death benefit usually cannot be reduced below the initial face amount of the policy. A producer must also *hold a license for securities and life insurance* to sell variable universal life.

Regulating Variable Products (SEC, FINRA, and Texas) – Both state and federal governments *regulate* Variable life insurance products. Due to the investment risk, the federal government has established that variable contracts are securities. Consequently, the Securities and Exchange Commission (SEC) and the Financial Industry Regulatory Authority (FINRA) regulate variable contracts. A state's Insurance Department also regulates variable life insurance as an insurance product.

Agents selling variable life insurance products must:

- Be registered with FINRA;
- Have a securities license; and
- Be licensed in a state to sell life insurance.

Interest-Sensitive Whole Life

Interest-sensitive whole life, also known as current assumption life, is a whole life insurance policy that delivers a guaranteed death benefit to age 100. The insurance provider sets the initial premium based on current risk, interest, and expenses assumptions. If the actual values change, the insurance provider will lower or raise the premium at specified intervals. Also, interest-sensitive whole life policies credit the cash value with the current interest rate. This rate is typically comparable to a money market rate and can be higher than the guaranteed levels. The policy also provides a minimum guaranteed interest rate.

Interest-sensitive whole life provides the same benefits as traditional whole life policies. It also has the added benefit of current interest rates, which may allow for either a shorter premium-paying period or greater cash value accumulation.

Indexed Life

The central feature of *indexed whole life*, or equity index whole life, is a guaranteed minimum interest rate. The cash value depends on the equity index's performance, like the S&P 500. The policy's face amount increases yearly to keep up with inflation as the CPI (Consumer Price Index) increases. Also, evidence of insurability is not required. Indexed whole life policies are categorized depending on whether the insurance provider or the policy owner assumes the inflation risk. If the insurance provider assumes the risk, the premium remains level. If the policyholder bears the risk, the policy premiums increase with the increases in the face amount.

The table below compares the key features and components of adjustable, universal, and variable life policies.

POLICIES COMPARED	
Adjustable Life	**Key Features** – Can be Term or Whole Life; can convert from one to the other
	Premium – Can be increased or decreased by policy owners
	Face Amount – Flexible; set by the policy owner with proof of insurability
	Cash Value – Fixed rate of return; general account
	Policy Loans – Can borrow cash value
Universal Life	**Key Features** – Permanent insurance with renewable term protection
	Premium – Flexible; minimum or target
	Face Amount – Flexible; set by the policy owner with proof of insurability
	Cash Value – Guaranteed at a minimum level; general account
	Policy Loans – Can borrow cash value
Variable Life	**Key Features** – Permanent insurance
	Premium – Fixed (if Whole Life); flexible (if Universal Life)
	Face Amount – Can increase or decrease to a stated minimum
	Cash Value – Not guaranteed; separate account
	Policy Loans – Can borrow cash value

Combination Plans and Variations

Joint Life

Joint life is a stand-alone policy that ensures two or more lives. A joint life policy can be in the form of permanent or term insurance. The premium payment for a joint life policy would be less than the same type and amount of coverage on the same insureds. It is also known as joint whole life, which performs similarly to an individual whole life policy with two noteworthy exceptions:

- Insurers base the premium payment on a *joint average age* of the insureds.
- Insurers only pay the death benefit upon the *first death*.

A premium based on a joint age is less than the sum of two premiums based on individual age. Therefore, it is common to find joint life policies purchased by husbands and wives. This situation is particularly the case if the need for insurance does not extend beyond the first death. Policy owners use joint life policies when there is a need for two or more individuals to be protected. However, the need for insurance is no longer present after the first insured dies.

For example, a married couple buying a house may purchase a joint life policy for mortgage protection if both spouses work and earn the same income. If one spouse dies, the policy covers the mortgage payments for the surviving spouse.

Business owners also use joint life to meet various business life insurance needs by insuring the lives of business partners through the funding of a buy-sell agreement. A buy-sell is a business continuation agreement that describes what will happen with the business if an owner becomes disabled or dies.

Survivorship Life

Survivorship life, also known as a "last survivor" or a "second-to-die" policy, is similar to joint life. It insures two or more lives for a *premium based on a joint age*. The primary difference is that survivorship life pays on the last death rather than the first death. Since the insurer does not pay the death benefit until the last death, the joint life expectancy, in a sense, is extended. This "extension" results in a lower premium payment for joint life, which pays upon the first death. Policy owners often use this insurance policy to *offset the estate tax liability* upon the death of the last insured.

Annuities

Annuity Principles and Concepts

Annuities are contracts that deliver income for a specified number of years or life. They protect an individual against outliving their money. An annuity is not a life insurance product but rather a vehicle for accumulating money and *liquidating an estate*. Life insurance companies will often market annuities, and licensed life insurance agents are authorized to sell certain annuities.

Annuities do not pay a face amount upon the annuitant's death—they do just the opposite. In most cases, the annuity payments stop upon the annuitant's death. Although annuities use mortality tables, these tables reflect a longer life expectancy than those used with life insurance. Mortality tables show the number of individuals within a specified group, including males, females, smokers, and nonsmokers, starting at a certain age, who expect to be alive at a succeeding age.

The Parties

Owner – The individual who purchases the annuity contract does not necessarily have to receive the benefits. *The annuity owner has all rights*, such as surrendering the annuity and naming the beneficiary. The annuity owner can be a corporation, trust, or legal entity.

Annuitant – The annuitant is the individual who receives payments or benefits from the annuity. Insurance providers use the annuitant's life expectancy when writing the annuity. The contract owner and the annuitant do not need to be the same person but are most of the time. A corporation, trust, or other legal entity can own an annuity, but *the annuitant must be a natural person.*

Beneficiary – The beneficiary is the individual who receives the annuity's assets (either the cash value or the amount paid into the annuity, whichever is greater) when the annuitant dies during the accumulation period. Beneficiaries also receive the balance of annuity benefits.

Accumulation Period vs. Annuitization Period – The *accumulation period* is also called the *pay-in period*. This period is when the annuity owner makes premium payments into an annuity. It is also when the premium payments earn interest on a tax-deferred basis.

The *annuity period* is also called the *annuitization, liquidation,* or *payout period*. It is when the total amount accumulated during the accumulation period converts into a stream of annuity income payments to the annuitant. The annuity period can last for the annuitant's lifetime or a specific time. The *annuitization date* starts when the annuity benefit payouts begin (trigger for benefits).

The amount of annuity income depends on the following:

* The amount of cash value accumulated or premium paid;
* The frequency of premium payments;
* The interest rate; and
* The gender and age of the annuitant.

An annuitant with a longer life expectancy will receive smaller income installments. For instance, all other factors are equal. A 65-year-old male will have higher annuity income payments than a 45-year-old male because he is younger than a 65-year-old female due to the statistical fact that women have a longer life expectancy.

Mostly, individuals purchase annuities to supplement or provide *retirement income*. They also buy annuities to help *fund a college education*. Individuals can use an annuity for any situation that requires a steady income stream at some future point in time. People also use annuities to provide *structured settlements*. A structured settlement would take on the form of a court settlement arising from a civil lawsuit, or it can take on the condition of the income provided to a state lottery winner. In addition, many settlement options for a life insurance policy involve choosing an annuity payment option. The primary function of an annuity is to *liquidate a principal sum, regardless of how it accumulated.*

Types of Annuities

Insurers classify annuities according to how they invest premiums, how annuity owners make premium payments, and when (and how) annuitants receive benefit payouts.

Premium Payment Options – Insurers classify annuities based on how they can be funded (paid for). Two options are a *single payment* (lump sum) or *periodic payments*. With periodic payments, the annuity owner pays premiums in installments over time. Periodic payment annuities can be either *level premium*, in which the annuitant/owner pays a fixed installment, or a *flexible premium*. With a flexible premium, the frequency and amount of each installment will vary.

Annuity Investment Options – Annuities can be fixed or variable based on how insurers invest the premium payment funds.

Fixed Annuities – A *fixed annuity* offers the following features:

- A guaranteed minimum interest rate to be credited to the purchase payment(s);
- Annuity (income) payments that do not vary from one payment to the next;
- The insurer guarantees the length of the period of payments and the specified dollar amount for each payment as determined by the settlement option chosen by the annuitant.

With a fixed annuity, the annuitant knows the exact amount of every payment they receive from the annuity during the annuitization period. Fixed annuities have a *level benefit payment amount*. A disadvantage to fixed annuities is that inflation could erode their purchasing power over time.

Variable Annuities – A *variable annuity* operates as a hedge against inflation. It is variable from the standpoint that the annuitant could receive different return rates on the funds paid into the annuity. The three main characteristics of variable annuities are listed below:

- **Underlying Investment** – An insurer invests the annuitants' payments into variable annuities in its separate account, not its general account. The separate account is not part of the insurer's investment portfolio. It is not subject to the restrictions on the insurer's general account.
- **Interest Rate** – The issuing insurance company does not guarantee a minimum interest rate.
- **License Requirements** – A variable annuity is considered a *security*. State regulators and the Securities Exchange Commission (SEC) regulate variable annuities. An agent selling variable annuities must have a securities license and a life insurance license. Companies or agents that sell variable annuities must also register with FINRA.

Like buying shares in a Mutual Fund, variable premiums purchase *accumulation units* in the fund. Accumulation units represent an ownership interest in the insurer's separate account. During the annuity period, the accumulation units convert to *annuity units*. The number of received annuity units remains level. However, the unit values will fluctuate until the insurer pays the annuitant.

FEATURES	FIXED ANNUITY	VARIABLE ANNUITY
Interest Rate	Guaranteed by insurer	No guarantee
Underlying Investment	General account (safe, conservative)	Separate account (equities)
License Needed	Life insurance	Life insurance PLUS securities
Expenses	Guaranteed	Guaranteed
Income Payment	Guaranteed	No guarantee

Indexed Annuities – *Indexed (or equity-indexed) annuities* are fixed annuities that invest fairly aggressively to achieve higher returns. Like fixed annuities, they have a guaranteed minimum interest rate. The current interest rate that is credited corresponds to a familiar index, such as the Standard and Poor's (S&P) 500.

Usually, the insurance providers reserve the initial returns for investment purposes but pay the excess to the annuitant. For instance, the company might keep the first 4% earned and credit any accumulation above 4% to the annuitant's account. Therefore, if the interest earned is 11%, the company keeps 4% and credits the client's account with 7%. Equity-indexed annuities are less risky than mutual funds or variable annuities. However, they expect to earn a higher interest rate than a fixed annuity.

Immediate vs. Deferred Annuities – Insurers classify annuities according to when the annuity's income payments start. An *immediate annuity* is purchased with one lump-sum payment and provides a stream of income payments that begin *within one year* from the purchase date. Usually, the first payment is made as early as one month from the date of purchase. This type of annuity is also known as a Single Premium Immediate Annuity (SPIA).

Income payments begin *one year after* the purchase date in a *deferred annuity*. Annuity owners fund deferred annuities through periodic payments, such as Flexible Premium Deferred Annuities (FPDAs), or a single lump-sum payment, like Single Premium Deferred Annuities (SPDAs). Periodic payments can vary annually. More flexibility for premium payments is allowed when an annuity's deferral is longer.

Payout Options

Annuity payment options specify how annuity funds will be paid. They are similar to the settlement options in life insurance that determine how the policy proceeds will be paid to the beneficiaries.

Life Contingency Options - Pure Life vs. Life with Guaranteed Minimum – The life annuity pays a specified amount for the remainder of the annuitant's life. With *pure life*, also called *life-only* or *straight life*, this payment ends at the annuitant's death (no matter how soon that occurs in the annuitization period). This option delivers *the highest monthly benefits* for an annuitant. Under this option, while the payments are guaranteed for the annuitant's lifetime, there is no guarantee that all proceeds will be fully paid.

With the *life with guaranteed minimum settlement option*, when the annuitant dies before the principal amount has been paid out, the insurance company will refund the remainder of the principal amount to the beneficiary. This option is also known as *refund life*. It guarantees that the insurer will pay out the entire principal amount.

The two refund life annuities include:

- **Cash Refund** — Once the annuitant dies, the beneficiary will receive a lump-sum refund of the principal minus any benefit payments already made to the annuitant. The cash refund option does not guarantee any interest will be paid.
- **Installment Refund** — Once the annuitant dies, the beneficiary receives guaranteed installments until the entire principal amount is paid out.

It is worth noting, however, that any unpaid annuity benefits after the death of an annuitant are taxable when paid to the beneficiary.

Life with Period (Term) Certain – *Life with period (term) certain* is an additional life contingency payout option. With this option, the annuity payments are guaranteed for the *annuitant's lifetime* and a specified period for the beneficiary. For instance, a life income with a 20-year period certain option would provide the annuitant with an income while they are alive (for the entire life). If the annuitant dies after payments start, the payments will continue to their beneficiary for the remainder of the period (a total of 20 years).

Single Life vs. Multiple Life – A *single* life annuity protects one life, and insurers make annuity payments for that life only. The annuity owner can contribute premiums with a single payment or periodic payments. Subsequent values will accumulate until the contract is annuitized.

A *multiple life* annuity protects two or more lives. Joint life and joint and survivor are the most common multiple life annuities.

Joint Life – *Joint life* is a payout option where two or more annuitants receive payments until the first death among the annuitants, and then payments end.

Joint and Survivor – The *joint and survivor* option is a modification of the life income option. It will guarantee an income for two recipients that neither can outlive. Although the surviving recipient(s) can receive payments in the same amount as the first recipient who dies, most contracts require the surviving recipients to accept a reduced payment after the first recipient dies. This option is usually written as "joint and ½ survivor" or "joint and 2/3 survivor," where the surviving beneficiary will receive ½ or 2/3 of the amount received when both beneficiaries were alive. A couple in retirement commonly selects this option. As with the life income option, there is no guarantee that all proceeds will be paid out if both beneficiaries die after the installments begin.

Annuities Certain (Types) – Unlike the life contingency benefit payment option, *annuities certain* is a *short-term annuity* that limits the amount paid to either a fixed period or until a fixed amount is liquidated.

- **Fixed Period** – With *fixed-period installments*, the annuitant selects the benefit period. The insurance provider determines the amount of each payment based on the account's value and future earnings projections. This option only pays for a specified amount of time, whether or not the annuitant is living.
- **Fixed Amount** – With *fixed-amount installments*, the annuitant chooses how much each payment will be. The insurance provider analyzes the account's value and future earnings to determine how long it will pay the benefits. This option pays a specified amount until funds are exhausted, whether or not the annuitant is alive.

Chapter Review

This chapter was chock-full of information about the different types of life insurance policies and annuities. Be sure that you are familiar with the various types of policies discussed and can compare and contrast the various policy types. Let's review all of these concepts:

	TERM LIFE
General Characteristics	• Pure protection • Lasts for specific term • No cash value • Maximum age above which coverage will not be offered or at which coverage cannot be renewed
Level Premium Term	• Level death benefit and level premium
Annually Renewable Term	• Renews each year without proof of insurability • Premiums increase due to attained age
Decreasing Term	• Coverage gradually decreases at predetermined times • Best used when the need for protection decreases from year to year

Features of Term Policies	• *Renewable* – can renew the policy without evidence of insurability • *Convertible* – the right to convert a term policy to a permanent policy without evidence of insurability
WHOLE LIFE	
General Characteristics	• Permanent protection • Guaranteed elements (premium, face amount, and cash value) until death or age 100 • Level premium • Cash value and other living benefits
Ordinary Whole Life (Continuous Premium)	• Basic policy • Level death benefit • The insured pays the premiums for life or until age 100
Limited Payment	• Premiums are paid until a certain time; coverage is in effect to age 100
Single Premium	• Premiums are paid in one single lump sum; coverage continues to age 100
FLEXIBLE PREMIUM	
General Characteristics	• A type of whole life insurance • Has a flexible premium
Universal Life	• An insurance component that comes in the form of annually renewable term • Two options for the death benefit: - Option A – level death benefit - Option B – increasing death benefit • Can make a partial surrender/cash withdrawal
OTHER TYPES OF POLICIES	
Variable Life	• Fixed premiums with a minimum death benefit • Cash value and the actual amount of the death benefit are not guaranteed • Assets are held in separate accounts • Agents must be dually licensed in both insurance and securities
Combination Plans	• *Joint Life:* - Premiums are determined by the joint average age of the insured - Death benefits are paid upon the first death only • *Survivorship Life:* - Premiums are determined by the joint average age of the insured - Death benefits are paid upon the last death
ANNUITIES	
Phases	• *Accumulation (pay-in)* – payments are made into the annuity • *Annuitization (pay-out)* – the annuitant receives payments from the annuity
Parties	• *Annuitant* – the insured (must be a person); policies are issued on the annuitant's life • *Beneficiary* – will receive any amount contributed to the annuity (plus any gain) if the annuitant dies during the accumulation period • *Owner* – has all rights to the policy (usually the annuitant); can also be a corporation or trust

ANNUITIES *(Continued)*	

Types of Annuities	• *Fixed annuities:*
	  - Guaranteed
	  - Fixed payments
	  - Premiums are held in a general account
	• *Variable annuities*
	  - Payment is not guaranteed
	  - Premiums are held in a separate account
	  - Invested in stocks and bonds
	• *Indexed annuities:*
	  - Interest rates are tied to an index
	  - Earn a higher rate than fixed annuities
	  - Are not as risky as mutual funds or variable annuities

Premium Payments	• *Single premium* – a single lump-sum payment; the principal is immediately created in both immediate and deferred annuities • *Periodic (Flexible) premium* – multiple payments; the principal is created over time (used for deferred annuities only)

Payment Options	• *Life Only:*
	  - An insured cannot outlive their income
	  - Any funds not paid out are retained by the insurer at the insured's death
	  - Pays the highest monthly amount
	• *Refund Life Annuity:*
	  - Guaranteed lifetime income
	  - If an annuitant dies, the balance is "refunded" to the beneficiary
	  - The installment option pays the beneficiary until the purchase amount is paid out
	  - The cash refund pays the balance of an original annuity's purchase amount minus payments made to the annuitant
	• *Life with Period Certain:*
	  - Specific monthly payments for life and a specific period
	  - If an annuitant dies before the payment period is up, the payment goes to the beneficiary
	• *Joint Life:*
	  - Two or more annuitants receive payments until the first death, then payments end
	• *Joint and Survivor:*
	  - Income for two or more individuals that cannot be outlived
	  - Often used with period certain
	  - When one annuitant dies, the other receives either ½ or 2/3 of the original payment amount
	• *Lump-sum:*
	  - Paid at annuitization; all accumulated interest is taxable
	  - An additional 10% penalty is imposed before annuitants reach age 59 ½
	• *Annuities Certain*
	  - Payments are guaranteed for a fixed period or until a certain fixed amount

Income Payments	<ul><li>*Immediate:* - Purchased with a single premium - Income payments begin within 12 months from the purchase date</li><li>*Deferred:* - Purchased with either a lump sum or periodic premium payments - Benefits start sometime after one year from the date of purchase - It is often used to accumulate funds for retirement</li></ul>
Interest Rate	<ul><li>*Guaranteed:* - The insurer must pay this minimum percentage, usually around 3%</li><li>*Current:* - Exceeds the guaranteed rate - Paid to the annuitant when an insurer's own investment is better than expected</li></ul>

CHAPTER 3:
Life Policy Riders, Provisions, Options, and Exclusions

You now know the different life insurance policies and their suitability for various insured individuals. Next, you will learn about available riders, provisions, options, and exclusions that can cause two policies of the same type to differ significantly. By the chapter's end, you will understand the following:

- Policy Provisions
- Policy Riders
- Policy Options

Provisions define an insurance contract's characteristics and are relatively universal from one policy to the next. *Riders* are added to a policy to amend existing provisions. *Options* offer insurance providers and insureds ways to invest or distribute a sum of money available in a life policy. You must understand the different provisions, riders, and options for future life insurance transactions.

Policy Provisions

The standard policy provisions adopted by the NAIC (National Association of Insurance Commissioners) create uniformity among life insurance policies. There is no "standard" policy form in life insurance.

Entire Contract

The *entire contract* provision states that *the policy, application copy, and any amendments or riders* make up the entire contract. Any statements made before the contract cannot be used to modify the agreement. The insurance provider and the insured can only change policy provisions once the policy is effective if both parties agree and the change is attached to the contract.

Insuring Clause

The *insuring clause*, or the insuring agreement, sets forth the basic contract between the insurance company and the insured. It states the insurance company's promise to pay the death benefit upon the insured's death. Policyholders can typically find the insuring clause on the policy's face page. It also defines the parties to the contract, the premium payment amount, the death benefit amount, and how long coverage is in force.

Free Look

This provision allows the policyholder a specified number of days from receipt to review the policy and return it for a full premium refund if dissatisfied. The *free-look period begins when the policyholder receives the policy*, not when the insurance company issues the policy. Specific policies might require a more extended free-look period, or state statutes can set the period.

Consideration

Both parties to a contract or agreement must provide some *consideration* or value for the contract to be valid. The consideration provision stipulates that the policy owner's consideration or value is the premium and the statements made in the application. The consideration offered by the insurance company is the promise to pay per the contract terms. A consideration clause does not always appear as a separate provision. It is often in the entire contract provision. A separate provision about the premium payments is also usually found in the policy.

Owner's Rights

The parties to the insurance contract are the insurance provider, the policy owner, the insured, and the beneficiary. The policy owner and the insured can be the same individual or different people. Regardless, only the policy owner has ownership rights under the policy, not the insured or the beneficiary. Ownership rights include:

- Naming and changing the beneficiary;
- Selecting a payment option for receiving benefits;
- Assigning the policy; and
- Receiving the policy's living benefits.

The policy owner is responsible for paying the policy premiums. When applying for insurance, the policy owner must also have an insurable interest in the insured. The insurance arrangement is known as third-party ownership if the policy owner and the insured are different individuals.

Assignments

Life insurance policy owners can transfer complete or partial ownership of the policy to another individual without the insurer's consent. However, the owner must inform the insurance provider of the assignment in writing. Transfer of the life insurance policy *does not change the amount of coverage or the insured*; it only changes who has the policy ownership rights.

The assignment provision stipulates the policy owner's right to assign the policy or transfer ownership rights. The policy owner must notify the insurance provider in writing of the assignment. The following two types of policy assignments include:

- **Absolute Assignment** – *Absolute Assignment* involves transferring *all ownership rights* to another person or entity. It is a permanent transfer, and the new policy owner does not need an insurable interest in the insured.
- **Collateral Assignment** – *Collateral Assignment* involves transferring *partial rights* to another individual to secure a loan or some other transaction. It is a temporary and partial assignment of some policy rights. Once the policy owner repays the loan or debt, they regain these rights.

Beneficiary Designations

The *beneficiary* is the individual or interest to which the insurer will pay policy proceeds upon the insured's death. The beneficiary can be a person, a class of individuals (sometimes used with children of the insured), the insured's estate, or an institution or other entity such as a corporation, charity, foundation, or trustee of a trust. Trusts are commonly used with beneficiary designations for estate tax purposes or to manage life insurance proceeds for a minor. However, naming a trust as a beneficiary does not avoid estate taxes.

The beneficiary does not need to have an insurable interest in the insured. Additionally, the policy owner does not have to name a beneficiary for the policy to be valid.

Primary and Contingent – The beneficiary designation can offer three levels of priority or choice. When the first beneficiary dies before the insured, the second (or sometimes third) level in the succession of beneficiaries is entitled to death benefits. Each level is only eligible for death proceeds if the beneficiary(s) in the level(s) above them predeceases the insured.

The *primary beneficiary* always has the first claim to the policy proceeds following the insured's death. Policy owners can name multiple primary beneficiaries and choose how the proceeds will be divided.

The *contingent beneficiary* is also known as a secondary or tertiary beneficiary. Contingent beneficiaries have the second claim if the primary beneficiary predeceases the insured. They do not receive anything if the primary beneficiary is still alive when the insured dies.

When none of the beneficiaries are alive, or if there are no named beneficiaries when the insured dies, the insured's *estate* will automatically receive the proceeds of a life insurance policy. If this occurs, the policy's death benefit could be factored into the insured's taxable estate.

Revocable and Irrevocable – Beneficiary designations can be either revocable or irrevocable. Without the knowledge or consent of the beneficiary, the policy owner can change a *revocable* designation at any time. Policy owners cannot change an irrevocable designation without the beneficiary's written agreement. An *irrevocable* beneficiary has a vested interest in the policy; therefore, the policy owner cannot exercise certain rights without the beneficiary's consent. In addition to being unable to change the beneficiary designation, the policy owner cannot borrow against the policy's cash value; this loan would reduce the policy's face value. Also, policy owners _ assign the policy to another individual without the beneficiary's consent.

Common Disaster – When both the insured and the primary beneficiary die at approximately the same time from a common accident with no clear indication of who died first, a problem could arise in identifying who is eligible for the death benefit. The *Uniform Simultaneous Death Law* addresses this problem in most states; it protects the policy owner's original intent and the contingent beneficiary. Suppose the insured and the primary beneficiary die in the same accident with insufficient evidence to demonstrate who died first. In that circumstance, the insurance company will distribute the policy benefits as if the primary beneficiary were the first to die.

When added to a policy, the Common Disaster Clause states that if the insured and the primary beneficiary die in a common disaster, the insurer will assume that the primary beneficiary died first. Insurance providers would presume this even if the beneficiary outlived the insured by one or more days. The insurer will pay the proceeds to the contingent beneficiary or the insured's estate if no contingent beneficiary is designated. Most insurance providers specify a certain period, typically 14 to 30 days, in which death must occur for this provision to apply. Following the insured's death, the insurer will assume that the beneficiary died first as long as the beneficiary dies within this specified time. The law intends to fulfill the wishes of the policy owner regarding the payment of proceeds to beneficiaries.

Example 3.1 – Jim has a life insurance policy that contains a Common Disaster Clause. Jim is the insured; his wife Margot is named the primary beneficiary. Jim's son Brandon is named as the contingent beneficiary. Sadly, Jim and Margot got in a terrible auto accident, and Jim died immediately; Margot died four days later from her injuries sustained in the same accident. The policy included the Common Disaster Clause; therefore, the death benefit would be paid to Brandon, the contingent beneficiary, as if Margot, the primary beneficiary, had died before Jim, the insured.

Minor Beneficiaries – An insurer will either pay benefits *designated to a minor* to the minor's guardian or the minor's trustee if the trust is the named beneficiary. The trustee and guardian can be the same individual. Having life insurance benefits payable to a minor is generally not a sound practice.

Designation by Class – A beneficiary class uses a designation like "my children." This term can often be vague if the insured has been married multiple times, has adopted children, or has children out of wedlock.

An example of a less vague class would be the "children of the union of Becky and Kyle Smith." Many insurance providers encourage the insured to name each child specifically and state the percentage of benefits they will receive.

When naming beneficiaries, it is essential to be specific by referring to each individual by name and designating the exact amount to be given to each individual. Two class designations are available when an insured decides to "group" the beneficiaries: per capita and per stirpes. *Per capita* means "by the head," which evenly distributes benefits among the living named beneficiaries. *Per stirpes* means "by the bloodline," which distributes the death benefits of a beneficiary who died before the insured to that beneficiary's heirs.

Premium Payment

Modes – The policy stipulates when the premium payments are due, whether they are to be paid monthly, quarterly, semiannually, or annually, and to whom.

The *premium mode* is the manner or frequency of the policy owner's premium payments. Most insurance policies allow annual, semi-annual, quarterly, or monthly payments. Suppose the policy owner selects a premium mode other than annual. In that instance, there will be an additional charge to offset the loss of earnings since the insurer does not have the entire premium to invest. Insurance providers will also pass down the administrative costs associated with recurring billing to policy owners.

Whenever an insured dies during the period when they have previously paid the premium, the insurance provider must *refund any unearned premium* and the policy proceeds.

Grace Period – A *grace period* refers to the time after the premium due date that the policyholder has to pay the premium before the policy lapses (typically 30 or 31 days). The grace period protects the policy owner against an unintentional policy lapse. If a policyholder dies during this period, the death benefit is payable; however, insurers will deduct any unpaid premiums from the death benefit.

Level or Flexible Premiums – Most life insurance policies have a *level premium*, which means the premium remains the same throughout the contract's duration. However, policies such as universal life allow the policyholder to pay more or less than the planned premium. These policies have a *flexible premium*.

Reinstatement

A *reinstatement provision* allows policy owners to reinstate a lapsed policy. The maximum time limit for reinstatement is typically *three years* after the policy has lapsed. If the policy owner reinstates their policy, they must provide evidence of insurability. The policyholder must pay all back premiums with interest and could be required to repay any outstanding loans and interest. The advantage of reinstating a lapsed policy instead of purchasing a new one is that the insurer restores the policy to its original state. The policy retains the values calculated at the insured's issue age, and a policy owner *cannot reinstate* a surrendered policy.

Incontestability

The *incontestability clause* prevents insurance companies from denying a claim due to statements within the application after the policy has been effective for *two years*. This provision is especially relevant when there is a concealment of a material fact or a material misstatement of facts. Insurers can contest a claim during the first two years of the policy if they feel the applicant was misleading or provided inaccurate information on the application. The incontestability period is not applicable in the event of premium nonpayment. It also does not typically apply to statements concerning sex, age, or identity.

Misstatement of Age and Gender

An insured's age and gender are essential to the premium the insurer will charge for a life insurance policy. Consequently, a policy provision allows the insurance provider to adjust the policy when a misstatement of age or gender occurs. When the applicant misstated their age or gender, in the case of a claim, insurers can adjust the policy benefits to an amount that the premium at the correct gender or age would have obtained. The insurer should base a proceeds calculation on their rate when the policy was issued.

Policy Loans and Withdrawals

The *policy loan option* is only in policies with a cash value. The policyholder can borrow an amount equal to the available cash value. Insurers deduct any outstanding loans and accrued interest from the policy proceeds upon the insured's death. An outstanding policy loan prevents the policy from lapsing unless the loan amount and accrued interest exceed the available cash value. However, the insurance company must give the policyholder *30 days of written notice* that the policy will lapse. Insurers can defer a policy loan request for up to six months unless the reason for the loan is to cover the policy premium. Policy loans are not subject to federal income taxation.

Automatic Premium Loans – The automatic premium loan provision is typically added to cash value contracts at no additional charge but is not required. This type of loan *avoids the unintentional lapse of a policy* because of the nonpayment of premiums. The insurance provider automatically generates a loan against the policy's cash value for the amount of premium due when the policy owner has not paid the premium by the end of the grace period. It is a loan for which the insurance provider will charge interest. When the insured does not repay the loan and interest and dies suddenly, the insurer will deduct this amount from the death benefit. While the insurer can defer requests for other loans for up to *six months*, loan requests to pay past-due premiums must be honored immediately. Generally, the policyholder must opt for this provision in writing to make it effective.

Exclusions

Exclusions are the kinds of risks the policy will not cover. Specific exclusions are standard in all policies, and policy owners can attach other exclusions as riders. The most common exclusions in life insurance policies are aviation, hazardous occupations or hobbies, and war or military service.

Aviation – Most life insurance policies insure a policy owner as a pilot on a regularly scheduled airline or a fare-paying passenger. However, they exclude coverage for noncommercial pilots or require an additional premium.

Hazardous Occupations or Hobbies – When the insured is employed in a hazardous occupation or participates in dangerous hobbies like auto racing or skydiving, insurers will exclude death from a hazardous occupation or hobby from coverage. The underwriter can also charge a higher premium for insuring these risks.

Military Service or War – Insurers do not exclude military service in most life insurance policies issued today. However, insurance providers can use two different exclusions to limit the death benefit if the policyholder dies because of war or serving in the military. The *status clause* of the policy excludes every cause of death while the policyholder is on active duty in the military. The *results clause* only eliminates the death benefit if the insured dies due to an act of declared or undeclared war.

Suicide

In life insurance policies, the *suicide provision* protects the insurance carriers from individuals who obtain life insurance intending to commit suicide. Insurance policies typically specify when the insurer will not pay death proceeds if the insured commits suicide. When the insured commits suicide within two years after the policy effective date (issue date), the insurance company's liability is limited to a premium refund. When the insured commits suicide after two years, the policy will pay the death benefit to the designated beneficiary as if the insured had died of natural causes.

Policy Riders

Riders are written modifications attached to a policy that provide benefits not included in the original policy. A rider sometimes requires an additional premium, which helps tailor a policy to meet the insured's needs. Insurers classify riders according to their primary purpose.

Disability Riders

Specific riders provide benefits in the event of the insured's disability. In contrast, other riders, also known as *accelerated or living benefits* riders, provide partial payment of the death proceeds before the insured's death.

Waiver of Premium – The *waiver of premium* rider waives the insured's policy premium when they become disabled. Coverage will remain in force until the insured can return to work. If the insured cannot return to work, the premium payments will continue to be waived by the insurer. Most insurance providers impose a 6-month waiting period from the moment of disability until they waive the first premium. When the insured is still disabled after this waiting period, the insurance provider will refund the premium paid by the policy owner from the start of the disability. This rider typically expires when the policy owner reaches the age of 65.

For the insured to be eligible for this benefit, they must meet the definition of total disability stated in the policy. Although this definition differs from one policy to another, insurers usually define total disability as the inability to engage in any work activity. More specifically, total disability refers to the insured's failure to complete the duties of their occupation for the first two years. It also refers to any gainful employment which reasonably suits the insured by training, education, and experience. Insurance providers do not make benefit payments for a partial disability.

Waiver of Monthly Deduction – The *waiver of monthly deductions* rider will pay all monthly deductions while insureds are disabled, following a 6-month waiting period. This rider only pays monthly deductions, not the total premium amount necessary to accumulate cash value. The period this rider will pay monthly deductions varies based on the age at which the insured becomes disabled. Insurers typically include this rider in Universal Life and Variable Universal Life policies.

Monthly deductions include expense charges, charges for the actual cost of insurance, and charges or expenses for any benefits added to the policy through endorsement, rider, or amendment. They are stipulated in the insurance policy for the insurer to deduct from the account value.

Payor Benefit – The *payor benefit* rider is mainly associated with juvenile policies or any life insurance policy written on the life of a minor. Otherwise, it functions as a waiver of premium rider. When the payor, typically a guardian or parent, becomes disabled for at least six months or dies, the insurance provider will waive the premium payments until the minor reaches a certain age, such as 21. This rider is also appropriate when the policy owner and the insured are different individuals.

Disability Income – Under the *disability income* rider, if a disability occurs, the insurance provider will waive the policy premiums and pay a monthly income to the insured. The amount paid is typically based on a percentage of the policy's face amount to which it is attached.

Cost of Living – The *cost-of-living* rider addresses the inflation factor by automatically increasing the amount of coverage *without requiring evidence of insurability* from the insured. A cost-of-living factor tied to an inflation index like the Consumer Price Index (CPI) can increase the policy's face value.

Riders Covering Additional Insureds

Specific riders allow the policy owner to add additional insureds to the original policy, such as children's term or family term. A nonfamily term rider lets the policy owner change the insured specified under the policy.

Spouse/Other Insured Term – The *other insured rider* offers coverage for one or more family members other than the insured. The rider is typically level term insurance attached to the insured's base policy. This rider is also called a family rider. When the rider covers only the insured's spouse, it can be specified as a *spouse term rider* that allows the spouse to be added to the coverage for a stated amount and a limited period. It generally expires when the spouse reaches the age of 65.

Children's Term – The *children's term rider* allows insurers to add any children (natural, stepchildren, or adopted) of the insured to the coverage for a specified amount. This coverage is also term insurance and typically expires when minors reach a certain age (18 or 21). Most riders allow the minor to convert to a permanent insurance policy without providing evidence of insurability.

A children's term rider provides temporary life insurance coverage for all family children for one premium. The premium does not change due to the inclusion of additional children since insurers calculate premiums based on an average number of children.

Family Term – The *family term rider* combines the spouse term rider and the children's term rider into a single rider. When added to whole life policies, the family term rider delivers level term life insurance benefits that cover the spouse and every child.

Nonfamily Insureds – Other riders are available to insure someone who is not a member of the insured's family. These individuals are known as *nonfamily insureds*. The change of insured or substitute insured rider does not allow an additional insured. Instead, it permits changing insureds, subject to insurability. It is mainly used with Key Person insurance when the key person or employee terminates employment or retires. The rider lets the policy owner, employer, or owner change the insured to another critical employee, subject to insurability.

Riders Affecting the Death Benefit Amount

Some riders affect the amount of the death proceeds paid out to the beneficiary. The death benefit will either increase through premium refunds or multiple indemnities or decrease if the insurer pays out a portion of the death benefit to the insured while they are still living.

Accidental Death – The *accidental death* rider will pay some multiple of the face amount if death is caused by an accident as defined by the policy. Generally, death must occur within 90 days of such an accident. The benefit is typically two times (*double indemnity*) the face amount. At the same time, some policies will pay triple the face amount (*triple indemnity*) for an accidental death.

All policies stipulate what will be considered accidental death. Accidental death does not include death caused by any disability or health problem. In addition, deaths resulting from war, self-inflicted injuries, or hazardous hobbies or avocations are generally not covered. They would be insured under the base policy unless expressly excluded.

This rider often expires when the insured reaches the age of 65. Because of this rider, no additional cash value can accumulate. The accidental death benefits will apply only to the face amount of the base policy and not to any extra benefits that policy owners can purchase from the policy's dividends.

Accidental Death and Dismemberment – *Accidental death and dismemberment (AD&D) riders* pay the face amount for accidental death. It pays a percentage of that amount, called a capital sum, for accidental dismemberment. The rider's dismemberment portion will typically determine the benefit amount according to the injury's severity. Insurance providers will generally pay the entire principal amount in the event of the loss of two hands, two arms, two legs or the loss of vision in both eyes. A capital sum is generally limited to half of the face amount. It is payable for losing one hand, arm, leg, or eye. The dismemberment can be defined differently by insurers, from the loss of use to the actual severance of the limb.

Guaranteed Insurability – The *guaranteed insurability* rider lets the policy owner purchase additional coverage at specified dates in the future. These purchases are typically allowed every three years or following events like marriage or the birth of a child for an additional premium without evidence of insurability. Whenever this option is exercised, an insured purchases the extra coverage at their attained age. This rider usually expires when the insured reaches the age of 40. The guaranteed insurability rider is not adjusted or overcome by the existence of other riders.

Example 3.2 – Bobby's life insurance policy includes the waiver of premium and guaranteed insurability riders. Three years after the policy was issued, Bobby became totally and permanently disabled, and his insurer waived the premium payments. However, at the specified times or events stipulated in the policy, Bobby can purchase additional insurance coverage, and the insurer will waive premiums on those increases.

Return of Premium – The *return of premium* rider uses increasing term insurance. When a policy owner adds this rider to a whole life policy, it specifies that the original face amount is payable when death occurs before a given age. Nevertheless, the insurer owes the beneficiary an amount equal to all previously paid premiums. The return of premium rider typically expires at a specified time, such as age 60.

Term Riders – *Term riders* allow policy owners to purchase temporary insurance without issuing another policy. They are typically attached to a whole life policy to provide more coverage at a reduced cost.

Accelerated (Living) Benefits and Long-Term Care Riders – Accelerated death benefits will allow the *early payment* of a portion of the death proceeds if insureds have any of the following conditions:

- A terminal illness;
- A medical condition requiring an extraordinary medical intervention for the insured to survive, such as an organ transplant;
- A medical condition that drastically limits the insured's lifetime without extensive treatment;
- Inability to perform or complete activities of daily living (ADLs);
- Confinement to a long-term care facility or permanent institutionalization; or
- Any other condition that the Department of Insurance approves.

The maximum benefit is usually a percentage of the face amount of insurance, typically 50%. However, the insurance provider can legally pay up to 100% of the policy death benefit before the insured dies. There could be a dollar limit, such as $100,000, and the face amount of insurance will decrease after the payments. Accelerated death benefit payouts will not necessarily reduce the premium; however, the insurer could waive the premiums.

The *Living Needs Rider* allows for the payment of a part of the policy's death benefit if the insured is ever diagnosed with a terminal condition that will result in death within two years. This rider aims to provide the insured with the necessary funds for all medical and nursing home expenses due to the terminal illness. Most insurers do not charge an additional premium for this rider because it is simply an advance payment of the death benefit. The beneficiary receives the remainder of the policy's proceeds at the insured's death.

Long-term care (LTC) coverage, often a separate standalone policy, can also be marketed and sold as a rider to a life insurance policy. These riders allow for the payment of part of the death benefit, also called accelerated benefits, to cover the insured's health care expenses incurred in a nursing or convalescent home. Like the living needs rider, LTC benefit payments will reduce the payable amount to the beneficiary upon the insured's death.

Effects on a Death Benefit – When an insured withdraws a portion of the face amount through the accelerated benefits rider, the insurer will reduce the death benefit by that amount and the earnings lost by the insurance provider in interest income.

Example 3.3 – The policy's face amount is $100,000. However, the policy owner had to withdraw $30,000 from the policy three years before his death because of a terminal illness. Since the policy owner pulled out this amount, the insurer lost $300 worth of interest. Upon the insured's death, the beneficiary received $69,700 in death benefits:

$100,000 (face amount) - $30,000 (accelerated benefit) - $300 (lost interest) = $69,700 (death benefit)

The following table includes a breakdown of available riders that can be attached to a life insurance policy to provide policy owners with additional benefits:

TYPE OF RIDER	AVAILABLE RIDERS
Disability Riders	• Waiver of Premium • Waiver of Monthly Deduction • Payor Benefit • Disability Income • Accelerated (Living) Benefit
Riders Covering Additional Insureds	• Spouse • Children • Family • Nonfamily
Riders Affecting Death Benefits	• Accelerated Death Benefit • Accidental Death or AD&D • Guaranteed Insurability • Return of Premium • Term Riders

Policy Options

Policy owners have to decide how they will make benefit payments and how they should protect the policy's cash value. Policy owners must also choose how to invest the return of excess premium (dividends). The different options available to policyholders are Nonforfeiture, Dividend, and Settlement.

Nonforfeiture Options

Because a permanent life insurance policy has a cash value, insurers write certain guarantees *the policy owner cannot forfeit*. These guarantees, called *nonforfeiture values*, are required by state law to be contained in the policy. Every policy has a table showing the nonforfeiture values for at least 20 years. Policy owners will select one of the following nonforfeiture options: cash surrender value, reduced paid-up insurance, or extended term.

Cash – The policy owner can surrender the policy for its current cash value when coverage is no longer affordable or needed. Upon receiving the cash surrender value, the excess is taxed as ordinary income if the cash value exceeds the premiums paid. The insured is no longer covered once the policy owner chooses this option. Policies surrendered for their cash value cannot be reinstated. When the policy owner surrenders a life policy or annuity for its cash value, the insurer charges a fee known as a *surrender charge*.

Reduced Paid-up Insurance – Under this option, the insurance provider uses the policy's cash value as a single premium to purchase a paid-up permanent policy with a *reduced face amount* from the previous policy. The new reduced policy will remain in force until death or maturity, building cash value.

Extended Term – Under the *extended-term* option, the insurance provider uses the policy's cash value to convert to term insurance for the *exact face amount* as the previous permanent policy. The new coverage term will last for a period equal to the amount of cash value it will purchase. When the policy owner has not chosen one of these nonforfeiture options, if the insurer terminates the original policy, it will *automatically* apply the extended-term option.

Example 3.4 – Review the table below. Suppose the insured decides to exercise the reduced paid-up option at the end of year 15. The cash value of $8,100 can be used as a single premium to obtain paid-up insurance of the same type as the original policy. The insured does not have to pay an additional premium while retaining some life insurance, which, in this case, is $21,750.

The extended-term option specifies using the policy's cash value to purchase a term insurance policy at a single premium equal to the original policy's face value. In this example, the term insurance policy has a $50,000 face amount. The insurer determines that $8,100 of cash value is the equivalent of 18 years and eight days of $50,000 worth of protection for this insured.

Table of Guaranteed Values – $50,000 Whole Life Nonforfeiture Table (20 years)				
End of Policy Year	Cash or Loan Value	Reduced Paid-up	Extended-Term	
			Years	Days
1	$0	$0	0	60
2	$50	$250	0	122
3	$400	$1,600	2	147
4	$950	$3,600	5	27
5	$1,550	$5.650	7	183
6	$2,150	$7,600	9	185
7	$2,750	$9,400	11	52
8	$3,350	$11,100	12	186
9	$4,000	$12,850	13	315
10	$4,650	$14,500	15	6
11	$5,300	$16,050	15	333
12	$6,000	$17,600	16	249
13	$6,700	$19,100	17	95
14	$7,400	$20,450	17	255
15	**$8,100**	**$21,750**	**18**	**8**
16	$8,650	$23,050	18	116
17	$9,850	$24,440	18	208
18	$10,400	$25,550	18	227
19	$11,200	$26,750	18	231
20	$12,000	$27,850	18	20

Dividends and Dividend Options

Dividends are paid only on participating policies. When the policy owner buys a policy from a participating insurance provider, they pay a higher premium. The higher premium is a safety measure if the insurance provider's losses exceed expectations. The insurance provider will return a dividend to the policy owner if the interest earned by the company exceeds the assumptions or the actual mortality experience improves. Dividends are a return of surplus premiums and are *not taxable* to the policy owner. Insurance providers *cannot guarantee* dividends.

Insurers could pay the first dividend as early as the first policy anniversary. However, it must occur by the end of the 3rd policy year. From then on, insurance providers typically pay dividends yearly. Policy owners can receive their dividends in one of several different ways.

Cash – The insurance provider usually sends the policy owner a check for the dividend amount as it is declared each year.

Reduction of Premiums – The insurance provider uses the dividend to reduce the following year's premium. For instance, if the policy owner typically pays an annual premium of $1,000 and the insurance provider declares a $100 dividend, the policyholder would only pay a $900 premium that year.

Accumulation at Interest – The insurer keeps the dividend in an account that accrues interest. The policy owner is allowed to withdraw the dividends at any time. The interest amount is specified in the policy and compounds annually. Although the dividends are not taxable, *the interest on the dividends is taxable* to the policy owner when credited to the policy, regardless of whether or not the policy owner receives the interest.

Paid-up Additions – Policy owners can use the dividends to buy a single premium policy in addition to the permanent policy's face amount. No new separate policies are issued. However, each small single premium payment *increases the original policy's death benefit* by the amount the dividend will purchase. Also, each paid-up policy builds cash value and pays dividends. The additional coverage that policy owners can buy with the dividend will depend on the insured's attained age when the dividend is declared.

When a policy owner does not select the dividend option, the insurance provider will *automatically* use paid-up additions to increase the death benefit of the original policy by the amount the dividend will buy.

Paid-up Option – Generally, the insurance company first accumulates the dividends at interest. It then uses the accumulated dividends, plus interest and the policy's cash value, to "pay up" the policy early. When the policy owner has a continuous premium whole life policy where premiums are paid to age 100, using the paid-up option, the insured can "pay up" the policy early.

One-year Term Option – The insurer uses the dividend to buy additional insurance in the form of *one-year term insurance* that increases the overall policy death benefit. The policy owner can use the dividend as a single premium on as much one-year term insurance as it will purchase. They can also buy term insurance equal to the policy's cash value for as long as it will remain in force. When the insured dies during the one-year term, the beneficiary receives both the death proceeds of the original policy and the death benefit of the one-year term insurance.

Settlement Options

Settlement options are the methods insurance companies use to pay a beneficiary the death proceeds upon the insured's death or to pay the endowment benefit should the insured live to the endowment date. When completing the application, the policy owner can choose a settlement option and may change that selection during the insured's life. Once the policy owner selects the settlement option, the beneficiary cannot change it. When the policy owner does not choose a settlement option, the beneficiary can pick one at the time of the insured's death.

Cash Payment (Lump Sum) – Upon the insured's death or at endowment, the contract pays the proceeds in a cash payment, known as a *lump sum*, unless the recipient chooses a different mode of settlement. Generally, payment of the principal face amount following the insured's death is not taxable as income.

Life Income – The *life-income option*, referred to as straight life, provides the recipient with an income the policyholder cannot outlive. Insurers guarantee installment payments for as long as the recipient lives, regardless of the date of death. They base each paid installment on the principal amount and the *recipient's* life expectancy. If the beneficiary lives long, payments can exceed the total principal. However, when the beneficiary dies after they start receiving installments, the policy owner forfeits the balance of the principal to the insurance provider. There is a chance that the beneficiary might not live long enough to receive all the life insurance proceeds.

Consequently, insurance companies make options available that provide at least a partial guarantee to pay out some or all of the benefits. With each of the guarantees, an insurer reduces the installment's size.

Under the *life income with period certain option*, the recipient has a lifetime income and a guaranteed installment period. Insurers guarantee these payments for the recipient's lifetime, but a specified period is also guaranteed. For example, a life income with a ten-year certain option will provide the recipient with an income for as long as they live. When the recipient dies shortly after beginning to receive payments, insurers will continue the installments to a beneficiary for the remainder of the ten years. As previously stated, the life income with period certain option's installment will be smaller than the life income only option.

The *life income joint and survivor* option will provide guaranteed income payments for two or more recipients as long as they live. Most contracts specify that the surviving recipient will receive a reduced payment after the first recipient's death.

Typically, insurers write the reduced option as "joint and 1/2 survivor" or "joint and 2/3 survivor." The surviving beneficiary will receive either 1/2 or 2/3 of the death benefit when both beneficiaries are alive. Policy owners who want to protect two beneficiaries, like elderly parents, usually choose this option. Unless a period certain option is also selected, there is no guarantee that the insurer will pay full life insurance benefits if all beneficiaries die soon after the installment payments begin. This option guarantees, however, a lifetime income for all beneficiaries.

Interest Only – Under the *interest-only option*, the insurer retains the policy proceeds. It pays interest on the proceeds to the recipient (beneficiary) monthly, quarterly, semiannually, or annually. The insurance provider typically guarantees a particular interest rate and pays interest over and above the guaranteed rate. An interest-only option is temporary because the insurance company retains the proceeds until it pays out in a lump sum or under another settlement option. When the beneficiary can choose a settlement option, the interest option is sometimes used as a temporary option if the beneficiary requires some time to decide which settlement option to select. For example, the policy owner can specify that interest only will be paid yearly to the surviving spouse. The policy owner's children receive the principal at the surviving spouse's death or when they reach a certain age.

Fixed Period – With the *fixed-period installments option*, also called *period certain*, a policy owner chooses a fixed period of years. The insurer pays equal installments to the recipient. These payments will continue for the stated period even if the recipient dies before the end of that period. If the recipient dies, the payments will continue to a beneficiary. The insurer will determine the size of each installment payment based on the principal amount, guaranteed interest, and the length of the period selected. The longer the period chosen, the smaller each installment payment will be. This option does not ensure income for the beneficiary's lifetime; however, it guarantees the entire principal gets distributed.

Fixed Amount – Under the *fixed-amount installments option*, a specified, fixed amount is paid in installments until the proceeds (principal and interest) are exhausted. The recipient pays a specified fixed dollar amount until the proceeds are gone. When the beneficiary dies before the proceeds are distributed, a contingent beneficiary will continue receiving the installments until all proceeds are exhausted. With this option, the size of each installment payment will determine how long the beneficiary will receive benefits. The larger the installment payment, the shorter the income period will be. Like the fixed-period option, this option does not guarantee the beneficiary will receive payments for their lifetime. However, it does ensure that the insurance company pays all proceeds.

The following table includes a breakdown of available options that policy owners can add to life insurance policies to provide additional benefits:

OPTION TYPE	AVAILABLE OPTIONS
Nonforfeiture Options	• Reduced Paid-up • Extended-Term (automatic) • Cash
Dividend Options	• Cash • Reduction of Premium • Accumulation at Interest • Paid-up Additions (automatic) • Paid-up Insurance • One-year Term
Settlement Options	• Cash (automatic) • Life Income • Interest Only • Fixed Period • Fixed Amount

Chapter Review

This chapter explained life insurance policy provisions, options, and riders. Remember that provisions stipulate the rights and obligations under the contract; riders modify provisions, and options specify ways to distribute a policy's proceeds. Let's review the major points of the chapter:

POLICY PROVISIONS	
Standard Provisions	• *Consideration* – the parties to a contract exchange something of value • *Entire contract* – policy (with amendments and riders) and copy of the application • *Grace period* – the period after the premium is due, during which the policy will not lapse • *Incontestability* – the insurance provider cannot contest misstatements on the application after a specified period • *Insuring clause* – the basic agreement between the insurer and the policy owner • *Misstatement of age or gender* – the death benefit is adjusted according to the correct age and gender at policy issue • *Payment of premiums* – the policy owner pays premiums in advance • *Reinstatement* – policy owners can restore a policy within a specified period with proof of insurability
Other Provisions	• *Assignment* – absolute or collateral • *Exclusions* – noncommercial aviation, hazardous occupation, war or military service, suicide within a specified period • *Free look* – applicants can return the policy for a refund of the premium within a specified period • *Ownership* – the policy owner has ownership rights

Beneficiaries	• *Designations* – can be a person (including minors), class of individuals, estates
	• *Succession* – the levels of priority or choice; each level in the succession is eligible only if the beneficiary in the level above has died:
	  - *Primary* – has first claim to the policy benefits
	• - *Contingent* (secondary, tertiary) – next claim after the primary
	• *Policy owner's right to change a beneficiary:*
	  - *Revocable* – the policy owner can change beneficiaries at any time
	  - *Irrevocable* – the policy owner can only change beneficiaries with the consent of the beneficiary
	• *Common disaster clause* – protects the rights of contingent beneficiaries; if the primary beneficiary and the insured died at approximately the same time, it is assumed that the primary beneficiary was the first to die

Policy Loans, Withdrawals and Partial Surrenders	• *Cash loans* – a policy's cash value with unpaid loans and interest deducted • *Automatic premium loans* – prevent an unintentional lapse in the policy due to nonpayment of premium
RIDERS	
Disability	• *Waiver of premium* – waives the premium if the insured becomes totally disabled; 6-month waiting period before benefits start • *Waiver of monthly deductions* – waives the insurance cost in the event of the insured's disability • *Payor benefit* – performs like a waiver of premium rider; used for juvenile policies • *Disability Income* – if a disability occurs, the insurer will waive the policy premiums and pay a monthly income to the insured typically based on a percentage of the policy's face amount • *Cost of Living* – this rider addresses inflation by automatically increasing the amount of coverage without evidence of insurability from the insured; the policy's face value can increase by a cost of living factor tied to the Consumer Price Index (CPI)
Accelerated Benefit	• Early payment if the insured is diagnosed with a specified catastrophic illness • The insured receives a portion of the death proceeds • Death benefits are reduced by the amount paid plus the insurer's lost earnings
Riders that affect the Death Benefit	• *Accidental death* – pays double or triple indemnity if accidental death takes place as defined in the policy; death must occur within 90 days of the accident • *Guaranteed insurability* – allows for the purchase of additional insurance at specified times at the attained age, without evidence of insurability • *Return of premium* – increasing term is added to a whole life policy that specifies if death occurs before a given age, not only is the death benefit payable to the beneficiary but all premiums are paid as well
Additional Insured	• *Spouse/other insured* – term rider (limited time, limited coverage); typically expires when the spouse turns age 65 • *Children's term* – covers all of the insured's children (limited time, limited coverage); can be converted to a permanent policy • *Nonfamily insured* – used by businesses (e.g., key person insurance)

OPTIONS	
Nonforfeiture	• *Reduced paid-up insurance* – uses a policy's cash value as a single premium to purchase a permanent policy with a reduced face amount • *Extended-term* – automatic option; uses a policy's cash value to convert to term insurance • *Cash surrender value* – no more insurance after that
Dividend	• *Cash* – insurance companies send a check to the insured • *Reduction of premium* – dividends are applied to the following year's premium • *Accumulation at interest* – insurance companies keep the dividend in an account where interest accumulates • *Paid-up addition* – dividends are used to increase the policy face amount • *Paid-up insurance* – dividends are used to pay up a policy early • *One-year term* – dividends are used to purchase additional insurance
Settlement	• *Cash* – a lump-sum payment that is usually not taxable • *Life income* – provides an income the beneficiary cannot outlive; if the beneficiary dies too soon, there is no guarantee that the entire principal will be paid out; available as either single life or as joint and survivor • *Interest only* – the insurance provider retains the principal and only pays out interest • *Fixed period* – payments are received for a specified period until all the proceeds are paid out • *Fixed amount* – payments are received in specified amounts until all the proceeds are paid out

CHAPTER 4:
Taxes, Retirement, and Other Insurance Concepts

This chapter will help broaden your knowledge of life insurance. It examines various topics, from group life insurance and specific plans for businesses to retirement plans and social security benefits. Finally, this chapter discusses the taxation rules for life insurance premiums and proceeds. After finishing the chapter, you will have learned the following topics:

- Third-Party Ownership
- Viatical Settlements
- Life Settlements
- Group Life Insurance
- Retirement Plans
- Life Insurance Needs and Analysis/Suitability
- Taxation of Insurance Premiums, Proceeds, and Dividends
- Social Security Benefits

Third-Party Ownership

Insurers write most insurance policies where the policy owner is also the insured. However, there are instances where someone other than the insured may own the contract. These contracts are also known as *third-party ownership*. "Third-party owner" is a legal term that identifies any person or entity not listed as an insured under the policy but has a legally enforceable right. Most third-party ownership policies are written in business situations or for minors whose parent is the policy owner.

Viatical Settlements

Viatical settlements allow a person with a life-threatening condition to sell their current life insurance policy and use the proceeds when needed before their death.

While a viatical settlement is not a policy option, it is a separate contract. The insured sells the death benefit to a *third party* at a discount. There are several essential concepts you must understand about viaticals:

- The insureds are known as *viators*;
- An individual, other than a viator, that enters into a viatical settlement contract is known as a viatical settlement *provider*;
- Viatical *producers* represent the providers; and
- Viatical *brokers* represent the insureds.

A viator typically receives a *percentage* of the policy's face value from the person who buys it. The new policy owner maintains the premium payments and will collect the full death benefit (income-tax-free).

Life Settlements

The term *life settlement* pertains to any financial transaction where a life insurance policy owner sells their policy to a third party for compensation, usually cash. A life settlement requires an absolute (permanent) assignment of all rights to the policy from the original policy owner to the new policy owner.

Policy owners can sell their policies because the premium costs have grown too high to continue the policy. They can also sell their policies if coverage is no longer needed. In many situations, however, life settlement transactions are offered to senior citizens with a life-threatening illness and a short life expectancy. In these cases, the policy owner can sell the policy to a life settlement provider for an amount more significant than what they would receive if they surrendered the policy for a cash value.

Example 4.1 – An insured, age 70, owns a $1,000,000 life insurance policy. He recently sold his small business for $5,000,000 and decided he no longer needed the life insurance coverage. The cash value is $390,000, which the insurance provider would give the policy owner if he cashed in the policy. After reviewing his medical records, a life settlement provider may offer him $575,000 for the policy. Once the policy owner transfers ownership and has received the funds, the life settlement company will assume the premium payments until the insured dies. The life settlement company will receive the $1,000,000 policy proceeds at that time.

Definitions

Life Settlements are not involved in establishing new life insurance coverage. The Life Settlement Act defines terms that do not conflict with the sale of the original life insurance but accurately identify the distinctions in the business of Life Settlement. Some of the more critical definitions include the following:

Business of Life Settlement – The term *business of life settlement* means any activity related to soliciting and selling a life settlement contract to a third party with no insurable interest in the insured.

Owner – The term *owner* refers to the life insurance policy owner seeking to enter into a life settlement contract. The term does not include an insurer, a financing entity, a qualified institutional buyer, a related provider trust, or a special purpose entity.

Insured – In a life settlement contract, an *insured* is a person covered under the policy considered for sale.

Life Expectancy – *Life expectancy* is an essential concept in life settlement contracts. It is a calculation based on the average number of months the insurer expects the insured to live due to mortality factors and medical history.

Life Settlement Contract – *Life settlement contracts* establish the terms under which the life settlement provider will compensate the policy owner in return for the transfer, assignment, sale, or release of any portion of any of the following:

- The death benefit;
- Policy ownership;
- Any beneficial interest; or
- Interest in a trust or other entity that is the policy owner.

Life Settlement Broker – A *life settlement broker* solicits, negotiates, or offers to negotiate a life settlement contract for compensation. Life settlement brokers only represent the policy owners. They have a fiduciary responsibility to act according to the owners' best interests and instructions.

Life Settlement Provider – A *life settlement provider* is an individual, besides the owner, who enters into a life settlement contract with the owner.

Group Life Insurance

Insurers write individual life insurance on a single life and base coverage on the underwriting of that individual's life. In contrast, the sponsoring organization obtains group life insurance, which covers the lives of more than one individual member of that group. Insurance providers generally write group insurance for employee-employer groups, but others also qualify for this coverage. They typically write this coverage as annually renewable term insurance. Two features that differentiate group insurance from individual insurance are:

- Evidence of insurability is generally not required unless an applicant is enrolling for coverage outside of the regular enrollment period; and
- The plan's participants (insureds) do not receive a policy because they do not control or own it.

Instead, all insured participants under the group plan receive a *certificate of insurance* as proof of coverage. It also includes policy benefits, exclusions, and procedures for filing a claim. The actual policy, or master policy/contract, is issued to the group's sponsoring organization, which is often an employer. The group sponsor is the policy owner and is the one that exercises control over the policy.

Group underwriting differs from individual insurance underwriting—it is based on the group's makeup and characteristics. Some of the factors that are of concern to group underwriters include the following:

- **Purpose of the Group** – The group must exist for a purpose other than obtaining group insurance.
- **Size of the Group** – Insurers base a group's size on the Law of Large Numbers of similar risks. The larger the number of people in the group, the more accurate the predictions of future loss experience will be.
- **Turnover of the Group** – For the underwriter, a group should have a steady turnover, with younger, lower-risk employees entering and older, higher-risk employees leaving.
- **The Group's Financial Strength** – Group insurance is costly to administer. The underwriter must consider whether the group's financial resources are sufficient to pay the policy premiums and whether the group can renew the coverage.

A unique aspect of group underwriting is that insurers base the cost of coverage on the ratio of men to women and the group's average age. In addition, to decrease adverse selection, the insurance company will require a minimum number of participants in the group, depending on whether the employees or the employer pay the insurance premium.

Conversion Privilege

The conversion privilege is another characteristic of group insurance. When an employer terminates an employee's membership in the insured group, the employee can convert to an individual policy at a standard rate *without proving insurability* based on the person's attained age. The group life policy can convert to any form of insurance issued by the insurance company (usually whole life), except for term insurance. The death benefit or face amount will equal the face amount of the group term insurance, but the premium will be higher. The employee typically has *31 days after terminating from the group* to exercise the conversion option. The employee still has access to coverage under the original group policy.

Additional rules that apply to conversion involve the insured's disability or death and the termination of the master policy. When the insured dies during the conversion period, whether or not the insured completed the application for an individual policy, the group policy has to pay a death benefit. Every individual who has been on the plan for at least *five years* can convert to individual permanent insurance of the same coverage in the event of the termination of the master contract.

Contributory vs. Noncontributory

The employer or other group sponsor can share premiums with the employees or pay all premiums. When an employer pays all premiums, the plan is called a *noncontributory plan*. Under a noncontributory plan, an insurance provider will require 100% of eligible employees to enroll. When employees and employers split group insurance premiums, the plan is called a *contributory plan*. Under a contributory plan, an insurance provider will require that 75% of eligible employees enroll.

Retirement Plans

Qualified vs. Nonqualified Plans

The IRS approved employer-sponsored *qualified retirement plans*, which offer benefits to employers and employees, including deductible contributions and tax-deferred growth.

Qualified plans included the following characteristics:

- Intended for the sole benefit of the employees and their beneficiaries;
- Are officially written and communicated to employees;
- Use a contribution or benefit formula that does not discriminate in the prohibited group's favor—stockholders, officers, or highly paid employees;
- Are not exclusively geared to the prohibited group;
- Are approved by the IRS;
- Are permanent; and
- Have a vesting requirement.

In contrast, nonqualified plans are not contingent upon the requirements regarding vesting, participation, and discrimination found in qualified plans. Nonqualified plans do not require government approval. They are a means for an employer to discriminate in favor of a valuable employee regarding employee benefits. Nonqualified plans accept after-tax contributions.

Some examples of nonqualified plans include:

- Individual annuities and deferred compensation plans for highly paid executives;
- Section 162 executive bonus plans; and
- Split-dollar insurance arrangements.

The table below shows the differences between qualified and nonqualified retirement plans.

QUALIFIED	NONQUALIFIED
Contributions currently tax deductible	Contributions NOT currently tax deductible
Plan APPROVED by the IRS	Plan DOES NOT NEED IRS APPROVAL
Plan CANNOT DISCRIMINATE	Plan CAN DISCRIMINATE
Earnings grow TAX DEFERRED	Earnings grow TAX DEFERRED
ALL WITHDRAWALS are TAXED	EXCESS over cost basis is TAXED

Individual Qualified Plans – IRA and Roth IRA

Traditional IRAs and Roth IRAs are the most common qualified individual retirement plans. Anyone with *earned income* is eligible to contribute to either plan.

A traditional *Individual Retirement Account (IRA)* lets individuals make tax-deductible contributions regardless of age. Previously, individuals could contribute to the account until age 70 ½; however, the SECURE Act of 2019 removed the prior age limit for all contributions. Plan participants can contribute up to a specified dollar limit each year or 100% of their salary if it is less than the maximum allowable amount. Individuals aged 50 or older are qualified to make additional (catch-up) contributions. A married couple can contribute double the amount for an individual, even if only one spouse has an earned income. Each spouse must maintain a separate account that does not exceed the individual limit.

In traditional IRAs, the owner can withdraw funds at any time. However, withdrawals before age 59 ½ are treated as early withdrawals and will be subject to the 10% additional tax. At 59 ½, the owner can withdraw assets without paying the 10% tax. However, the owner must start to receive distributions from the IRA at age 73 (the SECURE Act extended the required minimum distribution age from 72 to 73). At age 73, the owner must receive at least a minimum annual amount, known as the *required minimum distribution (RMD)*.

Roth IRAs are a type of individual retirement account funded with after-tax contributions. Like traditional IRAs, individuals can contribute 100% of their earned income up to an IRS-specified maximum (the dollar amounts change yearly). Roth contributions can continue irrespective of the account owner's age. Unlike a traditional IRA, distributions do not have to begin at age 73 (previously 72). Roth IRAs grow tax-free if the account is open for at least five years.

Taxation of IRAs and Roth IRAs – The following taxation rules apply to *contributions* made to traditional IRA plans:

- The income of the individual will determine the tax-deductible contributions for the year;
- Contributions must be made in *"cash"* to be tax-deductible (the term cash refers to any form of money, such as cash, check, or money order);
- As long as the excess amounts remain in the IRA, any excess contributions are taxed at 6% per year; and
- The IRS will not tax any money accumulated in the account (tax-deferred earnings) until withdrawal.

A *distribution* from an IRA is subject to income taxation when the withdrawal occurs. In case of an early distribution before 59 ½, a 10% penalty will also apply. There are certain conditions under which the 10% early withdrawal penalty would not be applicable (penalty tax exceptions):

- The participant is age 59 ½;
- The participant is disabled;
- The withdrawal goes toward the down payment on a home (not to exceed $10,000, and typically for first-time homebuyers);
- Withdrawals to pay for expenses relating to post-secondary education; and
- Withdrawals are used for catastrophic medical expenditures or upon death.

The following taxation rules apply to Roth IRAs:

- Contributions are not tax-deductible, and
- The IRS will assess a 6% tax penalty on excess contributions.

TRADITIONAL IRA	ROTH IRA
Contribute 100% of income up to an IRS-specified limit	
Excess contribution penalty is 6%	
Grows tax-deferred	Grows tax-free (if the account is open for five years)
Contributions are *tax-deductible* (Made with "pre-tax dollars")	Contributions are *not tax-deductible* (Made with "after-tax dollars")
10% penalty for early nonqualified distributions before age 59 ½ (some exceptions apply)	Qualified distribution cannot occur until the account has been open for 5 years and the owner is 59 ½
Distributions are *taxable*	Distributions are *not taxable*
Payouts must begin by 73	No required minimum age for payouts

Rollovers and Transfers – Situations arise where an individual may move the money from one qualified retirement plan to another. However, benefits withdrawn from any qualified retirement plan are taxable the year they are received if the individual does not move the money correctly. The two ways to accomplish this are through a *rollover* and a *transfer* from one account to another.

A *rollover* is a tax-free cash distribution from one retirement plan to another. Usually, participants must complete IRA rollovers within 60 days after withdrawing the money from the first plan. Whenever the distribution from the first plan is paid directly to the participant, the payor must withhold 20% of the distribution. Individuals can avoid the 20% withholding of funds by moving the distribution *from the first plan to the new IRA plan's trustee or administrator/custodian*. This transaction is known as a *direct rollover*.

A *transfer (or direct transfer)* is a tax-free transfer of funds from one retirement program to a traditional IRA. It can also directly transfer an interest in a traditional IRA *from one trustee to another*.

Plans for Employers

In addition to individual plans, different types of qualified plans are available for small and large employers.

Self-Employed Plans (HR-10 or Keogh Plans) – The *HR-10 or Keogh Plan* allows *self-employed individuals* to receive coverage under an IRS-qualified retirement plan. These plans let self-employed individuals fund their retirement programs with pre-tax dollars as if they were under a corporate pension or retirement plan. To be covered under a Keogh retirement plan, the individual must be self-employed or be a partner working full-time or part-time who owns at least 10% of the business.

Contribution limits are either the lesser of 100% of their total earned income or an established dollar limit. The contribution is tax-deductible, and it accumulates tax deferred until withdrawn.

Payouts can become available immediately upon a participant's death. If a participant becomes disabled, they may collect benefits directly, or the funds can be left to accumulate. When a participant enters retirement, funds distribution must occur no earlier than 59 ½ and no later than 73. If an individual withdraws funds before age 59 ½, there is a 10% penalty. Individuals can discontinue payments without incurring a penalty, and funds can be left to accumulate.

Under eligibility requirements, a person must be included in the Keogh Plan if they:

- Are at least 21 years old;
- Have worked for a self-employed individual for one year or more; and
- Have worked full-time at least 1,000 hours per year.

Employers must contribute the same percentage of funds to the employee's account as they contribute to their retirement account.

Simplified Employee Pensions (SEPs) – A *Simplified Employee Pension (SEP)* is a qualified plan for the self-employed or the small employer. An employee establishes and maintains an individual retirement account in a SEP to receive employer contributions. An employee's gross income does not include employer contributions. The primary difference between SEPs and IRAs is the larger amount participants can contribute each year to a SEP. This amount can be 25% of the employee's compensation or an annual dollar limit established by the IRS, whichever is less.

SIMPLE Plans – SIMPLE (Savings Incentive Match Plan for Employees) plans are available to eligible small businesses. They must have *no more than 100 employees* who earned at least $5,000 in compensation from the employer during the previous year. To set up a SIMPLE plan, the employer must not already have a qualified retirement plan. Employees who participate can defer up to a specified amount each year. The employer will make a dollar-for-dollar matching contribution up to an amount equal to 3% of the employee's yearly compensation. *Taxation is deferred* on earnings and contributions until funds are withdrawn.

Profit-Sharing and 401(k) Plans – Profit-sharing plans are qualified retirement plans. A portion of the company's profit is shared with employees and contributed to the plan. When the plan does not provide a definitive formula for calculating the profits to be shared, employer contributions must be *systematic and substantial*.

A 401(k) qualified retirement plan lets employees reduce their current salaries by remitting amounts into a retirement plan. The company can also match the employee's contribution, whether on a percentage or dollar-for-dollar basis. Under a 401(k) plan, participants can elect to either have the money contributed to the 401(k) or receive *taxable cash compensation*, referred to as cash or deferred arrangement plans (CODA). The employee's gross income does not include contributions up to a dollar ceiling amount into the plan. The ceiling amount is adjusted each year for inflation. The plan allows participants age 50 or older to make additional contributions up to a limit at the end of the calendar year.

401(k) plans allow early withdrawals for specific hardship reasons, such as disability or death. Sometimes, they allow loans up to 50% of the participant's vested accrued benefit or a particular dollar limit (established annually by the IRS).

403(b) Tax-Sheltered Annuities (TSAs) – A 403(b) plan or a tax-sheltered annuity (TSA) is a qualified plan available to employees of public school systems and employees of certain *nonprofit corporations under Section 501(c)(3)* of the Internal Revenue Code.

The employee or the employer makes contributions through a salary reduction. The employee's current income does not include their contributions. As with any other qualified retirement plan, 403(b) plans limit employee contributions to a maximum amount that changes annually, adjusted for inflation. The same catch-up provisions are also applicable.

	ELIGIBILITY	WHO CONTRIBUTES
HR-10 (Keogh)	Self-employed	Employer matches employee's contribution
SEP	Small employer or self-employed	Employer only
SIMPLE	Small employers (< 100 employees)	Employer matches employee's contribution
401(k)	Any employer	Employer matches employee's contribution
403(b) – TSA	Nonprofit organizations	Employer and employee

Life Insurance Needs and Analysis/Suitability

Personal Insurance Needs

Survivor Protection – The primary wage earner's death will typically stop the flow of income to a family. The death of a non-earning spouse who takes care of minor children may also cause significant financial hardship for the survivors. Life insurance can provide the required funds for survivors to maintain their lifestyle if the insured dies. This coverage is known as *survivor protection*, which requires a careful audit of current assets and liabilities and determining the needs of the survivors.

Cash Accumulation – Individuals can use life insurance to accumulate specific amounts of money for particular needs, guaranteeing that the funds will be available when needed. For instance, some life insurance policies, such as whole life, provide permanent protection and accumulate a cash value available to the policyholder during their term.

Liquidity – The cash accumulation feature allows some life insurance policies to provide *liquidity* to the policy owner. Policy owners can borrow against the policy's cash value for immediate needs.

Estate Creation – An individual can create an estate through savings, earnings, and investments. However, all of these methods require discipline and significant time. Purchasing life insurance, however, *creates an immediate estate*. Estate creation is consequential for young families who have not yet had time to accumulate assets. When individuals buy a life insurance policy, they will immediately have an estate of at least that face value when they pay the initial premium. No other legal method exists by which individuals can create an immediate estate at such a small cost.

Estate Conservation – The proceeds from life insurance can pay *federal estate taxes and inheritance taxes*. Beneficiaries do not need to sell off the deceased's assets.

Business Insurance Needs

For the same reason individuals use life insurance, businesses use life insurance to create an immediate payment upon the insured's death.

Businesses commonly use life insurance as an employee benefit, protecting employees and their beneficiaries. Other forms of life insurance can even cover the company itself and serve business owners and their survivors. These include compensating executives, funding business continuation agreements, and protecting the business against financial loss caused by the disability or death of key employees.

Key Person – Businesses can suffer a devastating financial loss due to the premature death of a key employee, who is someone with skills, business contacts, or specialized knowledge. A business can reduce the risk of such a loss using *key person insurance*. Under this coverage, the insured is the key employee, and the employer is the:

- Applicant;
- Policy owner;
- Premium payer; and
- Beneficiary.

If a key employee dies, the business will use the money for the additional costs of operating the company and replacing the employee. The business cannot take a tax deduction for the premium expense. However, in the event of a key employee's death, the benefits paid to the business are typically received as tax-free income. The employee does not require any special contracts or agreements. They only need to provide their permission for this coverage.

Buy-Sell Funding – In the event of the death of an individual owner or a partner, the surviving family members (or partners) will sell the business to settle the deceased's estate. Unless the business owner (sole proprietor) or partners make a prior arrangement, the surviving family members (or partners) may have to sell the business at a loss. *Buy-sell agreements* set a value, or purchase price, on a business and are used to establish someone else's intent to buy the company upon the insured's death. Businesses can purchase life insurance to provide the necessary funds for the buy-sell agreement. They can use insurance to fund the buy-sell agreement either fully or partially.

Partnership buy-sell agreements let the surviving partner or partners buy the deceased partner's share of the business from the deceased's family. A partnership buy-sell agreement can be either a cross-purchase or entity plan. In a *cross-purchase plan*, each partner buys insurance on each other's lives. Every partner is the owner, premium payer, and beneficiary of the life insurance on the lives of the other partners. The amount of life insurance equals each partner's share of the deceased partner's business interest purchase price. In contrast, the business must buy out the ownership interest of any disabled or deceased partner under the *entity plan*.

Executive Bonuses – An *executive bonus* is an arrangement in which the employer offers the employee a wage increase in the premium amount on a new life insurance policy taken out on the employee. The employee owns the policy and has all the control. Because the employer treated the premium payment like a bonus, that premium amount is *tax-deductible to employers* and *income taxable to employees*. The employer would only offer the benefit if the employee were willing to accept these conditions.

Taxation of Insurance Premiums, Proceeds, and Dividends

Generally speaking, the following taxation rules apply to individual life insurance policies:

- *Premiums* are not tax-deductible;
- *Death benefit:*
  - Tax-free if a named beneficiary takes the death benefit as a lump-sum distribution; and
  - The principal is tax-free; interest is taxable if the insurer pays the death benefit in installments other than a lump sum.

Amounts Available to Policy Owners

As previously discussed, permanent life insurance provides living benefits. Policyholders can receive those living benefits in several ways.

Dividends – Dividends are a return of unused premiums and are not considered income for tax purposes. When dividends are left with the insurance provider to accumulate interest, the interest on the dividend is taxed as ordinary income every year it earns. The policy owner does not need to be paid out the interest for this to be the case.

Cash Value Accumulations – A policyholder can borrow against their policy's cash value accumulations or receive the cash value upon policy surrender. Cash values grow tax-deferred, and any cash value over and above the premium payments is taxable as ordinary income upon endowment or surrender. The insurer pays the face amount upon the policy owner's death, and there is no more cash value. Death benefits are usually delivered to the beneficiary and are tax-free.

Policy Loans – The policy owner can borrow against the policy's cash value. Money borrowed against the cash value is not taxable as income; however, the insurer charges interest on outstanding policy loans. Policy loans, with interest, can be repaid to the insurance company in any of the following ways:

- By the policy owner while the policy is in force;
- At policy surrender or maturity, deducted from the cash value; or
- At the insured's death, deducted from the death benefit.

Surrenders – When a policy owner surrenders a policy for cash value, some of the cash surrender value is taxed as income if it exceeds the premiums paid into the policy. Should the policy owner withdraw cash value from a universal life policy through a partial surrender, the death benefit and the cash value are reduced by the surrender amount.

Example 4.1 – Consider the following scenario:

- Face amount: $300,000
- Premiums paid: $70,000
- Total cash value: $100,000

If the policy owner surrendered $30,000 of cash value, the $30,000 would be tax-free. If the policy owner took out $100,000, the last $30,000 would be taxable since the $100,000 exceeds the premiums paid in by $30,000.

Accelerated Benefits – A terminally ill insured receives accelerated benefits tax-free under a life insurance policy. When a chronically ill insured (e.g., Alzheimer's disease, cancer, or other severe illness) accepts accelerated benefit payments, these benefits are tax-free up to a specific limit. The insured must include any amount received over this dollar limit in their gross income.

Amounts Received by Beneficiaries

General Rule and Exceptions – Life insurance proceeds paid to named beneficiaries are usually *free of federal income tax* if received as a lump sum payment. An exception to this rule will apply if the benefit payment results from a transfer for value, which occurs when the life insurance policy owner sells the policy to another party before the insured's death.

Settlement Options – With *settlement options*, the interest portion of the payments is taxable as income when the beneficiary receives both principal and interest payments.

Example 4.2 – Suppose $100,000 of life insurance proceeds were used in a settlement option, paying $13,000 annually for ten years. In that case, $10,000 annually would be tax-free, and $3,000 per year would be taxable as income.

PERMANENT LIFE FEATURES	TAX TREATMENT
Premiums	Not tax-deductible
Cash value exceeding paid premiums	Taxable at surrender
Policy Loans	Not income taxable
Policy dividends	Not taxable
Dividend interest	Taxable in the year earned
Lump-sum death benefit	Not income taxable

Group Life and Employer-Sponsored Plans

The *premiums* that an employer pays for a policy on an employee, whereby the life insurance is for the employee's benefit, are *tax-deductible to the employer* as a business expense. When the group life policy coverage equals $50,000 or less, employees do not have to report the premium employers pay as income (not taxable to employees).

When a business is a life insurance policy's named beneficiary or has a beneficial interest in the policy, premiums that the company pays for such insurance are not tax-deductible. For businesses that pay the premiums for any of the following arrangements, the premiums will not be deductible:

- Key-person (key-employee) insurance;
- Stock-redemption or entity purchase agreement; and
- Split-dollar insurance.

The *cash value* of a life insurance policy owned by a business or an employer-provided policy accumulates on a tax-deferred basis and is subject to taxation like an individually owned policy.

Policy loans are not taxable to businesses. Unlike individual taxpayers, corporations can deduct interest on a life insurance policy loan for loans not exceeding $50,000.

Policy death benefits paid under a business-owned or employer-provided life insurance policy are received free of federal income tax by the beneficiary in the same manner as individually owned policies.

If the qualified plan meets the general requirements, the following tax advantages will apply:

- Employer contributions are not taxed as income to employees and are tax-deductible to employers;
- The plan's earnings accumulate tax-deferred; and
- Lump-sum distributions to employees are received tax-free.

Modified Endowment Contracts (MECs)

The Tax Reform Act of 1984 eliminated numerous traditional tax shelters. Consequently, single premium life insurance remained among the few financial products offering significant tax advantages. Many of these policies were purchased to set aside large sums of money for tax-deferred growth and the tax-free cash flow available via policy loans and partial surrenders.

The IRS established the 7-pay test to restrict this activity and identify if an owner has overfunded their insurance policy. A life insurance policy that fails a *7-pay test* is a *Modified Endowment Contract (MEC)*. It loses the standard tax benefits associated with a life insurance contract. In MECs, the cumulative premiums paid during the policy's first seven years exceed the net level premiums necessary to pay the policy up using guaranteed mortality costs and interest.

When a policy fails the 7-pay test and becomes a modified endowment contract, it remains an MEC.

Every life insurance policy is subject to the 7-pay test. When a material change to a policy occurs (e.g., an increase in the death benefit), a new 7-pay test is required. A beneficiary's death benefit is tax-free, whether from a life insurance policy or MEC.

The following taxation rules apply to the MEC's cash value:

- Accumulations are tax-deferred;
- Distributions are taxable, including policy loans and withdrawals;
- The IRS will tax distributions on a LIFO basis (Last In, First Out)—also called the "interest-first" rule; and
- Distributions before age 59 ½ are subject to a 10% penalty.

The table on the following page shows the tax considerations for insurance and annuities:

TAX CONSIDERATIONS FOR LIFE INSURANCE AND ANNUITIES	
Premiums	Not deductible (personal expense)
Death Benefit	Not taxable income (except for interest)
Cash Value Increases	Not taxable (as long as the policy is in force)
Cash Value Gains	Taxed at surrender
Dividends	Not taxable (return of unused premium; however, interest is taxable)
Accumulations	Interest is taxable
Policy Loans	Not income taxable
Surrenders	Surrender value - past premium = amount taxable
Partial Surrenders	First In, First Out (FIFO)*
Settlement Options – Death benefits are spread evenly over an income period (averaged). Interest payments in excess of the death benefit portion are taxable.	
Estate Tax – If the insured is the policy owner, it will be included for estate tax purposes. If the policy is given away (to a trust, for example) and the insured dies within three years of the gift, the death benefit will be included in the estate.	

* FIFO only applies to Life Insurance. Annuities follow a LIFO format.

Social Security Benefits

Social Security is a Federal program enacted in 1935, known as *Old Age Survivors Disability Insurance (OASDI)*. This program protects eligible workers and dependents against financial loss because of old age, disability, or death. With a few exceptions, Social Security covers almost every individual. In some aspects, Social Security plays a role in federal life and health insurance, which is essential to consider when determining an individual's life insurance needs.

Social Security uses the Quarter of Coverage (QC) system to determine whether or not a person qualifies for Social Security benefits. The number of credits or QCs a worker earns determines the type and amount of benefits. Anyone operating their own business or working in jobs covered by Social Security can earn up to 4 credits for each year of work.

Fully insured refers to anyone who has earned *40 quarters of coverage* and is entitled to Social Security retirement, Medicare, and survivor benefits. Forty quarters is the equivalent of working for ten years.

Individuals can attain a *currently insured* status (or partially insured) and qualify for certain benefits. They need to have earned six credits (or quarters) of coverage during the 13 quarters ending with the quarter wherein the insured either:

- Dies;
- Qualifies for disability insurance benefits; or
- Qualifies for old-age insurance benefits.

According to the table on the following page established by Social Security, the number of quarters required to be eligible for the benefits differs by age for younger workers.

CONDITIONS FOR PAYMENT	PAID TO	TYPE OF PAYMENT
RETIREMENT BENEFIT		
Fully insured at age 66* (or reduced benefits at age 62)	Retired individual and eligible dependents	Monthly benefit equal to the primary insurance amount (PIA)
DISABILITY BENEFIT		
Fully insured status and total and permanent disability prior to the retirement age	Disabled worker and spouse and eligible dependents	Monthly disability benefit after a 5-month waiting period
SURVIVOR BENEFIT		
Worker's death	Surviving spouse and dependent children	• Lump-sum burial benefit if fully or currently insured • Monthly income payments if fully insured

* The current full retirement age is 66, gradually increasing to 67. For anyone born in 1960 or later, full retirement benefits are payable at age 67.

Chapter Review

This chapter discussed different life insurance products, such as group plans, third-party plans, and qualified and nonqualified plans for individuals and businesses. You have also learned some basic principles of taxation for life insurance and annuities. Let's review the major points:

THIRD-PARTY CONTRACTS	
General Features	• The policy owner and the insured do not have to be the same person • Policies are typically written for businesses or minors
Viatical Settlements	• Viators are insureds with a terminal illness • Viators receive a percentage of the policy's face amount
Life Settlements	• Policy owners sell the life insurance policies they no longer need to a third party • The insured does not have to be terminally ill • Absolute assignment
GROUP LIFE INSURANCE	
General Features	• Employers are the policy owners; employees are the insureds • No evidence of insurability • *Conversion* – no evidence of insurability within a specified number of days (typically 30 or 31 days of termination) • *Noncontributory* – employer pays 100% of the premium; requires 100% employee participation • *Contributory* – employer and employees share the cost of the premium; requires 75% participation

QUALIFIED PLANS	
General Features	• Approved by the IRS • Tax benefits for employers and employees • Must be permanent and have a vesting requirement • Cannot discriminate in favor of the prohibited group

Individual Qualified Retirement Plans	*Traditional IRA:*
	• Earned income
	• Pretax contributions
	• Contributions:
	  - No limiting age (SECURE Act recently changed this law)
	  - *Dollar limit* – up to a maximum allowed amount
	  - Married couples – double the amount for singles
	• Withdrawals can begin at age 59 ½ but not later than age 73
	Roth IRA:
	• Earned income
	• After-tax contributions
	• Contributions:
	  - No limiting age
	  - *Dollar limit* – up to a maximum allowed amount
	• Withdrawals do not have to begin at age 73

Employer-Sponsored Qualified Plans	• Contributions up to an IRS-specified amounts • Both the employer and the employee can contribute *Types of plans:* • *HR-10 (Keogh)* – self-employed • *SEP* – small employer/self-employed; employer funds employee's IRA • *SIMPLE* – small employer (no more than 100 employees); set up as an IRA or as a 401(k) • *401(k)* – any employer; cash or deferred arrangements; profit sharing • *403(b)* – nonprofit organizations; a tax-sheltered annuity
TAXATION	
Life Insurance	• *Premiums* – not tax-deductible • *Cash value* – taxable only if the amount exceeds premiums (taxed on gains) • *Policy loans* – not taxable, interest not tax-deductible • *Dividends* – not taxable as a return of premium; any interest is taxable • *Death benefit* – not taxable if lump-sum; any interest is taxable
IRAs	• *Contributions* – pretax dollars, tax-deductible, must be made in "cash" • *Earnings* – tax-deferred • *Distributions* – taxable; 10% penalty for early withdrawals
Roth IRAs	• *Contributions* – after-tax dollars, not tax-deductible • *Distributions* – not taxable

Business Insurance	• Employer contributions:
	  - Tax-deductible to the employer; not taxed as income to the employee
	  - The earnings grow tax-deferred
	• Lump-sum distributions to employees have favorable tax treatment

OTHER RELATED CONCEPTS	
Rollovers and Transfers	• Tax-free transactions • Distribution of money from one qualified retirement plan to another • Must be completed within 60 days • If from the plan to the participant, 20% of the distribution is withheld • If from the plan to the trustee, no withholdings (direct rollover)
Modified Endowment Contract (MEC)	• Overfunded life insurance policy (7-pay test) • *Accumulation* – tax-deferred • *Distributions* – taxable (Last In, First Out) • Distributions before age 59 ½ – 10% penalty
SOCIAL SECURITY BENEFITS	
Types of Benefits	• Retirement • Disability • Survivor
Insured Status	• *Fully insured* (40 quarters of coverage) – qualify for Social Security retirement, Medicare, and survivor benefits • *Currently insured* (6 quarters of coverage) – qualify for some benefits

CHAPTER 5:
Field Underwriting Procedures

This chapter will examine the producer's first significant role in transacting insurance, completing the application, and delivering the policy. You will learn the application process's steps, including completing the application, collecting the premium, and providing the policy. This chapter also discusses the characteristics and requirements of contracts and some unique aspects of health insurance contracts. Finally, this chapter will also help you build the foundation of important health insurance concepts for your licensing exam and your role as an agent. After finishing the chapter, you will have learned the following topics:

- Completing the Application
- Explaining Sources of Insurability Information
- Policy Delivery
- Explaining the Policy and its Provisions, Riders, Exclusions, and Ratings
- Replacement

Completing the Application

An insurance application begins with a form provided by the insurance company, which the agent completes by asking the applicant questions and recording the applicant's responses. This form is also called the "app." The agent submits the application to the insurance provider for approval or rejection. The application is the applicant's written request to the insurer to issue a policy or contract based on the information found in the application. When insurance providers issue a policy, a copy of the application is stapled to the back, becoming a part of the *entire contract*.

A "notice to the applicant" has to be issued to every applicant for health insurance coverage. This notice informs the applicant that the insurance provider will order a credit report concerning their prior coverage history and previous health insurance applications. The agent is required to leave this notice with the applicant.

Completeness and Accuracy

Agents must take special care to ensure the accuracy of the application in the interest of both the insurance company and the insured. The application is often the primary source of underwriting information. The agent's responsibility is to ensure it is filled out completely, correctly, and according to the applicant's knowledge.

Signatures

The proposed insured must sign every application for *health insurance* (if they are not the insured) along with the agent who solicits the insurance policy.

Changes in the Application

Most insurance carriers require the applicant to fill out the application in ink. The applicant might answer a question incorrectly and want to change it, or the agent may need to correct a mistake when filling out the app. There are two ways to make corrections on an application. The first and best way is to start over with a new application. If that is not practical, the agent may correct an application by drawing a line through the incorrect answer and inserting the correct one. *The applicant must add their initials next to the updated answer.*

Premiums with the Application

Usually, an initial premium is collected for a health insurance policy and sent to the insurance company with the application. The agent provides a *conditional receipt* to the applicant. However, *the agent cannot bind coverage*, so the coverage begins once the insurance provider approves the application and issues the policy.

No Initial Premium with Application – There will be cases where the agent did not collect a premium with the insurance application. Upon delivery, the agent must collect the premium and obtain a statement of continued good health from the applicant before releasing the policy.

Submitting the Application for Underwriting

The agent should review the application to ensure the applicant answers every question and collects all necessary signatures. The agent then sends the application to the insurance company.

Explaining Sources of Insurability Information

To determine an applicant's insurability, the insurance provider can use several sources, such as a Medical Information Bureau (MIB) report, to collect underwriting information. The insurer must advise the applicant of the sources used and how they obtained this information. All sources used to verify applicants' insurability must adhere to the Fair Credit Reporting Act (FCRA).

Attending Physician Report

If the underwriter determines it is necessary, the insurance provider will send an attending physician's statement (APS) to the applicant's doctor for completion. The APS is the best source for accurate information about the applicant's medical history. The physician can clarify what the applicant was treated for, the necessary treatment, the length of treatment and recovery, and the prognosis.

Medical Exam Report

When required by the insurer, paramedics or physicians conduct medical examinations at the insurer's expense. Typically, insurance providers do not require such exams with health insurance underwriting, which stresses the importance of the agent in recording medical information on the application. With life insurance underwriting, the medical examination requirement is more common. An insurer is responsible for the exam costs when requesting a medical exam.

When an insurer requires an applicant to take an HIV test, the insurance provider must obtain the applicant's written consent. The consent form must explain the test's purpose and inform the applicant about the confidentiality of the results and procedures for notifying the applicant.

Underwriting for HIV or AIDS is allowed as long as it does not unfairly discriminate. An adverse underwriting decision is not permitted solely based on the appearance of symptoms. Insurers are required to maintain strict confidentiality regarding HIV-related test results or diagnoses.

HIPAA Privacy

The HIPAA Privacy Rule defines protected information as "individually identifiable health information" held or disseminated by a covered entity or its business associate, whether paper, electronic, or oral. It is also known as *protected health information (PHI)*.

Individually identifiable health information includes demographic data relating to payment information or physical or mental health conditions that could quickly identify the person.

A covered entity must obtain the person's written authorization to disclose information unrelated to healthcare operations, treatment, or payment.

Gramm-Leach-Bliley Act (GLBA) Privacy

The *Gramm-Leach-Bliley Act (GLBA)* mandates that, in general, an insurer cannot disclose nonpublic personal information to nonaffiliated third parties except for the following reasons:

- The insurer clearly and conspicuously discloses to the consumer in writing that information can be disclosed to a third party;

- The consumer is provided the opportunity, before the time that information is initially disclosed, to require that information not be disclosed to the third party; or
- The consumer receives an explanation of how to exercise a nondisclosure option.

The Gramm-Leach-Bliley Act requires two disclosures to a customer (a consumer with an ongoing financial relationship with a financial institution):

1. When the customer relationship is established (e.g., a policy is purchased); and
2. Before disclosing protected information.

The customer must receive an annual privacy disclosure and have the right to opt out or not share their private information with other parties.

Policy Delivery

The agent or producer is responsible for delivering the policy to the insured and collecting any premiums due at delivery. They may also be required to obtain a *statement of good health* from the insured. The insured must sign this statement verifying that the insured has not sustained an injury or illness since the application date.

Explaining the Policy and its Provisions, Riders, Exclusions, and Ratings

The agent must explain the policy's primary benefits and provisions to the insured. When an insurer issues the policy with a revision or amendment, the agent must explain these changes and obtain the insured's statement and signature acknowledging these changes.

Replacement

When a producer or agent attempts to replace the insured's current health insurance with a new policy, the agent must be careful not to mislead the insured or provide coverage to the insured's detriment. Producers must carefully compare the current and proposed replacement policy's benefits, limitations, and exclusions. The agent also must ensure that the policy owner does not cancel the existing policy before the new policy is issued.

Pre-existing conditions are an essential consideration when replacing a policy. A pre-existing condition is a medical condition for which an insured sought treatment or medical advice within a specified period before the policy issue. Due to pre-existing condition limitations, insurance providers may not cover health conditions covered under the current policy under the new policy. Insurers may require a new waiting period in a new policy.

Underwriting is necessary when replacement is involved; underwriters are responsible for evaluating risk and deciding whether a person is eligible for coverage. The insured may believe that a replacement policy is in their best interests. However, after an underwriter evaluates an exchange of premium and risk, insureds may pay a different premium or receive the same benefits.

Example 5.1 – When Morgan (a nonsmoker without health problems) applies for health insurance at age 25, the insurer will base premiums on his current age and health status. He would pay a different premium if he applied for a replacement policy at age 45 after suffering a heart attack and smoking for 15 years. Suppose, at the age of 25, Morgan paid an excessively high policy premium because he was issued an overpriced policy. What happens at age 45? Morgan is evaluated, and his age and health are considered (along with other factors). His premiums are higher due to these factors. Even though Morgan paid excessive premiums on his original policy, insurers would evaluate him based on the present rather than when the original policy was initially issued.

Chapter Review

This chapter explained field underwriting practices for health insurance policies. Let's review them:

EXPLAINING SOURCES OF INSURABILITY INFORMATION	
Sources of Insurability Information	• *Attending Physician Report* – provides the most accurate information on the applicant's medical history • *MIB report* – helps insurers share adverse medical information on insureds • *Credit Reports* – contain factors related to a risk's potential for loss, including consumer reports (information regarding a consumer's credit, character, reputation, or habits collected from employment records, credit reports, and other public sources) and investigative consumer reports (information obtained through an investigation and interviews with associates, friends, and neighbors of the consumer) • *Medical Exam Report* – conducted by paramedics or physicians • *Gramm-Leach-Bliley Act (GLBA) Privacy* – an insurer cannot disclose nonpublic personal information to a nonaffiliated third party except for a specific set of reasons
INITIAL PREMIUM PAYMENT AND RECEIPT	
Policy Issue and Delivery	• *Effective date of coverage* – if the premium is not collected with the application, the agent is required to obtain the premium and a statement of continued good health at the time of policy delivery
REPLACEMENT	
Agent's Responsibility	• Compare benefits, limitations, and exclusions contained in the current and the proposed replacement policy • Ensure that the current policy is not canceled before the new policy is issued

CHAPTER 6:
Types of Health Policies

This chapter will focus on different health insurance policies and compare each type of coverage, examining its advantages and disadvantages and their application to various individuals and their situations. Based on a person's finances, vocation, and health status, they may find a given type of health insurance more desirable than another. Keep this in mind as you progress through the chapter. By the chapter's end, you will understand the following:

- Medical Expense Insurance
- Disability Income
- Accidental Death and Dismemberment
- Long-Term Care
- Group Insurance
- Other Policies

Medical Expense Insurance

Healthcare insurance providers (carriers) include:

- Stock and mutual insurers;
- Blue Cross/Blue Shield;
- Health maintenance organizations (HMOs); and
- Preferred provider organizations (PPOs).

Care is administered not only in the doctors' offices or the hospital but also in surgical centers, urgent care centers, and skilled nursing facilities.

Basic Hospital, Medical, and Surgical Policies

Insurers often combine basic hospital, surgical, and medical policies with major medical policies, sold to consumers as *Medical Expense Insurance*. These policies deliver benefits for covering the cost of medical care resulting from sickness or accidents. The three basic coverages (hospital, surgical, and medical) can be obtained separately or as a package. These coverages are known as *first-dollar coverage* because they do not require the insured to pay a deductible. This coverage differs from Major Medical Expense insurance; however, the basic medical coverages generally have more limited coverage than the Major Medical Policies.

Basic Hospital Expense Coverage – Hospital expense policies cover hospital room and board charges and miscellaneous hospital expenses. These expenses include medicines, lab and x-ray charges, and using the operating room and supplies when a hospital admits the insured. The insurer sets the limits on room and board at a specific dollar amount per day up to a maximum number of days, and there is no deductible. These limits may not cover the total hospital room and board costs incurred by the insured. For instance, if the hospital expense benefit was $500 per day, and the hospital charged $600 per day, the insured would be responsible for the additional $100 per day.

Miscellaneous hospital expenses generally have a separate limit. This amount pays for the various costs associated with a hospital stay. This separate limit appears as a multiple of the room and board charges, such as ten times the room and board charges or a flat amount. A policy might specify the maximum limit for certain expenses, such as $100 for drugs or $150 for using the operating room. As with the room and board charges, the miscellaneous hospital expense limits may not cover the total amount the insured needs during a lengthy hospital stay.

Basic medical expense coverage is also known as Basic Physicians' Nonsurgical Expense Coverage. It offers coverage for nonsurgical services a physician provides. However, the benefits are typically limited to visits to patients confined in the hospital. Some policies will also cover office visits. There is no deductible, but coverage is usually limited to a certain number of visits per day, a specified limit per visit, or a specific limit per hospital stay.

In addition to nonsurgical physician's expenses, insureds can purchase basic medical expense coverage to cover maternity benefits, emergency accident benefits, mental and nervous disorders, home health care, hospice care, outpatient care, and nurses' expenses. Regardless of the type of plan or coverage purchased, these policies usually offer only limited benefits contingent upon time limitations. The insured must often pay a considerable sum in addition to the benefits paid by the medical expense policies.

Basic Surgical Expense Coverage – Insurers usually write this coverage together with Hospital Expense policies. These policies cover the costs of surgeons' services, whether they perform the surgery in or out of the hospital. Coverage includes the surgeons' fees, an anesthesiologist, and the operating room when it is not a miscellaneous medical item. Similar to the other basic medical expense coverage types, there is no deductible, but coverage is limited. All contracts have a *surgical schedule* that lists the types of operations covered and their assigned dollar amounts. The contract may pay for a similar operation if the procedure is not on the schedule. Special schedules may list a specified amount, express the amount payable as a percentage of the maximum benefit, or assign a relative value multiplied by its conversion factor.

Each surgical procedure receives a point value relative to the number of points assigned to the maximum benefit in the *relative value* approach. Major surgical procedures like heart surgery generally have maximum point values. This maximum benefit typically has a value of 1,000 points. Other surgical procedures, like an appendectomy, may have a lower point value (e.g., 200 points). To determine the amount payable for the appendectomy, multiply the assigned 200 points (relative value) by the *conversion factor*. This conversion factor is the total amount owed *per point*.

For example, if 10 were the conversion factor, the policy would pay $2,000 (200 x 10) for the appendectomy and the maximum benefit of $10,000 (1,000 x 10) for the heart surgery.

Major Medical Policies

Major Medical Expense Policies provide a *broad range of coverage* under one policy instead of the limited coverage available under the Basic Medical Expense Policies. Usually, these policies offer the following coverage:

- Comprehensive coverage for hospital expenses (physicians' services, nursing services, room and board, miscellaneous fees, etc.);
- Catastrophic medical expense protection; and
- Benefits to cover prolonged illness or injury.

Typically, insurers include a blanket limit for specific expenses in the policy. There is a per-person lifetime benefit limit. Unlike the basic medical expense plans, these policies usually carry coinsurance requirements, deductibles, and large benefit maximums.

Supplemental Major Medical Policies and Comprehensive Major Medical Policies are the two common types of Major Medical Policies available.

Supplemental Major Medical Policies can be purchased to supplement the coverage payable under a basic medical expense policy. The supplemental major medical policy covers any expenses not covered by the basic medical expense policy and any costs that exceed the maximum. The supplemental policy will provide coverage moving forward if the time limit has passed in the basic policy.

The basic expense policy does not have a deductible and will provide coverage on a first-dollar basis. After the basic coverage limits are exhausted, the insured must pay a *corridor deductible* before the major medical coverage pays benefits. The corridor deductible only applies to the coverage limits between the basic and major medical policies.

Health Maintenance Organizations (HMOs)

Through the Health Maintenance Act of 1973, Congress vigorously supported the growth of *Health Maintenance Organizations (HMOs)* in this country. The act required employers with over 25 employees to offer the HMO as an alternative to their regular health insurance plans.

Preventive Care Services – The HMO Act's primary goal was to lower health care costs by utilizing *preventive care*. While most insurance plans did not provide any benefits for preventive care before 1973, HMOs offer free annual check-ups for the entire family. Through these visits, the HMOs hope to identify diseases in the earliest stages, when treatment is most likely to succeed. The HMOs also offer members free or low-cost immunizations to prevent certain illnesses.

General Characteristics – The HMO offers benefits in the form of services rather than reimbursement for a physician's or hospital's services. Usually, the insurance carriers provide the financing, while the doctors and hospitals provide the care. The HMO concept is distinctive in that it offers both patient care and financing for its members.

Limited Service Area – The HMO provides health care services to individuals living within specific geographic boundaries, like city limits or county lines. Anyone living within the boundaries can enroll in the HMO. However, they are ineligible if they do not live within the service area.

Limited Choice of Providers – The HMO limits costs by only offering care from physicians who meet its standards and are willing to provide care at a pre-negotiated price.

Copayments – A *copayment* or copay is a flat dollar amount or a specific part of the cost of care that the member must pay. For example, the member might pay $5, $10, or $25 for each doctor's office visit.

Prepaid Basis – HMOs operate on a *capitation basis*. The HMO receives a flat monthly amount attributed to each member, whether they see a physician. Essentially, it is a prepaid medical plan. As a plan member, you will receive all the necessary services from the member physicians and hospitals.

Primary Care Physician vs. Referral (Specialty) Physician – Care is provided to the HMO's members by a limited number of physicians approved to practice in the HMO.

Primary Care Physician (PCP) – When a person becomes a member of the HMO, they select their *primary care physician (PCP)* or *gatekeeper*. Once selected, the insurer will pay the primary care physician or HMO regularly for being responsible for the care of that member, whether or not care is provided. It should be in the best interest of the primary care physician to keep this member healthy to prevent future disease treatment.

Referral (Specialty) Physician – For the member to see a specialist, the primary care physician (gatekeeper) must refer the member. The referral system prevents the member from seeing higher-priced specialists unless it is essential. Many HMOs impose a financial cost to the PCP for referring a patient to a more expensive specialist. Consequently, the primary care physician is incentivized to use an alternative treatment before providing a referral. HMOs must have mechanisms to handle complaints that sometimes result in the delay of a referral or complaints about coverage concerns or other patient care.

Hospital Services and Emergency Care – The HMO offers the member inpatient hospital care in or out of the service area. Services may be limited when treating mental, emotional, or nervous disorders, including drug or alcohol treatment or rehabilitation.

HMOs must provide emergency care for members whether they are in or out of the HMO service area. When a member receives emergency care outside the service area, the HMO will be eager to get the member back into the service area, so salaried member physicians can provide care.

Preferred Provider Organizations (PPOs)

Preferred Provider Organizations (PPOs) are the traditional medical systems' answer to HMOs. Under the PPO system, physicians are paid fees for their services instead of salaries. Nevertheless, the member is encouraged to visit approved member physicians who previously agreed upon the fees to charge. This incentive comes in the form of benefits. Members can utilize any physician they choose. However, the PPO will cover 90% of the cost of a physician on their approved list while only covering 70% of the cost if the member uses a physician not included on the PPO's approved list.

A PPO is a group of physicians and hospitals that contract with insurance companies, employers, or third-party organizations to provide medical services at a reduced fee. PPOs differ from HMOs in two ways. First, providers do not offer medical care on a prepaid basis, but physicians are paid a fee for service. Secondly, subscribers do not have to use physicians or facilities contracting with the PPO.

Any qualified physician or hospital that agrees to follow the PPO's standards and charges the appropriate fees that the PPO has established can join the PPO's approved list. Physicians and hospitals can belong to several PPO groups simultaneously.

PCP Referral (Gatekeeper PPO) – The insured does not have to choose a primary care physician in a PPO. The insured can select medical providers not on the preferred list and retain coverage. The insured can receive medical care from any provider. Yet, if the insured chooses a PPO provider, the insured will incur lower out-of-pocket costs. Conversely, if an insured utilizes a non-network provider, the insured's out-of-pocket costs will be higher. In a PPO, all network providers are "preferred." The insured can visit any of them, even specialists, without seeing a primary care physician first. Certain services might require plan pre-certification, which evaluates the medical necessity of an inpatient admission and the number of days needed to treat the condition.

Point-Of-Service (POS) Plans

The *Point-of-Service (POS)* plan is simply a combination of HMO and PPO plans. POS plans are also called "open-ended HMOs."

Nature and Purpose – With the Point-of-Service plan, employees are not locked into one plan or forced to choose between the two. When a need arises for medical services, an employee can make a different selection.

Out-of-Network Provider Access – Similar to HMOs, PPO plans enter into a contract with healthcare providers who form a provider network. Plan members do not have to use only in-network providers for their medical care.

In a Point-of-Service plan, the individuals can visit an in-network provider at their discretion. If they elect to utilize an out-of-network physician, they may do so. However, the member deductibles, copays, and coinsurance could be considerably higher.

With these plans, participants typically have access to a provider network controlled by a primary care physician (gatekeeper). However, plan members can seek care outside the network but at a reduced coverage level.

Indemnity Plan Features – Under the POS plan, if a participant uses a non-member physician, the attending physician will be paid a fee for service. However, the member patient must pay a higher coinsurance amount or percentage for using a non-member physician.

Flexible Spending Accounts (FSAs)

A *Flexible Spending Account (FSA)* offers benefits funded by employer contributions and salary reductions. Employees can deposit a certain amount of their income into an account before paying taxes. This account reimburses the employee for eligible health care and dependent care expenses for the year. FSA benefits are subject to "use-it-or-lose-it" and annual contribution rules; this plan does not offer a cumulative benefit beyond the plan year.

The two types of Flexible Spending Accounts are Health Care Accounts for out-of-pocket health care expenses and Dependent Care Accounts (subject to annual contribution limits) to help cover dependents' care expenses. These accounts allow employees and their spouses to continue working.

An FSA is not subject to federal income taxes, Social Security (FICA) taxes, or state income taxes, ultimately saving 1/3 or more in taxes. When the plan favors highly compensated employees, the benefits for these employees are not exempt from federal income taxes.

Child and dependent care expenses have to be for the care of one or more qualifying individuals:

- Dependents under the age of 13 who received care. Employees can claim these individuals as an exemption on their Federal Income Tax return;
- A spouse who was mentally or physically unable to care for themselves; or
- Dependents who are physically or mentally disabled and incapable of caring for themselves. They can be claimed as an exemption if the individual earns gross income less than an IRS-specified amount.

Individuals who cannot clean, dress, or feed themselves due to mental or physical problems are unable to care for themselves. Also, individuals who require constant attention to prevent injuring themselves or others cannot care for themselves as well.

The insured can change benefits during open enrollment. After that period, insureds cannot make other changes during the plan year. However, the insured may be able to make a change under one of the following conditions, referred to as qualified life event changes:

1. Marital status;
2. Number of dependents;
3. One of the dependents qualifies for or no longer satisfies the Medical Reimbursement plan's coverage requirements for unmarried dependents because of student status, attained age, or any similar circumstances;
4. The insured, the insured's spouse, or a qualified dependent changes employment status that impacts eligibility under the plan (at least a 31-day gap in employment status is required to qualify);
5. Change in dependent care provider; or
6. Family medical leave.

The IRS limits annual contributions to Dependent Care Accounts up to a specified amount adjusted annually for the cost of living. This limit is a family limit. Even if both parents contribute to flexible care accounts, their combined contribution cannot exceed the amount.

High Deductible Health Plans (HDHPs) and Health Savings Accounts (HSAs)

Individuals frequently use *High Deductible Health Plans (HDHPs)* in coordination with MSAs, HSAs, or HRAs. The high deductible health plan features higher out-of-pocket limits and annual deductibles than traditional health plans, lowering premiums. Except for preventive care, individuals must meet the yearly deductible before the plan pays benefits. Preventive care services are typically first-dollar coverage or paid after copayment. The HDHP credits a part of the monthly health plan premium into the coordinating MSA, HSA, or HRA. Individuals can pay the HDHP deductible with funds from the coordinating account plan.

Health Savings Accounts (HSAs) help individuals save for qualified health expenses their spouse or dependents may incur. An HDHP can make a tax-deductible contribution to an HSA to cover out-of-pocket medical expenses. The individual's taxable income does not include employer contributions to an HSA.

To be eligible for an HSA, a person:

- Must be covered by a high deductible health plan;
- Must not have coverage under other health insurance (excluding specific injury insurance and accident, disability, long-term care, dental care, vision care); and
- Must not qualify for Medicare and cannot be claimed as a dependent on anyone else's federal income tax return.

HSAs are associated with high deductible insurance. Individuals can obtain coverage under a qualified health insurance plan with minimum deductibles.

Each year, qualified individuals (or their employers) can save up to a specified limit, regardless of their plan's deductible. To open an HSA, a person must be under the Medicare eligibility age. For taxpayers age 55 and older, an additional contribution of $1,000 is allowed.

HSA holders who use the money for non-health expenditures will pay tax plus a 20% penalty. After age 65, withdrawals for non-health purposes will be taxed but not penalized.

Health Reimbursement Accounts (HRAs)

Health Reimbursement Accounts (HRAs) include funds set aside by employers to reimburse their employees for qualified medical expenses, like coinsurance amounts or deductibles. Employers qualify for the preferential tax treatment of funds put in an HRA in the same way they are eligible for tax advantages by funding an insurance plan. Employers may deduct the cost of a health reimbursement account as a business expense.

The following are fundamental characteristics of HRAs:

- They are contribution healthcare plans rather than defined benefit plans;
- HRAs are not a taxable employee benefit;
- Employer contributions are tax-deductible;
- Employees can roll over their unused balances at the end of the year;
- Employers do not have to advance claim payments to employees or healthcare providers during the plan year's early months;
- HRAs are funded with employer dollars, not employee salary reductions;
- They allow the employer to reduce health plan costs by combining the HRA with a high-deductible (and usually lower-cost) health plan; and
- HRAs balance the group purchasing power of larger and smaller employers.

HRAs are available to employees of companies of all sizes. However, the employer decides eligibility and contribution limits.

An HRA has no statutory limit. However, employers set limits so employees can roll over any unused balances at the end of the year based on the employer's discretion. Former employees (including those who have retired) can have continued access to unused HRAs, but only at the employer's discretion. HRAs stay with the originating employer and do not follow an employee to their new employment.

Disability Income

Individual Disability Income Policy

A significant risk individuals will face during their lifetime is becoming disabled and unable to perform work-related duties. Recent statistics show a 30% chance of a 25-year-old being disabled for more than 90 days before age 65. It is far less likely that the same 25-year-old will suffer a premature death before age 65.

For most people who cannot work, employment income would end after a brief period. Consequently, most individuals would have to use their savings to pay everyday expenses such as rent, food, and utilities. Each person should ask themselves how long they could survive without an income.

Disability income insurance replaces lost income in the event of a disability. It is a vital component of a comprehensive insurance program. Coverage is obtained individually or through an employer on a group basis.

Elimination and Benefit Periods – The *elimination period* is a waiting period imposed on the insured from the start of disability until benefit payments begin. It is a deductible that measures days instead of dollars. The elimination period eliminates coverage for short-term disabilities; insureds will be able to return to work relatively quickly. The elimination periods contained in most policies range from 30 days to 180 days. Just as choosing a higher deductible reduces medical expense insurance premiums, opting for a longer elimination period lowers disability income insurance premiums. An essential consideration in selecting the elimination period is stipulating payment in arrears. In other words, if the insured chooses a 90-day elimination period, the insured will be eligible for benefits on the 91st day; however, payments will begin on the 121st day. In selecting the duration of the elimination period, insureds must determine how long they can go without benefit payments following disability.

Under some disability income policies, a *probationary period* is another waiting period imposed in addition to the elimination period. The probationary period is a waiting period, usually 10 to 30 days from the policy's issue date, during which insurers will not pay benefits for disabilities related to illness. This period only applies to sickness, not injury or accidents. The probationary period intends to reduce the chances of adverse selection against the insurance carrier. This period protects insurers against individuals purchasing disability income policies shortly after developing a disease or other health condition requiring immediate medical attention.

The *benefit period* refers to how long the monthly disability benefit payments will last for each disability after the elimination period has been satisfied. Most policies include benefit periods lasting one year, two years, five years, and until age 65. Some plans offer a lifetime benefit period; however, a longer benefit period will have higher premiums.

Injury vs. Sickness – *Injury* can be defined using either the accidental means definition or the accidental bodily injury definition. The accidental means definition indicates that the cause of the accident must be unintended and unexpected. The accidental bodily injury definition suggests that the damage to the body is unintended and unforeseen. A policy that utilizes the accidental bodily injury definition provides broader coverage than one that uses the accidental means definition.

The definition of illness is a disease or *sickness* contracted after the policy has been effective for 30 days. It can also refer to a condition or disorder that manifests after the policy becomes effective (in force).

Most disability income policies include a *presumptive disability* provision specifying the conditions that will automatically qualify the insured for full disability benefits. Some disability policies provide a benefit when individuals meet specific qualifications, regardless of their capability to work. The presumptive disability benefit covers dismemberment (the loss of use of any two limbs), permanent and total blindness, or loss of hearing or speech. Some policies will specify a requirement of actual severance of limbs rather than loss of use.

A percentage of the insured's previous earnings determines the *benefit limitations* on the monthly benefit amount payable under most disability income policies. The benefit limits are the maximum benefits the insurance provider is willing to accept for individual risk. It is common for policies to limit benefits to roughly 66% of the insured's average earnings for two years immediately preceding disability.

An insurance provider rarely writes a disability income policy reimbursing the insured for 100% of lost income. Insurance providers will not pay benefits equal to the insured's previous earnings to reduce the chance of the insured pretending to be injured. If an insurance carrier provided benefit payments as much or more than the insured's earnings, the individual would have no incentive to return to work as quickly as possible. By paying the insured a benefit somewhat less than their previous earnings, they are motivated to return to work after recovering from a disability instead of collecting benefits.

Most insurance providers will adjust benefits according to the insured's amounts from workers compensation or Social Security. When the insured receives benefits from these programs, the insurance provider decreases the benefit amount paid under the policy so that the insured cannot profit from their disability.

Social Insurance Supplements (SIS) or *Social Security Riders* supplement or replace benefits that may be payable under Social Security Disability. These allow for the payment of income benefits, usually in three different circumstances:

- When the insured qualifies for Social Security benefits but before the benefits commence (typically, there is a 5-month waiting period for Social Security benefits);
- If the insured has been denied coverage under Social Security (roughly 75% of individuals who apply for Social Security benefits are denied coverage because of their rigid definition of total disability); or
- When the amount payable under Social Security is less than the amount payable under the rider (in this situation, the insurer will pay only the difference).

These riders can also supplement or replace benefits payable under a social insurance program like workers compensation.

Usually, disability income policies do not cover losses caused by military service, war, overseas residence, intentionally self-inflicted injuries, or injuries suffered while committing or attempting to commit a felony.

Disability income policies protect individuals against the possible loss of income because of a disability and also cover businesses. There are three types of disability income policies used for companies: Business Overhead Expense, Key Person Disability, and Disability Buy-Sell Insurance.

Business Overhead Expense Policy

The *business overhead expense (BOE)* policy is insurance sold to small business owners to meet overhead expenses. Such expenses can include employee salaries, rent, utilities, leased equipment, installment purchases, etc., following a disability. Business overhead expense policies reimburse the business owner for the incurred overhead expenses while the business owner is disabled. This policy does not reimburse the business owner for their compensation, salary, or other income lost due to a disability. There is generally an elimination period of 15 to 30 days, and benefit payments typically last for one or two years. The benefits are usually limited to the maximum monthly amount stated in the policy or the covered expenses incurred. The premiums paid for BOE insurance are tax-deductible to the business as a business expense; however, the benefits received by the company are taxable.

Business Disability Buyout Policy

A *buy-sell agreement* is a legal contract prepared by an attorney. When one of the owners becomes disabled or dies, the buy-sell agreement specifies how the business will pass between owners. It is common for the company to purchase insurance to provide the cash needed to accomplish the buyout when the owner becomes disabled or dies. The policies that fund buy-sell agreements have an extremely long elimination period, possibly one or two years. Typically, policies that fund buy-sell agreements also provide a sizeable lump-sum benefit rather than monthly benefits to buy out the business.

Like a life insurance buy-sell agreement, the *disability buyout agreement* specifies who will buy out a disabled partner's interest in the business. It legally obligates that individual or party to purchase the interest in the event of a disability. Policy owners can add a provision for the occurrence of a disability to a buy-sell agreement to eliminate the need for two separate contracts. It is common for a disability income policy that funds a buyout to include an elimination period of one or two years. The long elimination period provides time to determine if a disabled business partner is permanently disabled or can return to the business. With disability buy-sell insurance, the premium paid by the company is not tax-deductible, and benefits are received tax-free. Buyout plans typically allow for a lump-sum payment of the benefit.

Key Employee Policy

An employer can purchase a *key person disability policy* to cover the life of a key employee whose economic value to the business is mission-critical. Employers calculate this value based on the potential loss of business income and the cost of hiring and training the key person's replacement. *The business pays the premium, owns the contract, and is the beneficiary.* The key person is the insured, and the company must have the key person's written consent to be insured.

Group Disability Income Policy

Group plans differ from individual plans in a variety of ways. The most common differences between group and individual disability plans are listed below:

- *Group plans* typically specify the benefits based on a percentage of the worker's income. In contrast, individual policies typically specify a flat amount.
- *Short-term group plans* generally include maximum benefit periods of 13 to 26 weeks, with weekly benefits of 50% to 100% of the individual's income. Individual short-term plans include maximum benefit periods of 6 months to 2 years.
- *Group long-term plans* provide maximum benefit periods of more than two years, with monthly benefits typically limited to 60% of the individual's income.
- *Group disability plans* also contain minimum participation requirements. Generally, the employee must have worked for 30 to 90 days before qualifying for coverage.
- *Group plans* typically make benefits supplemental to any benefits received under workers compensation.
- Some *group disability plans* only offer benefits for non-occupational disabilities.
- In a *group disability plan* funded entirely by the employer, the employee's income benefits are included in their gross income and taxed as ordinary income.

Accidental Death and Dismemberment

Accidental Death and Dismemberment (AD&D) coverage can be written as a separate policy or as a rider. It is frequently a part of group health and group life plans. AD&D coverage provides a lump-sum benefit payment if the insured dies from an accident or in the event of losing particular body parts resulting from an accident.

Accidental Death and Dismemberment coverage is a pure form of accident insurance and only pays for accidental losses. The *principal sum* is the benefit amount paid for accidental death. This amount typically equals the insurance contract's face value or coverage amount. When a loss of sight or accidental dismemberment occurs, the policy pays a percentage of that principal sum, often called the *capital sum*. The benefit amount will vary according to the severity of the injury.

The policy will typically pay the entire principal for losing two or more limbs or sight in both eyes. However, it might only pay 50% for losing one hand or foot. Also, in cases of accidental death, some policies will pay a double or triple indemnity, which means the policy will pay twice or three times the face amount. Most policies will pay the accidental death benefit as long as the accident causes the death and occurs within *90 days*.

Limited Risk policies and *Special Risk* policies are the two particular policies that pay accidental death and dismemberment benefits only under specific circumstances. The Limited Risk policy defines the risk in which the insurer will pay benefits for accidental death or dismemberment. For example, the policy may be a Travel Accident policy; the benefits are only payable if the loss occurs due to travel. On the other hand, the Special Risk policy will cover unusual types of risks that AD&D policies usually do not cover. It only covers the specific risk or hazard the policy identifies, such as a racecar driver test-driving a new car.

Long-Term Care

Long-term care (LTC) policies (individual policies, group policies, or riders to life insurance) offer coverage to individuals who can no longer live independently. These individuals require living assistance at home or in a nursing home facility. A long-term care policy can vary in the number of days of confinement covered, the amount paid for nursing home care, the number of home health visits covered, and other contract provisions. LTC policies also must offer coverage for at least *12 consecutive months* in a setting other than a hospital's acute care unit.

Long-term care policies generally include a waiting period called an *elimination period*, similar to those found in disability income policies. Long-term care elimination periods can range from 0 to 365 days. The longer the waiting period, the lower the premium. Insurance providers typically give insureds an option to choose the elimination period that best suits their needs. LTC policies also include a *benefit period*, which is how long coverage applies following the elimination period. The benefit period is generally 2 to 5 years, with some policies offering lifetime coverage. A long-term care policy with a longer benefit period will have a higher premium.

Under most LTC policies, the benefit amount payable is typically a specific fixed dollar amount per day, irrespective of the cost of care. For instance, if an insured has $100 of fixed daily coverage and the care facility only charges $90, the insurer will pay $100 daily. Some policies pay the actual charge the insured incurs per day. Most LTC policies are also guaranteed renewable; however, insurance providers have the right to increase the premiums.

Optional benefits are obtainable with long-term care policies for an additional premium. The *prohibited provisions* or actions found in long-term care policies include the following:

- Cancel, nonrenew, or otherwise terminate a long-term care policy on the grounds of the insured's age or the deterioration of mental or physical condition;
- Establish a new waiting period when coverage is replaced or converted within the same company, except for increased benefits voluntarily selected by the insured; or
- Provide coverage only for skilled nursing care or offer significantly more coverage for skilled care than lower levels of care.

Long-term care policies may contain the following *exclusions*:

- Pre-existing conditions or diseases;
- Mental and nervous disorders or diseases except for organic cognitive disorders such as senile dementia, Alzheimer's disease, and Parkinson's disease;
- Drug addiction and alcoholism;
- Treatment or illness caused by war, attempted suicide, or participation in criminal activities; and
- Treatment is payable by the government, workers compensation, Medicare, or similar coverage.

Eligibility for Benefits

Typically, an insured must be unable to perform some activities of daily living (ADLs) to be eligible for long-term care policy benefits. ADLs include *bathing, dressing, toileting, transferring positions* (also called mobility), *continence,* and *eating.*

Levels of Care

Usually, long-term care policies will cover three care levels: skilled care, intermediate care, and custodial care. The long-term care policy may also provide additional care levels, all of which the insured receives in their home:

- Home health care;
- Adult daycare;
- Hospice care; or
- Respite care.

Skilled Care – *Skilled care* is daily rehabilitative and nursing care that only medical personnel can provide under the direction of a physician. It occurs in an institutional setting and includes changing a sterile dressing or physical therapy provided in a skilled nursing facility. *Care provided by non-professional staff is not skilled care.*

Intermediate Care – *Intermediate care* is occasional rehabilitative or nursing care given to insureds with stable conditions who need daily medical assistance less frequently than skilled nursing care. A physician orders it, and skilled medical personnel will monitor or deliver this care. Intermediate care could be as simple as providing the medication once daily to a group in physical therapy or changing a bandage. Skilled medical personnel can carry it out in the patient's home, an intermediate care unit, or a nursing home.

Custodial Care – *Custodial care* assists with personal needs such as eating, dressing, or bathing, which nonmedical personnel can give, such as home health care workers or relatives. They can provide custodial care in the patient's home or an institutional setting. In other words, it involves caring for an individual's ADLs, not surgical or hospital needs.

Home Health Care – *Home health care* is care given by skilled nursing or other professional services in one's home. It includes occasional visits to the person's home by licensed practical nurses, registered nurses, vocational nurses, or community-based organizations like hospice. Home health care includes occupational therapy, physical therapy, speech therapy, and medical services provided by a social worker.

Home Convalescent Care – *Home convalescent care* is provided in the insured's home under a planned program established by their attending physician. Insureds must receive such care in a hospital, long-term care facility, or home health care agency.

Residential Care – *Residential care* is provided while the insured resides in a residential care facility for the elderly (RCFE) or a retirement community. In some arrangements, independence is the same as living in one's home. However, this type of care offers a physical and social environment that contributes to continued intellectual, psychological, and physical growth. These facilities are common among the middle and upper classes.

Adult Daycare – *Adult daycare* is care given to functionally impaired adults on a less-than-24-hour basis by a community center or a neighborhood recreation center. Care includes various health, social, and related activities. Meals and transportation to and from the daycare center typically accompany the service.

Respite Care – *Respite care* intends to provide relief to the family caregiver. It can offer a service such as someone coming to the home to allow the caregiver to nap or go out for a while. The caregiver may also receive this relief from an adult daycare center.

Individual LTC Contracts

Individual LTC insurance is the most common form of long-term care in the private market. The advantages of an individual long-term care policy include:

- The ability to customize the plan to the individual's own needs;
- Guaranteed renewability; and
- State regulation of LTC plans.

Group and Voluntary LTC Contracts

Group long-term care policies are gaining in popularity. Group LTC offers less underwriting and lower rates than other group health insurance. These policies give someone denied individual coverage an opportunity to enroll during open enrollment periods. Not all states regulate group LTC, and many group plans do not allow employer contributions to premiums. Most group long-term care plans are voluntary, meaning the individual chooses whether or not to enroll in the plan.

Group Insurance

Eligibility for group coverage requires that the members form the group for a purpose other than obtaining group health insurance. In other words, the coverage needs to be incidental to the group. Usually, two types of groups qualify for group insurance, including employer-sponsored and association-sponsored.

Employers (e.g., sole proprietorships, partnerships, or corporations) offer group coverage to employees through an *employer-sponsored group*, like a multiple employer trust. Eligible employees must meet specific time of service requirements and work full-time. Group health insurance can be either contributory or noncontributory.

An *association group* (alums or professionals) can purchase group insurance for its members. The group must have been active for at least two years, be organized for reasons other than buying insurance, have at least 100 members, have a constitution and by-laws, and hold at least annual meetings. Examples of these groups include, but are not limited to, college alum associations, professional associations, labor unions, trade associations, veteran associations, customers of large retail chains, and saving account depositors. Association group plans can be contributory or noncontributory.

General Concepts

Group health insurance is similar to group life insurance provided by an employer or other group sponsor for eligible members or employees. The policy, or master contract, is issued to the group sponsor. In contrast, the individual insureds are issued *certificates of insurance* as proof of their coverage. Many group life insurance provisions are in group health insurance. Some notable ones include coverage for dependents and the right to *convert to an individual policy* following a group health contract termination.

Underwriting for group policies is unique. When insurers write a group policy, every eligible group member must be covered regardless of the member's age, sex, physical condition, or occupation. Therefore, the underwriting of group policies focuses on the entire group. The cost of the policy will vary according to the ratio of males to females and the group's average age. Evidence of insurability is not typically required. An annual reevaluation adjusts premiums based on the group's claim experience. Premiums are often allowed to be made retroactive for the year. Any group replacement underwriting will consider group stability, loss history, and composition.

The underwriting process uses the following requirements to *avoid adverse selection*:

- The insurance has to be incidental to the group. In other words, the members must not have formed the group for the sole purpose of buying insurance;
- There should be a steady flow of people through the group, with younger or healthier individuals replacing older or unhealthy individuals;
- The group's persistency (insurance providers do not want to write risks that frequently change insurers);
- A method of selecting benefits that avoids the individual selection of benefits;
- How insurers choose eligible participants (employees meet minimum service requirements and are typically full-time only);
- Identify whether the group is contributory or noncontributory;
- The group's size and composition, as well as the industry the group is involved in; and
- The group's prior claims experience.

Individual vs. Group Contracts

Individual health insurance contracts are issued to cover the applicant and dependents. Most policies are issued guaranteed renewable. Therefore, insurers complete the underwriting process with the utmost care to determine insurability.

Insurability factors include the applicant's gender, age, occupation, physical condition, habits, or lifestyle. Group insurance underwriting is less restrictive than individual contracts because the underwriting functions for the entire group. Annually renewable term insurance contracts would contemplate annual reevaluation of the risk and adoption of remedial measures if the initial underwriting evaluation proved incorrect.

The underwriter can adjust the benefits provided, the contract's conditions, and the premium rate on each contract anniversary date.

COBRA

In 1985, Congress passed the *Consolidated Omnibus Budget Reconciliation Act (COBRA), requiring all employers with 20 or more employees to* offer group health coverage to terminated employees and their families following a qualifying event. *Qualifying events* include the following:

- Voluntary termination of employment;
- Termination of employment for a cause other than gross misconduct (e.g., company downsizing); and
- A change in employment status from full-time to part-time.

Employers extend coverage for up to *18 months* if these qualifying events occur. The terminated employee has to exercise the extension of benefits under COBRA within 60 days of separation from employment. The employer collects a premium of no more than 102% of the individual's group premium rate from the terminated employee. The additional 2% charge covers the employer's administrative costs.

For events such as *death*, *divorce*, or *legal separation*, the coverage period for the terminated employee's dependents is *36 months*.

An important concept to remember is that COBRA benefits apply to group health insurance, not group life insurance. Furthermore, unlike the conversion privilege in which the individual converts coverage to an individual health insurance policy, COBRA continues the same group coverage. The terminated employee pays the group premium that the employer paid (or the employee and the employer paid if the plan was contributory).

Under the Affordable Care Act, coverage for the insured's children extends until the adult child reaches *age 26*. Under COBRA coverage, the same age limit applies to the insured's eligible children. Also, when dependent children lose "dependent child" status under the group plan, they qualify for a maximum of *36 months* of continuation coverage.

Several *disqualifying events* under which COBRA benefits will no longer continue include becoming covered under another group plan, failure to make a premium payment, becoming eligible for Medicare, or if the employer terminates all group health plans.

Other Policies

Various health insurance policies offer limited coverage for specific accidents or sicknesses. These contracts must specify the type of accident or sickness covered, the amount of coverage, and the limited perils. Insurers pay benefits on an *indemnity* or *expense-paid* (reimbursement) basis.

Short-Term Medical

Short-term medical insurance plans provide temporary coverage for individuals in transition (early retirees or those between jobs) and are available for terms ranging from one month up to 11 months, depending on the state or commonwealth. Unlike regular major medical plans, the Affordable Care Act does not regulate short-term medical insurance policies. Their enrollment is not limited to the open enrollment period.

Short-term health plans may have medical provider networks and impose premiums, benefit maximums, coinsurance, and deductibles like traditional health plans. They also cover outpatient and inpatient care, surgery, and physician services.

Accident

Accident-only policies are limited policies that offer coverage for disability, death, dismemberment, or hospital and medical care caused by accidents. Because they are limited medical expense policies, they will only cover losses caused by accidents, not sickness.

Critical Illness or Specified Disease

Critical illness policies cover multiple illnesses, such as renal failure, heart attack, and stroke. They pay a lump-sum benefit to the insured upon the diagnosis (and survival) of any illnesses the policy covers. The policy typically specifies a minimum number of days the insured must survive after a physician first diagnoses the condition.

Cancer

Cancer policies cover only one illness and pay a lump-sum cash benefit whenever the insured is first diagnosed with cancer. It is a supplemental policy designed to fill the gap between the additional costs of being diagnosed with the illness and the insured's traditional health coverage. There are no restrictions on how insureds can spend the funds. They can use the benefit for loss of income, personal living expenses, experimental treatment, to pay medical bills, a mortgage, etc.

Hospital Indemnity

A *hospital indemnity* policy offers a specific amount daily, weekly, or monthly for insureds confined in a hospital. Payment under this policy type is unrelated to incurred medical expenses that insurers determine based on the *number of days confined in a hospital*. This policy is also known as a hospital fixed-rate policy.

Dental Plans

Dental expense insurance is a type of medical expense health insurance that covers the prevention, care, and treatment of dental disease and injury to the insured's teeth. An important feature of dental insurance plans includes preventive and diagnostic care (teeth cleaning, fluoride treatment, etc.). Some dental plans require periodic exams as a condition for continued coverage.

Dental expense coverage may be integrated or packaged with other health insurance benefits similar to major medical. In that case, a standard deductible might apply to the integrated plan. However, some integrated plans carry separate deductibles for the medical and dental sections of the contract.

Under the Affordable Care Act, pediatric dental coverage is considered an essential health benefit. It *must be available* as part of a health plan or stand-alone plan for children 18 and under. However, insurance providers are not required to offer adult dental coverage.

Depending on the state, insureds can obtain pediatric dental benefits through any of the following types of plans:

- A qualified health plan which includes dental coverage;
- A stand-alone dental plan purchased with a qualified health plan; or
- A bundled/contracted plan.

Vision and Hearing Plans

Some employers offer their workers this type of group health insurance to cover eye exams, eyeglasses, and hearing aids on a limited basis. It is essential to know that pediatric vision benefits are mandatory under the Affordable Care Act.

Chapter Review

This chapter covered the major health insurance policies, including medical expense, disability, long-term care, and group. Let's review the key features of each insurance type:

MEDICAL EXPENSE INSURANCE	
Basic Hospital, Medical and Surgical Policies	• *Basic hospital expense coverage* – pays for hospital room and board, and miscellaneous expenses, including medicines and lab and X-ray charges while the insured is confined to a hospital • *Miscellaneous hospital expenses* – covers other miscellaneous expenses associated with a hospital stay; expressed as either a flat amount or a multiple of the room and board charge • *Basic medical expense coverage* – pays for nonsurgical physician's services. It can also be purchased to cover maternity benefits, emergency accident benefits, nurses' expenses, mental and nervous disorders, home health care, hospice care, and outpatient care • *Basic surgical expense coverage* – covers the costs of surgeons' services, regardless of whether the surgery is performed in or out of the hospital
Major Medical Policies	• Supplemental Major Medical Policies • Comprehensive Major Medical Policies • Offer a range of coverage (lifetime benefit per person limit) under one policy, including benefits for prolonged injury or illness, comprehensive coverage for hospital expenses, and catastrophic medical expense protection
Health Maintenance Organizations (HMOs)	• Preventive care • Limited service area • Limited choice of providers • Copayments • Prepaid basis • Primary Care Physician (PCP) acts as a gatekeeper • Referral (Specialty) Physician (PCP referral required)
Preferred Provider Organizations (PPOs)	• A group of hospitals and physicians contract to provide services at a reduced fee • Members can use any physician but are encouraged to use approved physicians who have previously agreed upon fees
Point-of-Service plans	• Combines HMO and PPO plans • Employees are not locked into one plan and are allowed to choose depending on the need for medical services
Flexible Spending Account (FSA)	• Funded by employer contributions and salary reduction • Employees deposit pre-tax funds into an account from which the employee is reimbursed for eligible expenses related to health care and dependent care during the year • FSA benefits are subject to "use-it-or-lose-it" and annual maximum rules
High Deductible Health Plans (HDHPs) and related Health Savings Accounts (HSAs)	• *High-deductible health plans (HDHPs)* – used in conjunction with MSAs, HSAs, or HRAs; features higher out-of-pocket limits and annual deductibles than traditional health plans, which result in lower premiums • *Health savings accounts (HSAs)* – individuals with high deductible health plans can make a tax-deductible contribution to an HSA and use it to cover out-of-pocket medical expenses

DISABILITY INCOME	
Disability Income Insurance	• Replaces lost income if a disability occurs • *Presumptive disability* – specifies the condition that qualifies an insured for full disability benefits • *Recurrent disability* – specifies the period during which the recurrence of an illness or injury will be considered a continuation of a prior disability • *Elimination period* – waiting period that lasts from the onset of disability until benefit payments begin • *Probationary period* – the period after the policy begins during which benefits won't be paid for illness-related disabilities • *Benefit period* – the length of time after the elimination period has been satisfied during which the monthly disability benefit payments will last for each disability • *Benefit limitations* – the maximum benefits an insurer is willing to accept for an individual risk; benefits are based on a percentage of the insured's past earnings • *Social Insurance Supplement (SIS) or Social Security Riders* – supplement or replace benefits payable under Social Security Disability
Business Overhead Expense Policy	• Pays for a small business owner's overhead expenses incurred while the business owner is totally disabled
Business Disability Buyout Policy	• Specifies who will buy out a partner's interest in a business in the event disability occurs
Key Person Disability	• Covers the potential loss of business income and the expense of hiring and training the replacement for a key person • The business pays the premium, owns the contract, and is the beneficiary

ACCIDENTAL DEATH AND DISMEMBERMENT	
Coverage	• AD&D is viewed as a pure form of accident insurance • It pays for accidental losses only • Accidental death is paid for by the principal sum • Dismemberment is paid for by the capital sum (percentage of the principal sum)

LONG-TERM CARE	
Levels of Care	• *Skilled care* – rehabilitative and daily nursing care by licensed medical personnel • *Intermediate care* – occasional rehabilitative or nursing care for insureds that require daily medical assistance less frequently than skilled nursing care • *Custodial care* – care for a person's activities of daily living given in an institutional setting or the patient's home • *Home health care* – provided in one's home by licensed vocational nurses, registered nurses, licensed practical nurses, or community-based organizations • *Home Convalescent Care* – given by a long-term care facility, a home health care agency, a hospital, or in the insured's home under a planned program established by their attending physician • *Residential Care* – given while the insured lives in a retirement community • *Adult daycare* – provides care for functionally impaired adults on less than a 24-hour basis • *Respite Care* – provides relief to the family caregiver; adult daycare centers can also offer this type of relief

Policies	• Available as an individual policy, group policy, or as a rider to life insurance policies • Coverage for insureds who require living assistance at home or in a nursing home facility • Must provide at least 12 months of consecutive coverage in a setting other than a hospital's acute care unit • Guaranteed renewable, but insurance companies may increase premiums
GROUP INSURANCE	
Basics	• Group must be formed for a purpose other than purchasing insurance • Two types of group insurance include employer-sponsored and association-sponsored
Underwriting	• Every eligible member of the group must be covered regardless of age, sex, physical condition, or occupation • Cost varies by the average age of the group and the ratio of males to females • Evidence of insurability is usually not required
COBRA	
Qualifying Events	• Voluntary termination of employment • Termination of employment for other reasons besides gross misconduct (e.g., company downsizing) • A change in employment status from full time to part time
Length of coverage	• 18 months – after a qualifying event • 36 months – for dependents after events such as divorce, legal separation, or death of the employee
LIMITED BENEFIT PLANS	
Types of Plans	• *Accident* – coverage for a disability, medical care, death or dismemberment resulting from an accident • *Dread disease policy* – provides a variety of benefits for a specific disease, such as heart disease policies or cancer policies • *Critical illness* – a lump-sum payment is made to the insured upon the diagnosis and survival of a critical illness • *Employer-sponsored plan* – employer-provided group coverage; employees must work full-time and meet service requirements • *Hospital indemnity* – provides a specific amount on a daily, weekly, or monthly basis while the insured is hospitalized • *Dental plans* – covers the prevention, treatment, and care of dental disease and injury to the insured's teeth • *Short-term medical* – temporary coverage for individuals in transition • *Vision/hearing plans* – a type of group health plan that covers eye exams and eyeglasses or hearing aids on a limited basis

CHAPTER 7:
Health Policy Provisions, Clauses, and Riders

You should be able to list the different types of health insurance policies and their defining characteristics. Health insurance policies include provisions, clauses, and riders that significantly affect their terms and benefits. Some policy provisions are mandatory, while others are optional. Part of your responsibility as a producer is to be able to explain the different policy provisions and riders to your clients. The knowledge you share with prospective customers will help them make educated decisions about their health insurance policies. This chapter will discuss the following topics:

- Mandatory Provisions
- Other Provisions and Clauses
- Riders
- Rights of Renewability

Mandatory Provisions

The NAIC (National Association of Insurance Commissioners) established the *Uniform Individual Accident and Sickness Policy Provisions Law*, which every state adopts. This law introduced standard provisions that are included in every individual health insurance policy. Although the wording may differ from one insurance carrier to another, the basic provisions are the same. Some of these provisions are similar to those in a life insurance policy.

These provisions define the duties and rights of the policy owner and the insurance provider. The insurance provider may reword any provision so long as the modification does not make the provision less favorable to the policy owner or beneficiary.

Entire Contract

The *entire contract* provision stipulates that the health insurance policy, a copy of the signed application, and any attached riders and amendments make up the entire contract. Neither party can change the policy without the express written consent of both parties, and any changes must also be a part of the contract. Only an insurance company's executive officer, not an agent, has the authority to make any changes to the policy.

Grace Period

The *grace period* is the time beyond the premium due date. Policyholders can still pay premiums before the policy lapses for nonpayment. Grace periods may differ according to individual state laws. In most cases, the grace period cannot be less than *seven days for policies with a weekly premium, ten days for policies with a monthly premium, and 31 days for every other mode*. During the grace period, coverage continues in force.

Reinstatement

When the policy owner does not pay the premium by the end of the grace period, the policy will lapse (terminate). This provision states under what conditions the insured may *reinstate coverage*. If the insurance company or an authorized representative accepts the policy premium and does not require a reinstatement application, reinstatement is automatic. However, when a reinstatement application is needed, and an insurer issues a conditional receipt for the premium payment, the insurance company may approve or disapprove the reinstatement application. Insurers automatically reinstate coverage if they do not refuse the reinstatement application within 45 days from the date the conditional receipt was issued. Accidents will be covered immediately following the reinstatement; however, *insurance providers will cover sickness after ten days*. This stipulation helps to protect the insurance provider from adverse selection.

Change of Beneficiary

The change of beneficiary provision states that policy owners can change the beneficiary by providing a written request to the insurance carrier. Unless the beneficiary is *irrevocable*, the beneficiary's consent is not required. If the beneficiary designation is irrevocable, the policy owner must obtain the beneficiary's permission before making any changes.

Claims Procedures

The *notice of claim* provision specifies the insured's responsibility to provide the insurance company with reasonable notice in the event of a loss. Notice is required immediately or within 20 days of the loss. Notice to the agent is the same as notice to the insurance company.

Upon receiving a notice of claim, the insurance company must supply *claims forms* to the insured within a specified number of days (typically 15, but this may vary from state to state). When the claimant does not furnish these forms, the insurer considers the claimant to have complied with the policy's requirements if they submit *written proof* of the occurrence and the nature and extent of the loss.

Following a loss, the claimant must submit *proof of loss* as soon as reasonably possible or within 90 days, not exceeding one year. However, the 1-year limit only applies if the claimant is legally competent to comply with this provision.

The *time of payment of claims* provision states that claims are to be paid immediately upon written proof of loss. Different policies typically state the time of payment of claims as 60 days, 45 days, or 30 days. However, if the claim involves disability income benefits, the benefits have to be paid no less frequently than monthly.

The *payment of claims* provision specifies who receives the claims payments. All benefits are payable to the insured while they are alive. If the insured is deceased, insurers will pay pending claims to the beneficiary. If there is no beneficiary, benefits are paid to the deceased's estate unless the insured has allocated the benefits to be paid directly to a doctor or hospital for services rendered.

Some policies allow a provision called the *facility of payment* clause. This provision gives insurers the right to expedite urgently needed claim payments and pay up to a specified limit to a relative or another individual who is justifiably entitled to benefits.

Physical Examination and Autopsy

The *physical exam and autopsy* provision allows insurance providers to examine the insured as often as possible while a claim is pending at their own expense. The insurer also typically has the right to conduct an autopsy if state law does not prohibit it.

Time Limit on Certain Defenses (Incontestable)

The *time limit on certain defenses* provision is analogous to the incontestability provision in a life insurance policy. Insurance providers cannot use any statement or misstatement made in the application (except fraudulent ones) to deny a claim when the policy has been effective for *two years*.

Insurers *cannot deny or reduce claims* for losses or disabilities that began two years after the policy issue date. They also cannot reject or lower claims even though a physical condition or disease not explicitly excluded from coverage existed before the effective date of coverage.

Legal Actions

This provision limits when a claimant can seek recovery from an insurance provider under a policy. The policy owner must wait *60 days*, but no later than two or three years (in most states) after proof of loss before they can bring legal action against the insurance company.

Misstatement of Age or Sex

If the insured misstated their age or gender in the application, the insurer would *adjust* the benefits paid under the policy to what the paid premiums would have purchased at the correct age.

Change of Occupation

The insured's occupation is essential during underwriting, particularly for disability income insurance. Health insurance policies generally include a provision that lets the insurance provider adjust benefits if the insured changes occupations. When the policyholder changes to a more hazardous occupation, upon filing a claim, the insurer will reduce benefits to what the paid premiums would have purchased, assuming the more hazardous occupation. The insured can apply to the insurance provider for a rate reduction whenever the change is to a less dangerous profession.

Illegal Occupation

This provision specifies that the insurance provider will deny liability if the insured engages in an illegal occupation or is injured while committing an unlawful act.

Relation of Earnings to Insurance

The relation of earnings to insurance provision lets an insurer limit the insured's benefits to their average income for the past 24 months. If necessary, the insurer decreases benefits on a pro-rata basis.

When the total benefits for a single loss under all policies exceed the insured's monthly or average monthly earnings for the previous two years, the insurance provider will only be liable for a proportionate amount of the benefit. The insurer must return premiums for that part of the benefit, which is not payable. Also, the insurer can never reduce the monthly benefit to less than $200.

Other Provisions and Clauses

All individual health insurance policies must include specific standard provisions. These are called *Uniform Mandatory Provisions*. In addition to these mandatory provisions, some provisions, such as the free look provision, are required in individual policies. In contrast, other provisions are necessary for both individual and group policies. Insurance providers can use additional provisions that do not conflict with the uniform provisions if they receive approval from the state where the policy is delivered. Although listing all the provisions insurance companies use is impossible, the following are the most commonly used:

Insuring Clause

The *insuring clause* or agreement is typically on the first page of the policy. It is a general statement identifying the basic contract between the insured and the insurer. It identifies the insured and the insurer and specifies what kind of loss (peril) is covered.

Free Look

The *free look* or *right to examine* provision gives the insured several days to review the policy and return it for a full refund if dissatisfied. It is typically *ten days* from the policy's delivery date but can vary for different policies. Most states mandate this provision for individual policies.

Consideration Clause

The *consideration clause*, which is usually on the first page of the policy, makes it clear that both parties to the contract are required to give some valuable consideration. The consideration given by the applicant is the payment of the premium and the statements in the application. The insurance provider's consideration is the promise to pay claims under the contract terms.

Probationary Period

The *probationary period* provision stipulates that a specific time must pass before coverage for specified conditions goes into effect. This provision is generally in disability income policies. The probationary period also applies to new employees who have to wait a specific time before they can enroll in the group plan. This provision intends to prevent unnecessary administrative expenses in cases of employee turnover.

Elimination Period

The *elimination period* is a type of deductible usually found in a disability income policy. It is a specific number of days that have to expire after an accident or onset of an illness before benefits are payable. Longer elimination periods will result in a lower cost of coverage.

Waiver of Premium

Insurers typically include the *waiver of premium* provision or rider with guaranteed renewable and noncancelable disability income policies. It specifies that in the event of total and permanent disability, the insurer will waive premiums for the duration of the disability. The insured must be disabled for a specified period, typically six months, to be eligible. The insured must continue paying the policy premium during this 6-month waiting period. However, the waiver is usually retroactive to the date the disability began, and any paid premiums during the waiting period are refunded. This provision or rider usually expires when the insured reaches age 65. As long as the insured becomes disabled before age 65, the insurer will waive premiums for the duration of the disability.

Pre-Existing Conditions

Pre-existing conditions are those for which the insured has received a diagnosis, advice, treatment, or care during a specific period before the application for health coverage. Until January 2014, health insurance policies could exclude these conditions from coverage. However, the Affordable Care Act eliminated pre-existing conditions and restrictions on individual and group health insurance plans. Long-term care insurance and Medicare Supplement policies may have pre-existing condition limitations.

Coinsurance

Most major medical policies contain a *coinsurance provision* that allows for sharing expenses between the insured and the insurer. After the insured satisfies the policy deductible, the insurer usually pays most of the costs, typically 80%, with the insured paying the remaining 20%. Other coinsurance arrangements, such as 90/10, 75/25, or 50/50, are also available. The larger the percentage covered by the insured, the lower the required premium. This provision enables the insurer to control costs and discourage policy overutilization.

Most policies also limit the insured's out-of-pocket expenses during a policy year. A *stop-loss limit* is a stated dollar amount beyond which the insured no longer contributes to sharing costs. The insurer pays 100% of the expenses above the stated stop-loss limit.

Copayments

This *copayment* provision is similar to the coinsurance feature, as the insured shares part of the service cost with the insurance company. Unlike coinsurance, a copayment has a *fixed dollar amount* the insured will pay each time they use certain medical services.

Deductibles

A *deductible* is a stated dollar amount the insured must pay before the insurer pays the policy benefits. Insurers intend to have the insured absorb the more minor claims while the coverage provided under the policy absorbs the more significant claims—the larger the deductible, the lower the premium the policy owner must pay.

Most major medical policies have an *annual deductible* (also known as a calendar year deductible) that is paid once in any year, regardless of the number of claims. These policies may contain an *individual deductible*, where each insured is responsible for a specified deductible amount each year. They may also include a *family deductible*.

The annual deductible is met if two or more family members pay a deductible in a given year, regardless of the number of claims incurred by other family members. Some policies contain what is known as a *per-occurrence deductible* or *flat deduct*ible, which the insured must pay for each claim. This type of deductible could result in the policy owner paying more than one deductible in a given year.

The policy may also contain the *common accident* provision, which applies when more than one family member is involved in a single accident. In this case, only one deductible will apply to all family members injured in the same accident.

Some supplemental major medical plans also contain an *integrated deductible*. The amount an insured will pay under basic medical expense coverage may satisfy the deductible. For example, suppose the supplemental coverage includes a $1,000 integrated deductible, and the insured has $1,000 in basic medical expenses. In that case, they will have met the deductible. If the basic policy only covers $800 of the basic costs, the insured must satisfy the remaining $200 difference.

Specific policies also include a *carry-over provision*. When the insured did not incur enough expenses during the year to satisfy the deductible, the policy owner could carry over any costs during the final three months to the following year to meet the new annual deductible.

Example 7.1 – An insured has a $500 deductible. Billy incurs $100 in the first half of the year and another $250 during the last quarter, ultimately not reaching the total deductible for the year. He could carry the $250 forward to the following year, making him eligible for claim payments if he incurs an additional $250 in the new year.

Long-term care and disability income policies typically have a time deductible as an elimination period.

Exclusions and Limitations

Exclusions specify what an insurance provider will not cover. These causes of loss are expressly not included in the coverage. *Reductions* are a decrease in benefits due to certain specified conditions. The most common exclusions in a health insurance policy are injury or loss that results from any of the following:

- Military duty;
- War;
- Self-inflicted injury;
- Cosmetic medical expenses;
- Dental expense;
- Eye refractions; or
- Care in government facilities.

Also, most policies temporarily suspend coverage while a policyholder is serving in the military or residing in a foreign country.

Mental and Emotional Disorders – Typically, the lifetime benefit for major medical coverage limits the amount payable for mental or emotional disorders. The benefit is commonly a separate lifetime benefit, and there usually is a limit on the number of outpatient visits per year. The benefit might also pay a maximum limit per visit. Inpatient treatment is generally not subject to these limitations.

Substance Abuse – Like mental and emotional disorders, outpatient treatment of substance abuse is usually subject to a maximum limit.

Eligible Expenses

Medical expenses covered by a health insurance plan are eligible expenses, which insurance providers will state in the policy.

Pre-Authorizations and Prior Approval Requirements

Some health insurance policies will require the prior approval or pre-authorization of certain tests, medical procedures, or hospital stays. The insured must obtain the insurance provider's approval before the test, procedure, or hospital stay to ensure the policy will pay the expenses.

Usual, Reasonable, and Customary (URC) Charges

Specific medical expense insurance plans include a benefit schedule that explicitly states the covered procedures and their costs. Other plans may use the term *"usual, reasonable, and customary,"* which means the insurer will pay an amount for a specified procedure based on the average charge in that geographic region.

Lifetime, Annual, or Per-Cause Maximum Benefit Limits

The largest benefit amount a policy will pay is called the maximum benefit. This limit can be a lifetime limit, an annual limit, or a per-cause limit.

- **Lifetime Limit** – The *lifetime limit* specifies a maximum benefit amount the policy will pay during the insured's lifetime.
- **Annual Limit** – An *annual limit* is the most a policy will pay each year that the policy remains in force.
- **Per-Cause Limit** – The *per-cause* limit is the most a policy will pay for any expenses incurred from the exact cause or related causes.

Riders

Impairment (Exclusion) Rider

The *impairment (exclusion)* rider can be attached to a contract to eliminate coverage for a defined pre-existing condition, such as back injuries. Impairment riders can become a permanent part of the policy or be temporary. Attaching this rider to a policy excludes coverage for a condition that the insurer would otherwise cover. Often, a person's only means of obtaining insurance at a reasonable cost when they have a current impairment is through a policy that excludes coverage for the specific impairment.

Example 7.2 – A surgeon may have suffered a back injury before applying for a disability policy. The insurance company may agree to issue a disability policy with an exclusion rider, excluding coverage for any claim related to the surgeon's back. The policy would cover any other disability that may be incurred in the future, as long as it is unrelated to the surgeon's back. This scenario may be the only way the insured can obtain coverage. When writing the contract, the underwriter will decide whether to make the exclusion permanent or only for a short time, such as if the insured can go for a stated period without further treatment. Underwriters will specify the terms of the rider in the policy.

Most riders in life and health insurance policies *add* some form of additional coverage, and often, an extra cost is added to the premium. The impairment (exclusion) rider is an exception because it *removes* something from the standard coverage. There is no additional charge for this, nor is the premium lowered to reflect a reduction in coverage.

Guaranteed Insurability Rider

The guaranteed insurability rider is also called the *Future Increase* or *Guaranteed Purchase Option*. This option, also available on life insurance policies, will let the insured buy additional amounts of disability income coverage *without evidence of insurability*. The insured typically receives several option dates, such as every two years, to exercise the additional purchase option. Most insurers do not allow the insured to exercise the additional purchase option beyond a certain age, typically 50. They will base the premium for the extra coverage on the insured's attained age when they exercise the option. The insured must meet an earnings test before each purchase to prevent over-insurance. Also, the insurance provider will usually limit the amount purchased at each option date to some specified amount, such as $500-$5,000.

Rights of Renewability

The *face page* of the individual health insurance contract must clearly state under what conditions the insured can renew the policy. When the insurance provider reserves the right to refuse renewal, insurers must deliver or mail a written notice not to renew the policy beyond the premium payment period.

Since an individual health insurance policy provides coverage for a specified term, the absence of a cancellation provision does not guarantee continuing protection. Even when the insurance provider cannot cancel a policy, the insurer can retain the right to refuse to renew the policy.

Insureds should carefully examine every policy to determine which renewal provision it includes, as this is essential.

Noncancelable

The insurer cannot cancel a *noncancelable* policy, nor can the premium be raised beyond what is in the policy. The policy may call for an increase in a particular year, like "age 65," which the insurer must write in the original contract. The insured can renew the policy for the contract's life. The insurance company cannot increase the premium above the amount for which the insurer initially issued the policy. However, the guarantee to renew coverage typically only applies until the insured reaches age 65. At this time, the insured is usually eligible for Medicare. For disability income insurance, the policy will be renewed beyond age 65 only if the insured can prove that they have continued working full-time.

Cancelable

This provision allows the insurance company to *cancel* the policy at any time or at the end of the policy period. There are no guarantees that the insurance provider will continue coverage at the end of the policy period. Insurers must provide the insured with proper written notice of the cancellation and a refund of any unearned paid premiums. When the insured is in the middle of a claim at the time of cancellation, the insurance provider must continue to honor the claim. This renewability provision is illegal and rare in many states.

Guaranteed Renewable

The *guaranteed renewable* provision is similar to the noncancelable provision, except the insurance company can raise the policy premium on the anniversary date. However, the policy owner has the unilateral right to renew the policy for the contract's life. The insurance provider can only raise premiums *on a class basis*, not on an individual policy. As with noncancelable policies, coverage usually is not renewable beyond the insured's age of 65. Insurers must write long-term care policies and Medicare Supplements as *guaranteed renewable contracts*. The insurance company cannot cancel them when the insured reaches age 65.

Chapter Review

This chapter discussed different health insurance policy provisions and riders that modify coverage. Let's review some of the central concepts:

POLICY PROVISIONS	

Mandatory Provisions	• *Entire contract* – the policy (with riders and amendments) and a copy of the application
	• *Grace period* – the period after the premium is due during which the policy will not lapse
	• *Reinstatement* – policy owners can restore a policy within a stated period with proof of insurability
	• *Change of beneficiary:*
	  - Revocable – the beneficiary can be changed at any time
	  - Irrevocable – the beneficiary can be changed with the beneficiary's consent
	• *Notice of claim* – the insured must provide the insurer with reasonable notice after a loss within 20 days or as soon as possible
	• *Claim form* – the insurance company must supply the insured with claims forms within a specified period
	• *Proof of loss* – the claimant has to submit proof of loss within 90 days of the loss
	• *Time of payment of claims* – specifies that claims have to be paid upon written proof of loss
	• *Payment of claims* – states to whom claims insurers will make payments
	• *Physical examination and autopsy* – the insurance company has the right to examine the insured as often as necessary while a claim is pending
	• *Time limit on certain defenses* – misstatements on an application cannot be used to deny a claim after the policy has been effective for two years
	• *Legal action* – the insured has to wait 60 days after written proof of loss before bringing legal action against the insurer
	• *Misstatement of age* – insurers will adjust benefits according to what the premium paid would have purchased at the correct age
	• *Change of occupation* – allows the insurance provider to adjust benefits if the insured changes their occupation
	• *Illegal occupation* – liability will be denied if the insured is engaged in an illegal occupation or is injured while committing an illegal act

Other Provisions and Clauses	• *Insuring clause* – a basic agreement between the policyholder and the insurer • *Free look* – policy owners can return the policy for a refund of the premium within a specified period • *Consideration* – the parties to a contract exchange something of value • *Probationary period* – states that a period must pass before coverage for specified conditions goes into effect • *Elimination period* – commonly found in disability income policies; a specified number of days that must pass after the occurrence of an accident or onset of an illness before benefits will be payable

POLICY PROVISIONS *(Continued)*	
Other Provisions and Clauses *(Continued)*	• *Waiver of premium* – in the event of total and permanent disability, premiums will be waived for the duration of the disability • *Pre-existing conditions* – coverage does not apply to pre-existing conditions • *Recurrent disability* – specifies the time that must pass between two illnesses for a new set of benefits to be available for the second illness • *Deductible* – a specified dollar amount the policy owner pays before the insurance provider will pay the policy benefits • *Coinsurance* – allows the sharing of expenses between the insured and the insurance carrier; expressed as a percentage after the insured pays the policy deductible • *Copayments* – establishes the sharing of expenses between the insured and the insurer; expressed in a set dollar amount the insured pays for each medical service • *Eligible expenses* – the specified medical expenses covered by a health plan • *Pre-authorization or prior approval* – tests, medical procedures, or hospital stays for which the insured requires approval from the insurer • *Usual/reasonable/customary charges* – states what amount the insurance provider will pay for a given procedure • *Lifetime, annual, per cause maximum benefit limits* – specifies the largest benefit amount a policy will pay per year, per lifetime, or per cause • *Exclusions* – specifies causes of loss for which the insurance company will not pay, including losses that result from military duty, war, self-inflicted injuries, cosmetic medical expenses, dental expenses, eye refractions, or care in government facilities
RIDERS	
Impairment Rider	• Eliminates coverage for pre-existing conditions that are specifically defined, such as back injuries • Can be temporary or can become a permanent part of the policy
Guaranteed Insurability Rider	• Allows the insured to buy additional amounts of coverage without providing evidence of insurability • Premium for an additional amount is based on the insured's attained age at the time the option is exercised
RIGHTS OF RENEWABILITY	
Noncancelable	• An insurance company cannot cancel or increase premiums beyond the amount stated in the policy
Cancelable	• Insurance providers can cancel the policy at any time or the end of the policy period with proper written notice and a refund of any unearned premiums
Guaranteed Renewable	• Insurance carriers can raise the policy premium (on a class basis only) on the policy anniversary date • The insured has the unilateral right to renew the policy for the life of the contract

CHAPTER 8:
Social Insurance

This chapter will discuss social insurance and its government-sponsored Medicare, Medicaid, and Social Security programs. You will learn about basic benefits, eligibility requirements, and services each provides. This chapter includes many medical terms, acronyms, and numbers. Remember that the dollar amounts for different Medicare deductibles change frequently and serve as a reference only. What is essential for you to remember is who qualifies for each type of plan and what kind of coverage they can expect. When you complete this chapter, you will be familiar with the following:

- Medicare
- Medicare Supplement Policies
- Medicaid
- Social Security Benefits

Medicare

Medicare is a federal medical expense insurance program for individuals age 65 and older, even if they continue to work. Medicare benefits are also available to anyone, regardless of age, with a permanent kidney failure known as End-Stage Renal Disease (ESRD) or who is entitled to Social Security disability income benefits for two years.

Recent green card holders (permanent residents) aged 65 years or older or new immigrants who have never worked in the U.S. may not immediately qualify for Medicare. When they are not eligible for free Medicare, these individuals can still purchase it if they meet the following eligibility requirements:

- Are 65 years of age or older;
- Have recently become a U.S. citizen by naturalization and have not worked enough quarters to have social security coverage; and
- Are lawfully admitted aliens (green card holders) who have constantly lived in the United States *for five years* or longer and do not qualify for Social Security benefits.

The Center for Medicare and Medicaid Services (CMS), a United States Department of Health and Human Services (HHS) division, manages Medicare which includes the following four parts:

- **Part A (Hospital Insurance)** receives a subsidy through a portion of the payroll tax (FICA);
- **Part B (Medical Insurance)** is funded from monthly premiums paid by insureds and from the general revenues of the federal government;
- **Part C (Medicare Advantage)** allows individuals to receive all of their health care services through available provider organizations; and
- **Part D (Prescription Drugs)** is coverage for prescription drugs.

It is necessary to note that the term *Original Medicare* refers to Part A (Hospital Insurance) and Part B (Medical Insurance) only. It covers health care from any healthcare provider, doctor, hospital, or facility that accepts Medicare patients. Typically, it does not cover prescription drugs. Original Medicare does not require the patient to choose a primary care provider. It also does not require the patient to obtain a referral to a specialist as long as the specialist accepts Medicare.

The following are claims terminology and other key terms that apply to Medicare:

- **Actual Charge** – The amount a supplier or physician bills for a particular supply or service.
- **Ambulatory Surgical Services** – Care given at an ambulatory center. Unlike inpatient hospital surgery, these are surgical services provided at a center that do not require a hospital stay.
- **Approved Amount** – The amount Medicare finds reasonable for a service covered under Part B of Medicare.
- **Assignment** – A medical supplier or the physician agrees to accept the Medicare-approved amount as full payment for the covered services.
- **Carriers** – Organizations that process claims submitted by suppliers and doctors under Medicare.
- **Coinsurance** – The portion of Medicare's approved amount the beneficiary must pay.
- **Comprehensive Outpatient Rehabilitation Facility Services** – Outpatient services received from a Medicare-participating facility.
- **Deductible** – The expense a beneficiary must first incur before Medicare begins paying for covered services.

- **Durable Medical Equipment** – Medical equipment such as wheelchairs, oxygen equipment, and other medically necessary equipment that a doctor prescribes for use in the home.
- **Excess Charge** – The difference between the actual charge and the Medicare-approved amount for a supply or service.
- **Intermediaries** – Organizations that process inpatient and outpatient claims on patients from hospitals, home health agencies, skilled nursing facilities, hospices, and certain other providers of health services.
- **Limiting Charge** – The maximum amount a physician can charge Medicare beneficiaries for a covered service if the physician does not accept the assignment.
- **Nonparticipating** – Suppliers or doctors who can choose whether or not to accept assignment on each claim.
- **Outpatient Physical and Occupational Therapy and Speech Pathology Services** – These are medically necessary services prescribed by a therapist or doctor.
- **Pap Smear Screening** – Provides a screen for cervical cancer once every two years.
- **Partial Hospitalization for Mental Health Treatment** – An outpatient mental health care program.
- **Participating Doctors or Suppliers** – Doctors and suppliers who agree to accept assignment on all Medicare claims.
- **Peer Review Organizations** – Groups of practicing doctors and other health care professionals that the government compensates to review the care received by Medicare patients.

Part A

Medicare *Part A* assists with paying for inpatient hospital care, inpatient care in a skilled nursing facility, home health care, and hospice care.

An individual is eligible for Medicare Part A - Hospital Coverage if they qualify for one of the following conditions:

- A citizen or a legal resident of the United States age 65 or over and eligible for Social Security or Railroad Retirement benefits (Aged);
- Is 65 years old or over and entitled to monthly Social Security benefits based on the work record of their spouse, and the spouse is at least 62;
- Is younger than 65 years old but also has been entitled to Social Security disability benefits for 24 months (Disabled);
- Has ESRD (End-Stage Renal Disease), which is permanent kidney failure requiring dialysis or a transplant; or
- Has Amyotrophic Lateral Sclerosis (ALS), or Lou Gehrig's disease, which automatically qualifies for Part A during the month disability benefits begin.

Individuals not receiving those specific benefits must sign up for Part A, even if they are eligible for premium-free Part A.

In addition, monthly Part A premiums are mandatory when a beneficiary is not "fully insured" under Social Security. In other words, they have not earned *40 quarters* of coverage (equal to 10 years of work) and, therefore, are eligible to receive Social Security retirement, premium-free Medicare Part A, and survivor benefits.

Individuals who want to sign up for Medicare Part A have the following three options:

- **Initial Enrollment Period** – When an individual first becomes eligible for Medicare, starting three months before turning age 65 and ending three months after the 65th birthday;
- **General Enrollment Period** – Between January 1st and March 31st each year; and

- **Special Enrollment Period** – Any time during the year if the person or their spouse is still employed and covered under their group health insurance plan.

Those who do not qualify for premium-free Part A can purchase the coverage for a monthly premium. When a person fails to sign up for Part A when they are first eligible, the monthly premium can go up 10% unless the individual becomes eligible for a special enrollment period.

Inpatient Hospital Care – Hospital insurance helps pay for up to 90 days in a participating hospital during any benefit period, subject to a deductible. After the deductible is satisfied, the first 60 days are covered at 100% of approved charges. The insurance provider will pay the next 30 covered days, but they pay with a daily copayment. Each Part A insured has a lifetime reserve of 60 days of hospital care. The lifetime reserve days have a copayment double that of days 61 through 90 and are nonrenewable. Covered services include a semi-private room, meals, regular nursing services, operating and recovery room costs, hospital costs for anesthesia, intensive care and coronary care, X-rays, lab tests, drugs, medical supplies, appliances, rehabilitation services, and preparatory services related to kidney transplant surgery. Blood is also covered, excluding the first 3 pints.

Under the inpatient hospital stay, Part A does not include private duty nursing, a television, or a telephone in the hospital room. It only provides a private room if it is medically necessary. Also, inpatient mental health care within a psychiatric facility is limited to 190 days in a person's lifetime.

After sixty days of non-use of the inpatient hospital care benefit, a new benefit period and deductible will start.

Skilled Nursing Facility Care – Part A helps pay for up to 100 days in a participating skilled nursing facility during each benefit period, following a 3-day inpatient hospital stay for a related illness. The insured's doctor must certify that daily skilled care is medically necessary to receive this care. Covered expenses include. Covered expenses include:

- A semi-private room;
- Meals;
- Regular nursing and rehabilitation services; and
- Other medical supplies.

Home Health Care – For individuals confined to their homes, hospital insurance can pay the total approved costs for home health visits from a participating home health agency. There is no limit to the number of covered visits to a person's home. Covered services include physical therapy, speech therapy, and part-time skilled nursing care. Hospital insurance also covers:

- Occupational therapy;
- Part-time services of home health aides;
- Medical social services; and
- Medical supplies and equipment.

Hospice Care – Under certain conditions, hospital insurance can help pay for *hospice care* for terminally ill insureds if a Medicare-certified hospice provides the care. Covered services include doctor and nursing services and supplies, including outpatient drugs for pain relief, medical appliances, home health aides, therapies, homemaker services, medical social services, short-term inpatient care, respite care, and counseling.

The table on the following page is a reference chart for covered hospital services under Medicare Part A.

BENEFITS	MEDICARE PAYS	YOU PAY
HOSPITALIZATION		
First 60 days	All but the deductible	Deductible
Days 61-90	All but the daily deductible	Daily deductible
After day 90 (up to 60 days)*	All but the daily deductible	Daily deductible
After lifetime reserve days	Nothing	All costs
SKILLED NURSING FACILITY CARE		
First 20 days	100% of the approved amount	Nothing
Days 21-100	All but the daily deductible	Daily deductible
Beyond 100 days	Nothing	All cost
HOME HEALTH CARE		
For as long as you meet Medicare requirements for home health care benefits.	100% of the approved amount; 80% of the approved amount for durable medical equipment	Nothing for services; 20% of the approved amount for durable medical equipment
HOSPICE CARE		
For as long as a doctor certifies the need	All but limited costs for outpatient drugs and inpatient respite care	Limited cost sharing for outpatient drugs and inpatient respite care
BLOOD		
Unlimited if medically necessary	All but the first 3 pints per calendar year	For the three 3 pints**

* Sixty lifetime reserve days. For every lifetime reserve day, Medicare will pay for all covered costs except for daily coinsurance.
** To the extent that 3 pints of blood are replaced or paid for under one part of Medicare during the calendar year. They do not have to be replaced or paid for under the other part.

Part B

Medicare *Part B* will pay for doctor's services and various other medical services and supplies that hospital insurance does not cover. Medical insurance covers most of the services needed by individuals with permanent kidney failure.

Part B is optional and offered to everyone who enrolls in Medicare Part A. Part B is subsidized by monthly premiums and the federal government's general revenues. Most people enrolled in Medicare Part B pay the *standard monthly premium*. However, when an insured's modified adjusted gross income reported on their IRS tax return is above a certain amount, the insured might have to pay a higher premium.

Once a person becomes eligible for Part A, they will receive and have to pay for Part B unless they decline it. When the person decides they want Part B after initially refusing it, they must wait until the next general enrollment period (January 1st through March 31st) to enroll.

After the annual medical insurance deductible is satisfied, medical insurance usually pays 80% of the approved charges for covered expenses for the remainder of the year. The 20% coinsurance payable for Part B expenses has no maximum out-of-pocket limit.

Doctor Services – Part B pays for doctor services no matter where a person receives them in the United States. Covered doctor services include:

- Diagnostic tests and X-rays related to the treatment;
- Surgical services;
- Medical supplies furnished by a doctor's office; and
- Services of the office nurse.

Outpatient Hospital Services – Part B pays for outpatient hospital services received for diagnosis and treatment, such as care in a hospital, emergency room, or outpatient clinic.

Home Health Visits – Medicare will cover home health services as long as the insured is eligible, which are recommended by the insured's doctor. Such services limit the number of hours per day and days per week on a part-time basis. The services that Medicare does not fully cover will receive coverage from Medicaid.

Other Medical and Health Services – Under certain conditions or limitations, medical insurance pays for other medical services and supplies. Some examples include periodic support services, ambulance transportation, home dialysis equipment, supplies, independent laboratory tests, outpatient physical therapy, speech pathology services, oral surgery, and X-rays and radiation treatments.

Prescription Drugs (Limited Coverage) – Only medicines administered in a hospital outpatient department under certain circumstances, such as injected drugs at a doctor's office, medications requiring durable medical equipment (e.g., nebulizer or infusion pump), or some oral cancer drugs, are covered. Other than these examples, insureds under Part B will pay 100% for most prescription drugs unless Part D of Medicare covers them.

Outpatient Treatment of Mental Illness – Medicare pays for outpatient treatment of an approved condition such as anxiety or depression in a doctor's office (or other health care provider's office) or hospital outpatient department. Generally, the enrollee pays 20% of the Medicare-approved amount (coinsurance) and the Part B deductible. It is essential to note that Part A also covers inpatient mental health care.

Yearly "Wellness" Visit – In addition to a "Welcome to Medicare" preventive visit during the first 12 months, Medicare Part B covers an annual "wellness" visit. During this visit, the provider and the insured can create or update a personalized plan for disease prevention. The insured has no out-of-pocket cost for these visits if the doctor or other qualified healthcare provider accepts Medicare assignment. When the doctor or the health care provider performs additional services or tests during the same visit that the preventive benefit does not cover, the insured might have to pay coinsurance, and the Part B deductible might apply.

Medical insurance under Medicare Part B *does not cover* the following:

- The cost of skilled nursing home care beyond 100 days per benefit period;
- Private duty nursing;
- Intermediate nursing home care;
- Physician charges over Medicare's approved amount;
- Most outpatient prescription drugs;
- Custodial care received in the home;
- Care received outside the United States;
- Dental care, excluding dental expenses resulting from an accident only, cosmetic surgery, hearing aids, eyeglasses, orthopedic shoes, and acupuncture expenses; or
- Expenses incurred because of war or act of war.

The table below is a reference chart for covered medical services under Medicare Part B.

BENEFITS	MEDICARE PAYS	YOU PAY
MEDICAL EXPENSES		
Medicare pays for medical services in or out of the hospital	80% of the approved amount after the deductible	Deductible*, plus 20% of the approved amount and limited charges above this amount
CLINICAL LABORATORY SERVICES		
Unlimited if medically necessary	100% of the approved amount	Nothing for services
HOME HEALTH CARE		
For as long as the enrollee meets the Medicare requirements for home health care benefits	100% of the approved amount; 80% of the approved amount for durable medical equipment	Nothing for services; 20% of the approved amount for durable medical equipment
OUTPATIENT HOSPITAL TREATMENT		
Unlimited if medically necessary	The Medicare payment to hospital is based on the hospital cost	20% of the billed amount after the deductible
BLOOD		
Unlimited if medically necessary	80% of the approved amount after the deductible, and starting with the 4th pint	The first 3 pints plus 20% of the approved amount for additional pints after the deductible**

* Once the Medicare recipient reaches a specified dollar amount in expenses for covered services, the Part B deductible does not apply to any other covered services the enrollee receives for the rest of the year.
** To the extent that any of the 3 pints of blood are replaced or paid for under one part of Medicare during the calendar year. They do not have to be replaced or paid for under the other part.

Part C

In 2003, the Medicare Modernization Act changed the name of *Part C* from Medicare+Choice to *Medicare Advantage*. Medicare Advantage plans must cover all of the services under Original Medicare, excluding hospice care and some care received in qualifying clinical research studies. They may offer extra coverage, such as dental, vision, hearing, and other health and wellness programs.

Beneficiaries must be enrolled in Medicare Parts A and B to be *eligible* for Medicare Advantage. Medicare Advantage is Medicare provided by approved Health Maintenance Organizations or Preferred Provider Organizations. Many HMOs or PPOs will not charge a premium beyond what Medicare pays. The advantages of an HMO or PPO for a Medicare recipient may be that they cover most medical problems for a set fee, allowing insureds to budget for healthcare costs. Claim forms are not required, and the HMO or PPO pays for services not usually covered by Medicare or Medicare supplement policies. Such services include dental care, eye exams, hearing aids, or prescriptions.

Most Medicare HMOs require beneficiaries to receive medical services through the plan, except in emergencies. A few HMOs allow for greater freedom of choice through point-of-service plans.

A *Medicare Private Fee-for-Service Plan* is a Medicare Advantage Plan offered by a private insurer. Medicare pays the insurer a set monthly amount to provide health care coverage, and the insurance company decides how much enrollees pay for the services they receive.

Another section of Medicare Advantage, known as *Special Needs Plans*, provides more focused and specialized health care for specific groups of individuals. This group includes people with Medicare and Medicaid who live in nursing homes or have certain chronic medical conditions.

Part D

In November 2003, Congress passed the *Medicare Prescription Drug, Improvement, and Modernization Act (MMA)*. This act executed a plan to add Part D, a Prescription Drug Benefit, to the standard Medicare coverage. This *optional coverage* is offered through private Prescription Drug Plans (PDPs) with Medicare contracts. Beneficiaries must sign up with a plan offering this coverage in their area to receive the benefits provided and enroll in Medicare Part A or Parts A and B. The government will provide a standard plan in areas where private plans are unavailable. Medicaid recipients are automatically enrolled.

When Medicare beneficiaries do not enroll when they are first eligible, they must pay a 1% penalty for each month they delay enrollment.

Medicare beneficiaries can choose *stand-alone plans* that provide fee-for-service coverage or *integrated plans* that group coverage together, including HMOs and PPOs. These plans are known as Medicare Advantage.

Some Medicare standards restrict the plans offered by private insurance companies. However, they still have the freedom to customize their plans. Providers are required to cover drugs for specific classes but do not have to pay for every drug in each class.

Those who sign up for Part D will have a monthly premium and a deductible, which will vary by plan. After the deductible is satisfied, the plan will provide prescription drug benefits until the insured reaches a benefit limit. Under the standard drug benefit, once the beneficiary and their plan spend a specific amount combined on drugs (including the deductible), the beneficiary will typically pay no more than 25% of the cost for prescription drugs until they reach the annual out-of-pocket spending amount.

Catastrophic coverage starts automatically once the beneficiary has satisfied the plan's out-of-pocket cost requirements for the year. It covers 95% of prescription drug costs. The beneficiary will pay the greater of the specified amount or 5%. The cost limit for generic drugs would be lower than for name-brand drugs.

Additional assistance is available for those with lower incomes. These beneficiaries will not have a gap in their coverage.

Primary, Second Payor

While a person becomes eligible for Medicare upon turning 65, federal laws extend primary coverage benefits under the employer's plan to active older employees regardless of age. In other words, employer plans are typically *primary* coverage, and Medicare is *secondary* coverage.

Medicare and the Affordable Care Act

Medicare is not part of the Health Insurance Marketplace, a vital component of the Affordable Care Act. The Marketplace allows qualified individuals, families, and small business employees to obtain health insurance. When considered eligible for Medicare Part A, an individual will not qualify for Marketplace tax credits to help pay for premiums or reductions in cost-sharing. An insured can keep a Marketplace plan after Medicare coverage begins; however, any premium tax credits and reduced cost-sharing through the Marketplace will end.

Medicare Supplement Policies

Medicare supplement plans, also called *Medigap*, are policies issued by private insurers to fill in some of the gaps in Medicare. These plans intend to fill the gap in coverage attributable to Medicare's co-payment requirements, deductibles, and benefit periods. The federal Social Security program does not administer these plans. Instead, they are sold and serviced by private insurance companies and HMOs. These policies must meet specific requirements and receive approval from the state insurance department. Medicare supplement policies pay some or all of Medicare's co-payments and deductibles.

Under the *Omnibus Budget Reconciliation Act (OBRA)* of 1990, Congress passed a law authorizing the NAIC to create a standardized model for Medicare supplement policies. This model requires Medigap plans to meet specific requirements regarding participant eligibility and the benefits provided. This law aimed to eliminate questionable marketing practices and provide consumers with protection by standardizing coverage.

Anyone who qualifies for Medicare can also purchase a Medicare supplement and pay the necessary premium for those additional benefits. Under OBRA, Medicare supplement insurance cannot discriminate in pricing or be denied based on an applicant's claims experience, health status, receipt of health care, or medical condition. An *open enrollment* period is a 6-month period that guarantees the applicants the right to purchase Medigap after signing up for Medicare Part B.

The NAIC established standard Medicare supplement benefit plans identified with the letters A through N to standardize the coverage offered under Medicare supplement plans. *The core benefits found in Plan A must be in every plan*, as well as the variety of benefits these other plans offer. Any insurer selling Medigap plans must at least provide Plan A, while the other plans are optional.

Once an individual becomes eligible for a Medicare supplement policy, and during the open enrollment period, insurance carriers offer coverage on a guaranteed issue basis. Under these circumstances, an insurance provider must do the following:

- Sell the patient a supplement policy;
- Identify all pre-existing conditions incurred more than six months from the effective date of coverage; and
- Not charge more for a Medicare supplement policy due to past or present health conditions.

Medicare Supplement Plan A includes only the *core benefits*. The core benefits, also called basic benefits, cover the following:

- Part A coinsurance/copayment (not the Part A deductible);
- Part A hospital costs up to an additional 365 days after Medicare benefits are exhausted;
- Part A hospice care coinsurance/copayment;
- Part B coinsurance/copayment; and
- The "blood deductible" for Parts A and B (first 3 pints of blood).

In addition to Plan A, which includes only the core benefits, most insurance companies offer some or every additional plan. Insurance providers are not permitted to change the benefits provided in these supplemental plans, nor can they change the designation letter of any of the following plans:

Plan B – Core benefits plus the Medicare Part A deductible.

Plan D – Core benefits, Medicare Part A deductible, skilled nursing facility coinsurance, and the foreign travel benefit.

Plan G – Core benefits, Medicare Part A deductible, skilled nursing facility coinsurance, 100% of Medicare Part B excess charges, and the foreign travel benefit. This plan has to pay for services of activities of daily living (ADL) that Medicare does not cover.

Plans C, E, F, H, I, and J are no longer available. However, these plans will remain in force for insureds who purchased them when they were available.

Medicare Supplement Plans K and L have lower premiums with higher out-of-pocket costs. The core benefits of these two plans are different as well:

- Approved hospital costs for the copayments for days 61 through 90 during any Medicare benefit period.
- Approved hospital costs for the copayments for lifetime reserve days 91 through 150.
- Approved hospital costs for an additional 365 days after all Medicare benefits are used.
- 50% of charges for the first 3 pints of blood in Plan K, 75% of charges for the first 3 pints of blood in Plan L.
- 50% of the Part B coinsurance amount in Plan K, 75% of the Part B coinsurance amount in Plan L.
- 50% of respite care and hospice cost-sharing expenses for Part A in Plan K, 75% of respite care and hospice cost-sharing expenses for Part A in Plan L.

Plan K provides 50% of the Medicare Part A deductible and 50% of skilled nursing facility coinsurance.

Plan L provides 75% of the Medicare Part A deductible and 75% of skilled nursing facility coinsurance.

Plans M and N include benefits similar to Plan D, but the co-pays and deductibles may differ.

The table below outlines the benefits provided under each Medigap plan.

Medigap Plan	Basic Benefit	Skilled Nursing Coinsurance	Part A Deductible	Part B Excess (100%)	Foreign Travel Emergency
A	•				
B	•		•		
D	•	•	•		•
G	•	•	•	•	•
K	•	50%	50%		
L	•	75%	75%		
M	•	•	50%		•
N	•	•	•		•

Other Requirements – Insurance providers must describe each Medigap plan's benefits using the same format, language, and definitions. They must also use a standardized outline and chart that summarizes the benefits.

Insurers are not permitted to alter the standardized benefits of each plan. However, they are allowed to offer new, innovative benefits that can be cost-effective but are not currently available in the marketplace.

Every Medigap policy is *guaranteed renewable*. The insurer may not cancel or nonrenew coverage except for material misrepresentation on the application or because of nonpayment of the premium. Also, although the benefits provided by these plans are identical from one insurer to the next, the premiums vary considerably. Depending on how the insurance provider determines the premium charge, premiums can usually be raised on the policy anniversary date. Medigap policies must also contain a *30-day free look* provision that lets the insured return the policy to the insurance company within 30 days for a full refund of the premium paid.

Medigap policies cannot include a provision limiting coverage for pre-existing conditions for more than six months. When the insured has had a Medigap policy for at least six months and decides to switch to another one, the new policy cannot have a waiting period for pre-existing conditions for the same coverage as the old policy. Also, when the replacement policy offers additional coverage not included in the old policy, the 6-month waiting period applies only to the additional coverage.

Medicaid

Medicaid is a federal and state-funded program for individuals whose income and resources are insufficient to cover the cost of necessary medical care. Individual states design and administer their Medicaid programs, usually through the state's Department of Public Welfare, under broad guidelines developed by the federal government.

Individuals must meet specific income and other eligibility requirements to be eligible for Medicaid. Once someone qualifies as having low income and assets, they must meet other qualifiers, including disability, blindness, pregnancy, age (over 65), or caring for children receiving welfare benefits. Income is calculated according to a Federal Poverty Level (FPL) percentage for many eligibility groups.

New, modernized rules regarding Medicaid eligibility verification meant that state Medicaid agencies would rely primarily on information available through specific data sources. These data sources include the Social Security Administration, the Department of Labor, and the Department of Homeland Security rather than paper documentation from individuals and families. Each state has prepared a verification plan for Medicaid to comply with the new rules.

Certain income and asset levels, as well as other non-financial criteria, can determine eligibility for Medicaid. To qualify for Medicaid, individuals must satisfy federal and state requirements regarding U.S. citizenship, residency, and immigration status documentation.

Medicaid directs the states to provide at least the following services:

- Inpatient hospital care;
- Outpatient hospital care;
- Laboratory and X-ray services;
- Physician's services;
- Skilled nursing home services;
- Home health care services;
- Rural health clinic services;
- Periodic screening, diagnosis, and treatment;
- Family planning services; and
- Medicaid also pays for private duty nursing services, check-ups, prescription drugs, dental services, eyeglasses, and medical supplies and equipment.

Social Security Benefits

Social Security provides disability income benefits to eligible individuals under age 65, known as Old Age, Survivors, and Disability Insurance (OASDI). The person must have the proper insured status, meet the definition of disability, and satisfy the waiting period. It is difficult to qualify for disability income benefits under Social Security due to the strict definition of total disability that individuals must meet.

Those who apply for Social Security Disability Benefits will contact state agencies called Disability Determination Services (DDS) to evaluate their disability. When the state agency is satisfied that the worker is disabled as defined by the Social Security Act, the person is certified. In that situation, Social Security pays benefits after the waiting period has been satisfied.

Definition of Disability – Under Social Security, to be considered disabled, one's disability must meet the following definition: *the inability to participate in any gainful work in the national economy. The disability must occur due to a medically determinable impairment (physical or mental) that is expected to cause early death or has lasted or will last for 12 consecutive months.*

To be eligible for Social Security *disability benefits*, the disabled person must have earned a certain number of credits. Each year, an individual can earn a maximum of 4 work credits. Usually, a person needs 40 credits, 20 of which they acquired in the last ten years before the disability. In other circumstances, the amount of required credits varies by age, as shown in the following table:

- **Before age 24** – Individuals can qualify for benefits with only six credits earned three years before the disability occurred.
- **Ages 24 - 31** – Individuals can qualify for benefits if they have credit for having worked half the time between age 21 and the start of the disability. For example, if a person becomes disabled at age 27, they would need 12 credits (or three years' worth) out of the previous six years (between ages 21 and 27).
- **After age 31** – The required work credits vary even more. However, a person must have earned at least 20 credits in the ten years before becoming disabled.

AGE	CREDITS NEEDED
31-42	20
44	22
46	24
48	26
50	28
52	30
54	32
56	34
58	36
60	38
62+	40

Assuming an individual meets these stringent requirements, they must wait *five months* (waiting period) before Social Security will pay any benefits. Actual benefit payments will begin the *6th month of disability*.

Social Security will determine the disability benefit based on the individual's *Primary Insurance Amount (PIA)*. The PIA is determined by the individual's average indexed earnings on which a person pays Social Security taxes. Higher average earnings will result in a larger absolute benefit. Lower-paid workers will receive a greater percentage of their pre-disability income than higher-paid workers.

The Social Security Administration estimates that disabled employees earning the minimum wage can expect a Social Security benefit of approximately 57% of earnings at the time of disability. Employees paying the maximum Social Security tax can expect a benefit of roughly 30% of pre-disability earnings subject to Social Security taxation.

Social security benefits end when the person's retirement benefits start when the person dies or is no longer disabled. At death, family benefits will continue as survivor benefits. Benefits will continue for a 3-month adjustment period if a person no longer satisfies the definition of a disability.

Example 8.1 – An employee earning minimum wage is involved in an accident and cannot perform their regular duties. Before the disability, the employee earned $10,712 each year. As a result, the employee can expect Social Security benefits totaling 57% of their income or $6,105.84.

In this example: 57 / 100 = *Benefit / Pre-disability earnings*

57 / 100 = Benefit / $10,712 therefore,
Benefit = (57 x $10,712) / 100 or $6,105.84

Let us assume the employee earned more money ($25,000) and could pay the maximum Social Security tax. The employee could anticipate receiving approximately 30% of that income or $7,500.

In this example: 30 / 100 = *Benefit / Pre-disability earnings*

30 / 100 = Benefit / $25,000 therefore,
Benefit = (30 x $25,000) / 100 or $7,500

Chapter Review

This chapter discussed social health insurance, such as Medicare, Medicare Supplements, Medicaid, and Social Security Disability, available to senior citizens and individuals with special needs. Let's review some of the key points:

MEDICARE	

Basics	• Federal medical expense insurance program for individuals who:
	  - Are age 65 or older
	  - Have been qualified to receive Social Security disability benefits for two years
	  - Have a permanent kidney failure called End-Stage Renal Disease (ESRD)
	• Four parts:
	  - *Part A, Hospital Insurance*, financed through the payroll tax (FICA)
	  - *Part B, Medical Insurance*, financed by insureds and the general revenues
	  - *Part C, Medicare Advantage*, allows for the receipt of health care services through available provider organizations
	  - *Part D, Prescription Drug* coverage

MEDICARE (Continued)	
Part A	• Enrollment: - *Initial enrollment period* – when a person first becomes eligible for Medicare (starting three months before turning 65, ending three months after the 65th birthday) - *General enrollment period* – between January 1st and March 31st every year - *Special enrollment period* – at any time during the year if the person or their spouse is still employed and insured under a group health plan • Coverage: - Inpatient Hospital Care - Skilled Nursing Facility Care - Home Health Care - Hospice Care
Part B	• Optional; offered to everyone who enrolls in Part A • Coverage: - Doctor Services - Outpatient Hospital Services - Home Health Visits - Other Medical and Health Services - Prescription Drugs (limited coverage) - Outpatient Treatment of Mental Illness - Yearly "Wellness" Visit
Part C	• *Medicare Advantage* – requires enrollment in Parts A and B • Care is provided by an approved Health Maintenance Organization or Preferred Provider Organization
Part D	• Prescription drug benefit • Optional coverage through private prescription drug plans that have contracts with Medicare
Primary, Secondary Payor	• For individuals eligible for Medicare coverage who continue to work, their employer's health insurance plan would be considered primary coverage, while Medicare would be secondary coverage
MEDICARE SUPPLEMENT POLICIES	
Basics	• Also referred to as Medigap • Policies issued by private insurance providers to fill in the gaps in Medicare
Coverage	• *Plan A* – includes core benefits, including coinsurance/copayment; additional Part A hospital costs; hospice care coinsurance/copayment; Part B coinsurance/copayment; 3 pints of blood under Parts A and B • *Plans B - N* – includes core benefits plus various additional benefits
MEDICAID	
Purpose	• Provide medical care for people whose income and resources are insufficient • Federal and state-funded • To qualify for Medicaid, individuals must satisfy federal and state requirements regarding U.S. citizenship, residency, and immigration status documentation

SOCIAL SECURITY BENEFITS	
Basics	• *OASDI* – Old Age, Survivors, and Disability Insurance • Provides disability income benefits • Individuals are required to satisfy insured status, the definition of disability, and waiting period requirements
Qualifying for Disability Benefits	• Individuals must have earned 40 work credits (four per year), 20 of which were earned in the ten years before the disability • 5-month waiting period • Benefits are based on Primary Insurance Amount (PIA)

CHAPTER 9:
Other Health Insurance Concepts

This chapter discusses various characteristics that apply to most health insurance policies. You will review the owner's rights, benefits for dependents, coordination of benefits, and different types of disability coverage. This chapter will continue the discussion of tax issues as they pertain to health insurance, specifically the tax treatment of premiums and proceeds. You will also read about managed care and workers compensation. This chapter will provide a comprehensive review of the following policy features and provisions to complete your studies on health insurance:

- Owner's Rights
- Dependent Children Benefits
- Primary and Contingent Beneficiaries
- Modes of Premium Payment
- Nonduplication and Coordination of Benefits
- Occupational vs. Nonoccupational
- Total, Partial, Recurrent, and Residual Disability
- Managed Care
- Workers Compensation
- Subrogation
- Taxation of Premiums and Proceeds of Insurance

Owner's Rights

When an individual health insurance policy offers a death benefit, the policy owner can designate a beneficiary and change the beneficiary unless the beneficiary designation is irrevocable. The *change of beneficiary provision* specifies the power to change a policy's beneficiary. The policy owner also has the right to make any other change without the beneficiary's or beneficiaries' consent.

Dependent Children Benefits

The Affordable Care Act mandates that every insurance company offer health insurance policies covering the insured's dependent children. These policies must cover children *up to the age of 26*.

The law extends coverage for the insured's children to age 26. This coverage is available regardless of residency, marital status, financial dependence on their parents, or eligibility to enroll in their employer's health plan.

A policy providing dependent child coverage until a specified age cannot terminate coverage if the child is dependent upon the insured due to a physical or mental disability. A parent or legal guardian must provide proof of the dependency within 31 days of the child attaining the maximum age. Upon request, proof of dependency is required each year after two years after reaching the maximum age.

Primary and Contingent Beneficiaries

The insurance provider pays the death benefits available in a policy to a beneficiary. A *primary beneficiary* is the first person designated. However, when the primary beneficiary dies before the benefits become payable, these benefits will go to a *contingent* or *secondary beneficiary*. The insurer will pay benefits to the deceased's estate if no beneficiary is designated.

When an individual health insurance policy provides a death benefit, it must also contain a *change of beneficiary* provision. This provision gives the policy owner the right to change any primary and contingent beneficiary or make any other change without the beneficiary's or beneficiaries' consent. However, this change will not be possible if the policy owner chooses an irrevocable designation of a beneficiary.

Modes of Premium Payment

Regarding insurance premiums, mode refers to the policy owner's *frequency* of premium payments. Insurers base a policy's rates on the assumption that policy owners will pay the premium annually at the beginning of the policy year. This practice allows the insurance company to invest the premium for an entire year before paying any claims. When the policy owner decides to pay the premium more frequently than annually, there will be an additional charge because the insurer will have other expenses in billing the premium. However, the policy owner can pay *annual, semi-annual, quarterly*, or *monthly premiums*.

Nonduplication and Coordination of Benefits

The *Coordination of Benefits (COB)* provision (only in group health plans) avoids over-insurance and duplication of benefit payments for individuals covered under multiple group health plans. This provision limits the total amount of paid claims from all insurance providers covering the patient to an amount that does not exceed the total allowable medical expenses.

This provision sets up which plan is the primary coverage or which is responsible for providing the total benefit amount as specified. Once the primary plan has paid its full benefit, the insured will submit the claim to the *secondary* or *excess* insurance provider for additional payable benefits, including coinsurance and deductibles. In no case will the total amount the insured receives surpass the costs incurred or the maximum benefits available under all plans.

If every policy has a COB provision, the order of payments is determined as follows:

- If a married couple has group coverage and each is a named dependent on the other's policy, the individual's group coverage is considered *primary*. The *secondary* coverage (spouse coverage) will pick up where the first policy's coverage ends.
- If both parents name their children as dependents under their group policies, the *birthday rule* will typically determine the payment order. The coverage of the parent whose birthday falls first in a calendar year will be considered primary). On occasion, the *gender rule* can also apply where the father's coverage is primary.
- If the parents are separated or divorced, the policy of the parent who has custody of the children will be the primary coverage.

Occupational vs. Nonoccupational

Health insurance, including disability insurance, is written on an occupational or nonoccupational basis. *Occupational* coverage provides benefits for injury, illness, or disability resulting from accidents or sicknesses occurring on or off the job. On the other hand, *nonoccupational* coverage only covers claims resulting from accidents or illnesses occurring off the job. Insurers write many individual health policies on an occupational or nonoccupational basis. Most group plans are only nonoccupational; they assume that workers compensation coverage will cover accidents or injuries on the job.

Total, Partial, Recurrent, and Residual Disability

Total Disability – Under some disability income policies, the definition of *total disability* differs. Some policies use a relatively strict definition like the *"any occupation"* definition, similar to Social Security. This definition of total disability requires the insured to be unable to perform any occupation for which they are reasonably suited because of experience, training, or education. Other insurance providers have adopted a more liberal definition of total disability as the inability to perform the duties of one's own occupation. As expected, the more liberal *"own occupation"* definition of disability means it is easier to qualify for disability benefits.

Partial Disability – *Partial disability* covers full-time working insureds and refers to the inability to work full-time or perform some, but not all, of one's regular job duties, resulting in a loss of income. The partial disability benefit covers a partial loss of income when the insured's disability allows them to work; however, they cannot perform their regular job. The partial disability benefit is usually 50% of the total disability benefit and is limited to a specific period, as noted in the policy.

Insurers pay the benefits under a partial disability policy in a flat or residual amount.

Recurrent Disability – *Recurrent disability* is a policy provision that specifies the period (typically within six months) during which the recurrence of an illness or injury will be considered a continuation of a previous disability period. This feature is important because the recurrence of a disabling condition will not be treated as a new period of disability, so the insured is not subject to another elimination period.

Residual Disability – *Residual disability* is a disability income policy that helps pay for income loss when a person returns to work after a total disability. The individual is still unable to work at the same level or as long as they worked before becoming disabled. Many insurers have replaced partial disability with residual disability, which provides benefits for a loss of earnings. When the individual can only work part-time or at a lesser-paying position, residual disability will make up the difference between their current earnings and those before the disability.

Managed Care

A *managed care* program is any medical expense plan that contains costs by controlling participants' behavior. An adequately managed care plan should have the following five essential characteristics:

1. Controlled access to providers;
2. Comprehensive case management;
3. Preventive care;
4. Risk sharing; and
5. High-quality care.

Workers Compensation

Workers compensation is a benefit provided and regulated by the states. It will vary to some degree from state to state.

Eligibility

To qualify for workers compensation benefits, a worker must work in an occupation covered by workers compensation and have had a work-related accident or sickness. Workers compensation benefits are payable when an employee is injured by a work-related injury, regardless of fault or negligence.

Benefits

Workers compensation laws offer four types of benefits:

1. Medical benefits;
2. Income benefits;
3. Death benefits; and
4. Rehabilitation benefits.

Subrogation

Subrogation is the legal process by which an insurer seeks recovery of the amount paid to the insured from a third party who may have caused the loss. Through subrogation, the *insured is unable to collect twice.*

Taxation of Premiums and Proceeds of Insurance

Personally-Owned Health Insurance

Taxation of benefits received from an insurance policy is often determined by whether or not the premiums were taxed. Individuals *cannot deduct premium payments* on a personally-owned disability income policy. However, disability *income benefits are received free of federal income tax* by the individual.

In *long-term care* or *medical expense* insurance policies, an insured can deduct unreimbursed medical expenses paid for themselves, their spouse, and their dependents. These deductions are acceptable, provided the expenses exceed a percentage of the insured's adjusted gross income (AGI). The law allows deductions for unreimbursed expenses over 7.5% of the adjusted gross income.

This provision will only apply if the insured itemizes these deductions on their tax return.

Employer-Provided Health Insurance

Employer-paid premiums for disability income insurance for employees are deductible as business expenses. They are not taxable income to the employee.

Benefits received by an employee are fully taxable to the employee as income if they are attributable to employer contributions.

When the employee and employer share in premium contributions, the employee's contribution is not deductible; however, benefits attributable to their portion of the contribution are not taxable as income. The taxation of income received by the employee will depend on the type of group plan:

- **Noncontributory** – The employer pays the entire premium cost, so the income benefits are included in the employee's gross income and taxed as ordinary income.
- **Fully Contributory** – The employee pays the entire cost of the premium. Consequently, the employee receives the income benefits free of federal income tax.
- **Partially Contributory** – The cost is partially paid by the employee and the employer. The portion paid by the employee is free of federal income tax. The amount paid by the employer is included in the employee's gross income and taxed as ordinary income.

For example, if an employee funds 40% of the premium and receives a benefit of $1,000, only $600 (60% employer contribution) of the benefit payment will be taxed to the employee as income. In comparison, $400 (40% employee contribution) will be received free of federal income tax.

Short-term disability (STD) group plans typically have a benefit period of fewer than two years. In this type of disability income plan, it is standard to place a maximum dollar amount on the benefit that the insurer will pay regardless of earnings. It is also standard to have an elimination period except for a disability caused by accidents.

Long-term disability (LTD) group plans generally pay benefits for two years or longer.

For *group medical and dental expense insurance*, employer-provided premiums are deductible as a business expense. However, any premiums paid by the employee are only deductible if the employee premium and other unreimbursed medical expenses exceed a certain percentage of the insured's AGI (Adjusted Gross Income).

Most individuals who itemize their deductions can claim deductions for unreimbursed medical expenses not covered by health insurance exceeding *10%* of their adjusted gross income. If the insureds are 65 or older, they can continue deducting any medical expenses exceeding 7.5% of their AGI.

Employees receive group medical and dental expense benefits free of federal income tax.

The following general rules apply to the taxation of long-term care policies:

- Premiums may be deductible;
- Daily benefits from the LTC policy are received free of federal income tax as long as they do not exceed the daily cost of long-term care; and
- Benefits paid over the cost of care received are taxed as ordinary income.

Sole proprietors and partners can deduct 100% of the cost of a medical expense plan for themselves and their families because they are considered self-employed individuals, as opposed to employees. The deduction cannot exceed the taxpayer's earned income for the year.

Key person disability income premiums are *not deductible* to the business. However, the company receives policy benefits free of federal income tax.

Business overhead expense (BOE) insurance policies are sold to small business owners to reimburse them for the overhead expenses incurred following a disability. The *premiums* paid to the BOE policy are a business expense and are *tax-deductible* to the business. The *benefits* are typically limited to covered costs incurred or the maximum monthly benefit stated in the policy and are taxable to the company.

Disability buy-sell insurance covers partners or corporate officers of a privately held business. The policy pays the organization to purchase the business interest of a disabled partner. In a disability buy-sell policy, whether a cross-purchase or entity plan, the premiums are *not deductible* to the business, but the company receives policy benefits free of federal income tax.

TAX CONSIDERATIONS FOR HEALTH INSURANCE		
	PREMIUMS	**BENEFITS**
Individual Disability Income	Not deductible	Not taxable
Group Disability Income	Deductible for employer	Taxable
Individual Medical	Not deductible	Not taxable
Group Medical	Deductible for employer	Not taxable
Individual Long-Term Care	Not deductible*	Not taxable
Group Long-Term Care	Deductible for employer	Not taxable
Individual Medicare Supplement	Not deductible*	Not taxable
Group Medicare Supplement	Deductible for employer	Not taxable

TAX CONSIDERATIONS FOR HEALTH INSURANCE *(Continued)*		
	PREMIUMS	**BENEFITS**
Buy-Sell	Not deductible	Not taxable
Key Person	Not deductible	Not taxable
Business Overhead Expense (BOE)	Deductible for employer	Taxable
MSAs	Deductible	Not taxable when used for medical expenses
		Taxable when taken out at end of year
FSAs	Not deductible	Not taxable
HRAs	Deductible	Not taxable
HSAs	Deductible	Not taxable when used for medical expenses
		Taxable plus 20% penalty under 65, no penalty over 65 for nonmedical use

* Unless combined premiums and unreimbursed medical expenses exceed 10% of adjusted gross income (or 7.5% for individuals age 65 or older) and are subject to the tax-qualified limitations.

Chapter Review

This chapter described several additional concepts that apply to health insurance. Let's review them:

MISCELLANEOUS FEATURES AND PROVISIONS	
Owner's Rights	<ul><li>Designate and change a beneficiary</li><li>Make other changes without consent from the beneficiary</li></ul>
Dependent Children Benefits	<ul><li>*Eligible dependents* – coverage cannot be terminated if a child is incapable of self-support because of a physical or mental disability</li></ul>
Primary and Contingent Beneficiaries	<ul><li>*Primary beneficiary* – the first person designated</li><li>*Contingent or secondary beneficiary* – receives benefits if the primary beneficiary dies before benefits are payable</li><li>*No beneficiary* – benefits go to the deceased's estate</li></ul>
Premium Payment	<ul><li>*Mode* – more frequent premium payments will result in a higher premium</li></ul>
Coordination of Benefits (COB) provision	<ul><li>*Purpose* – avoid over-insurance and duplication of benefit payments when a person is covered under multiple group health plans</li><li>Establishes the primary plan (responsible for providing benefit amounts) and the secondary, or excess, provider (responsible for any additional benefits)</li></ul>
Occupational vs. Nonoccupational	<ul><li>*Occupational coverage* – benefits for injury, illness, or disability resulting from accidents or sicknesses that happen on or off the job</li><li>*Nonoccupational coverage* – only pays claims that result from accidents or sicknesses occurring off the job</li></ul>

MISCELLANEOUS FEATURES AND PROVISIONS *(Continued)*	
Total, Partial and Residual Disability	• *Total disability* – the definition is different under different policies • *Partial disability* – unable to perform one or more regular duties of one's own occupation • *Residual disability* – provides benefits for loss of income when the employee returns to work after a total disability but cannot yet work at a pre-disability level
Managed Care	• Attempts to manage costs by controlling participant behavior
Subrogation	• The process by which an insurance company attempts to recover the amount paid to the insured from a third party who may have caused the loss
WORKERS COMPENSATION	
Eligibility	• Employed in an occupation covered by workers compensation • Suffer a work-related sickness or injury (regardless of negligence or fault)
Benefits	• Medical benefits • Income benefits • Death benefits • Rehabilitation benefits
TAXATION OF PREMIUMS AND PROCEEDS	
Personal Health Insurance	• Premium payments are not deductible • Benefits are received tax-free
Employer-provided Health Insurance	• Premium payments made by the employer are deductible as a business expense • Benefits received by the employee are taxable to the employee as income • Types of employer health plans: - *Noncontributory* – the employer pays the entire cost; benefits are a part of the employee's gross income and are taxed as income - *Fully contributory* – employee pays the cost; benefits are received tax-free - *Partially contributory* – the cost is shared by the employer and the employee; the portion paid by the employee is received tax-free, and the portion paid by the employer is part of the employee's gross income and is taxed as ordinary income

CHAPTER 10:
Texas Statutes and Rules Common to Life and Health Insurance

The concepts you have learned apply to the life and health insurance industry. Now that you have studied these insurance policies and their provisions, you can focus on regulations and definitions that apply only to Texas. You will examine various topics, from the duties of the Insurance Department to licensing laws. This chapter contains definitions and numbers for dollar amounts and time limits. Be sure that you know them for your exam.

Unless otherwise noted, all references are to the Texas Insurance Code (Ins.) or the Texas Administrative Code (TAC), Title 28.

- **Insurance Definitions**
  Ref.: Ins. 101.051; 547.001; 801.051-.053, .057, 885.001-706; TAC § 3.9704
- **Commissioner of Insurance**
  Ref.: Ins. 31.001-.002, 31.021-.022, 38.001, 82.001-.056, 86.001-.002, 401.051-.056, 404.003, 051-.053, 521.003- .004, 541.107-108, 546.151, 4001.005, 4005.102, 83.051-.054; TAC § 1.88
- **Licensing Requirements**
  Ref.: Ins. 4001.003, .006; 4001.104-.106, 4001.151-.156, 4001.201 - .206, 4001.252, 4001.254-255, 4002.003, 4003.001, 4003.004, 4003.006-.007, 4004.051-.054, 4005.101-.102, 4005.105, 4052.001, 4054.301-.303, 1115.056; TAC § 1.502, 19.1001-.1030
- **Marketing Practices/Claims Methods and Practices**
  Ref.: Ins. 541.051-.61, .101-.111; 542.001-.014, .054- .058; 544.002; 701.001-.005, .051-.052, .101-.109, .151- .154; 1104.024; 4005.053, 4005.101; TAC § 21.4, 21.115, 21.201-.205
- **Texas Life and Health Guaranty Association**
  Ref.: Ins. 443.004, 463.205

Insurance Definitions

Transacting Insurance

Transacting insurance in Texas includes any of the following by mail or any other means:

- Solicitation;
- Negotiations;
- Sale (the production of a contract of insurance); and
- Advising a person regarding coverage or claims.

The following acts, when performed by agents or insurers, constitute the *business of insurance* in this state:

- Creating or proposing to create an insurance contract;
- Receiving or taking an insurance application;
- Collecting or receiving any consideration for insurance, including a commission, a premium, an assessment, a membership fee, or dues;
- Delivering or issuing an insurance policy;
- Directly or indirectly acting as a producer or agent for an insurance provider; or
- Conducting any business recognized as transacting insurance within the Insurance Code's statutes.

Types of Insurers

An *insurer* (or principal) is the organization or company that issues an insurance policy.

Insurance departments classify insurers in various ways based on authority to transact business, ownership, marketing and distribution systems, location of incorporation (domicile), or rating (financial strength).

As you read about different classifications of insurers, remember that these categories are not mutually exclusive. Such categories include who owns it, where it conducts insurance business, and what type of agents it appoints.

Domestic, Foreign, and Alien Companies

Insurance departments classify insurers according to where they are incorporated. An insurance company must obtain a certificate of authority before transacting insurance within the state, regardless of the location of incorporation (domicile).

Domestic – A *domestic* insurer is an insurance company incorporated in this state. In most cases, the company's home office is in the state it formed (domicile). For instance, a company chartered in Colorado would be considered a Colorado domestic company.

Foreign – *Foreign* insurers are insurance companies incorporated in another state, the District of Columbia, or a territorial possession. Presently, the United States has five major U.S. territories, including Puerto Rico, the Northern Mariana Islands, Guam, American Samoa, and the U.S. Virgin Islands.

For example, a company chartered in New York would be a foreign company within California, and a company chartered in Puerto Rico would be foreign in any state.

Alien – An *alien* insurer is an insurance company incorporated outside the United States.

Stock and Mutual Companies

Stock Company – Stockholders own *stock companies*. These individuals supply the capital necessary to establish and operate the insurance company. They also share any profits or losses. Officers manage stock insurance companies, and the stockholders elect them. Stock companies generally issue *nonparticipating policies*, in which policy owners do not share losses or profits.

Policy owners of nonparticipating policies do not receive dividends; however, stockholders receive taxable dividends.

Mutual Company – Policy owners retain ownership of *mutual companies* that issue participating policies. Policy owners are entitled to dividends, a return of excess premiums that are not taxable. Dividends accrue when the combined earnings and premiums create a surplus that exceeds the actual costs of providing coverage; they are not guaranteed.

Fraternals – A *fraternal benefit society* is a group formed to provide insurance benefits for members of a religious organization, affiliated lodge, or fraternal organization with a representative government. Fraternals only sell to their members and are considered charitable institutions, not insurers. They are not subject to all the regulations that apply to insurance providers offering coverage to the public.

Certificate of Authority

Before insurance providers can transact business in a specific state, they must apply for and receive a license or *Certificate of Authority* from the Texas Department of Insurance (TDI). They must also meet the state's financial (capital and surplus) requirements. Insurance providers who meet these financial requirements and receive approval to conduct business in the state are *authorized* or *admitted* as legal insurance companies. Insurance providers not approved to conduct business in Texas are considered *unauthorized* or *non-admitted*. Most states do not allow unauthorized insurance companies to do business in the state, except through licensed excess and surplus lines brokers.

An insurer must hold a certificate of authority issued by the Commissioner to conduct insurance business in Texas. The certificate remains in effect until canceled, revoked, or suspended. When an insurance provider fails to file an annual statement as required by law, the Department may revoke or suspend the provider's certificate of authority.

Commissioner of Insurance

General Powers and Duties

The Commissioner is the chief executive and administrative officer of the Texas Department of Insurance (TDI). This individual must be:

- A citizen of the state of Texas;
- Knowledgeable and accomplished in the field of insurance and insurance regulation; and
- Have at least *five* years of experience in government or business administration or as a certified public accountant or practicing attorney.

The Governor appoints the Commissioner for a 2-year term ending on February 1 of every *odd-numbered year*.

The Commissioner of Insurance has the following powers and duties:

- Manage the internal affairs of the Department of Insurance;
- Prescribe forms and procedures to be followed during proceedings held before the Department;
- Assist in the interpretation of any state insurance law;
- Issue insurance licenses and certificates of authority; and
- Enforce fines, penalties, denials, revocations, or suspensions of licensees and certificates of authority.

Examination of Records

The Commissioner regulates insurance companies authorized to transact business in this state. Examining insurance providers' records and books ensures that the companies remain solvent and that they conduct business in compliance with state laws and regulations regarding licensing, rates, policy forms, claims, and market conduct.

The Commissioner must examine every authorized insurer at least once every *five years*. This examination requirement applies to each domestic insurer organized under Texas laws and admitted foreign and alien insurers.

The examination costs are the responsibility of the insurance carrier under examination.

Complaints – The Commissioner and the Department of Insurance must establish a program to resolve policyholder complaints. If the Department receives a written complaint, it will notify each party of the complaint's status at least once per quarter. The Department must also keep an information file about every complaint filed with the Department.

Investigations, Hearings, and Penalties

Because the Commissioner's role is to protect the public from unfair trade practices and to enforce insurance laws, if the Commissioner suspects that its agent or an insurer has committed a violation or is engaged in unfair trade practices, the Commissioner can issue a statement of charges and hold a hearing for any reason deemed necessary within the scope of the Insurance Code.

When the Commissioner believes a licensed agent is engaging in any form of unfair trade practice or method of competition or that a person is selling insurance without a license, the Commissioner can serve an *emergency cease and desist order* by registered or certified mail. The order must state the charges and require the person to stop committing the acts, practices, or methods in violation. The order must also explain the rights of the person charged with the order.

Unless the individual in violation requests a hearing, the emergency cease and desist order is final *61 days* from the date it is received.

The charged individual can request a hearing to contest or review the charges. They must make the written request *within 60 days* of receiving the emergency cease and desist order. The Commissioner must hold the hearing within *30 days* of receiving the request.

After a hearing, the Department will determine whether the method of competition or the act or practice considered in the hearing is an unfair method of competition or a false, misleading, or deceptive act or practice. The Department will also determine if the charged individual engaged in the method of competition, action, or practice violating the Insurance Code or the Business and Commerce Code.

When determining that a person committed such a violation, the Department will make written findings and issue a *cease and desist order* to the individual. If the agent disagrees with the order, they must appeal to the court system. It is essential to note that this cease and desist order differs from the emergency cease and desist order as it comes after a hearing determines the person is guilty of the violation.

When an individual does not comply with an issued subpoena concerning a hearing, a district court in the county where the individual resides can order the individual to comply with the subpoena or testify. If a person refuses to comply with a subpoena, the court can punish the person's failure to obey as *contempt*.

Any person *in violation of a cease and desist order* of the Commissioner will be subject to an administrative penalty:

- $1,000 for each violation; or
- $5,000 for all violations.

When a court finds an individual violated a cease and desist order, that individual must pay a civil penalty of $50 or $500 for willful violations. The state can recover the penalty in a civil action.

Along with revoking or suspending a license, the Commissioner can levy any or all of the following penalties:

- Order the payment of an administrative penalty; and
- Order the licensee to make complete restitution.

The Commissioner may order the licensee to make full restitution to each Texas insured, resident, and entity operating in this state harmed by a violation of or failure to comply with the Insurance Code or a rule of the Commissioner. The licensee must make the restitution in the form and amount and within the period determined by the Commissioner.

The Commissioner can assess an administrative penalty on a licensee who violates any of the following:

- The Insurance Code;
- Another insurance law of Texas; or
- An order or rule adopted under the Insurance Code or another Texas insurance law.

A violation penalty *cannot exceed $25,000* unless the Insurance Code or another insurance law specifies a lesser or more significant penalty. The Commissioner will notify other state Commissioners or similar officers of any penalties. The following factors determine the amount of the penalty:

- The severity of the violation, including the circumstances, nature, extent, and gravity of the violation, and the hazard or potential hazard created to the safety, health, or economic welfare of the public;
- The economic harm to the public confidence or public interest caused by the violation;
- The history of previous violations;
- The necessary amount to prevent a future violation;
- Efforts to correct the violation;
- Whether the violation was intentional; and
- Any other matter that justice requires.

After identifying a violation, the Department can issue a report to the Commissioner providing the facts that led to the determination. The Department may also recommend levying an administrative penalty, including a recommended penalty amount. The Department must give written notice of the report to the affected individual within 14 days after the date of the report. This notice must contain a summary of the alleged violation and a statement of the recommended penalty amount. The notice must inform the individual of their *right to a hearing* on the penalty amount, the violation's occurrence, or both. The individual has 20 days after receiving the notice to accept the determination and recommended penalty or request a hearing.

After a hearing, the Commissioner will, by order, find that a violation occurred and assess an administrative penalty or determine that a violation did not happen. Notice of the Commissioner's order must include a statement of the person's right to judicial review of the order. The individual must pay the penalty or file a petition for judicial review no later than 30 days after the date the Commissioner's order becomes final.

Other available remedies for violating the Insurance Code, another insurance law of Texas, or a rule of the Commissioner may include:

- Denying an application for a license;
- Suspending, revoking, or denying renewal of a license;
- Placing on probation an individual with a suspended license;
- Assessing an administrative penalty; or
- Reprimanding a license holder.

Licensing Requirements

Types of Licenses

The Texas Department of Insurance may issue an insurance license to the following qualified individuals or entities.

Agent – Insurance providers consider an *agent* to be anyone who solicits insurance, takes or transmits an insurance application or policy, examines risk or loss, or collects, receives, or transmits premiums. Insurers typically compensate agents through commissions, where a percentage of the premium is paid to the agent by the insurer.

Applicants for an original insurance agent license in Texas must submit a written application and nonrefundable filing fee to the Commissioner. The application must include the applicant's full name, age, occupation, place of residence, business for the past five years, and a statement as to whether the applicant has ever held a license before had one revoked or been refused a license. The Department can deny an application if the applicant does not provide a set of fingerprints.

The Department can issue an insurance license to applicants who meet all of the following requirements:

- Is at least 18 years old;
- Has passed the required licensing exam within the last 12 months;
- Has submitted the application, fees, and any other required information requested by the Department; and
- Has not committed any acts which may cause a license to be denied.

The following applicants do not have to take an examination:

- The application is for the renewal of an unexpired license issued by the Department;
- The applicant's license expired less than one year before the date of application, and if the previous license was not denied, suspended, or revoked;
- The applicant is a corporation, partnership, or depository institution;
- An applicant applying for a life, accident, and health license is specified as a chartered life underwriter (CLU);

- An applicant applying for a life and health counselor license is specified as a chartered life underwriter (CLU), certified financial planner (CFP), or chartered financial consultant (ChFC);
- An applicant applying for a property and casualty license is specified as a chartered property casualty underwriter (CPCU);
- A nonresident individual who is exempt from the exam under regulations for nonresident producers; or
- An applicant for a life agent license or a general life, accident, and health license who was authorized to solicit insurance on behalf of a fraternal benefit society.

The applicant must hold a license to which these exemptions are applied individually and are not transferable.

Nonresident Agents – A *nonresident agent* does not reside in Texas. In other words, they claim a different home state. When the agent's home state gives Texas residents the same privilege (reciprocity), a nonresident can obtain an insurance agent license. The applicant must meet specific Texas licensing requirements and hold a license in good standing in their resident state.

The Commissioner can enter into reciprocal agreements with officials of other states to *waive the written examination* requirements for applicants who reside in those states as long as they meet the following conditions:

- The other state orders licensing applicants to pass a written exam;
- A suitable official of the other state certifies that the applicant's insurance license is valid in that state and either held a license before examinations were required or passed a written exam; and
- The agent licensing applicant has no physical place of business in Texas as an insurance agent.

When the state line runs through a town, agents who live in the adjoining state may be licensed as resident agents in Texas if they maintain their business office in Texas.

If the licensee's home state suspends, cancels, or revokes the licensee's resident license, a nonresident license will be automatically suspended, canceled, or revoked.

The Department may also grant a nonresident license to individuals not licensed in other states or commonwealths as long as the applicant has:

- Passed the exam for an agent's license;
- Satisfied eligibility requirements after an exam of the applicant's criminal history records; and
- Met all requirements for an individual license as required under law.

Counselor – A life and health insurance *counselor* offers to examine a life, accident, or health insurance policy, pure endowment policy, or annuity for a fee or commission. They recommend or provide information regarding the policy's benefits, coverage, terms, conditions, or premiums.

Temporary – The Commissioner may issue a *temporary agent's license* to an applicant being considered for appointment as a producer by another agent, insurance company, or health maintenance organization (HMO) without a written exam. An agent, insurer, or HMO considering the appointment of a temporary license applicant must provide the applicant with at least 40 hours of training to the applicant within 30 days of applying for the license.

Temporary licenses are valid for *180 days* after the date of issuance. They can only be issued to those who intend to apply for a producer license to sell insurance products to the general public.

Corporations or Partnerships

An agent license can be issued to a corporation or partnership if admitted to transact insurance business in Texas, applied to the Department, and paid all the required fees. Also, the entity must meet the following requirements:

- At least one active partner of the partnership or one officer of the corporation is licensed separately from the corporation or partnership;
- A director, officer, manager, member, partner, or another person who can control the corporation or partnership has not had a license revoked or suspended or been the subject of any other disciplinary action by an insurance or financial regulator of any state in the United States, or committed an act for which the Department can deny a license;
- Corporations or partnerships can pay any amount up to $25,000 on a claim or compensation for an error, omission, or negligent act; and
- Every location where the corporation or partnership will engage in business in Texas is registered separately with the Department.

Exemptions/Exceptions

An insurance license is not required if an insurer's employee, director, or officer is not involved with selling insurance contracts and does not receive commissions.

In addition, the following individuals do not have to hold an insurance producer license:

- An employee or director of an insurer whose activities are limited to administrative, executive, managerial, or clerical;
- The employee or director of a special agent who assists insurance producers by providing technical assistance and advice to licensed insurance producers;
- A person who furnishes and secures information for group insurance or performs administrative services related to property and casualty insurance that is mass-marketed;
- An association or employer involved in operating or administering employee benefits for the employees of an association or employer;
- Employees of organizations or insurers engaged in the rating, inspection, or classification of risks or in the supervision of training insurance producers who are not individually involved in the sale of insurance;
- A person who solely performs advertising actives without an intention to solicit insurance business;
- A nonresident agent who solicits, sells, or negotiates an insurance contract to an insured for commercial property and casualty risks located in more than one state; or
- A full-time salaried employee who advises an employer about their insurance interests or those of its subsidiaries.

License Expiration and Renewal

The Commissioner will issue an initial license after the applicant passes a written exam. If the Commissioner denies the license, they must notify the applicant and insurer in writing that the license will not be issued.

An agent's license must be renewed every two years on the licensee's birthday, whether odd-numbered or even-numbered years, depending on when the license was issued. It will continue until the Commissioner revokes, refuses, or suspends the license.

The Commissioner will send an agent whose license is about to expire a notice of expiration at least *30 days* before that date.

If an agent allows their license to expire, the following reinstatement rules apply:

- If expired for *no more than 90 days* – The license can be renewed by filing a renewal application, paying the renewal fee, and paying an additional fee equal to one-half of the renewal fee.
- If expired for *more than 90 days but less than one year* – The licensee can obtain a new license by filing a new application, paying the licensing fee, and paying an additional fee equal to one-half of the license fee. A license exam is not required.
- If expired for *over one year* – The individual may not renew the license. They must go through a complete licensing process required by the State for any new applicants. Also, the agent cannot use continuing education credits obtained before the department grants the new license to satisfy any certification course or CE requirements.

Continuing Education

Continuing education (CE) rules aim to maintain high standards of professionalism and competence within the insurance industry and protect the public by improving and preserving licensed producers' insurance knowledge and skills.

Unless otherwise exempt, licensees must complete *24 hours* of continuing education each renewal period before the license expiration date. At least *3 hours* of CE must cover *ethics*. When a licensee holds more than one license, they must complete 24 hours of continuing education for all licenses during the license period.

Licensees must complete continuing education hours *during the reporting period*. They cannot carry over any excess hours to the next reporting period or receive credit from duplicate courses during the same licensing period.

A licensee who cannot complete the 24 hours of CE before the license expiration date will have 90 days to complete the deficient number of hours and pay a fine per deficient hour. When these conditions are not satisfied within 90 days of the license expiring, the license will become inactive, and the licensee must apply for a new license.

The continuing education requirements *do not apply in the following cases*:

- Agents who have held a license for 20 years or more as of December 31st, 2002, are exempt from continuing education requirements. Agents whose renewal date is after 12/31/2002 could still be exempt from CE requirements if they have held a license for over 20 years without gaps in licensure longer than 90 days;
- Agents who are only licensed to receive renewal or residual commissions;
- Nonresident agents who are subject to CE requirements in their home state if their home state applies reciprocity with the CE requirements of Texas;
- Agents who qualify for an exemption due to medical disability, illness, or circumstances beyond their control; and
- Retired agents.

Licensees must complete at least half (50%) of all required CE hours in a *classroom* or *a setting equivalent to a classroom* approved by the Department of Insurance. The Department can accept continuing education hours completed in other professions.

New applicants who were previously licensed must provide the Department with evidence of completing the previous license's CE requirements or proof of payment of fines for failing to meet the CE requirements.

Producers must maintain records of completion of continuing education courses for four years from the course completion date. Those records must be readily available to the Department of Insurance for audit or investigation.

To be certified as a continuing education course, the course must enhance the producer's knowledge, understanding, and professional competence regarding identified topics for an insurance product. There are also specific requirements for *product certification courses*, such as long-term care or Medicare product certification.

Producers who transact Medicare and Medicare supplement insurance business must complete an *8-hour* Medicare-related product certification course as part of their CE requirement. In each reporting period after the reporting period where the licensee completed the certification course, license holders must complete at least *4 hours* of certified continuing education for Medicare-related products.

Approved Medicare-related product certification courses are required to cover, at a minimum, the following topics related to Medicare products:

- Types, features, and availability of Medicare products;
- State and federal laws;
- Prohibited sales practices;
- Sales suitability rules; and
- Fraudulent and unfair trade practices.

Resident agents who intend to solicit, sell, or negotiate *annuity* contracts must complete a *4-hour* training course on annuities before initiating any transactions. Producers who continue to sell annuities must complete 4 hours of annuity-related continuing education every year. Agents can use these hours to satisfy a producer's general continuing education requirements.

Notifying the Department of Certain Information

A person licensed as an agent must notify the Texas Department of Insurance (TDI) every month of any of the following:

- A change in their mailing address;
- A felony conviction; or
- An administrative action was taken against the licensed agent by an insurance or financial regulator of Texas, another state, or the United States.

A corporation or partnership licensed as an agent has to file biographical information with the Department:

- For each director, executive officer, or unlicensed partner who manages the entity's operations;
- For each partner with the right or ability to control the partnership or shareholder who owns the corporation; and
- If another entity owns the corporation or partnership, it must file biographical information for each person who controls the parent entity.

A corporation or partnership is required to notify the Department no later than *30 days* after the date of:

- A felony conviction of a license holder; and
- The addition or removal of a partner, director, officer, member, or manager.

Records Maintenance

An agent must maintain all insurance records (including all records relating to customer complaints) separate from the records of any other agent's business.

License Termination, Denial, Suspension, and Revocation

Denial of License – The Commissioner can discipline a license holder or deny an application to an individual who has done any of the following:

- Intentionally violated any provision of the Texas Insurance Code;
- Willfully made a material misstatement in the licensing application;
- Obtained, or endeavored to obtain, the license by misrepresentation or fraud;
- Misappropriated or converted to personal use any money belonging to an insurance provider, insured, or beneficiary;
- Been guilty of dishonest or fraudulent practices;
- Materially misrepresented the terms and conditions of a life insurance policy or contract;
- Made or issued any statement misrepresenting or making incomplete comparisons regarding the terms of an insurance or annuity contract in an attempt to induce the owner to surrender or forfeit the contract and replace it with another (also called twisting); or
- Been convicted of a felony.

Surrender of License – The *surrender of an agent's license* to the Department of Insurance will not avoid any offense committed before the effective date of the surrender, and it will not prevent the agent from being penalized.

Suspension, Revocation, or Refusal to Renew – The Commissioner will suspend or revoke an existing license or deny a new license for any of the following reasons:

- Intentional violations of state insurance laws;
- Willful material misstatements in the license application;
- Attempting to obtain a license by misrepresentation or fraud;
- Felony conviction; or
- Rebates of insurance premiums.

Anyone with a revoked insurance license must wait to apply for another license in Texas for *five years*.

When an individual agent or a corporate official of an insurer is convicted of a felony involving moral turpitude or a breach of fiduciary duty, the individual's license or the company's application for a certificate of authority can be denied or revoked. If the insurer terminates the official, the company cannot have its certificate of authority revoked. They can petition for issuance or reinstatement of a certificate of authority any time after the convicted corporate official is no longer with the company.

The petition for reinstatement or issuance should be filed with the associate commissioner and must include the following information:

- The date of final conviction and the date the probation or sentence ends; and
- The petitioner's reasons why they believe the license should be issued or reinstated.

The office of the associate commissioner can order an investigation into the matter. It can grant the petition if the petitioner demonstrates that it would be in the public's best interest and that justice would be served if the license was issued or reinstated.

Agent Appointment

A licensee can only act as an agent if a designated insurance company authorized to conduct business in Texas appoints them. When an insurance company terminates an agent's appointment, it must immediately file a statement of the facts related to the termination and the date and cause with the Commissioner.

When a licensed local recording agent with no appointment from an insurer refers an insurance application to a local recording agent who has an appointment with that insurance company, the appointed agent can share the commission with the agent who does not have an appointment if the referral results in the issuance of an insurance policy.

Controlled Business

Insurance licenses are issued with the intention that the license holder will engage in the insurance business with members of the general public. The licensee will not primarily earn commissions on personal business from the licensee's close associates or immediate family, also referred to as *controlled business*.

In Texas, at least 25% of a licensee's total premiums in a calendar year must be from businesses other than controlled business. This business includes individuals other than the applicant and from property besides that which the applicant controls the placing of insurance through employment, family relationship, sale, mortgage, or ownership.

Marketing Practices

Unfair and Prohibited Trade Practices

Insurance companies and producers cannot engage in any trade practice defined as, or determined to be, a deceptive or unfair act or practice or an unfair method of competition in the insurance business.

It is an unfair trade practice to deliberately engage in an unfair method of competition. Participating in such actions with enough frequency that the commission of unfair marketing practices indicates a general business practice is also considered an unfair trade practice.

When the Department of Insurance determines, after a hearing, that a producer or an insurance company has committed an unfair trade or competition practice, the Department can issue a cease and desist order requiring the individual to stop engaging in the method of competition, act, or practice and impose penalties for violating insurance laws.

Misrepresentation – It is illegal to publish, issue, or circulate any information, illustration, or sales material that is intentionally misleading, false, or deceptive regarding the policy benefits or terms, the payment of dividends, etc. This illegal activity also refers to oral statements and is known as *misrepresentation*.

False Advertising – Advertising covers a wide range of communication, from publishing an ad in a magazine or newspaper to broadcasting a commercial on television or the Internet. Advertisements cannot include deceptive, untrue, or misleading statements that apply to the insurance business or anyone conducting it. Violating this rule is called *false advertising*.

Advertising or circulating any materials that are deceptive, untrue, or misleading is prohibited. Deceptive or false advertising specifically includes *misrepresenting* any of the following:

- Benefits, terms, conditions, or advantages of any insurance policy;
- Financial condition of any individual or the insurance carrier;
- Dividends from the policy or any dividends previously paid out; or
- The true intention of an assignment or loan against a policy.

Portraying an insurance policy as a share of stock or utilizing names or titles that could misrepresent its true nature will be considered false advertising. Also, a person or entity cannot use a name that deceptively suggests it is an insurance provider.

Defamation of Insurer – *Defamation* occurs when an oral or written statement intends to injure a person engaged in the insurance business. This activity also applies to statements that are maliciously critical of the financial condition of any individual or company.

Rebating – *Rebating* is an inducement (kickback) offered to the insured during the sale of insurance products not specified in the policy. Both the offer and the acceptance of a rebate are illegal. Rebates can include, but are not limited to, the following:

- Rebates of premiums on the policy;
- Special services or favors;
- Offer to pay for referrals;
- Advantages in dividends or other benefits; and
- Stocks, bonds, securities, and their profits or dividends.

State regulations do not prohibit producers from giving or providing promotional materials, articles of merchandise, educational items, or traditional courtesy commonly extended to consumers valued at *$25 or less.*

Boycott, Coercion, and Intimidation – Engaging in any activity of *boycott, coercion, or intimidation* intended to create a monopoly or restrict fair trade is illegal. This activity would include unfair behavior that influences clients, competing brokers, and agents.

Coercion is requiring the applicant to purchase insurance from a specific insurer as a condition of a loan.

Commingling – Because producers and agents handle the funds of the insured and the insurance provider, they have fiduciary responsibility. A *fiduciary* is a person in a position of trust. Insurance agents and producers cannot commingle premiums collected from applicants with their personal funds.

A trustee named as the policy beneficiary can combine the life insurance policy proceeds with any other assets coming into the trust.

Unfair Discrimination – It is illegal to discriminate regarding premiums, rates, or policy benefits for individuals within the same class or with the same life expectancy. Insurers cannot discriminate based on race, national origin, marital status, sexual orientation, gender identity, creed, or ancestry. An exception to this rule would be if the distinction is required by law or made for a business purpose.

While not a complete list of acts that might be considered *unfair discrimination*, the following practices in life and health insurance constitute unfair discrimination between individuals of the same class:

- Discriminating solely based on a mental or physical impairment;
- Discrimination because of blindness or partial blindness; or
- Investigating a proposed insured's sexual orientation as part of the underwriting process.

Fraud – *Fraud* is the intentional concealment or misrepresentation of a material fact used to induce another party to make or refrain from making a contract or cheat or deceive a party. It is considered grounds for voiding an insurance contract.

The Texas Department of Insurance has an *Insurance Fraud Unit* to enforce laws relating to fraudulent insurance acts. A fraudulent insurance act is any illegal act that has been:

- Committed in support of or as a part of an insurance transaction;
- Committed while engaging the business of insurance; and
- A part of an attempt to defraud an insurance company.

Through the Insurance Fraud Unit, the Commissioner is responsible for developing fraud prevention educational programs and disseminating materials necessary to educate the public effectively about antifraud programs. The Insurance Fraud Unit must report annually to the Commissioner in writing regarding the number of cases completed by the unit and recommendations for statutory and regulatory responses regarding fraudulent activities encountered by the unit.

When the Commissioner believes that an individual has engaged in, is engaging in, or is about to engage in an act that could constitute a fraudulent insurance act or insurance fraud, the Commissioner can conduct any necessary investigation to determine whether the act occurred or to aid the enforcement of the insurance fraud laws. Should the Commissioner believe a fraudulent insurance act has occurred, the Commissioner will take the appropriate disciplinary measures and report the information to the proper law enforcement authorities.

When a person believes that a fraudulent insurance act has been or is about to be committed in Texas, the individual must report the details in writing to the Insurance Fraud Unit within *30 days*. A report submitted to the Insurance Fraud Unit of the insurance department constitutes notice to every other authorized governmental agency.

An individual cannot be liable in a civil action, including an action for slander or libel. A civil action cannot be brought against the individual for furnishing information relating to an anticipated, suspected, or completed fraudulent insurance act if they provided the information to any of the following:

- An authorized governmental agency or the Department of Insurance;
- A law enforcement officer or an employee or agent of the officer;
- The National Association of Insurance Commissioners;
- A state or federal government agency established to detect and prevent fraudulent insurance acts; or
- A special investigative unit of an insurance carrier.

Commission Sharing

Both agents and insurers must understand the rules regarding commission payments. A licensed agent or insurer conducting business in Texas cannot pay commissions to a person or corporation unless they hold a valid agent's license for the same line of insurance. Temporary license holders cannot receive commissions from a sale made to a colleague, business associate, or family member.

A person or corporation that is not a licensed insurance agent cannot accept commissions or other valuable considerations.

An agent may charge a client a reasonable fee for services rendered, such as the following:

- Special delivery or postal charges;
- Electronic mail costs;

- Telephone transmission costs; or
- Similar costs incurred by the producer on behalf of a client.

If the agent charges fees for these services, they must inform the client and obtain their written consent for each fee charged. An unlicensed individual can refer a customer or potential customer to an agent. This activity does not constitute acting as an agent. It is legal if the unlicensed person does not review specific insurance policy terms or conditions with the customer.

It is *illegal* for an agent or insurance provider to pay an unlicensed person to perform the duties of an agent. This compensation can include a commission, a rebate of payable premiums, employment, a contract for service, or any other inducement not specified in the insurance policy. Deferred compensation or commissions if the unlicensed individual once held an agent's license do not apply.

When a licensed local recording agent with no appointment from an insurer refers an insurance application to a local recording agent who has an appointment with that insurance company, the appointed agent can share the commission with the agent who lacks an appointment if the referral results in the issuance of an insurance policy.

Claims Methods and Practices

The following acts, practices, or omissions are unfair and deceptive claim settlement practices when intentionally committed or performed with such frequency as to demonstrate a general business practice and are prohibited:

- Misrepresenting to insureds relevant facts or policy provisions relating to coverage.
- Failure to acknowledge and act promptly upon communications concerning an insurance claim.
- Failure to adopt and implement practical standards for promptly investigating and processing claims.
- Failure to affirm or deny coverage of claims within a reasonable period after an insured submits proof of loss.
- Not attempting in good faith to produce fair, prompt, and equitable claim settlements on which liability is reasonably clear.
- Delaying or refusing a settlement solely because other insurance is available to partially or entirely satisfy the claim. The claimant has the right to recover from more than one insurance provider and to choose the coverage from which to recover and the order of payment.
- Compelling insureds to initiate lawsuits to recover amounts due under an insurance policy by offering considerably less than the amount recovered in those lawsuits.

TDI might require an insurance provider to file periodic reports based on complaints of unfair settlement practices. The reports have to include the following information:

- The total number of claims during the past three years and information regarding how or if the insurer resolved them; and
- The total number of complaints, the nature of each complaint, their classification by line of insurance, the disposition of these complaints, and the time it took to process each complaint.

Failing to maintain records of complaints is an unfair claim settlement practice.

Prompt Payment of Claims – Insurers must settle and pay claims promptly within *60 days*. No later than the 15th business day following receipt of a notice of a claim, the insurance provider must do the following:

- Acknowledge receipt of the claim;
- Launch an investigation; and
- Request all forms, statements, and items the insurance provider believes it will require from the claimant.

Surplus lines insurers have until the 30th day following receipt of a notice of a claim to perform the previously listed requirements.

The insurer must notify the claimant in writing of its acceptance or rejection of the claim no later than the 15th business day after the insurance company receives all requested forms, statements, and items. When the insurance provider suspects that arson is involved, the insurer has until the 30th day to notify the claimant of its acceptance or rejection.

If the insurance provider rejects a claim, the notice to the claimant must contain the reasons for the rejection. Let's presume the insurer requires more time to make a claim decision. In that situation, it must give the claimant the reasons for the delay and accept or reject a claim no later than the 45th day after the insurer notifies the claimant of a delay.

Once a claim is approved, the insurance provider must pay it within *five business days* after the insurer notifies the claimant that it will pay a claim. Under these circumstances, surplus lines insurers have until the 20th business day to settle the claim. Insurance providers who delay payments can be subject to additional damage payments.

For a good cause shown, insurance carriers may have additional time to settle related claims.

When an insurer delays payment of a claim later than 60 days from receiving the required forms and statements from the insured, the insurance provider must pay the claim with an additional interest of 18% per year, including any potential attorney's fees due to the delay. This situation does not apply to cases arising from litigation or arbitration.

Texas Life and Health Insurance Guaranty Association

The *Texas Life and Health Insurance Guaranty Association* protects insureds, policyholders, beneficiaries, and anyone entitled to payment under an insurance policy from insurers' insolvency and incompetence. The Association is a nonprofit entity subject to the applicable provisions and laws of the state Insurance Code and the immediate supervision of the Commissioner. The Association receives funding from its members through assessment, and all authorized insurers must be members. The Association pays covered claims up to certain limits established by state law.

It is an unfair trade practice to advertise protection afforded by the Life and Health Insurance Guaranty Association when selling any insurance product the Association covers.

Numbers, Dollars, Days, and Dates

To perform your best on the state regulations portion of the licensing exam, memorize the numbers and their definitions on the following page.

DEPARTMENT OF INSURANCE REGULATIONS

2 years	Commissioner's term of office
5 years	Administration, attorney, or CPA experience required before applying to become the Commissioner
60 days	For agent to request a hearing after receiving a cease and desist order
30 days	After receiving the request for Commissioner to hold the hearing
5 years	Commissioner must conduct annual examinations of authorized insurers

LICENSING AND APPOINTMENT REQUIREMENTS

18	Minimum required age for licensing
12 months	Results of the licensing examination are valid
90 days	Maximum duration of temporary licenses
6 months	No more than one temporary license issued per person
2 years	Duration of reporting period
5 years	After license revocation or denial before another license application can be filed
5 years	After felony conviction for breach of fiduciary duty before another license application can be filed
2 years	Duration of an agent's license

MISCELLANEOUS PRODUCER REGULATIONS

90 days	After license renewal date for agents to pay fees and complete CE before license expires
24 hours	CE to be completed during each reporting period
3 hours	Minimum requirement for ethics training

IMPORTANT DOLLAR AMOUNTS

$50	Maximum agent licensing fee
$25,000	Maximum fine for violating the Insurance Code
$2,500	Fine for willful violation of the Fair Credit Reporting Act

Chapter Review

This chapter focused on state-specific regulations for producers and insurers. Let's review some of the essential requirements and processes:

TYPES OF INSURERS	
Domicile	• *Domestic* – the home office is chartered or incorporated in the same state where policies are being sold • *Foreign* – the home office is located in a different state than the one where policies are being sold • *Alien* – the home office is chartered in any country other than the United States; considered an alien insurer in all U.S. states and territories

TYPES OF INSURERS *(Continued)*	
Ownership	• Stock: - Owned and controlled by stockholders - Sell participating and nonparticipating policies - Stockholders have voting rights and elect the Board of Directors - Dividends are a share of profits and are taxable • Mutual: - Owned and controlled by its policyholders - Sell only participating policies - Policyholders have voting rights and elect a Board of Directors - Dividends are a return of premium and are not taxable • Fraternal Life Insurance Organizations/Fraternal Benefit Society: - Operates as a Corporation, Association, or Society - Is for the benefit of its members and beneficiaries - Not for profit; lodge system - Life Insurance is in the form of a Certificate of Membership instead of a policy (Group Insurance)
LICENSING REQUIREMENTS	
Licensing Process	• Pass examination • Submit application and fees
Types of Licenses	• *Individuals* – resident and nonresident • Temporary licenses are valid for 90 days - Issued to maintain the existing business
Maintenance and Duration	• Must be renewed every two years • Can be reinstated within a short period if expired • *Continuing education* – has to be completed every reporting period • Disciplinary actions: - Suspension, revocation, or refusal to renew license - Cease and desist order - Monetary penalties
STATE AND FEDERAL REGULATIONS	
Commissioner of Insurance	• Appointed by the Governor for two years • Regulates the internal affairs of the Department of Insurance • Does not write laws • Examines all authorized insurers
Agent Regulation	• Only one license of the same type is allowed per agent • Must be licensed in the line of authority for which the agent transacts insurance • Avoid unfair trade practices
Company Regulation	• Certificate of Authority • *Domestic/foreign/alien* – location of incorporation • *Ownership* – stock or mutual • Avoid unfair trade practices or unfair claims settlements

UNFAIR TRADE PRACTICES	
Misrepresentation	• Untrue, deceptive, or misleading information regarding the terms of an insurance contract, the insurance company, or the insurance agent, including the financial standing of any insurance provider • Omission of a material fact • Non-willful misrepresentation of a material fact is grounds to void a contract; misrepresentations of immaterial facts may also make the contract voidable
False Advertising	• Circulating any material that is untrue, deceptive, or misleading • Misrepresenting policy terms, benefits, dividends, or advantages • Presenting an insurance policy as a share of stock • Using names or titles that could misrepresent the true nature of a policy
Rebating	• *Kickbacks* – giving anything of value in exchange for buying a policy • Most insurance providers do not allow rebating
Coercion	• Imposing one's will on another • Falsely stating that a client must purchase one product to qualify for another • A prime example of coercion is a loan officer who claims that a client must purchase mortgage life insurance to qualify for the loan
Defamation	• Making false statements in writing (libel) or verbally (slander) with the intent of injuring anyone involved in the business of life insurance
Fraud	• Intentional deception that results in injury for financial gain

CHAPTER 11:

Texas Statutes and Rules Pertinent to Life Insurance Only

This chapter will explain some of Texas's major regulations that apply exclusively to life insurance. By the end of this chapter, you should be able to explain the basic laws that apply to the different types of life insurance products.

Unless otherwise noted, all references are to the Texas Insurance Code (Ins.) or the Texas Administrative Code (TAC), Title 28.

- **Marketing and Solicitation**
  Ref.: TAC § 3.303, 21.104-.105, 21.107, 21.111, 21.114, 21.122, 21.2201-.2214
- **Policy Provisions**
  Ref: Ins. 1101.003-.009, .053 .055, .156; 1101.011, 1103.055; 1108.101; 1111.052; 1551.254; TAC § 3.101- .106, 3.111-.112, 3.119, 3.121, 3.123, 3.4301-.4317, 3.804 (5)(A)
- **Individual Life and Annuity**
  Ref: Ins. 1101.001, .105, .009, .051; 1116.002; TAC § 3.9711
- **Group Life**
  Ref: Ins. 1101.053; 1131.001-.806
- **Credit Life**
  Ref.: Ins. 1153.003, .004,.151, .153, .155, .157, .201-.204, TAC § 3.5001 – 3.5206
- **Replacement**
  Ref.: Ins. 1114.001-.102
- **Nonforfeiture Law**
  Ref.: Ins. 1105.001 - .153, TAC § 3.3844

Marketing and Solicitation

The process of issuing a life insurance policy starts with solicitation. Soliciting insurance means persuading an individual to purchase an insurance policy, which can be done orally or in writing. This process also includes offering information about available products, explaining the policy benefits, recommending a specific type of policy, and trying to secure a contract between the applicant and the insurer.

Any sales presentations that insurance carriers or agents use in communication with the public must be complete and accurate.

Advertisements

Primarily, advertising must be accurate and not misrepresent the facts. Advertising rules apply to any insurance advertisement intended for presentation, distribution, or dissemination when used or made by or on behalf of the insurer.

All insurers must create and maintain a system of control over the content, form, and method of disseminating all advertising of its policies. The *insurer is responsible for all policy advertisements*, regardless of who created, wrote, presented, or distributed them.

Duty of Insurers – Insurance providers marketing policies in Texas must maintain a system of control over the content, form, and dissemination of all advertisements on their policies. Every insurer is responsible for all advertisements prepared and approved by the insurance company. No insurer can avoid responsibility for advertisements by authorizing or directing anyone else to prepare or approve them.

Duty of Agents – Before using an advertisement, an agent must file its contents with the insurance provider's home office and receive written approval.

Specific Insurance Code regulations for advertisements of life insurance policies in Texas include, but are not limited to, the following:

- Advertisements cannot make any incomplete or unfair comparisons with other policies, rates, benefits, or dividends;
- Advertisements must use language that is clear and understandable by the general public;
- Advertisements must identify the actual insurance provider before using trade names, insurance designations, or names of any parent companies;
- Insurers cannot use any combination of words or symbols similar to those of state or federal government agencies if they may imply that the solicitation is associated with a government agency;
- Advertisements cannot contain false statements regarding the payment of claims, imply that claim settlements will be liberal or generous, or that the insurer will provide special treatment beyond the policy terms; and
- Testimonials must be genuine, accurately reproduced, and represent the author's opinion. The testimonial must include "Paid Endorsement if the individual receives compensation."

Illustrations

The term *illustration* refers to a depiction or presentation that includes non-guaranteed elements of a life insurance policy over the years.

General Rules – An illustration used during the sale of a life insurance policy is required to contain the following basic information:

- Name of the insurance company;
- Name and business address of the producer or the insurance provider's authorized representative, if any;
- Name, age, and sex of the proposed insured, except when a composite illustration is allowed under this regulation;
- Rating classification or underwriting used to create the illustration;
- Generic name of the policy, the product name (if different), and form number;
- Initial death benefit;
- Dividend option or application of non-guaranteed elements (if applicable)
- Illustration date; and
- A prominent label stating "Life Insurance Illustration."

Regulation of Illustrations – The purpose of regulating life insurance illustrations is to establish standards for formats, content, and disclosure that will protect consumers and promote consumer education. This regulation aims to make illustrations more understandable and ensure that they do not mislead life insurance consumers. For example, insurance companies must eliminate the use of caveats and footnotes as much as possible and define the illustration's terms in language that a typical person would understand.

Illustrations must differentiate between guaranteed and projected amounts and disclose the following information:

- **Not Part of the Contract** – Illustrations must clearly state that it is not a part of the insurance contract.
- **Values Not Guaranteed** – Values not guaranteed have to be identified.

Agents can only use illustrations approved by an insurance provider and cannot change them.

Prohibited Practices – When using an illustration during the sale of a life insurance policy, an insurer or its agents may not:

- Depict the policy as anything other than a life insurance policy;
- Describe non-guaranteed elements in a way that could be misleading;
- Use an illustration that portrays a policy's performance as being more favorable than it is;
- Provide an incomplete illustration;
- Claim that premiums will not be required for each policy year unless that is the case;
- Use the term "vanish" or "vanishing premium," or a similar term that suggests the policy becomes paid-up; or
- Use illustrations that are not self-supporting.

When an illustration displays an interest rate used to determine the illustrated non-guaranteed elements, it cannot be greater than the earned interest rate underlying the disciplined current scale.

Life Insurance Policy Cost Comparison Methods

The industry established specific methods and indexes that measure and compare the actual policy costs to help consumers make educated decisions about buying life insurance. Insurers typically illustrate these comparisons in policy documents. Traditional methods of comparing costs include the interest-adjusted net cost method and the comparative interest rate method.

Interest-Adjusted Net Cost Method – The interest-adjusted net cost method considers the time value of money or the investment return on the insurance premium had it invested elsewhere. It applies an interest adjustment to annual premiums and dividends. The *net payment cost index* and the *surrender cost index* are two versions of the interest-adjusted method.

Comparative Interest Rate Method – In a *buy term invest the difference plan*, the comparative interest rate (CIR) is the rate of return that must be earned on a "side fund." At a chosen time, the value of the side fund will equal the surrender value of the higher premium policy.

Policy Provisions

You have previously learned about life insurance policy provisions, options, and clauses that apply to most policies. Here is a list of standard provisions adopted by Texas that must be in life insurance policies issued in this state:

- The policy, a copy of the application, and any attached riders comprise the entire contract.
- All statements of the insured are considered representations and not warranties.
- Individual and group life insurance policies are incontestable after the policy has been effective for two years.
- In the case of a misstatement of an insured's age, the policy will pay benefits based on what the premiums paid would have purchased at the insured's correct age. This provision allows the insurance provider to make the change even though they discovered the error beyond the incontestability period. When the misstatement of age causes an insurance provider to continue coverage beyond the maximum age stated in the policy, the insurer's only duty is to return any premiums received after the insured reaches the maximum age.
- A life insurance policy with cash value must have a provision for the policyholder to borrow from those values. Any unpaid loans at the time of the insured's death will be subtracted from the death benefit paid to the beneficiary.
- Any life insurance policy with cash value must have a nonforfeiture provision.
- A policy owner can request reinstatement of a lapsed policy within three years by paying the back premiums with interest and proving insurability.
- Life insurance policies stipulate that the initial premium be paid in advance to effect coverage.
- Settlement of a death benefit cannot be for less than the face amount of the policy, less any indebtedness.
- The policy owner can assign the policy to another party without the insurance company's consent.

All individual life insurance policies and annuities issued or delivered in Texas must also contain the following provisions:

Free Look – When an agent does not give the applicant a buyer's guide and disclosure document at or before the time of application, the applicant must be allowed a free look of at least *15 calendar days*, during which the applicant can return the policy for an unconditional refund without penalty. A notice on or attached to the cover page must prominently disclose information regarding the free-look period. The free look period starts on the day the consumer receives the contract.

Individuals who purchase a fixed annuity must have a free-look period of at least 20 days. If the applicant returns the policy during this time, the insurer must refund premiums and contract fees. Individuals who purchase variable or modified guaranteed annuities must be refunded an amount equal to the policy's cash surrender value, plus additional contract fees.

Grace Period – Insurers must provide consumers a one-month grace period to pay a premium while the policy remains effective. When an insured dies during the grace period, the insurer will deduct the unpaid premium from any settlement under the policy.

Policy Loans – A life insurance policy must allow the policyholder to take out a *policy loan* from the policy's cash value as long as:

- The policy is effective;
- The premiums have been paid for at least three full years; and
- The policy is assigned correctly.

Failure to repay the policy loan or the loan's interest will not void the policy until the amount owed under the loan equals or exceeds the policy's cash value.

The policy loan provision only applies to policies that provide cash values or nonforfeiture values (not pure endowment contracts or term policies).

Viatical Settlement Disclosures

A viatical settlement provider is required to disclose the following information to the viator before the execution of the viatical settlement contract:

- How viatical settlements operate;
- Possible alternatives to viatical settlements for individuals with life-threatening or catastrophic illnesses, including, but not limited to, accelerated benefits provided by the issuer of the life insurance policy and loans secured by the life insurance policy;
- The fact that the viatical settlement might be subject to the claims of creditors;
- The fact that the proceeds from a viatical settlement can unfavorably affect the recipient's eligibility for Medicaid or other government benefits. Individuals should seek advice from the appropriate agencies;
- Tax consequences that can result from entering into a viatical settlement;
- Consequences of an interruption of assistance as provided by medical or public assistance programs;
- The viator's right to rescind a viatical settlement within 15 days of receiving the proceeds from the viatical settlement; and
- The identity of any individual who will receive any compensation or fee from the viatical settlement company concerning the viatical settlement and the amount and terms of such compensation.

Prohibited Provisions

Certain Limitations Periods – A life insurance policy cannot include a provision limiting the period during which the policy owner can file a lawsuit to less than *two years* after the cause of action.

Retroactive Issuance, Exchange, or Conversion – A life insurance policy cannot contain a provision under which the policy is issued more than *six months* before the application date (backdating) if it causes the policy owner to rate at an age younger than their age on the application. For this subsection, the age of the policy owner on the date of the application is the age the policy owner was/will be on the birthday closest to the application date.

If the policy owner agrees, an issuer can exchange or convert a policy as of a date not earlier than the original policy's effective date. When a policy owner exchanges or converts a policy, and the insurer issues a new policy on a date earlier than the application date for exchange or conversion, the amount under the new policy cannot exceed the amount of the original policy. It also cannot exceed the amount that the paid premiums would have purchased at the policy owner's age on the effective date of the original policy.

Settlement upon Maturity – The life insurance policy cannot contain a settlement at maturity provision less than the policy face amount plus earned dividends and minus owed debt or unpaid premiums. However, the policy can allow a settlement below the face amount if the insured dies by suicide, by a hazardous occupation, or as a result of aviation activities under certain conditions stipulated in the policy.

Group Life

A group policy in Texas must cover at least *two employees* on its issue date. The policy must insure every eligible employee if the insured employees do not pay any portion of the premium.

The following provisions apply to the *termination and conversion* of group life policies issued in Texas:

- Those eligible and covered under a group policy for at least *five years* must apply for an individual policy and pay the first premium within 31 days after the person's membership in a group plan terminates.
- The individual policy has to be issued without evidence of insurability.
- The insured has the right to choose any individual policy offered by the insurance provider, except for term insurance.
- The amount of coverage in an individual policy cannot exceed the lesser of the prior group coverage, or $2,000.

When the individual insured dies during the conversion period, the insured's beneficiary is entitled to the death benefit, which the group policy will pay.

The insured can assign all rights and benefits under the policy to any individual, corporation, firm, association, trust, or legal entity other than the insured's employer.

Under a group life insurance policy, employers can extend coverage to the insured's *spouse and eligible children*. A natural or adopted child qualifies if the child is younger than 25 years of age, mentally or physically disabled, and under the parents' supervision. Biological or adopted grandchildren are eligible for coverage as long as they are younger than 25 years old.

Only one certificate of insurance is required when delivering a group life policy that contains a statement concerning the coverage of a spouse or children.

Whenever a spouse's group life insurance coverage terminates, they have the same conversion rights as the insured. Termination can be because the insured's employment ends, the insured's eligibility for insurance terminates, the insured dies, or the group life insurance policy terminates.

Group Policy Provisions

Group policies have similar provisions to individual policies, such as a 2-year incontestability period and a 31-day grace period. However, the *Misstatement of Age* provision included in group policies differs from the one in individual policies. In group insurance, if the insured participant misstates their age, the insurance provider will adjust the premium and the benefit to the correct age. The benefit is adjusted only in individual insurance.

Group insurance participants are typically allowed to cover dependents on their policies. *Dependent coverage* generally applies to the insured's spouse and children; however, it may also include dependent parents or anyone else on whom participants can prove dependency.

Group life insurance policies cannot include any provision reducing the period during which an insured can start an action to less than two years. Insureds must be permitted to file a lawsuit under the policy within two years of a cause of action.

Credit Life

Credit insurance is a type of coverage written to insure the debtor's life and pay off the loan balance in the event of the debtor's death. Insurers typically write credit life as decreasing term insurance and as an individual policy or a group plan. When insurers write coverage as a group policy, the creditor owns the master policy, and each debtor receives a certificate of insurance.

The creditor is the policy's owner and beneficiary. However, the borrower (or the debtor) usually pays the premiums. Credit life insurance cannot pay out more than the debt balance, so there is no financial incentive for the insured's death. The creditors can require the debtor to have life insurance; however, they cannot require that the debtor purchases insurance from a specific insurance company.

In Texas, insurance companies will refund any unearned gross premiums if they terminate credit life insurance for all plans in which death benefits are not payable due to a policy exclusion. When a policy ends because of the death benefit payout, the premiums paid to the insurance provider are earned, and no refund is required.

Replacement

Replacement is any transaction in which a new life insurance policy or annuity is purchased, causing the existing life insurance policy or annuity to be any of the following:

- Surrendered, forfeited, lapsed, or otherwise terminated;
- Reissued with a reduction in cash value;
- Converted to reduced paid-up insurance, continued as extended-term insurance, or reduced in value by using nonforfeiture benefits or other policy values;
- Amended to affect either a reduction in benefits; or
- Used in a financed purchase.

The *replacing insurer* is the company that issues the new policy.

The *existing insurer* is the company whose policy is being replaced.

Duties of the Replacing Producer
- Present the applicant with a *Notice Regarding Replacement* signed by both the applicant and the producer. Producers must leave a copy with the applicant;
- Acquire a list of all existing life insurance and annuity policies to be replaced, including policy numbers and the names of all insurers being replaced;
- Give the applicant the original or a copy of the written or printed communications used for presentation; and
- Submit a copy of the replacement notice with the new insurance application to the replacing insurer.

Every producer who initiates the application must submit the following to the insurer with or as part of every application:

- A statement signed by the applicant confirming whether replacing an existing life insurance policy or annuity is involved in the transaction; and
- A signed statement confirming whether the producer knows the transaction could involve replacement.

Duties of the Replacing Insurance Company

- Require the producer to provide a list of the applicant's life insurance or annuity contracts to be replaced and a copy of the replacement notice given to the applicant; and
- Send each existing insurer a written communication advising of the proposed replacement within a specified period from the date the replacing insurer's home or regional office receives the application. The replacing insurer must include a policy summary or ledger statement containing policy data on the proposed life insurance policy or annuity.

Nonforfeiture Law

Nonforfeiture benefits are built into the policy and guarantee that the policyholder *cannot forfeit them*. State law mandates insurers to include these guarantees in the policy.

State regulations apply to nonforfeiture benefits in individual and group life insurance policies and annuities offering long-term care insurance. According to these state regulations, the policy must stipulate the provision for nonforfeiture. It must allow for a benefit available in the event of a default in the premium payment. All insurance providers must offer at least one of the following nonforfeiture options:

- Reduced paid-up;
- Extended-term; and
- Shortened benefit period.

All life insurance policies must ensure the following:

1. That upon surrendering the policy no later than *60 days* after the due date of premium payment, the insurer will pay a *cash surrender value* (rather than a paid-up nonforfeiture benefit), provided the premiums have been paid for at least three full years for ordinary life insurance policies, or five years for industrial life insurance;
2. That a specified paid-up nonforfeiture benefit is in force as defined by the policy unless the eligible person chooses a different option within 60 days after the premium due date; and
3. Upon surrender of the policy no later than 30 days after the policy anniversary, the insurer will pay a cash surrender value as long as the policy is paid up or continued under a paid-up nonforfeiture benefit.

The insured has the right to reject or accept the nonforfeiture benefit. The agent must provide information to the prospective policyholder to help them understand and accurately complete the rejection statement.

Any paid-up nonforfeiture benefit available upon default in paying a premium due on any policy anniversary must be such that its present value is equal to the available cash surrender value. When a cash surrender value is unavailable, insurers will utilize the value that would have been required if there were no premium payment conditions for at least a specified period.

Nonforfeiture requirements *do not apply* to the following insurance products:

- Group insurance;
- Most term policies;
- Annuities;
- Reinsurance;
- Pure endowment;
- Policies delivered outside of the state of Texas through an agent or other company representative; or
- Any policy that does not allow for cash values or nonforfeiture values.

Chapter Review

This chapter focused on the state-specific regulations of life insurance products. Let's review some of the essential requirements and processes.

MARKETING AND SOLICITATION	
Advertisements	• Accurate and not misleading • Insurance providers are responsible for all advertisements
Illustrations	• Presentation of non-guaranteed elements • *General rule* – includes information about the insurer, insured, underwriting classifications, and policy benefits • Needs to be clearly labeled "Life Insurance Illustration"
Life Insurance Policy Comparison Methods	• *Interest-Adjusted Net Cost method* – time value of money • *Comparative Interest Rate method* – rate of return
POLICY PROVISIONS	
Required Provisions	• *Free-look period* – 15 calendar days • *Grace period* – one month • *Policy loans* – from the policy's cash value after three full years of paid premiums • *Backdating* – 6 months • *Legal action* – within two years after the loss occurs • *Payment of claims* – within 60 days of the claim

Nonforfeiture Law	• Guarantees benefits that cannot be forfeited (lost) by the policyholder
	• Three minimum nonforfeiture options:
	  - Reduced paid-up
	  - Extended-term
	  - Shortened benefit period

OTHER LIFE POLICIES AND LAWS	

Group Life	• Termination and conversion rules
	• Policy provisions:
	  - Incontestability period – two years
	  - Grace period – 31 days
	  - Misstatement of age – insurance provider adjusts the premium and benefits

OTHER LIFE POLICIES AND LAWS *(Continued)*	
Credit Life	<ul><li>The creditor is the owner and the beneficiary</li><li>The borrower pays the premium</li></ul>
Viatical Settlements	<ul><li>Third-party contracts</li><li>The viator is paid a percentage of the policy's face amount</li><li>May be rescinded within 15 days of receiving the payment</li></ul>
REPLACEMENT	
General Rules	<ul><li>A transaction involving a new policy replacing an existing policy that is: - Surrendered, forfeited, lapsed, or terminated - Reissued with a lower cash value - Converted to reduced paid-up insurance</li><li>Notice Regarding Replacement (provided by the producer)</li></ul>
Exemptions	<ul><li>Credit life</li><li>Group life and annuities</li><li>Existing policy replaced by the same insurance provider</li><li>Existing nonconvertible nonrenewable term policy that expires within five years</li><li>Immediate annuities</li></ul>

CHAPTER 12

Texas Statutes and Rules Pertinent to Accident and Health Insurance Only

Texas has insurance regulations that apply only to accident and health insurance policies. This chapter explains some of these laws, including state programs and organizations that serve the insured.

Unless otherwise noted, all references are to the Texas Insurance Code (Ins.), Texas Administrative Code (TAC), Title 28, or the Affordable Care Act.

- **Required policy provisions**
  Ref.: Ins. 1551.004; 1367.003; 1368.005, TAC § 3.3403
- **AIDS testing requirements**
  Ref: TAC § 21.704 - .705
- **Medicare supplements**
  Ref.: TAC § 3.3301- 3310, 3.3312-.3313, 3.3315-.3325
- **Long-Term Care**
  Ref: TAC § 3.3804, 3.3822, 3.3832
- **Small group health insurance**
  Ref: TAC § 26.8; Ins 1501
- **Affordable Care Act**
  Section 1302, 1321, 1401, 1402, 1511-1515, 18022

Required Policy Provisions

Coverage for Newborns

All individual and group health insurance policies in Texas covering the insured's or subscriber's family members must pay health insurance benefits for the insured's newly born children from birth. Insureds must notify the insurance provider of newborn children within 31 days of delivery. Policies cannot exclude or limit coverage for congenital disabilities of a newborn child.

This provision does not apply to accident-only policies, limited policies covering specific diseases, dental or vision insurance, motor vehicle medical payment insurance, hospital indemnity, or long-term care policies.

Coverage for Drug and Alcohol Treatment

All group health benefit plans in Texas must provide drug and alcohol addiction treatment on the same basis as the benefits covering physical illness. Coverage amounts can be less but must be sufficient to treat the chemical dependency.

This provision does not apply to self-funded groups, employer groups with fewer than 250 employees, or limited benefit plans.

AIDS Testing Requirements

Insurers or agents cannot use the medical application or underwriting to establish the proposed insured's sexual orientation or use the medical application or underwriting to determine if the proposed insured has AIDS or AIDS-related complex. Insurers must keep the HIV-related test results confidential.

An insurer can only disclose the results of the test under the following conditions:

- As required by law; or
- Upon the authorization or written request of the proposed insured to the following:
  - The proposed insured or a person legally authorized to consent to the test;
  - A licensed physician, medical practitioner, or another individual designated by the insured;
  - An insurance medical information exchange;
  - A reinsurer if the reinsurer is involved in the underwriting process;
  - Outside legal counsel who needs the information to represent the insurance company effectively.

The insurance carrier must provide written notice of a positive HIV-related test result to either a designated physician of the proposed insured or to the Texas Department of Health.

Medicare Supplements

Minimum Standards and Cancellation

A Medicare supplement policy cannot deny any claim for losses incurred more than six months beyond the effective date of coverage because of a pre-existing condition. It cannot indemnify against losses caused by sickness on a different basis than losses caused by accidents.

A Medicare supplement policy cannot terminate a spouse's coverage solely because of the occurrence of an event specified for termination of the insured's coverage, other than nonpayment of premium.

Each Medicare supplement policy must be at least guaranteed renewable. When an insurer provides Medicare supplement policies, applicants must receive a policy form offering the basic core benefits (Plan A). Insurers are not required to issue supplement plans B through N. In Texas, insurers cannot offer any groups, packages, or combinations of benefits other than plans A through N.

The standard benefit plans A through N must be uniform in structure, designation, language, and format.

Medicare supplement policies must have a notice prominently printed on the first page. It must state that the policy owner has the *right to return* the policy within *30 days* (free-look period).

Medicare supplement policies must include a *continuation or renewal provision* on the policy's first page and be appropriately captioned. It must consist of any reservation by the insurance carrier of the right to change premiums and any automatic renewal premium increases based on the policy owner's age (attained age policies). Issue age policies do not allow an increase in premiums based on age; they will enable an increase in premiums only when *benefits increase*.

Medicare supplement policies cannot allow for the payment of benefits based on standards described as reasonable and customary, usual and customary, or similar words.

Any limitations regarding pre-existing conditions must appear as a separate paragraph of the policy labeled pre-existing conditions.

Long-Term Care

Renewability Provision

A renewal provision must appear on the policy's first page and be appropriately captioned. The duration of renewability and the duration of coverage must also be listed.

All long-term care policies or certificates issued in Texas must be *guaranteed renewable* or *noncancelable*. Insureds have the right to keep their long-term care insurance in force by making timely premium payments. The insurance provider cannot change the policy or decline to renew it.

Outline of Coverage

The *outline of coverage* must follow the standard format set out in the insurance regulations. It must include information about the insurer, the policy number, and its essential features. An agent must deliver this separate document to the insured before the application or enrollment form.

In Texas, with individual or group LTC policies, producers must deliver outlines of coverage to the applicant at the time of initial policy solicitation or before the producer presents the application. The outline of coverage must be a separate document and contain no advertising material. It must be written in a font size no smaller than 12-point type and follow the format approved by the Department of Insurance.

The outline of coverage must specify the terms under which the policyholder can return the policy and receive a premium refund and provide a description of the *right to return (free look)* provision under the policy. LTC policies must allow the policyholder *30 days* to review the policy and return it for a full premium refund.

Small Group Health Insurance

A *small employer* is any person, firm, partnership, corporation, or association that employed *at least 2 but no more than 50* eligible employees on business days during the *previous calendar year.*

Insurance providers can require a small employer to contribute to the employee's group health insurance premium under the insurance company's standard requirements for all small employer groups. Coverage under a small employer group plan is available if 75% of the eligible employees choose to be covered. The insurer can waive the 75% participation requirement if it offers another plan that allows a lower participation percentage for other small employer groups. Small employers with only two employees must have 100% participation in the plan.

Insurers can terminate a small employer group's health benefit plan if the small employer group fails to meet the participation requirement for six months.

Small group health insurance is renewable for its eligible employees and their dependents *except* for the following reasons:

- The employer fails to pay premiums when expected;
- The employer makes an intentional misrepresentation of a material fact or performs a fraudulent act;
- The number of eligible enrollees falls below the insurance provider's minimum participation number;
- The employer fails to comply with the insurance company's contribution requirements; or
- The insurer meets the state requirements for terminating the insurance coverage in the small employer market.

Insurance carriers cannot increase any requirement for minimum employer participation or minimum employer contributions after the plan is in force.

Every small employer carrier (except HMOs) must offer small employers two standard benefit plans. As provided by the Insurance Code, the insurance carrier must include the basic coverage benefit plan and the catastrophic care benefit plan as a condition of conducting business in Texas with small employers.

Instead of standard benefit plans, HMOs can offer health benefit plans that comply with the Texas Consumer Choice of Benefits Health Insurance Plan Act.

Affordable Care Act

Exchanges and Marketplace

The Patient Protection and Affordable Care Act (PPACA, ACA, or the Act) was signed into law on March 23rd, 2010, as part of the Health Care and Education Reconciliation Act of 2010. The ACA is a comprehensive bill implemented in phases until fully effective in 2018. Since the bill is a federal law, it supersedes state regulations and must conform accordingly.

The Act mandates increased educational, preventive, and community-based health care services. To help lower health insurance costs, the ACA intends to do the following:

- Establish a new competitive private health insurance market;
- Hold insurance companies accountable by keeping premiums low, preventing denials of care, and allowing applicants with pre-existing conditions to obtain coverage (the ACA eliminated pre-existing conditions exclusions as of January 2014);
- Help stabilize the economy and the budget by reducing the deficit by cutting government overspending; and
- Extend coverage for dependent children until age 26 in individual and group health plans.

Also, it gives small businesses and nonprofits a tax credit for an employer's contribution to health insurance for employees. It prohibits insurers from rescinding health coverage when an insured becomes ill and eliminates lifetime benefit limits.

Specific health coverage plans, such as stand-alone dental, retiree-only, Medigap, and long-term care insurance, are usually *exempt* from the ACA changes.

These provisions are controversial, and healthcare laws are constantly being challenged in the courts. Agents should review current laws to ensure they give up-to-date information and advice.

Eligibility – The Health Insurance Marketplace makes health coverage available to uninsured individuals. To be eligible for health coverage through the Marketplace, the person:

- Has to be a U.S. citizen or national or be legally present in the United States;
- Has to live in the United States; and
- Cannot be currently incarcerated.

If a person has Medicare coverage, that person is *not eligible* to use the Marketplace to buy a health or dental plan.

The Act established *insurance exchanges* that administer health insurance subsidies and facilitate enrollment in private health insurance, Medicaid, and the Children's Health Insurance Program (CHIP). An insurance exchange can assist the applicant in doing the following:

- Compare private health plans;
- Obtain information concerning health coverage options to make educated decisions;
- Obtain information concerning eligibility or tax credits for the most affordable coverage; and
- Enroll in a health plan that meets the applicant's needs.

When health insurance providers set their premium rates, they are only allowed to base those rates on four standards:

1. Location of residence within the state (geographic rating area);
2. Single or family enrollment (family composition);
3. Age; and
4. Tobacco use.

For individual plans, the location refers to the insured's home address; for small group plans, the location relates to the employer's principal place of business.

Taxes, Penalties, and Subsidies

Enrollment in the Health Insurance Marketplace began in October 2013, and tax credits for eligible people became available in 2014.

After applying for health insurance for a qualified health plan, *individuals* can take an advance tax credit to lower the cost of their health care coverage if purchased through an exchange. For the premium tax credit, household income refers to the Modified Adjusted Gross Income (MAGI) of the taxpayer, spouse, and dependents. This calculation includes income sources such as salary, wages, interest, dividends, foreign income, and Social Security.

Legal residents and citizens with incomes *between 100% and 400%* of the Federal Poverty Level (FPL) qualify for the tax credits. States can extend Medicaid coverage to people under 138% of the FPL. Individuals who receive public coverage like Medicare or Medicaid do not qualify for the tax credits.

Individuals who qualify for a premium tax credit and have a household income *between 100% and 250%* of FPL are eligible for cost-sharing subsidies (reductions). To receive the subsidy, eligible individuals must purchase a silver-level plan.

The tax credit is sent to the insurance provider, reducing the insured's monthly health care premiums. Tax credits are based on the individual's or family's expected annual income.

Small employers that offer health plans may qualify for federal tax credits, depending on their average wages and size. These tax credits, available to low-wage employers with under a $50,000 average per employee and 25 or fewer workers, can cover up to 50% of paid premiums for small business employers and 35% of paid premiums for small tax-exempt employers.

To qualify for the credit, a small employer must pay the premiums for all employees enrolled in a qualified health plan through a Small Business Health Options Program (SHOP).

The credit is available to qualified employers for two consecutive taxable years.

The Affordable Care Act initially required every U.S. citizen and legal resident to have qualifying health insurance. This requirement was the *individual mandate* and part of the Act's Shared Responsibility Provision. If a person did not have qualifying health care, a federal tax penalty would result. The individual's taxable income, the number of dependents, and the joint filing status determined the penalty amount.

As of 2019, the individual mandate and shared responsibility penalty *no longer apply*. However, many states have their own health insurance mandate. Individuals must have qualifying health insurance or pay a *state tax penalty* in these states.

Employer Penalties – Employers with fewer than 50 full-time employees are not subject to employer penalties. The following table shows the penalties for an employer with more than 50 full-time employees if at least one employee receives premium tax credits for health insurance:

COVERAGE	PENALTY TAX
Employer *does not* offer coverage	$2,000 per full-time employee (first 30 employees are excluded)
Employer *offers* coverage	The lesser of $3,000 per employee who receives a premium tax credit or $2,000 per each full-time employee (first 30 employees are excluded)

Essential Health Benefits

The Affordable Care Act (ACA) stipulates that all healthcare plans include the following *ten essential benefits*:

- Emergency services;
- Ambulatory patient services;
- Hospitalization;
- Maternity and newborn care;
- Rehabilitative and habilitative services and devices;
- Mental health and substance abuse disorder services, including behavioral health treatment;
- Laboratory services;
- Prescription drugs;
- Pediatric services, including vision and oral care; and
- Preventive and wellness services and chronic disease management.

Mental Health Parity – The Affordable Care Act passed guidelines on how health insurance providers implement the Mental Health Parity and Addiction Equity Act of 2008 (MHPAEA). MHPAEA stipulates that financial requirements (e.g., coinsurance) and treatment limitations cannot be more restrictive than those that apply to other medical and surgical benefits.

Pediatric Services – Pediatric dental coverage is an essential health benefit under the Affordable Care Act. It must be available as a stand-alone plan or health plan for children 18 or younger. However, insurance providers do not have to offer adult dental coverage.

Depending on the state, insurers can offer pediatric dental benefits through one of the following types of plans:

- A qualified health plan that contains dental coverage;
- A stand-alone dental plan obtained in conjunction with a qualified health plan; or
- A contracted/bundled plan.

Preventive Services – Most health insurance plans, including private insurance plans available through the Marketplace, must cover *preventive services* like screening tests and shots at no cost to the insured.

The following preventive services must be offered without coinsurance or copayment, even if the insured has not met the annual deductible. The no-cost condition will only apply if a network provider delivers the services.

REQUIRED PREVENTATIVE CARE SERVICES	
For ALL Insureds	Screening for blood pressure, alcohol misuse, depression, and HIV for those at higher risk
	Immunization vaccines
	Prevention counseling for sexually transmitted infection (STI) for those at higher risk
For Adults	Screening for cholesterol for specific ages or those at higher risk, aspirin use for certain ages, colorectal cancer screening for adults over 50, obesity, Type 2 diabetes for adults with high blood pressure, and tobacco use for all adults and cessation interventions
	Diet counseling
For Men	Abdominal aortic aneurysm one-time screening (for men of specified ages who have never smoked)

REQUIRED PREVENTATIVE CARE SERVICES *(Continued)*	
For Women	Gynecological and obstetrical care, including screenings when needed for anemia, breast cancer mammography, BRCA genetic testing, cervical cancer (for women at higher risk beginning at age 40), and other conditions
	Contraception with FDA-approved contraceptive methods, sterilization procedures, and education and counseling, excluding abortifacient drugs
	Well-woman visits and comprehensive support and counseling for breastfeeding for pregnant and nursing women
For Children	Screenings for behavioral disorders, autism, blood disorders, developmental progress including height, weight, and body mass index, congenital hypothyroidism, lead poisoning, vision, hearing, oral health, phenylketonuria (PKU), and tuberculin testing

Employer Notification Responsibilities

All employers offering their employees health insurance must provide information about the ACA and the Health Insurance Marketplace exchanges. The notification aims to help employees evaluate health coverage options for themselves and their dependents.

Chapter Review

This chapter focused on the state-specific regulations of health insurance products. Let's review some of the essential points:

INDIVIDUAL INSURANCE	
Required Provisions	• Same as the NAIC mandatory and optional provisions
State Mandatory Coverages	• Newborn children of the insured are covered from the moment of birth • Drug and alcohol addiction treatment
GROUP COVERAGE	
Certificate of Insurance	• Evidence and length of coverage • Policy benefits and exclusions • Procedures for filing a claim • Must be given to all insureds
Small Employer	• Between 2 and 50 employees • *Two standard benefit plans* – basic coverage and catastrophic care benefit
SPECIFIC PRODUCTS	
Medicare Supplement Plans	• Cannot duplicate Medicare benefits • Coverage must be guaranteed renewable • Must include a 30-day free-look period (right to return) • Pre-existing condition exclusion – no longer than six months
Long-Term Care	• Coverage must be noncancelable or guaranteed renewable • Must include a 30-day free-look period (right to return) • Pre-existing condition exclusion – no longer than six months • *Outline of coverage* – must be given at the time of initial policy solicitation

AFFORDABLE CARE ACT	
Eligibility	• Must be a U.S. citizen or national or be lawfully present in the U.S. • Must live in the U.S. • Cannot be currently incarcerated
Features and Coverages	• Coverage for the insured's children until age 26 • No pre-existing conditions exclusions • Premium rates can only be based on age, geographic area, family composition, and tobacco use
Insurance Exchanges (Marketplace)	• Federally-facilitated marketplace • State exchange • Helps applicants to: - Compare private health insurance plans - Obtain information about health coverage options and eligibility for tax credits - Enroll in an appropriate health plan
Essential Health Benefits	• Ten essential health benefits: - Emergency services - Ambulatory patient services - Hospitalization - Pregnancy, maternity, and newborn care - Mental health and substance abuse services - Prescription drugs - Rehabilitative and habilitative services and devices - Laboratory services - Chronic disease management and preventive and wellness services - Pediatric services, including oral and vision care

CHAPTER 13:
Texas Statutes and Rules Pertinent to Health Maintenance Organizations (HMOs)

This chapter will focus on Health Maintenance Organizations (HMOs). You will learn about the major principles that govern HMO plans and their general provisions, services, and state-specific regulations. By the end of this chapter, you should be able to compare HMOs with other medical plans based on their advantages and disadvantages for consumers.

Unless otherwise noted, all references are to the Texas Insurance Code (Ins.) or the Texas Administrative Code (TAC), Title 28.

Ref.: TAC Chapter 11; 11.501, 11.1611; Ins. 843, 1271

- **Definitions**
- **Evidence of Coverage**
- **Nonrenewal/Cancellation**
- **Enrollment**

Definitions

Health Maintenance Organizations (HMOs) fund health care for their members primarily on a prepaid basis. They also organize and deliver the services. Subscribers pay a fixed periodic fee (typically monthly) and receive a broad range of health services, from routine doctor visits to emergency and hospital care. The HMO receives payment whether or not the subscribers use the services.

The cost of preventive care, such as annual physicals and periodic immunizations, is included in the services.

Other health insurance plans provide expense coverage, typically on a reimbursement basis, to the insured for medical and hospital expenses covered under the plan. Preventive health care is not covered under these plans.

HMOs seek to identify medical problems early by offering preventive care. They encourage early treatment and provide care on an outpatient basis whenever possible rather than admitting members to the hospital.

In Texas, if the medically necessary covered service is unavailable through network providers or physicians, all HMOs must allow referrals to a non-network provider or physician and fully reimburse the non-network provider or physician at the usual, customary, or agreed-upon rate.

Cost-Sharing Methods

Copayments are a specific dollar amount or a percentage of the cost of care that the member must pay. For example, the member could pay $5 or $10 for each office visit.

Deductibles and Coinsurance – Most private insurance plans include both deductibles (expressed in dollar amounts) and coinsurance provisions (expressed in a percentage) to indicate the required financial participation of an insured. This requirement is a cost-containment tool used by the insurance carrier.

While HMOs typically contain copayments, they do not use deductibles or coinsurance provisions. They emphasize preventive care to reduce the need for expensive hospital care.

Nature of Benefits

Prepaid Services – The theory behind an HMO is that the member pays a fixed periodic fee for all necessary medical services from member physicians and hospitals.

Indemnity – Indemnity health insurance plans offer broad coverage for medical expenses from any provider selected by the insured. These plans are also known as *first-dollar insurance* because they provide benefits without requiring the insured to meet a deductible. Most insurance companies no longer offer this type of coverage because the insured has no reason to restrict the use of their coverage or search for lower-cost providers.

Gatekeepers and Network-Model HMOs

Gatekeepers – Initially, the member selects a primary care physician or gatekeeper. The primary care physician must refer the member if the member requires a specialist. This practice helps prevent the member from seeing the higher-priced specialists unless it is critically needed.

Network-Model HMOs – A *Network-Model HMO* differs from a group-model HMO in that it contracts with two or more independent groups of physicians to offer medical services to its subscribers. Usually, physician groups that enter into this arrangement treat non-HMO patients on a fee-for-service basis.

Evidence of Coverage

The Texas Department of Insurance and Department of Health have enacted regulations to protect HMO patients.

Texas HMOs are required to provide each enrollee with *evidence of coverage* that includes the following:

- The HMO's name, address, and phone number, including a toll-free number on the first page of the policy;
- A schedule of benefits, deductibles, and copayments; and
- Policy cancellation and nonrenewal provisions and the minimum notice period.

Each evidence of coverage must also specify the information that will appear in any blanks, except for single-case forms, which must be ready for use.

Texas HMOs cannot charge for immunizations for children from birth through age six. When the Health Maintenance Organization is part of a small employer health benefit plan covering children's immunizations, the HMO can charge a copayment or deductible.

Certificate of Authority

A *certificate of authority* issued by the Commissioner is required to establish or operate the HMO. The application for a certificate of authority must include the following:

- A notarized copy of the applicant's primary organizational documents;
- A copy of the applicant's rules, bylaws, and rules regarding internal affairs;
- A list of the names, addresses, and official titles of anyone responsible for the applicant's affairs;
- A copy of any contract made or to be made between the applicant and any of its directors and officers, or with health care providers, any exclusive agent or agency, or any individual providing administrative, management, or data processing services;
- A description of the quality assurance program, including peer review, to fulfill the quality of health care requirements;
- A copy of the forms of evidence of coverage to be provided to enrollees;
- Financial statements listing assets, liabilities, and sources of financial reports;
- The schedule of charges during the first 12 months of operation;
- A statement acknowledging that the Commissioner can serve lawful process;
- A description and map of the geographic region to be served;
- A description of complaint procedures;
- A description of programs used to fulfill health care quality requirements; and
- Any information required by the Commissioner.

Nonrenewal, Cancellation, and Prohibited Practices

HMO policies must include a statement specifying the following acceptable grounds for canceling or renewing a policy:

- Nonpayment of premiums due under the policy;
- Fraud in the use of services or facilities;

- Failure to meet eligibility requirements (insurers can cancel coverage *immediately*);
- Misconduct that is detrimental to the delivery of services or safe plan operations;
- Failure of a plan physician and the subscriber to establish a satisfactory patient-physician relationship; and
- When the enrollee does not reside or work in the HMO service area.

When an insurer cancels a policy for nonpayment of premium, the insurance company must provide a 30-day written notice to the insured. If an insurer cancels a policy due to fraud, the notice must be at least 15 days.

HMOs are not allowed to engage in any of the following activities:

- Causing or knowingly allowing the use of advertising or solicitation that is misleading or untrue;
- Causing or knowingly allowing the use of any form of evidence of coverage that is deceptive;
- Canceling or nonrenewing coverage except for the failure to pay the coverage charges or another reason promulgated by the Insurance Code; and
- Using in its name, literature, or contracts the words insurance, mutual, casualty, surety, or any other words that describe the insurance business. This activity is permissible if the HMO is a licensed insurance provider.

Enrollment

Most HMOs operate solely through a group enrollment system. Each group member pays a premium, whether or not the individual uses the HMO's services. By prepaying the services, the person is encouraged to see a doctor early to take preventive measures. Insurers expect that the general health of every HMO member will benefit from early detection and treatment by promoting preventive medicine. This assumption means that individuals can avoid costly procedures that become necessary when a condition worsens.

Most HMOs either operate their own clinics and hospitals staffed by healthcare professionals employed by the HMO or enter into volume discount arrangements with providers and hospitals and agreements with physicians to provide service on a prearranged per capita basis (known as capitation).

The Commissioner can issue HMO investment rules to ensure enrollees have sufficient access to health care providers. The Commissioner can also set primary and specialty care mileage requirements, minimum physician-patient ratios, maximum travel time, and maximum appointment waiting times.

Chapter Review

This chapter focused on the state-specific regulations of Health Maintenance Organizations (HMOs). Let's review some of the key points:

DEFINITIONS	
Cost Sharing	• *Coinsurance* – expressed in a percentage • *Copayment* – a specific dollar amount or a percentage of the cost of care that the member must pay • *Deductible* – expressed in dollar amounts
Features and Coverages	• *Gatekeeper* – if the member requires the attention of a specialist, the primary care physician or gatekeeper must refer the member • *Indemnity* – these plans are also known as first-dollar insurance because they provide benefits without requiring the insured to meet a deductible • *Network* – it contracts with two or more independent groups of physicians to offer medical services to its subscribers
EVIDENCE OF COVERAGE	
Texas HMOs	• Must provide each enrollee with evidence of coverage, including the HMOs contact information, a schedule of benefits, deductibles, copayments, and policy cancellation and nonrenewal provisions
Certificate of Authority	• Issued by the Commissioner and is required to establish or operate an HMO
NONRENEWAL AND CANCELLATION	
Grounds for Policy Nonrenewal or Cancellation	• Fraud, nonpayment of required premiums or cost-sharing, or failure to meet eligibility requirements • 30-day notice of cancellation, except for fraud (15 days)

KEY FACTS

Knowing the key facts can be the difference between passing and failing your licensing exam. Read through each point for a quick review of essential terms and concepts in this book.

Completing the Application, Underwriting, and Policy Delivery

Completing the Application

- An incomplete application is typically returned; however, coverage begins should the underwriter approve it. In this instance, the insurer gives up some of its ability to contest a claim.
- An applicant's statements on an insurance application are considered representations and not warranties.
- A warranty is a guarantee of truth.
- Although a conditional receipt can be issued, coverage does not begin until the applicant satisfies all the conditions and the application is approved.
- Although producers must sign the application, they are not parties to the contract.

Underwriting

- Insurable interest must exist at the time of the application but not necessarily at the time of a claim.
- Insurable interest can be based on economics or family relationships.
- HIPAA's privacy rule protects all personally identifiable health information, called protected health information.
- Protected health information includes name, birth date, Social Security Number (SSN), address, and health data.
- An insurance provider must have written pre-authorization to pull the applicant's credit report.
- Stranger-originated life insurance (STOLI) and investor-originated life insurance (IOLI) are outlawed in many states. In STOLI or IOLI, the investor can potentially profit from the insured's death.

Risk Classification

- Surcharges (rate-ups) can be accomplished using a rate charge for a different sex, a higher age, a flat fee, or a percentage adjustment to the manual rate.
- A surcharge is representative of a counteroffer. Coverage does not take effect until the applicant accepts the policy at a higher rate and pays the increased premium.
- The underwriter determines the final rating classification, not the agent.
- A standard risk has an average life span.
- A rated policy is issued to a substandard risk.
- Marital status is not an acceptable underwriting factor in life insurance.
- Avocation (hobby) is an acceptable underwriting factor in life insurance.

Delivering the Policy

- Coverage can never start unless the applicant pays the premium. Furthermore, even though the applicant pays the premium, coverage will not begin until they have met all of the conditions of the conditional receipt.
- The earliest coverage could begin would be the application date, assuming the applicant paid the first premium, had no conditions to fulfill, and was found insurable.
- It is the agent's responsibility to explain the policy provisions, riders, and exclusions to the policyholder or the insured.

Life Policies

Term Life

- The limits of an increasing term policy increase yearly by the premiums paid. An increasing term policy is also sometimes called a return of premium policy.
- Term insurance is renewable without requiring a physical examination up to a certain age.
- Insureds can convert term insurance to whole life, but not the reverse. The conversion is based on the insured's current age.
- In a level term policy, the coverage amount and the premium are level throughout the term.
- On an annual renewable level term policy, the premium will increase annually, although the face amount will remain the same.
- On a decreasing term policy, the face amount decreases, not the premium.

Traditional Whole Life Products

- Premiums used to obtain whole life insurance are kept in the insurance company's general account, which is invested more conservatively.
- Whole life policies must include a table showing their guaranteed cash value at the end of each year (anniversary date) for the first 20 years. Insurers must also display the interest rate and mortality table used to determine those values.
- A whole life insurance policy is designed to deliver protection until an individual dies or reaches age 100.
- Whole life and limited-pay life both reach maturity at age 100.
- A single premium can purchase a policy that is paid up for life.
- Single premium policies yield an immediate cash value.
- Limited-pay whole life policies, while paid up earlier, do not mature until the insured dies or reaches age 100, whichever happens first.
- On a 20-pay life policy, the cash value will equal the face amount at age 100 (maturity).
- A 20-pay life policy is a whole life policy in which the premium is paid up in 20 years.

Interest-Sensitive, Market-Sensitive, and Adjustable Life Products

- A universal life insurance policy has two choices of death benefits: option A or B.
- Policyholders can reduce, increase, or skip premium payments on universal life insurance policies. The policy will not lapse if there is enough cash value to pay for expense deductions.
- Universal life offers a minimum guaranteed rate of return and flexible premiums.
- Universal life, variable life, and variable/universal life are interest-sensitive whole life insurance products.
- The state guaranty fund does not back variable products and has no guarantees.
- A producer must be registered with FINRA to sell a variable product.
- Variable life products offer a hedge against inflation.
- Premium funds invested in a variable annuity or variable life contract must be kept in the insurance company's separate account, similar to a mutual fund.
- Variable whole life is an insurance and a securities product; therefore, it is regulated at the state level by the Department of Insurance and at the federal level by the Securities and Exchange Commission (SEC).
- Applicants with incomes that often fluctuate can benefit from purchasing an adjustable whole life policy.

Combination Plans and Variations

- A joint life policy pays when the first insured dies, and a joint and survivor life policy pays when the second insured dies.
- Survivorship life insurance is generally used in estate planning. The policy's death benefit allows the beneficiary to pay estate taxes when due.
- Survivorship life is usually purchased to fund estate taxes.

Annuities

- Annuities are the opposite of life insurance. Life insurance creates an estate, while annuities liquidate an estate over time.
- An annuitant cannot outlive the income from an annuity.
- An immediate annuity is funded with a single premium, and payments will begin one month later.
- The state guaranty fund backs fixed annuities and guarantees a fixed rate of return.
- On a variable annuity, the annuity is valued in annuity units during the payout period.
- A refund annuity has the least amount of risk to the annuitant.
- If an annuitant dies during the accumulation period of an annuity, the insurer will pay the account value to the beneficiary of the annuitant or the annuitant's estate.
- A life income annuity, also known as a straight or pure life annuity, has no beneficiary and is the riskiest option for the annuitant.
- A joint and survivor annuity will pay while either party is alive.
- Annuity tables are different than mortality tables because there is no insurance protection.
- Annuities are frequently used as life insurance settlement options.
- An annuity does not require underwriting.

Life Policy Provisions, Riders, and Options

Policy Provisions

- The entire contract includes the policy, a copy of the application, and any associated riders.
- The purpose of the entire contract provision is to protect the insured from the insurance company making changes to the policy after issuance.
- The insuring clause is the insurance provider's legally enforceable promise to pay.
- A policyholder can exercise the free-look provision without giving any reason.
- The free-look period begins upon policy delivery. When the insurance company mails the policy to the policyholder, the free-look period starts on the date of mailing (known as constructive delivery).
- A life insurance policy's owner's rights section specifies who has the right to change the beneficiary, who can take out a loan, and who can take a cash surrender.
- Upon reinstatement, both the suicide and incontestability clauses start over.
- If the insured lies on an application for life insurance, the insurance provider can contest the policy within two years (in most states). After two years have passed, the policy is incontestable.
- When an insured makes an absolute assignment, they are the assignor. The assignee is the party to which the assignor assigns the policy.
- The misstatement of age provision lasts for the duration of the policy. The discovery of a misstated age will cause an adjustment of the benefit amount rather than cancellation of the policy.

Policy Loans, Withdrawals, and Surrenders

- Insurance providers have six months to defer a request for a policy loan or cash surrender. However, they typically do not exercise this right.
- An insured's policy is the only collateral for a policy loan.
- Policy owners can take out a policy loan during the grace period.
- Failure to repay a policy loan will permanently affect the policy's cash value accumulation.

Beneficiaries

- Creditors cannot attach life policy proceeds left to a beneficiary. If there is no beneficiary, proceeds will go into the estate, which creditors can attach.
- An irrevocable beneficiary has a vested interest in the policy, and the policy owner cannot change it without their consent.
- The policy owner can change a revocable beneficiary at any time.
- Under the common disaster provision, the insured is presumed to die last.
- The beneficiary does not have to be of the age of majority (18 or 21, depending upon the state) to receive policy proceeds. However, proceeds cannot be directly paid to a minor child because they cannot sign the release.

Policy Riders

- The guaranteed insurability rider allows insureds to obtain additional insurance without a physical examination at specified dates.
- The payor benefit rider expires when the child reaches age 18 or 21, depending on the state, or when the payor recovers from their disability.
- An accidental death and accidental death and dismemberment rider can be attached to either a term or whole life insurance policy.
- A long-term care rider allows insureds to withdraw money from a policy's cash value to pay for qualifying home health care or nursing home care expenses.
- Any amount used for approved long-term care expenses lowers the policy's death benefit.
- When an insured includes the return of premium rider, should the insured live to the end of the policy term, the insurer will return the premium to the insured free of federal income tax.
- The accelerated benefits rider will pay out part of the proceeds before death. The proceeds are not taxable.

Policy Options

- If a policy with a cash value lapses for nonpayment, the insured has 60 days from the premium due date to choose a nonforfeiture option. Extended-term is the automatic nonforfeiture option the insurance provider selects if the insured does not specify otherwise.
- The policy owner can take the paid-up nonforfeiture option whenever there is a cash value.
- The owners of a mutual insurance company are the policy owners. Dividends received by the policy owners of a mutual policy are not taxable.
- Dividends received by stock owners in a stock company are taxable as ordinary income; dividends are never taxed as capital gains.
- If a beneficiary chooses the interest option, the taxable interest payments will vary. However, the beneficiary can withdraw the principal at any time.
- A fixed period payout does not guarantee payments for the beneficiary's entire life.

Taxes, Retirement Plans, and Other Insurance Concepts

Third-Party Ownership

- Key person and partnership insurance, as well as a policy written on the life of a spouse or minor child, are examples of third-party policy ownership.
- Third-party administrators (TPAs) are more common today because of the growth of self-funded plans.

Viatical Settlements and Life Settlements

- A viator is a person who seeks to sell their life insurance policy in a viatical settlement.
- A viatical settlement is an agreement where a terminally ill insured (a viator) sells their life insurance policy to an investor for less than its face value amount but more than its cash value.
- Life settlement contracts are between the life insurance policy owner and a third party.
- Life settlement transactions arise from existing life insurance policies.

Group Life Insurance

- Group policies are generally less expensive than individual policies.
- An individual cannot form a group only to buy insurance.
- Group insurance is typically written as an annually renewable term policy.
- A group sponsor (generally the employer) receives the master policy.
- Group participants (insureds) receive a certificate of insurance as evidence of coverage.
- Experience rating, based upon previous claims, is often used in group insurance.
- When an individual terminates employment, conversion from a group life policy to an individual policy is allowed for 31 days, regardless of health.
- In a contributory group life plan, employees pay part of the premium, and 75% of those eligible must participate. In a noncontributory plan, the employer pays the premium in full, and 100% of those eligible must participate.

Retirement Plans

- Qualified plans have early withdrawal penalties. The IRS levies a 10% penalty for full or partial cash surrenders on annuities, IRAs, 401(k)s, TSAs, and Keogh plans before age 59 ½ unless the insured has died or becomes disabled.
- Regarding an IRA, anyone with earned income can contribute up to 100% of earned income or the current contribution limit (subject to change by the IRS), whichever is less.
- There is no minimum annual contribution to an IRA.
- Small firms frequently use SEP IRAs as qualified tax plans for employees.
- IRA contributions can be tax-deductible if income is below a certain level, even if the client is an active participant in another qualified plan.
- Distributions from qualified plans can be rolled into an IRA (no dollar amount limit).
- Owners can fund IRAs with annuities but not whole life policies.
- Keogh (or HR-10) plans are available to self-employed sole proprietors, partners, and their employees; they are not available to a corporation's officers.
- TSAs are also called 403(b) plans.
- The IRS limits contributions to qualified plans.
- An example of a nonqualified plan is deferred compensation.

Social Security

- The Old Age, Survivors, Disability and Health Insurance Act (OASDHI) provides coverage for old age (social security), survivor benefits, disability income, and health insurance (Medicare). However, it does not include Medicaid coverage.
- To be fully insured for disability benefits under Social Security, a worker must have contributed to It for at least 40 quarters (10 years).

Tax Treatment of Insurance Premiums, Proceeds, and Dividends

- Upon a cash surrender, amounts paid over premiums paid are taxable.
- In all life insurance, death benefits paid to beneficiaries are received tax-free.
- Unpaid death benefits continue earning interest for the beneficiary. The interest is taxable.
- A trustee-to-trustee rollover excludes the withholding tax requirement.
- There is no 10% IRS penalty for annuitization before age 59 ½. Only cash surrenders are subject to the penalty.
- In individual life insurance, premiums paid are not tax-deductible; however, the proceeds are not taxable.
- Cash value life policies that fail the 7-pay test are considered modified endowment contracts (MECs) for the contract's life.
- Modified endowment contracts (MECs) include a 10% penalty for premature distributions.

Field Underwriting Procedures

Applications, Premiums, Underwriting

- The earliest coverage can start would be the application date, assuming the applicant paid the first premium, had no conditions to fulfill, and did not lie.
- An incomplete application is typically returned. Should the underwriter approve the application as is, coverage begins. If this happens, the insurance company gives up some of its ability to contest a claim.
- The Medical Information Bureau (MIB) collects information about claims.
- Coverage cannot begin unless the applicant pays the premium. Even though the applicant paid the premium, coverage will not start until they meet all the conditions of the conditional receipt.
- The underwriter establishes the final rating classification, not the producer.
- A buyer's guide and policy summary must be left with the applicant before accepting the initial premium.
- Although the producer must sign the application, they are not parties to the contract.
- It is the responsibility of the producer to explain the policy provisions, riders, and exclusions to the policy owner or the insured.

Contract Law

- The application answers and the premium are both the applicant's consideration. In return, the insurance company promises to provide coverage. Consideration does not have to be equal.
- An insurable interest must exist at the time of application but not necessarily at the time of a claim.
- Insurable interest can be based on economics or family relationships.
- A warranty is a guarantee of truth.

Types of Health Policies

Disability Income

- Permanent disability never goes away (such as losing a limb).
- A short-term disability policy has a shorter elimination period than a long-term disability policy.
- Under an individual disability income policy, premiums paid by the insured are not tax-deductible. However, any received benefits would be free of federal income tax.
- A blanket disability policy can be written to cover an employee group, a student group, a debtor group, passengers on a common carrier, or a sports team. Blanket policies do not require individual applications, and certificates of insurance are issued to those covered.

Business Disability Insurance

- Business overhead insurance will pay for the ongoing business expenses of a self-employed person, such as salaries or rent, while the self-employed person is disabled.
- Key person disability insurance indemnifies the business for the loss of services from a key employee because of a disability.

Accidental Death and Dismemberment

- On an Accidental Death & Dismemberment (AD&D) policy, loss of eyesight because of an accident is covered. Loss of hearing is not covered.
- Loss of a limb is covered, but the loss of the use of a limb is not covered (because that would not be dismemberment).
- A limited health insurance policy (like AD&D) will only cover limited perils and amounts.

Medical Expense Insurance

- Base plans cover in-hospital only. There is no coinsurance or deductible on a base plan.
- When calculating how much the insurance company will pay on a claim, the deductible is subtracted first, and then the coinsurance percentage is applied.
- Medical expense policies cover both sickness and accidents.
- Basic medical expense policies offer first-dollar coverage without a deductible.
- Health insurance excludes cosmetic surgery, self-inflicted injury, and war.
- Health insurance underwriters can discriminate based on an applicant's health history.
- Surgical expense policies will pay a claim up to the policy limit. They are the only health insurance policies using a relative value schedule.
- Major medical and Medicare Part B policies contain deductibles and coinsurance requirements.
- The stop loss feature on a major medical policy applies after the insured pays the deductible first.
- HMOs, PPOs, and POS plans are types of managed care.

Group Insurance

- Groups cannot form only to buy insurance. They must exist for another reason.
- Group health insurance typically has no probationary period and little underwriting. Group rates usually are lower than individual rates because administration costs are much lower.
- Experience rating, based on previous claims experience, is used on group health plans.

- COBRA (a federal regulation that applies to group medical expense policies) lets employees continue group coverage for 18 months if they quit or are terminated.
- Under COBRA, the family of a disabled or deceased employee can continue group coverage for another 36 months.

Individual/Group Long Term Care (LTC)

- LTC policies will pay for skilled nursing, intermediate care, and custodial care.
- Optional LTC coverage provides home health care, adult daycare, and hospice care.
- A person who cannot perform the activities of daily living (ADLs) will need a long-term care policy.
- ADLs include mobility, eating, bathing, dressing, toileting, and continence.

Other Policies

- Travel accident insurance will pay if an insured dies in a commercial aircraft (common carrier).
- Dental and vision insurance can be a family plan, individual policy, or offered as a group policy.
- Dental and vision insurance can require the insured to go to an in-network dentist to receive maximum benefits.
- Vision and dental insurance can have coinsurance amounts, deductibles, and annual maximum benefit amounts.
- Critical illness plans pay a lump-sum benefit directly to the insured.
- Interim policies are short-term health insurance plans to fulfill temporary needs (six months or less). They are frequently used to cover gaps in insurance between jobs.

Health Policy Provisions, Riders, and Options

Mandatory and Optional Provisions

- Mandatory provisions, like the grace period, protect the insured. Optional provisions, like probationary periods, protect the insurance company.
- If an insurance carrier proves fraud, it can contest a claim after two years. Insurers are typically reluctant to charge fraud because it requires proof of intent to deceive and is generally difficult to prove.
- The purpose of the incontestability clause is to protect the insurance company.
- Another name for the incontestability clause is the time limit on certain defenses clause.
- The longest grace period will be 31 days.
- If a reinstatement application is required, the insured is reinstated when the insurance company says so or after 45 days, whichever comes first. When the insurer reinstates an insured, a 10-day probationary period will begin on sickness only.
- If no reinstatement application is required, the insurer reinstates the insured effective upon payment of their late premium to either the insurance company or the producer.
- Insurers can deny claims if they occur after policy expiration.
- Under the time payment of claims provision, issuers must pay claims immediately. They must pay disability income claims at least monthly.
- The time payment of claims provision gives the claims department time to investigate (a maximum of 60 days).
- Under the legal actions provision, if an insurer does not pay a claim immediately, the claimant must wait at least 60 days before filing a lawsuit for failure to pay. Such lawsuits have to be filed within three years of the original loss.

Other Provisions and Riders

- In the insuring clause, the insurance provider promises to pay.
- A policy's maximum probationary period varies by state.
- The probationary period differs from the time limit on certain defenses provision, which is a maximum of two years.
- To reduce the premium on disability income policies, an insured can choose a longer waiting period.
- On disability income insurance, the waiting period is just another name for the elimination period.
- If insurance providers want fewer claims, they should lengthen the waiting period.
- The waiting period on a disability income policy is waived if the same recurrence occurs within 90 days.
- Waiver of premium does not pay money to the insured; it pays the premium to the insurance company on behalf of the insured.
- A family deductible limits the total amount the family must pay during the year, no matter how many family members become injured or sick.
- If an insurance provider wants to emphasize preventive care, they should waive the deductible for office visits.
- To find what is covered on a health insurance policy, the insured will look at the eligible expenses section.
- URC stands for usual, reasonable, and customary.
- The guaranteed purchase option is a rider that allows the insured to buy additional coverage at certain intervals without a physical examination. This rider is also called the guaranteed insurability rider (GIR).

Rights of Renewability

- Insurers must renew a conditionally renewable policy if certain conditions are satisfied.
- Optionally renewable policies offer the most significant disadvantage for the insured.
- On a noncancelable policy, the insurance carrier cannot change the coverage or the rates but can decline to offer renewal.
- Medical expense policies are typically written as cancelable, which means the company can cancel at any time as long as it provides advance notice.
- A cancelable policy can be canceled at any time by either party with proper advance notice.
- Cancellation will not affect a pending claim, only future claims.
- On a guaranteed renewable policy, the insurance provider cannot change the coverage; however, it can change the rates by class, not individually.
- If a policy is noncancelable and guaranteed renewable (the best kind), the company cannot change the coverage or rates and has to offer renewal.
- At the insured's option, a guaranteed renewable policy is renewable by paying the premium to a specified age (usually 65).

Social Insurance

Medicare and Medicare Supplements

- Certain people under age 65 with a disability or End-Stage Renal Disease are eligible for Medicare.
- Part A of Medicare offers hospital insurance.
- User premiums partially finance part B of Medicare (medical insurance).
- Medicare Part B has a premium, a deductible, and coinsurance, all set annually. The amount paid by Social Security depends upon the insured's primary insurance amount (PIA).

- Medigap core benefits must cover the 20% Medicare Part B coinsurance deductible.
- The federal government heavily subsidizes Medicare Parts B and D and requires the insured to pay a monthly premium.
- Medicare Part C sometimes has a premium, while in some cases, it does not.
- Individuals who enroll in Medicare Part C (Medicare Advantage) do not have to purchase a Medicare supplement.
- To be eligible for Medicare Part D (prescription drug insurance), a person must be enrolled in Medicare Part A or Parts A and B.
- A retiree can supplement Medicare by staying enrolled in their former employer's group health plan, purchasing a Medigap policy, or enrolling in a managed care plan through an HMO.
- Individuals age 65 or older cannot be denied Medigap coverage for health issues during open enrollment.
- There is a 6-month open enrollment period for purchasing Medigap policies.
- If the insured's medical bills exceed what Medicare covers, the insured needs a Medigap policy.
- An insured can only be covered by one Medicare supplement at a time. Selling more than one Medigap policy to the same individual is illegal.
- Long-term care policies and Medicare supplements have a 30-day free look.
- Medigap plan A covers 365 additional days of hospital care as a core benefit beyond what Medicare Part A covers during the policy owner's lifetime.

Medicaid

- Medicaid eligibility is based on a person's financial need. There is no age limit.
- Medicaid is medical welfare funded by local, state, and federal funds. It is available to low-income individuals and families.
- Medicaid provides the most coverage for nursing homes.

Social Security Benefits

- A disabled person must be fully insured to qualify for Social Security disability benefits.
- The waiting period before Social Security disability benefits begin is five months.
- Social Security disability benefits require that a disabled person cannot work any job. The disability is anticipated to last at least one year or result in death.

Other Health Insurance Concepts

Miscellaneous Health Insurance Concepts

- A recurrent disability is a prior injury that returns within a certain period (typically six months). The waiting period does not apply in the case of reoccurrence because it is the same injury.
- If a policy has residual disability coverage, it will pay the difference between what the insured used to earn before the disability and what the insured can currently earn.
- Health policies cover newborns from the moment they are born.
- The annual mode of payment for an insurance policy is the most inexpensive.
- In a medical expense policy, the coordination of benefits provision states that if the insured has two group policies, one is primary coverage, and one is excess coverage.
- Occupational coverage protects against both on- and off-the-job injuries for those not covered by workers compensation. Nonoccupational coverage protects off-the-job injuries only for those covered by workers compensation on the job.

- Workers compensation is mandatory on-the-job coverage for disability, sickness, or death.
- Subrogation allows the insurance provider to sue the negligent party to recover damages they have paid.

Tax Treatment of Premiums and Proceeds

- Premiums for AD&D or individual disability income policies are not tax-deductible.
- Premiums paid by individuals on medical expense policies can be tax-deductible if they exceed a certain percentage of their income.
- Premiums paid by an employer on a group health policy, like medical expenses, are tax-deductible since this is a fringe benefit to the employees.
- Benefits from an AD&D policy paid to a beneficiary are not taxable. They are treated similarly to life insurance proceeds.
- If the employer deducts the premium on a group policy, benefits are taxable.

Texas Statutes and Rules Common to Life and Health Insurance

Definitions

- Insurance transactions involve soliciting, negotiating, selling, and advising insurance products.
- Domestic insurance companies are those incorporated in the state of Texas.
- A foreign insurance company is an insurer with a home office in another state that has obtained a license from this state's insurance commissioner.
- An alien insurance company is an insurer based in another country with a Certificate of Authority admitting it to conduct business in Texas.
- An incorporated insurer owned by shareholders is called a stock insurer.
- Stock insurers sell nonparticipating policies and pay dividends to policy owners.
- Mutual insurers issue participating policies, which could pay a dividend.
- Mutual insurers can pay dividends to policy owners; however, dividends are not guaranteed.
- Dividends are a return of excess premiums in participating policies.
- A fraternal benefit society offers insurance benefits for members of affiliated religious organizations, lodges, or fraternal organizations with a representative form of government.
- A Certificate of Authority is a license issued by the Commissioner of Insurance to insurance carriers who meet the requirements to conduct business in a state.

Commissioner of Insurance

- The Commissioner's primary duty is to enforce state insurance laws and regulations to protect the general public.
- The insurance commissioner issues Certificates of Authority to insurance companies, allowing them to conduct business legally in a specific state.
- The Governor appoints the Commissioner for a 2-year term.
- The Commissioner must audit all authorized insurance companies no less frequently than once every five years.
- The Commissioner is responsible for determining if an insurance provider is insolvent.
- The insurance commissioner can issue a cease and desist order without a prior hearing.
- Emergency cease and desist orders become final 31 days after receiving them.
- Upon receiving the Commissioner's cease and desist order, the aggrieved party can request a hearing within 30 days.

- The Commissioner must hold hearings no more than ten days after receiving a hearing request.
- The Commissioner must enforce or annul the cease and desist order within 30 days after a hearing.
- After a hearing, the Commissioner can suspend, revoke, refuse to renew, or place a licensee who has violated the Insurance Code on probation.
- Violating a cease and desist order will carry a maximum penalty of $1,000 per violation, not exceeding $5,000 for all offenses.
- Violating the Insurance Code will carry a maximum penalty of $25,000.

Licensing Requirements

- A producer is a licensed individual who solicits, negotiates, or sells insurance contracts on behalf of an insurance provider.
- Producers only require a license in the state where they reside and any state where they transact insurance business.
- To obtain a license, an applicant must be 18, pass the licensing exam, pay the required licensing fees, and provide a complete set of fingerprints upon request from the Department of Insurance.
- A reciprocal agreement between Texas and other states allows Texas resident producers to obtain nonresident licenses in those states without passing a state licensing exam.
- An insurance counselor is a person who, for a fee, provides advice about the advantages or disadvantages of any insurance policy issued in Texas.
- Temporary licenses are available for up to 90 days without requiring a written examination.
- Corporations can hold agent licenses if eligibility requirements are satisfied.
- Employees, officers, or directors not involved in and compensated for selling insurance are not required to obtain a producer license.
- Salaried full-time employees who provide advice or counsel on the purchase of insurance are not required to be licensed as long as they do not receive commissions.
- An insurance carrier cannot appoint any person to act as their agent unless licensed.

License Maintenance and Duration

- Insurance licenses expire every two years on the license holder's birthday.
- Applicants whose license has expired for less than one year can obtain a new license without an exam.
- Agents must earn 24 hours of continuing education credits every two years, including 3 hours of ethics.
- Agents must maintain records of completed CE courses for at least four years.
- Producers must notify the Commissioner monthly of any change in address, felony conviction, or adverse administrative action against them in another state.
- Examples of actions that warrant license revocation, suspension, or probation include but are not limited to, intentional misstatements on a license application, felony convictions, and premium rebates.
- A producer with a revoked license must wait five years to file a new license application.

Marketing Practices

- An agent can only share commissions with another agent licensed for the same lines of insurance.
- Insurance providers must request forms, statements, and other items to begin an investigation within 15 business days of receiving a notice of a claim.

Unfair and Prohibited Trade Practices

- Misrepresentation is an unfair trade practice, including making misleading statements, ads, or illustrations. It also includes guaranteeing future dividends.

- Agents can be subject to license revocation or suspension for misrepresentation.
- Circulating deceptive sales material to the general public is considered misleading, deceptive, or false advertising and an unfair trade practice.
- A form of misrepresentation is false advertising.
- Defamation is making written or oral statements that are false or maliciously critical of an insurance company's or agent's financial condition.
- Rebating is giving something of value to induce the client to obtain an insurance policy, typically part of the paid premium or the commission received.
- Providing educational items, promotional materials, or merchandise is not considered rebating if the materials are given to every applicant or insured and do not exceed a $25 value.
- Combining premiums collected from insurance carriers with an agent's personal funds is commingling.
- Coercion is illegal and is considered to be a restraint of trade.
- Refusing coverage for individuals of the same class would be considered unfair discrimination.
- The availability or amount of coverage cannot be denied or reduced based on marital status.
- Fraud is intentional concealment or misrepresentation used to induce a party.
- An agent must report insurance fraud to the Insurance Fraud Unit of the Department of Insurance within 30 days.

Insurance Guaranty Association

- The Insurance Guaranty Association is designed to protect consumers if an insurer cannot fulfill contractual obligations due to insolvency.
- All insurance carriers must be members of the Insurance Guaranty Association.
- Producers are not allowed to make statements that the existence of the Insurance Guaranty Association guarantees an insurance company's policies.

Texas Statutes and Rules Pertinent to Life Insurance Only

Marketing and Solicitations

- Insurance providers are responsible for the content of their advertisements, regardless of who created them.
- Insurers must identify the name of the insurance company, agency, or agent in every advertisement.
- Illustrations are depictions or presentations that include non-guaranteed elements of a policy.
- Illustrations cannot represent the policy as anything other than life insurance.
- The comparative interest rate (CIR) is the rate of return that has to be earned on a hypothetical "side fund" in a buy-term-invest-the-difference plan. At a specified point in time, the value of the side fund will be equal to the illustrated cash surrender value of the policy with a higher premium.

Policy Provisions

- A new life insurance policy is contestable for two years from the issue date and incontestable after that.
- Both individual and group life insurance policies must contain a 31-day grace period during which the death benefit is payable.
- A policy owner has the right to borrow cash value from a policy on the condition that the policy has been effective for three years and no premium defaults have occurred.
- If an agent does not provide a disclosure and buyer's guide before delivering the application, the applicant must be allowed a 15-day free-look period.

- Viators can rescind a viatical settlement within 15 days of receiving proceeds.
- Life insurance policies cannot limit the time an insured can file a lawsuit against the insurance provider to less than two years after the cause of action.
- Insurers cannot backdate a policy more than six months before the application date.

Nonforfeiture Law

- In the event of the policy owner's default in premium payments, the insurance provider will allow a paid-up nonforfeiture benefit. A cash surrender benefit can be paid instead of the nonforfeiture benefit.
- After a policyholder surrenders an ordinary life policy, an insurer must pay a cash surrender value no later than 60 days after the premium due date. The policyholder must have paid premiums for three full years.

Group Life

- Group life coverage has to include every eligible employee.
- Group life requires a minimum of 2 employees as of the issue date.
- If the employer terminates a group policy, anyone impacted who has been insured for at least five years can convert to an individual policy without evidence of insurability.
- Upon termination of employment, group term life insurance must be convertible for 31 days to an individual life insurance policy, without evidence of insurability, at the insured's current age.
- If an insured misstates their age on a group life insurance application, the insurer will adjust the policy's face amount to what the paid premiums would have obtained if the insurer knew the correct age.
- Employers can extend coverage under a group life policy to the insured's spouse and eligible children.

Credit Life Insurance

- Most credit life policies are written as decreasing term insurance.
- The creditor is the owner and beneficiary of a credit life policy.
- Credit life cannot pay more than the balance of the debt.
- Creditors cannot require a debtor to purchase insurance through a specific insurer.

Replacement

- Replacement refers to any transaction in which a new life insurance policy or annuity is purchased while an existing policy has lapsed, been forfeited, surrendered, or terminated.
- A replacing insurer is the insurance provider who issues a new policy.
- An existing insurer is an insurance provider whose policy is replaced.
- Agents must give applicants a Notice Regarding Replacement at the time of application.
- Both the agent and the customer must sign the Notice Regarding Replacement.
- Replacing insurers must produce a list of policies being replaced and send a written communication to the existing insurer of the insured's intention to replace the policy.

Texas Statutes and Rules Pertinent to Accident and Health Only

Required Policy Provisions

- An insured's newborn children must be covered from birth.
- Insureds must notify insurers of a newborn within 31 days of birth.
- Insurers must provide coverage for alcohol and drug treatment on the same basis as physical illness.

- HIV test results cannot be released without the applicant's consent.
- Testing labs must provide written notice of positive HIV-related test results to the insured's designated physician or the Texas Department of Health.

Medicare Supplement

- A Medicare supplement policy cannot deny a claim for losses incurred within six months before the effective date of coverage.
- Coverage on a spouse cannot be terminated upon terminating the insured's coverage, except for nonpayment of premium.
- Medicare supplement policies are guaranteed renewable.
- Medicare supplement policies are required to give notice of the insured's right to return a policy within 30 days for a full refund (free look period).
- Medicare supplement policies must include a continuation or renewal provision stating the insurance company's rights to change premiums and any automatic renewal premium increases based on the insured's age.

Long-Term Care

- The renewability and duration of long-term care coverage must appear on the policy's first page.
- Long-term care policies must be noncancelable or guaranteed renewable.
- Agents must give prospective customers an outline of coverage when selling long-term care insurance.
- LTC policies must include a 30-day free-look period, during which the insured can return the policy for a full refund.

Small Group Health Insurance

- Small employer refers to a person, firm, partnership, corporation, or association that employs at least two but no more than 50 eligible employees during the preceding year.
- Coverage under a small employer group plan can only be available if at least 75% of employees participate.
- If a small group fails to meet participation requirements for six months, the insurance provider can terminate the group's health benefits.
- Small group insurance is not renewable if the number of employees does not qualify, an employer performs fraudulent acts, fails to pay premiums, fails to comply with contribution limits, or the insurer meets other state nonrenewal requirements.
- Small employer insurers must provide at least two standard benefit plans.

Affordable Care Act

- The Patient Protection and Affordable Care Act (PPACA) is also called the Affordable Care Act (ACA).
- This legislation requires children to remain as dependents on their parents' health plan until age 26, regardless of dependency, college status, or marital status.
- The Marketplaces are websites allowing individuals and small businesses to procure health insurance coverage.
- Premiums can vary based on the following factors:
  - Age (older individuals could be charged more than younger individuals)
  - Geographic location
  - Tobacco use
  - Individual vs. family enrollment
  - Plan category (bronze, silver, gold, platinum, catastrophic)

- Two cost reduction measures are available when a person qualifies based on need and purchases coverage on a Marketplace, including a Premium Tax Credit and a cost-sharing subsidy.
- The ACA requires health benefit plans to include coverage for the following ten essential health benefits:
  1. Emergency services
  2. Ambulatory patient services
  3. Laboratory services
  4. Hospitalization
  5. Prescription drugs
  6. Pediatric services, including vision and oral care
  7. Maternity and newborn care
  8. Mental health and substance abuse disorder services, including behavioral health treatment
  9. Rehabilitative and habilitative services and devices
  10. Chronic disease management and preventive and wellness services.
- The coverage must also include coverage for the employee's dependents.
- A full-time employee under the ACA is any person who works 30 hours or more on average per week.
- An employer subject to the ACA that does not offer health coverage to full-time employees and dependents will face an Employer Shared Responsibility Payment (penalty).
- An employer that offers health coverage to only employees but not dependents could also face a penalty.

Texas Statutes and Rules Pertinent to Health Maintenance Organizations (HMOs)

Overview and Definitions

- Health maintenance organizations (HMOs) finance health care for members on a prepaid basis.
- Individuals covered by an HMO contract are called subscribers.
- Subscribers pay a fixed periodic fee, regardless of the services used.
- HMOs usually operate through a group enrollment system, with each member paying a premium.
- Health maintenance organizations encourage preventive care.
- If medically necessary services are not covered through network providers or physicians, an HMO must allow referrals and fully reimburse referred non-network providers or physicians.
- Copayments are specific dollar amounts or percentages of the cost of care that has to be paid by a member.
- Coinsurance and deductibles are participation requirements that the insured must meet before the insurance policy pays.
- Copayments are expressed as a percentage; deductibles are expressed in dollar amounts.
- Prepaid services refer to the payment of a periodic membership fee, allowing the member to receive the services of member physicians and hospitals.
- Indemnity health insurance plans offer broad coverage for the medical expenses of any provider the insured selects.
- As an enrollee in an HMO, a subscriber has to choose a primary care physician (PCP), the person the subscriber must go to for their initial and primary care.
- Enrollees in an HMO need a referral from the PCP to see a specialist.
- Network-model HMOs contract with independent groups of physicians to provide medical services to subscribers.

Evidence of Coverage

- Evidence of coverage must include the HMO's name, address, phone number, schedule of benefits, deductibles, copayments, and policy cancellation and nonrenewal provisions.
- HMOs cannot charge for the immunizations of children younger than six years old unless a small employer health benefit plan covers children's immunizations.
- An HMO certificate of authority must include the schedule of charges to be used in the first year of operation.

Nonrenewal, Cancellation, and Prohibited Practices

- To cancel an HMO contract because of nonpayment of premiums, the insurer must provide the insured with 30 days advance written notice.
- Fifteen days' advance written notice is required to cancel an HMO contract due to material misrepresentation or fraud.
- HMOs are prohibited from allowing deceptive evidence of coverage or using misleading or untrue advertisements.

GLOSSARY

Accelerated Benefits – Riders attached to a life insurance policy that will allow death benefits to be used to pay for nursing or convalescent home expenses.

Accident – An unforeseen, unplanned event that occurs suddenly and at an unspecified place.

Accident Insurance – A type of insurance that protects the insured against loss caused by accidental bodily injury.

Accidental Bodily Injury – An unforeseen, unplanned traumatic injury to the body.

Accidental Death and Dismemberment (AD&D) – An insurance policy that pays a specific amount or a specific multiple of the insured's benefit amount if the insured dies, loses two limbs or loses sight due to an accident.

Accidental Death Benefits – A policy rider specifying that the cause of death will be examined to conclude if it complies with the policy's accidental death description.

Accidental Death Insurance – Insurance policies that pay if the insured's death is caused by an accident.

Accumulation Period – The period when the annuitant makes investments or payments in an annuity, and those payments earn tax-deferred interest.

Acquired Immunodeficiency Syndrome (AIDS) – An incurable and infectious disease caused by the human immunodeficiency virus (HIV).

Activities of Daily Living (ADLs) – Activities individuals need to do daily, such as getting dressed, moving about, eating, bathing, etc.

Actual Cash Value (ACV) – The required amount for property loss or to pay damages, which is calculated by subtracting depreciation from the property's current replacement value.

Actual Charge – The amount a supplier or physician bills for a particular supply or service.

Actuary – An individual trained in the technical aspects of insurance and related fields, particularly in insurance mathematics; an individual who, on behalf of the insurer, determines the mathematical probability of loss.

Adhesion – An insurance provider offers a contract on a "take-it-or-leave-it" basis. The insured's only choice is to accept or reject the agreement. Any contract ambiguities will be settled in the insured's favor.

Adjustable Life – Life insurance that allows changes in the premium amount, face amount, protection period, and duration of the premium payment period.

Adjuster – A representative of an insurance carrier who investigates and acts on the insurer's behalf to obtain agreements for the insurance claim amount.

Administrator – A person appointed by a court as a fiduciary to settle a deceased individual's financial affairs and estate.

Admitted (Authorized) Insurer – An insurer authorized to conduct business in a particular state.

Adult Daycare – A program for impaired adults that attempts to meet their functional, social, and health needs while away from home.

Adverse Selection – The tendency of risks with a higher probability of loss to buy and maintain insurance more often than the risks that present a lower probability.

Agency – An insurance company or sales office.

Agent – A person with a license to negotiate, sell, or effect insurance contracts on behalf of an insurance company.

Agent's Authority – Special powers granted to an agent by their agency contract.

Aleatory – A contract where the participating parties agree to exchange unequal amounts. Insurance contracts are aleatory; the amount the insurance company will pay in the event of a loss is unequal to the amount the insured will pay in premiums.

Alien Insurer – An insurance provider incorporated outside the U.S.

Alzheimer's Disease – A disease that causes victims to become dysfunctional because of the degeneration of brain cells, causing severe memory loss.

Ancillary – Additional, miscellaneous services provided by a hospital, such as lab work, X-rays, and anesthesia, but not hospital room and board expenses.

Annual Statement – An insurer must submit a detailed financial report each year to the Department of Insurance in any state where it conducts business.

Annuity – A contract that provides income for life or a specified period of years.

Apparent Authority – The appearance or assumption of authority based on the principal's words, actions, or deeds or due to circumstances the principal created.

Applicant – A person who submits an application for themselves or another individual to be insured under an insurance contract.

Application – A document that gathers information for underwriting purposes. Once a policy is issued, the insurance company considers any unanswered questions waived.

Approved Amount – The amount Medicare decides is reasonable for a service covered under Part B.

Assignment (Life) – The transfer of a life insurance policy's ownership rights from one person to another.

Assignment (Health) – A claim to a medical supplier or provider to receive payments directly from Medicare.

Attained Age – The age of the insured at a specified date.

Attending Physician's Statement (APS) – A statement commonly obtained from the applicant's doctor.

Authorized (Admitted) Insurer – An insurance provider authorized and licensed to conduct business in a specific state or commonwealth.

Avoidance – A method to deal with risk by deliberately avoiding it (e.g., if an individual wanted to avoid the risk of being killed in a helicopter crash, they might choose never to fly in a helicopter).

Back-End Load – A fee charged when a sale, transfer, or withdrawal from a life insurance policy or an annuity occurs.

Basic Hospital Expense Insurance – Coverage for doctor visits, emergency room visits, x-rays, and lab tests; benefits are limited to specified dollar amounts.

Basic Illustration – A proposal or ledger used to sell a life insurance policy that shows guaranteed and non-guaranteed elements.

Basic Medical Expense Insurance – Coverage for doctor visits, emergency room visits, x-rays, and lab tests; benefits, however, are limited to specified dollar amounts.

Beneficiary – The individual to receive the policy's proceeds when the insured dies.

Benefit Period – The period during which the insurer will pay the insurance benefits for each disability, illness, or hospital stay.

Binder (Binding Receipt) – A temporary contract that binds a policy before the premium is paid (puts an insurance policy into force).

Birthday Rule – A method of determining a dependent child's primary coverage. The parent with the health plan whose birthday occurs first in the calendar year will be designated as primary coverage.

Blanket Medical Insurance – A policy covering all medical costs, including hospitalization, doctor visits, and drugs.

Boycott – An unfair trade practice where one party refuses to do business with another until they agree to certain conditions.

Broker – An individual representing an insured in negotiating and obtaining an insurance contract.

Buy-Sell Agreement – A legal contract determining what will happen to a business if an owner becomes disabled or dies.

Buyer's Guide – A booklet describing insurance policies and concepts that provides general information to help applicants make educated decisions.

Cafeteria Plan – A selection of health care benefits from which employees can select the benefits they need.

Capital Amount – A percentage of a policy's principal amount paid to the insured if they suffer the loss of an appendage.

Carriers – Entities that process claims and pay benefits in an insurance policy.

Cash Value – The amount a policy owner is entitled to when the policy is surrendered before maturity.

Cease and Desist Order – A demand for an individual to stop committing an action violating a provision.

Certificate – A statement (or booklet) describing the coverage and confirming that a policy has been written.

Certificate of Authority – A document that authorizes insurers to conduct business and specifies the kind of insurance a carrier can transact. It is illegal for an insurer to transact insurance without this certificate.

Certificate of Insurance – A legal document indicating that an insurance policy has been issued. It specifies the types and amounts of insurance provided.

Claim – A request to receive benefits provided by an insurance policy.

Coercion – An unfair trade practice in which an insurance company uses physical or mental force to persuade applicants to purchase insurance.

Coinsurance – An agreement between insureds and insurers in which both parties are expected to pay a portion of the possible loss and other expenses.

Coinsurance Clause – This provision specifies how the insured and the insurer will share the losses covered by the policy. The proportions are agreed upon in advance.

Commingling – A practice in which individuals in a fiduciary capacity illegally mix their personal funds with funds they hold in trust.

Commission – The payment made by insurers to producers or brokers for selling and servicing policies.

Commissioner (Director, Superintendent) – The chief executive and administrative officer of a state Department of Insurance.

Comprehensive Policy – A plan that provides health care services, including immunization, routine physicals, preventive care, outpatient services, and hospitalization.

Comprehensive Major Medical – A combination of basic coverage and major medical coverage that features high maximum benefits, low deductibles, and coinsurance.

Concealment – Intentionally withholding known facts that can void a contract if the facts are material.

Conditional Contract – An agreement in which both parties must perform specific duties and follow rules of conduct to make the contract enforceable.

Consideration – A contract's binding force that requires exchanging something of value for the transfer of risk. The insured's consideration is the representations made in the application and the payment of the premium; the insurer's consideration is the promise to pay in the event of a loss.

Consideration Clause – A part of the insurance contract that specifies both parties must give something of value for the transfer of risk and stipulates the conditions of the exchange.

Consolidated Omnibus Budget Reconciliation Act (COBRA) of 1986 – The law allows for the continuation of group health care benefits for insureds for up to 18 months if they terminate employment or are no longer eligible and for dependents of insureds for up to 36 months in cases of the loss of eligibility because of the insured's death, divorce, or attainment of the limiting age.

Consumer Reports – Written or oral statements about a consumer's character, credit, reputation, or habits collected by a reporting agency from credit reports, employment records, and other public sources.

Contract – A legal agreement between two or more parties that is enforceable under the law.

Contributory – A group insurance plan requiring the employees to pay a portion of the premium.

Controlled Business – An entity that acquires and possesses a license solely to write business on the owner, relatives, immediate family, employer, and employees.

Convertible – A policy that can be exchanged for another type of policy by a contractual provision, at the policy owner's option, and without evidence of insurability (e.g., term life converted to a form of permanent life).

Coordination of Benefits – This provision determines the primary insurer in situations where an insured is covered by more than one policy, ultimately avoiding claim overpayments.

Co-pay – An arrangement in which an insured pays a specified amount for services "up front," and the insurance provider pays the remainder of the cost.

Countersignature – The act of signing an insurance contract by a licensed agent.

Coverage – The inclusion of perils (causes of loss) covered within a policy's scope.

Credit Life Insurance – A special type of insurance written to pay off a loan balance in the event of the debtor's death.

CSO Table – (The Commissioner's Standard Ordinary Table) A mortality table in life insurance that mathematically predicts the probability of death.

Custodial Care – Care to help an insured complete their activities of daily living (ADLs).

Death Benefit – The amount payable upon the death of the individual whose life is insured.

Decreasing Term – A type of life insurance with a level premium and a death benefit that decreases yearly throughout the policy.

Deductible – The portion of the loss paid by the insured before the insurer can pay any claim benefits.

Defamation – An unfair trade practice where one agent or insurance provider makes a defamatory statement about another, intending to harm the person or company's reputation.

Dependent – An individual who relies on another for support and maintenance.

Director (Commissioner, Superintendent) – The head of the state Department of Insurance.

Disability – A mental or physical impairment, either congenital or resulting from a sickness or injury.

Disability Income Insurance – Health insurance that provides periodic payments to replace an insured's income when ill or injured.

Disclosure – Identifying the name of the producer, representative, limited insurance representative, firm, or temporary insurance producer on any policy solicitation.

Domestic Insurer – An insurance provider that conducts business in the state of incorporation.

Domicile of Insurer – An insurer's location of incorporation and the legal capacity to write business in a state.

Dread (Specified) Disease Policy – A policy with a high maximum limit that covers certain diseases named in the contract (such as meningitis and polio).

Dual Choice – A federal requirement for employers with 25 or more employees that pay minimum wage and offer a health plan within a qualified HMO's service area to provide HMO coverage and an indemnity plan.

Earned Premium – The portion of the premium for which the insurer delivers policy protection.

Effective Date – When an insurance policy begins (called the inception date).

Eligibility Period – The period in which an employee can enroll in a group health care plan without evidence of insurability.

Elimination Period – A waiting period imposed on the insured from the onset of a disability until benefit payments begin.

Emergency – An injury or disease that occurs suddenly and requires treatment within 24 hours.

Employee Retirement Income Security Act (ERISA) – A law stipulating federal standards for private pension plans.

Endodontics – An area of dentistry that deals with preventing, diagnosing, and treating the dental pulp within natural teeth at the root canal.

Endorsement – A form that changes the provisions of a life insurance policy (also called a rider).

Endow – To reach the maturity date or time when the face amount equals the cash value.

Enrollment Period – The time employees have to enroll in a contributory group health plan.

Errors and Omissions Policy (E&O) – A professional liability insurance policy that protects the insurance provider from claims by the insured for mistakes or oversights on the insurer's part.

Estoppel – A legal obstruction to denying a fact or restoring a right that has been previously waived.

Excess Charge – The difference between the amount approved by Medicare for a service or supply and the actual charge.

Excess Insurance – Insurance that will pay over and above or in addition to the basic policy limits.

Exclusions – Causes of exposures, losses, conditions, etc., for which insurers will not pay insurance benefits.

Executory Contract – A contract that has not yet been fulfilled by one or both parties and promises action in the event of a specified future event.

Expiration – The date of termination listed in the policy.

Explanation of Benefits (EOB) – A statement outlining the services rendered, insurance company payments, and the insured's billing amounts.

Explanation of Medicare Benefits – A statement to a Medicare patient specifying how the insurer will settle the Medicare claim.

Exposure – A unit of measure used to calculate insurance coverage rates.

Express Authority – The authority granted to an agent due to the agent's written contract.

Extended Care Facility – A facility licensed by the state to provide 24-hour nursing care.

Extension of Benefits – A provision allowing coverage to continue beyond the policy expiration date for employees not at work because of a disability or who have hospitalized dependents on that date. This coverage continues until the employee returns to work or the dependent leaves the hospital.

Face – The policy's first page.

Fair Credit Reporting Act – A federal law establishing procedures for consumer-reporting agencies to follow to ensure that records are accurate, confidential, relevant, and properly used.

Fiduciary – An agent or broker handling an insurance company's funds in a trust capacity.

Fixed Annuity – An annuity offering fixed payments that guarantees a minimum interest rate will be credited to the annuity purchase.

Flexible Premium – A policy feature allowing the policy owner to vary the amount and frequency of premium payments.

Flexible Spending Account (FSA) – A salary reduction cafeteria plan that uses employee funds to offer various health care benefits.

Foreign Insurer – An insurance provider incorporated in another state or commonwealth.

Fraternal Benefit Societies – Life or health insurance carriers formed to provide insurance for members of an affiliated religious organization, lodge, or fraternal organization with a representative form of government.

Fraud – Intentional deceit or misrepresentation to induce an individual to part with something of value.

Free Look – A period during which a policy owner can inspect a newly issued individual life or health insurance policy for a specific number of days and surrender it in exchange for a full premium refund.

Front-End Load – A fee or commission charged when purchasing a security or an annuity.

Gatekeeper Model – A model of HMO and PPO organizations that uses the insured's primary care physician, also known as a gatekeeper, as the patient's initial contact for medical care and referrals.

Grace Period – The time after the premium due date during which policy owners can still pay premiums, and the policy and its riders remain in force.

Group Disability Insurance – A type of insurance that covers a group of people against loss of pay due to sickness or an accident.

Group Health Insurance – Health coverage offered to members of a group.

Group Life – Life insurance provided to members of a group.

Hazard – A situation that increases the probability of a loss.

Hazard (Moral) – A person's character, reputation, living habits, etc., affect their insurability.

Hazard (Morale) – The impact of a person's indifference to loss on the insured risk.

Hazard (Physical) – A type of hazard arising from a person's physical characteristics, such as a physical disability caused by either current circumstances or a condition present at birth.

Health Insurance – Protection against loss because of sickness or bodily injury.

Health Maintenance Organization (HMO) – A prepaid medical service plan in which specified providers contract with the HMO to deliver services. The focus of the HMO is preventive medicine.

Health Reimbursement Accounts (HRAs) – Health plans that let employers set aside funds to reimburse employees for qualified medical expenses.

Health Savings Accounts (HSAs) – Health plans intended to help individuals save for qualified health expenses.

Home Health Agency – An agency certified by the insured's health plan that delivers health care services under the contract.

Home Health Care – A type of care in which a home health aide or part-time nursing services, speech therapy, occupational therapy, or physical therapy services are provided in the insured's home.

Home Health Services – A covered expense under Medicare Part A in which a licensed home health agency provides home health care to an insured.

Hospice – A facility for the terminally ill that offers supportive care such as symptom relief and pain management to the patient and their family. Medicare Part A covers hospice care.

Hospital Confinement Rider – An optional disability income rider that waives the elimination period when an insured is admitted to a hospital as an inpatient.

Implied Authority – Authority not expressed or written in the contract. The agent is assumed to transact insurance business on behalf of the principal.

Income Replacement Contracts – Policies that replace a certain percentage of the insured's pure income loss due to a covered accident or sickness.

Indemnify – To restore the insured to the same condition as before the occurrence of loss with no intent to lose or gain.

Illustration – A proposal or ledger used to sell a life insurance policy that presents guaranteed and non-guaranteed elements.

Insolvent organization – A member organization that cannot pay its financial obligations and is placed under a final liquidation or rehabilitation order by a court.

Insurability – The acceptability of an applicant who satisfies an insurance company's underwriting requirements.

Insurable Interest – A financial interest in the life of another individual. It involves the possibility of losing something of value if the insured dies. Insurable interest must be specified at the time of policy issue.

Insurance – A contract under which one party (insurer) indemnifies or guarantees another party (insured) against a loss caused by a specified future peril or contingency in return for a premium payment.

Insured – The individual or organization covered by insurance; the party to be indemnified.

Insurer – An entity that indemnifies against losses, pays benefits, or provides services. It is also known as an "insurance company," "insurance provider," or "insurance carrier."

Insuring Clause – A general statement identifying the basic agreement between the insurer and the insured, generally located on the first page of the policy.

Integrated LTC Rider – A rider attached to a life insurance policy to pay long-term care benefits. The benefits available for LTC depend upon the life insurance benefits available; however, the benefits paid toward LTC will decrease the life insurance policy's benefits.

Intentional Injury – An act that intends to cause an injury. Self-inflicted injuries are not covered, but intentional injuries inflicted on the insured by another person are protected.

Intermediaries – Organizations that process inpatient and outpatient claims on individuals from hospitals, home health agencies, skilled nursing facilities, hospices, and certain other providers of health services.

Intermediate Care – A level of care one step down from skilled nursing care; it is given under the supervision of physicians or registered nurses.

Investigative Consumer Report – Reports similar to consumer reports in that they also deliver information on the consumer's reputation, character, and habits.

Issue Age – The person's age when a policy is issued.

Joint Life – A single policy insuring two or more lives.

Juvenile Life – A life insurance policy written on the life of a minor child.

Lapse – Terminating a policy because the premium was not paid by the end of the policy grace period.

Law of Large Numbers – A principle that states the larger the number of similar units of exposure, the more closely the reported losses will equal the probability of loss.

Legal Reserve – The accounting measurement of an insurance provider's future obligations to pay claims to policy owners.

Level Premium – A policy premium that remains the same during the period premiums are paid.

Life Expectancy – The average number of years remaining for an individual of a given age to live, as displayed on the mortality table.

Limited-Pay Whole Life – This type of whole life insurance charges a low annual premium and offers a guaranteed death benefit until the insured reaches the age of 100. It will endow for the face amount if the insured reaches age 100. A limited-pay life policy allows the policy owner to pay up the premiums for coverage entirely before age 100.

Limited Policies – Health insurance policies that only cover specific diseases or accidents.

Limiting Charge – The maximum amount a physician can charge a Medicare beneficiary for a covered service if the physician does not accept the assignment for the Medicare-approved amount.

Liquidation – Selling assets as a means of raising capital.

Living Benefits Rider – A rider added to life insurance policies that provide LTC benefits or benefits for the terminally ill.

Lloyd's Associations – Organizations that offer support facilities to underwriters or groups that accept insurance risk.

Loan Value – The amount of money a policy owner can borrow using the cash value of their life insurance policy as collateral.

Long-Term Care (LTC) – Health and social services provided under the supervision of physicians and medical health professionals for individuals with disabilities or chronic diseases. Care is usually given in a long-term care facility, a state-licensed facility that offers such services.

Long-Term Disability Insurance – A type of individual or group insurance that covers illness until the insured reaches age 65 and for life in the event of an accident.

Loss – The decrease, reduction, or disappearance of value to a person or property insured under a policy by a peril insured against.

Loss of Income Insurance – This insurance pays benefits for the inability to work due to a disability resulting from accidental bodily injury or sickness.

Lump-Sum – A settlement method that pays the beneficiary the proceeds of a life insurance policy in one lump-sum payment rather than in installments.

Major Medical Insurance – A type of health insurance that typically carries a large deductible and pays covered expenses up to a high limit whether the insured is in or out of the hospital.

Maturity Date – When the life insurance policy's face amount becomes payable.

Medicaid – A medical benefits program for individuals whose income and financial resources are insufficient to cover the cost of necessary medical care jointly administered by the individual states and the federal government.

Medical Expense Insurance – Insurance that pays benefits for medical, hospital, and surgical costs.

Medical Information Bureau (MIB) – An information database that contains the health histories of individuals who have applied for insurance in the past. Most insurers subscribe to this database for underwriting purposes.

Medical Savings Account – An employer-funded account connected to a high deductible medical insurance plan.

Medicare – A United States federal government plan that pays for qualified individuals' specific hospital and medical expenses.

Medicare Supplement Insurance – A type of individual or group insurance that fills the gaps in the level of protection provided by Medicare.

Medigap – Medicare supplement plans issued by private insurers designed to fill in some of the Medicare coverage gaps.

Misrepresentation – A lie or false statement that can void the contract.

Mode of Payment – The premium payment method, whether monthly, quarterly, semiannually, or annually.

Morbidity Rate – The ratio of sickness incidents to the number of healthy individuals in a given group over a particular period.

Morbidity Table – A table listing the incidence of sickness at specified ages.

Mortality Table – A table listing the probability of death at specified ages.

Multiple-Employer Trust (MET) – A group of small employers not eligible for individual group insurance. It is formed to establish a self-funded plan or group health plan.

Multiple Employer Welfare Association (MEWA) – Any organization of at least two employers, other than an admitted insurer, that establishes an employee benefit plan to provide accident, sickness, or death benefits to employees.

Mutual Companies – Insurance companies with no capital stock but are owned by the policy owners.

Natural Premium – The amount of premium needed from each group member of the same risk, age, and sex to pay $1,000 for every death that occurs in the group each year.

Nonadmitted (Nonauthorized) – An insurer who has not applied for or has been denied a Certificate of Authority and cannot transact insurance business in a particular state.

Nonauthorized (Nonadmitted) – An insurer who has not applied for or has been denied a Certificate of Authority and cannot transact insurance business in a particular state.

Noncancelable – An insurance policy that the insured has a right to remain effective by paying premiums that stay the same for a substantial period.

Nonforfeiture Values – Those guaranteed values in a life insurance policy that cannot be taken from the policy owner, even if they cease to pay the premiums.

Nonmedical – A life or health insurance policy underwritten based on the insured's statement of health, not a medical exam.

Non-Participating Policies (Non-Par) – Insurance policies that do not pay dividends.

Nonqualified Plan – A benefit plan that can discriminate, is not required to be filed with the IRS and does not offer a tax deduction for contributions.

Nonrenewal – Terminating a policy by an insurance provider on the renewal or anniversary date.

Nonresident Agent – An agent licensed in a state or commonwealth where they are not a resident.

Notice of Claim – A provision specifying an insured's responsibility to provide the insurer with reasonable notice in the event of a loss.

Omnibus Budget Reconciliation Act – A federal law that authorized the NAIC to create a standardized model for Medicare Supplement policies.

Option – A choice of how owners receive death benefits, policy dividends, nonforfeiture values, or cash values.

Oral Surgery – Operative mouth treatment, including teeth extractions and related surgical treatment.

Orthodontics – A unique field in dentistry that involves treating natural teeth to prevent or correct dental anomalies with appliances or braces.

Out-of-Pocket Costs – Amounts an insured has to pay for deductibles and coinsurance before the insurance provider will pay its portion.

Over Insurance – An excessive amount of insurance resulting in the insured being overpaid if a loss occurs.

Paid-Up Insurance – Policies for which all premiums have been paid but have not yet matured due to death or endowment.

Parol – A legal term that differentiates oral statements from written statements.

Parol Evidence Rule – This rule states that a contract cannot be altered without the parties' written consent. In other words, an oral agreement cannot change the contract.

Partial Disability – The ability to perform some but not all of the duties of the insured's occupation because of sickness or injury.

Participating Policies (Par) – Insurance policies that pay dividends to policy owners.

Payment of Claims – A provision that states to whom insurers will make claims payments.

Payor Benefit – A rider in juvenile policies waives the premiums if the individual paying them (usually the parent) is disabled or dies while the child is a minor.

Peril – The cause of a potential loss.

Periodontics – A specialty of dentistry that involves treatment of the supporting and surrounding tissue of the teeth, such as treatment for gum disease.

Permanent Disability – Disability from which the insured never recovers.

Permanent Life Insurance – A term used to refer to various whole life insurance policies that remain effective to age 100 as long as the premium is paid.

Persistency – The tendency or likelihood of an insurance policy not lapsing or being replaced by insurance from another provider.

Personal Contract – An agreement between an insurance provider and an individual stating the insurance policy will cover the individual's insurable interest.

Physical Exam and Autopsy – A provision allowing an insurer to have an insured physically examined when a claim is pending at its own expense. Insurers can also have an autopsy conducted where not prohibited by law.

Policy Loan – A nonforfeiture value in which an insurance provider loans a part or all of the policy's cash value assigned as security for the loan to the policy owner.

Policyholder – The individual who possesses the policy, generally the insured.

Policy owner – The individual entitled to exercise the owner's rights and privileges in the policy. This person does not have to be the insured.

Pre-Existing Condition – A physical condition existing before the policy's effective date and is typically excluded from coverage.

Preferred Provider Organization (PPO) – An organization of medical professionals and hospitals that offers services to an insurer's clients for a set fee.

Preferred Risk – A classification for insurance applicants who are less likely to incur a loss and are covered at a reduced rate.

Premium – A periodic insurance payment to keep the policy in force.

Presumptive Disability – A provision found in most disability income policies specifying the conditions that will automatically qualify the insured for full disability benefits.

Primary Beneficiary – The individual named the first beneficiary to receive benefits from a policy.

Primary Policy – A basic, fundamental insurance policy paying first out of other outstanding policies.

Principal Amount – The entire face value of a policy.

Private Insurance – Insurance provided by a nongovernmental insurance organization.

Pro Rata Cancellation – Terminating an insurance policy and adjusting the premium proportionate to the exact coverage in force.

Probationary Period – The time between a health insurance policy's effective date and when coverage begins.

Proceeds – The amount payable by the insurer, typically at the insured's death or when the policy matures.

Producer – An insurance broker or agent.

Proof of Loss – A claim form claimants must submit after a loss occurs.

Prosthodontics – A unique area of dentistry involving replacing missing teeth with artificial devices like dentures or bridgework.

Provider – Any individual or group who provides health care services.

Pure Protection – Insurance in which premiums are paid for protection in the event of disability or death rather than for cash value accumulation.

Pure Risk – The uncertainty or chance of a loss taking place in a circumstance that can only result in a loss or no change.

Qualified Plan – A retirement plan that satisfies the IRS guidelines for receiving favorable tax treatment.

Rate Service Organization – An organization formed by or on behalf of a group of insurance providers to develop and file rates with the Department of Insurance. It can also act as a collection point for actuarial data.

Rebating – Any inducement offered while selling insurance products not stated in the policy.

Reciprocal Exchange – An unincorporated group of people who mutually insure one another, with each separately taking on a share of each risk.

Reciprocity – A situation in which two parties provide each other the same advantages or help. For example, Producer A, who lives in New Jersey, can transact business as a nonresident in Virginia if Virginia's resident producers can transact business in New Jersey.

Recurrent Disability – A policy provision specifying the period during which the recurrence of an illness or injury will be a continuation of a prior period of disability.

Reduction – Decreasing the possibility or severity of a loss.

Reinsurance – A form of reinsurance in which one insurer (the reinsurer) indemnifies another insurer (the ceding insurer) for part or all of its policy liabilities in exchange for a premium.

Renewability Clause – A clause defining the insurance provider's and the insured's right to renew or cancel coverage.

Renewable Term – Insurance that can, at the insured's direction, be renewed at the end of a term without providing evidence of insurability.

Representations – An applicant's statements on the insurance application that are believed to be accurate but are not guaranteed to be true.

Rescission – Terminating an insurance contract due to material misrepresentation by the insured or misrepresentation, fraud, or duress on the agent's or insurer's part.

Reserve – An amount representing potential or actual liabilities kept by insurance providers in a separate account to cover debts to policy owners.

Residual Disability – A disability income policy that pays benefits for the loss of income when a person returns to work following a total disability but is still unable to perform at the same level as before the disability.

Respite Care – Temporary health or medical care provided by a nursing facility where a patient stays or by paid workers who go to the caregiver's home to give them a short rest.

Restorative Care – An area of dentistry involving treatments such as crowns or fillings that restore the functional use of natural teeth.

Retention – A method to deal with risk by intentionally or unintentionally retaining a portion of it for the insured's account. It is the amount of responsibility assumed but not reinsured by the insurance provider.

Rider – A supplemental agreement attached to and made a part of the policy indicating the policy's expansion by added coverage or a waiver of a condition or coverage.

Right to Return (Free Look) – The period during which a policy owner can inspect a new individual life or health insurance policy for a specified number of days and surrender it for a full refund of the premium if they are unsatisfied.

Risk – Uncertainty regarding the outcome of an event when two or more possibilities exist.

Risk Retention Group – A liability insurance provider owned by its members, who are exposed to similar liability risks because they are in the same industry or business.

Rollover – Withdrawing the money from a qualified plan and depositing it into another qualified plan.

Secondary Beneficiary – The individual named to receive benefits upon the insured's death if the (primary) first-named beneficiary is no longer living or does not collect all the benefits because of their death.

Service Plans – Insurance plans where the health care services are the benefits rather than the monetary ones.

Settlement Options – Choices are available to the insured/policy owner to distribute insurance proceeds.

Sharing – A method to deal with risk for a group of individuals or businesses with a similar or the same exposure to loss who share the losses within that group.

Short-Rate Cancellation – Canceling a policy with a less than proportionate return of premium.

Short-Term Disability Insurance – A group or individual policy that covers disabilities lasting 13 to 26 weeks and, in some cases, for up to two years.

Sickness – A physical disease, illness, or pregnancy, but not a mental illness.

Single Premium Whole Life (SPWL) – A life insurance policy that provides a level death benefit to the insured's age 100 for a one-time, lump-sum payment.

Skilled Nursing Care – Daily skilled care or nursing care, such as medication administration, diagnosis, or minor surgery, performed by or under the supervision of a qualified professional.

Speculative Risk – The uncertainty or opportunity of a loss occurring in a situation involving the chance for a loss or gain.

Spendthrift Clause – A clause preventing the debtors of a beneficiary from collecting the benefits before the beneficiary receives them.

Standard Provisions – State-approved requirements that must appear in every insurance policy.

Standard Risk – An insured or applicant with an average probability of loss based on their health, vocation, and lifestyle.

Stock Companies – Companies owned by stockholders whose investments provide the necessary capital to establish and operate the insurer.

Straight Life – A basic policy charging a level annual premium for the insured's lifetime and providing guaranteed level death benefits.

Subrogation – The legal process by which an insurer seeks recovery of an amount paid to the insured from a third party who might have caused the loss.

Substandard Risk – An insured or applicant who has a higher than average probability of loss and who may be charged an increased premium.

Superintendent (Director, Commissioner) – The head of a state's insurance department.

Supplemental Illustration – An illustration given in addition to a basic illustration that can be presented in a different format than the basic illustration but can only show a scale of non-guaranteed elements allowed in a basic illustration.

Surrender – An act of giving up a life policy, in which the insurance provider will pay the insured the policy's accumulated cash value.

Term Insurance – Insurance that offers protection for a specified period.

Terminally Ill – A patient with a terminal diagnosis who is expected to die within a specified amount of time listed in the policy.

Tertiary Beneficiary – The third in line to receive the death benefits of a life insurance policy.

Total Disability – A condition that prevents a person from performing the duties of any occupation due to sickness or injury.

Transfer – An insurance principle where the risk of financial loss is assigned to another party.

Twisting – A misrepresentation where a producer persuades an insured/policy owner to lapse, cancel, or switch policies, even to the insured's disadvantage.

Underwriter – Reviewing, accepting, or rejecting insurance applications.

Underwriting – The process of reviewing, accepting, or rejecting insurance applications.

Unearned Premium – The portion of a premium for which policy protection has not yet been provided.

Unilateral Contract – A contract legally binding only one party to contractual obligations once the premium is paid.

Universal Life – A combination of adjustable life insurance and a flexible premium.

Utmost Good Faith – The fair and equitable bargaining by both parties when forming the contract, where the applicant must disclose risk to the insurer, and the insurer must be fair in underwriting the risk.

Valued Contract – A disability insurance/life insurance contract that pays a specified amount in the event of a loss.

Viatical Settlement – An arrangement that allows a person with a life-threatening condition to sell an existing life insurance and use the proceeds when they are needed most, before death.

Waiting Period – The time between the start of a disability and when an insured starts receiving disability insurance benefits.

Waiver – The voluntary abandonment of a known advantage or legal right.

Waiver of Cost – A disability rider in Universal Life Insurance that waives the insurance cost. It does not waive the cost of premiums needed to accumulate cash values.

Waiver of Premium – A continuation of life insurance coverage if the policy owner becomes disabled and cannot pay the premiums.

Warranty – A stipulation in the policy that, if breached, can void the coverage.

Whole Life Insurance – Insurance that remains in force for a person's entire life and pays a benefit upon their death, whenever that may be.

Workers Compensation – Benefits required by the state to be paid to an employee by an employer in case of a disability, injury, or death resulting from an on-the-job hazard.

PRACTICE EXAM:

1

Test your readiness

You are about to take a Texas Life, Accident, and Health practice exam. This exam consists of *145 questions (130 scoreable questions plus 15 pretest questions)* and is *2 hours and 30 minutes* long. It is better to wait until you can fully devote your attention to completing it in the allotted time if you do not have enough time to complete this exam right now.

Any skipped questions will be graded as incorrect. The following chart breaks down the number of questions in each chapter and by topic.

General Knowledge *(100 scoreable questions plus 10 pretest questions)*	# of Questions
Completing the Application, Underwriting, and Delivering the Policy	12
Types of Life Policies	15
Life Policy Riders, Provisions, Options, and Exclusions	15
Taxes, Retirement, and Other Insurance Concepts	8
Field Underwriting Procedures	8
Types of Health Policies	16
Health Policy Provisions, Clauses, and Riders	15
Social Insurance	6
Other Insurance Concepts	5
Texas State Law *(30 scoreable questions plus 5 pretest questions)*	
Texas Statutes and Rules Common to Life and Health Insurance	14
Texas Statutes and Rules Pertinent to Life Insurance Only	6
Texas Statutes and Rules Pertinent to Accident and Health Insurance Only	7
Texas Statutes and Rules Pertinent to Health Maintenance Organizations (HMOs)	3

Raw scores will be converted to scaled scores that range from 0 to 100. The scaled score you receive is neither the number of correctly answered questions nor the percentage of questions correctly answered. A passing score is 70. Any score below 70 demonstrates how close you came to passing. The exam score is not based on each portion separately but on each exam as a whole.

Your exam is divided into multiple parts. You will now be presented with the General Knowledge portion.

#1. Who is responsible for bearing all the investment risk in a fixed annuity?

a) The beneficiary
b) The annuitant
c) The insurance company
d) The owner

#2. Which of the following best describes the annuity period?

a) The length of time from the accumulation period to the annuitization period
b) The length of time during which money is accumulated in an annuity
c) The length of time from the contract's effective date to the date of termination
d) The length of time during which accumulated money is converted into income payments

#3. Which nonforfeiture option delivers coverage for the longest period?

a) Accumulated at interest
b) Reduced paid-up
c) Extended-term
d) Paid-up option

#4. Under an individual disability policy, the MINIMUM schedule of time in which claim payments have to be made to an insured is

a) Within 45 days.
b) Weekly.
c) Biweekly.
d) Monthly.

#5. Which of the following descriptions accurately describes equity-indexed annuities?

a) They are riskier than variable annuities
b) They are security instruments
c) Equity-indexed annuities invest conservatively
d) Equity-indexed annuities seek higher returns

#6. Concerning group health insurance, COBRA stipulates that

a) Terminated employees have to be allowed to convert their group coverage to individual policies.
b) Group coverage has to be extended for terminated employees up to a certain period of time at the expense of the employer.
c) Group coverage must be extended for recently terminated employees up to a certain period of time at the former employee's expense.
d) Retiring employees have to be allowed to convert their group coverage to individual policies.

#7. When the insured purchased her health policy, she was a window washer. She has since changed occupations and now manages a library. If the insurance provider is notified of the insured's change of occupation, the insurer should

a) Replace the policy with a new one.
b) Return any unearned premium.
c) Increase the premium.
d) Adjust the benefit according to the reduced risk.

#8. An insured commits suicide one year after his life insurance policy was issued. The insurer will

a) Pay nothing.
b) Refund the premiums paid.
c) Pay the policy's cash value.
d) Pay the full death benefit to the beneficiary.

#9. Which of the following is NOT provided by a Health Maintenance Organization?

a) Services
b) Financing
c) Patient care
d) Reimbursement

#10. An insured stated on his application for life insurance that he had never had a heart attack when, in fact, he had a series of minor heart attacks last year, for which he sought medical attention. Which of these will explain why a claim for death benefits is denied?

a) Waiver
b) Utmost Good Faith
c) Estoppel
d) Material misrepresentation

#11. Who is a third-party owner?

a) An insurance provider who issues a policy for two people
b) An employee in a group policy
c) An irrevocable beneficiary
d) A policy owner who is not the insured

#12. An agent makes a mistake on the application and then corrects their mistake by physically entering the necessary information. Who has to initial that change, then?

a) Executive officer of the company
b) Insured
c) Agent
d) Applicant

#13. Which of the following is allowed under the free-look provision?

a) A right to return the policy for a full refund of the premium
b) Immediate coverage when the application is submitted
c) A guarantee that the policy will not lapse if the premium is past due
d) A guarantee that the policy will be issued

#14. COBRA applies to employers with

a) At least 60 employees.
b) At least 50 employees.
c) At least 20 employees.
d) At least 80 employees.

#15. Who picks the primary care physician in an HMO?

a) An HMO's subscribers do not have a primary care physician
b) The insurance provider
c) A referral physician
d) The individual member

#16. Which of these is true regarding elimination periods and the cost of coverage?

a) A longer elimination period means a higher cost of coverage
b) An elimination period does not affect the cost of coverage.
c) A longer elimination period means a lower cost of coverage
d) A shorter elimination period means a lower cost of coverage

#17. Many producers try to collect the initial premium to submit with the application. When a producer collects the initial premium from the applicant, the producer should issue the applicant a

a) Warranty.
b) Premium receipt.
c) Statement of good health.
d) Backdated receipt.

#18. The minimum rate of interest on an equity-indexed annuity is often based on

a) An index like the Standard & Poor's 500.
b) The returns from the insurer's separate account.
c) The annuitant's individual stock portfolio.
d) The insurer's general account investments.

#19. Which provision states that the insurance provider must pay Medical Expense claims immediately?

a) Legal Actions
b) Relation of Earnings to Insurance
c) Time of Payment of Claims
d) Payment of Claims

#20. | What is the purpose of COBRA?

a) To deliver continuation of coverage for terminated employees
b) To deliver coverage for the dependents
c) To deliver health coverage for people with low income
d) To protect insureds against insolvent insurance providers

#21. | An insured is hospitalized with a back injury. Upon checking her disability income policy, she learned she would not be eligible for benefits for at least 30 days. This scenario indicates that her policy is written with a 30-day

a) Probationary period.
b) Waiver of benefits period.
c) Elimination period.
d) Blackout period.

#22. | A prospective insured signs an application for a $50,000 life insurance policy, pays the initial premium and receives a conditional receipt. If the prospective insured dies the following day, which of the following is TRUE?

a) The beneficiary receives the full death benefit if it is determined that the prospective insured qualified for the policy
b) The insurer would return the premium to the insured's estate because the policy was not issued
c) The death claim will be rejected
d) The application will be voided

#23. | The section of a health insurance policy that specifies the causes of eligible loss under which an insured is assumed to be disabled is the

a) Consideration clause.
b) Probationary period.
c) Insuring clause.
d) Incontestability clause.

#24. | What settlement option should the beneficiary select if they want a guarantee that benefits paid from principal and interest would be paid for ten years before being exhausted?

a) Life with period certain
b) Fixed amount
c) Interest only
d) Fixed period

#25. | A policy owner purchased a 10-year level term life policy that is guaranteed renewable and convertible. What happens at the end of the 10-year term?

a) The insured has to provide evidence of insurability to renew the policy
b) The insured can only convert the policy to another term policy
c) The insured can renew the policy for another ten years at the same premium rate
d) The insured can renew the policy for another ten years but at a higher premium rate

#26. | What is the purpose of the buyer's guide in an insurance policy?

a) To list all policy riders
b) To provide information about the issued policy
c) To let the consumer compare the costs of different policies
d) To provide the name and address of the producer or agent issuing the policy

#27. | In an annuity, during which period is the accumulated money converted into a stream of income?

a) Payment period
b) Amortization period
c) Conversion period
d) Annuitization period

#28. Which of the following is a generic consumer publication explaining life insurance in general terms to assist the applicant while making an informed decision?

a) Illustrations
b) Buyer's Guide
c) Insurance Index
d) Policy Summary

#29. As it pertains to an annuity owner, all of the following are true EXCEPT

a) The owner needs to be the party to receive benefits.
b) The owner pays the premiums on the annuity.
c) The owner has the right to name the annuity beneficiary.
d) The owner is the party who can surrender the annuity.

#30. A producer is ready to deliver a policy to an applicant but has not received payment. Upon delivery, the producer collects the applicant's premium check, answers any questions the applicant might have, and then leaves. What did the producer forget to do?

a) Collect a late payment fee
b) Ask the applicant to sign a statement of good health
c) Offer the applicant a secondary policy
d) Ask the applicant to sign a statement that acknowledges the policy has been delivered

#31. In disability income insurance, the time between the onset of an injury or sickness and when benefits begin is known as the

a) Elimination period.
b) Qualification period.
c) Enrollment period.
d) Probationary period.

#32. What describes the specific information about a policy?

a) Illustrations
b) Buyer's guide
c) Producer's report
d) Policy summary

#33. What is the waiting period for a Waiver of Premium rider in life insurance policies?

a) 30 days
b) 3 months
c) 5 months
d) 6 months

#34. An insured pays his Major Medical Insurance premium each year on March 1st. Last March, he forgot to mail his premium to the insurer. On March 22nd, he had an accident and broke his leg. The insurance company would

a) Keep the claim pending until the end of the grace period.
b) Deny the claim.
c) Pay half of his claim because the insured had an outstanding premium.
d) Pay the claim.

#35. Which of the following statements regarding changing an irrevocable beneficiary is correct?

a) It can be changed at any time
b) It can never be changed
c) It can be changed only on the policy's anniversary date
d) It can only be changed with the written consent of that beneficiary

#36. All of the following losses are covered under a typical Accidental Death & Dismemberment policy EXCEPT

a) Income.
b) Eyesight.
c) Limb.
d) Life.

#37. An annuity owner funds an annuity that will supplement his retirement. Because he does not know what effect inflation can have on his retirement dollars, he would like a return that equals the performance of the Standard and Poor's 500 Index. He would likely purchase a(n)

a) Flexible Annuity.
b) Immediate Annuity.
c) Equity-Indexed Annuity.
d) Variable Annuity.

#38. Maria was injured in an accident. Although she still received benefits from her policy, she does not have to pay the premiums. Her policy includes a

a) Benefit of Payment clause.
b) Waiver of Benefit rider.
c) Waiver of Premium rider.
d) Return of Premium rider.

#39. An applicant for a health insurance policy returns a completed application to his agent and a check for the first premium. He receives a conditional receipt two weeks later. Which of the following has the insurance provider done by this point?

a) Approved the application
b) Issued the policy
c) Neither approved the application nor issued the policy
d) Both approved the application and issued the policy

#40. Which statement is INCORRECT concerning Medicare Part B?

a) It offers limited prescription drug coverage.
b) It provides partial coverage for medical expenses not fully covered by Medicare Part A.
c) It is fully funded by Social Security taxes (FICA).
d) It is known as medical insurance.

#41. A life insurance policy that develops cash value faster than a seven-pay whole life contract becomes a(n)

a) Nonqualified annuity.
b) Modified endowment contract.
c) Accelerated benefit policy.
d) Endowment.

#42. In a guaranteed renewable provision, which of the following is NOT a feature?

a) Coverage cannot be renewed beyond the insured's age of 65
b) The insured's benefits cannot be reduced
c) The insurance provider can increase the policy premium on an individual basis
d) The insured has a unilateral right to renew the policy for the life of the contract

#43. Twin sisters are starting a new business. They know it will take several years to grow the business to a point where they can pay off the debt incurred when starting the business. What type of coverage would be the most affordable and still provide a death benefit in the event one of them dies?

a) Whole Life
b) Ordinary Life
c) Joint Life
d) Decreasing Term

#44. The practicing providers are compensated on a fee-for-service basis under which of the following organizations?

a) Open panel
b) PPO
c) HMO
d) Blue Cross/Blue Shield

#45. Which of the following policies is called a "second-to-die" policy?

a) Juvenile life
b) Joint life
c) Survivorship life
d) Family income

#46. Under the mandatory Notice of Claim provision, the first notice of injury or sickness covered under an accident and health policy must contain

a) A clear statement that identifies the insured and the nature of the claim.
b) A statement from the insured's employer stating that the insured could not work.
c) An estimate of the total medical and hospital expenses incurred for the loss.
d) A complete physician's statement.

#47. When an insured withdraws a portion of the face amount through accelerated benefits due to a terminal illness, how will that affect the policy's payable death benefit?

a) The death benefit would be forfeited.
b) The death benefit would be the same as the original face amount.
c) The death benefit would be larger.
d) The death benefit would be smaller.

#48. To comply with the Fair Credit Reporting Act, an agent must notify an applicant that the insurer might request a credit report

a) At the time of application.
b) When the applicant's credit is checked.
c) When the policy is delivered.
d) At the initial interview.

#49. Zoe's health insurance policy year begins in January. Her policy contains a carry-over provision. In November, she had a small claim that was less than her deductible. Which of the following is true?

a) The insured can carry over the amount of this year's expenses to next year, which will help meet next year's deductible
b) The deductible will be waived
c) The insured is currently eligible for an integrated deductible until the new policy year
d) The insured must meet this year's deductible. However, next year's deductible will begin when or if Zoe makes a claim in the following calendar year

#50. Which of the following statements is correct concerning a standard risk classification in the same age group and with similar lifestyles?

a) A standard risk will pay a higher premium than a substandard risk.
b) A standard risk requires an extra rating.
c) A standard risk is also called high exposure risk.
d) A standard risk is representative of the majority of people.

#51. Under which of the following circumstances would an insurance provider pay accelerated benefits?

a) A couple wants to build a home and make a larger down payment
b) An insured is diagnosed with a terminal illness and needs help paying for medical treatment
c) A couple nearing retirement would like a steady income stream
d) An insured is looking for a way to put her son through college

#52. An insured's long-term care policy is scheduled to pay a fixed coverage amount of $120 per day. The LTC facility only charged $100 per day. How much will the insurer pay?

a) $100 a day
b) 80% of the total cost
c) 20% of the total cost
d) $120 a day

#53. Children's riders attached to whole life policies are typically issued as what type of insurance?

a) Adjustable life
b) Whole life
c) Term
d) Variable life

#54. The settlement option that pays throughout the lifetimes of two or more beneficiaries is called

a) Fixed amount.
b) Joint life.
c) Joint and survivor.
d) Fixed period.

#55. Which provision allows the policy owner time, while coverage is in force, to review a health insurance policy and determine whether or not to keep it?

a) Elimination Period
b) Probationary Period
c) Free Look Period
d) Grace Period

#56. Which of the following describes the specified dollar amount beyond which the insured no longer has to participate in the sharing of expenses?

a) Stop-loss limit
b) Out-of-pocket limit
c) First-dollar coverage
d) Corridor deductible

#57. Under a health insurance policy, benefits that have not otherwise been assigned, other than death benefits, will be paid to

a) The insured's spouse.
b) The insured.
c) Creditors.
d) The beneficiary of the death benefit.

#58. Most policies will pay the accidental death benefits as long as the death resulted from the accident and occurs within

a) 30 days.
b) 60 days.
c) 90 days.
d) 120 days.

#59. What is the purpose of key person insurance?

a) To provide health insurance to the key employees' families
b) To ensure retirement benefits are available to all key employees
c) To maintain an account that ensures a company's owner remains solvent
d) To reduce the risk of financial loss because of the death of a key employee

#60. All of the following are true of key person insurance EXCEPT

a) The plan is funded by permanent insurance only.
b) There is no limitation on the number of key employee plans in force at any time.
c) The employer is the policy's owner, payor, and beneficiary.
d) The key employee is the insured.

#61. A policy owner pays a monthly premium of $100 for their health insurance policy. What would be the duration of the grace period under their policy?

a) 7 days
b) 10 days
c) 31 days
d) 60 days

#62. The dividend in a paid-up addition option is used

a) To accumulate additional savings for retirement.
b) To purchase a smaller amount of insurance than the original policy.
c) To purchase a one-year term insurance policy in the amount of the cash value.
d) To reduce the following year's premium payment.

#63. Which of the following would provide an underwriter with information about an applicant's health history?

a) A medical examination
b) The agent's report
c) The inspection report
d) The Medical Information Bureau

#64. The producer may be required to obtain any of the following upon policy delivery EXCEPT

a) Signed waiver of premium.
b) Statement of good health.
c) Payment of premium.
d) Delivery receipt.

#65. Which life insurance policy provision states the insurance provider's duty to pay benefits upon the insured's death, and to whom will the benefits be paid?

a) Beneficiary clause
b) Consideration clause
c) Insuring clause
d) Entire contract clause

#66. Which of the following is an agent's responsibility when delivering a policy?

a) Issue the policy if the applicant is present
b) Approve or decline the risk
c) Collect a medical statement from the applicant's physician
d) Collect payment at the time of delivery

#67. The premium for exercising the Guaranteed Insurability Rider is based on the policy owner's

a) Average age.
b) Issue age.
c) Attained age.
d) Assumed age.

#68. Who has to pay for the cost of a medical exam required in the underwriting process?

a) Department of Insurance
b) Insurer
c) Applicant
d) Underwriters

#69. Which of these documents does a producer give to the policy owner that includes information about cash values, premium amounts, surrender values, and death benefits for specific policy years?

a) A notice regarding replacement
b) A privacy notice
c) A buyer's guide
d) A policy summary

#70. What happens to the face amount of the policy when a reduced paid-up nonforfeiture option is chosen?

a) It is lowered to the amount the cash value would purchase as a single premium
b) It is increased when additional premiums are paid
c) It decreases over the policy term
d) It stays the same as the original policy, regardless of any differences in value

#71. Under a health insurance policy's Physical Exam and Autopsy provision, how often can an insurer examine the insured at its own expense while a claim is pending?

a) Unlimited
b) None at all
c) One examination per week during the claim processing period
d) Two examinations per week during the claim processing period

#72. Which Medicare supplemental policies include the core benefits?

a) All plans
b) Plans A and B only
c) Plan A only
d) Plans A–D only

#73. In a life insurance contract, which of the following is an example of liquidity?

a) The flexible premium
b) The money in a savings account
c) The cash value available to the policy owner
d) The death benefit paid to the beneficiary

#74. When an employee terminates coverage under a group insurance policy, coverage remains in force

a) Until the employee can obtain coverage under a new group plan.
b) Until the employee informs the group insurance provider that a coverage conversion policy is issued.
c) For 31 days.
d) For 60 days.

#75. Which policy provision allows an insured to reactivate their lapsed life insurance policy if they take action within a certain period and provide proof of insurability?

a) Waiver of premium provision
b) Incontestable clause
c) Grace period
d) Reinstatement provision

#76. Which of the following terms describes an applicant's written request for the insurer to issue an insurance contract based on the information given?

a) Insurance Request Form
b) Request for Insurance
c) Application
d) Policy Request

#77. Regarding the consideration clause, which of the following is the consideration on the insurance company's part?

a) Offering the applicant a secondary policy
b) Offering an unconditional contract
c) Explaining policy revisions to the applicant
d) Promising to pay as per the contract terms

#78. If an insured consistently uses the automatic premium loan option to pay the policy premium,

a) The cash value will continue to increase.
b) The insurance provider will increase the premium amount.
c) The policy will end when the cash value is reduced to nothing.
d) The automatic premium loan amount will reduce the policy's face amount.

#79. What happens to the total premium if a policy owner changes their payment plan from monthly to annually?

a) Doubles
b) Increases
c) Decreases
d) Stays the same

#80. Which of the following is a risk classification underwriters use for life insurance?

a) Poor
b) Normal
c) Excellent
d) Standard

#81. The nonforfeiture option with the highest amount of insurance protection is called

a) Decreasing Term.
b) Reduced Paid-up.
c) Extended-Term.
d) Conversion.

#82. An individual purchased a $90,000 annuity with a single premium and began receiving payments two months later. What type of annuity is it?

a) Flexible
b) Deferred
c) Variable
d) Immediate

#83. The main eligibility requirement for Medicaid benefits is based on which of the following?

a) Number of dependents
b) Need
c) Whether the claimant is insurable throughout the private market
d) Age

#84. Which of these life insurance settlement options will guarantee payments for the recipient's lifetime but also provide a guaranteed period during which the payments will continue to a designated beneficiary if the original recipient dies?

a) Fixed-amount
b) Life income with period certain
c) Single life
d) Joint and survivor

#85. Which of the following is true of a Preferred Provider Organization (PPO)?

a) Members complete claim forms on every claim.
b) PPOs do not involve copayment fees.
c) Its goal is to direct patients to providers that offer discount services.
d) The staff model is the most common type of PPO.

#86. What is the name of the insured who participates in a viatical settlement?

a) Viatical broker
b) Viator
c) Third party
d) Contingent

#87. Respite care is what type of care?

a) 24-hour care
b) Relief for a major caregiver
c) Daily medical care given by medical personnel
d) Institutional care

#88. An applicant for life insurance is given a conditional receipt but dies before the insurer issues the policy. The insurance provider will

a) Pay the policy proceeds up to a specified limit.
b) Not pay the policy proceeds in any case.
c) Automatically pay the policy proceeds.
d) Pay the policy proceeds only if it would have issued the policy.

#89. An applicant for a life insurance policy and an agent fill out and sign the application. However, the applicant declined to give the agent the initial premium, and no conditional receipt was issued. When will coverage begin?

a) When the agent submits the application to the insurer, and the insurer issues a conditional receipt
b) When the agent delivers the policy, receives the initial premium, and the applicant provides a Statement of Good Health
c) On the specified effective date
d) On the application date

#90. What is the primary difference between coinsurance and copayments?

a) With coinsurance, the insurance provider pays the entire cost.
b) Coinsurance is a set dollar amount.
c) Copayment is a set dollar amount.
d) With copayments, the insured pays the entire cost.

#91. Which documents describe an insured's medical history, including diagnoses and treatments?

a) Individual Medical Summary
b) Comprehensive Medical History
c) Attending Physician's Statement
d) Physician's Review

#92. Under a continuous premium whole life policy, an insured would like to use the policy dividends to pay off the policy sooner. What dividend option could the insured use?

a) Reduction of premium
b) Accumulation at interest
c) Paid-up option
d) One-year term

#93. The provision that allows for the sharing of expenses between the insurance company and the insured is

a) Stop-loss.
b) Deductible.
c) Divided cost.
d) Coinsurance.

#94. An agent selling variable annuities is required to be registered with

a) The Guaranty Association.
b) SEC.
c) FINRA.
d) Department of Insurance.

#95. What statement best describes the free look provision?

a) The insurance company can obtain a medical exam of the proposed insured before issuing the policy
b) It allows the proposed insured to review the policy before applying
c) It allows the insured to return the policy if dissatisfied for any reason within ten days for a full refund of premiums
d) It allows the proposed insured to review the application before filling it out

#96. Which policy component decreases when the term insurance is decreased?

a) Dividend
b) Premium
c) Face amount
d) Cash value

#97. All of these statements regarding Accidental Death and Dismemberment coverage are correct, EXCEPT

a) Accidental death and dismemberment insurance is considered to be limited coverage.
b) Death benefits are only paid if death occurs within 24 hours of an accident.
c) Accidental death benefits are only paid if death results from accidental bodily injury as defined in the policy.
d) Dismemberment benefits are paid for specific disabilities presumed to be total and permanent.

#98. A survivorship life policy's premium compared with that of a joint life policy would be

a) As high.
b) Half the amount.
c) Lower.
d) Higher.

#99. Under an Accidental Death and Dismemberment (AD&D) policy, what type of benefit will be paid to the beneficiary in the event of the insured's accidental death?

a) Capital sum
b) Double the amount of the death benefit
c) Refund of premiums
d) Principal sum

#100. The long-term care policy's home health care coverage will NOT cover intermittent visits by which of the following medical professionals?

a) Licensed practical nurses
b) Community-based organization professionals
c) Attending physician
d) Registered nurses

#101. The mode of premium payment

a) Is the method used to calculate the policy's cash surrender value.
b) Does not affect the amount of the premium payment.
c) Is defined as the premium payment frequency and amount.
d) Is the factor that determines the amount of a policy's dividends.

#102. Which of the following would be a proper action when an agent replaces the insured's current health insurance policy with a new one?

a) The policies should have at least a 10-day gap between them
b) Policies have to overlap to cover pre-existing conditions
c) The old policy must be canceled before the new one is issued
d) The old policy should remain in force until the new policy is issued

#103. Regarding partial disability, which of the following is NOT true?

a) This is a form of insurance that covers part-time employees
b) The insured can still go to work and receive benefits
c) Benefit payments are usually 50% of the total disability benefit
d) An insured would qualify if they couldn't perform some of their regular job duties

#104. When a policy includes an automatic premium loan provision, what will happen if the policy owner dies before the loan is paid back?

a) The beneficiary of the policy takes over the loan payments
b) The policy is considered null and void
c) The loan balance will be deducted from the death benefit
d) The policy beneficiary receives the full death benefit

#105. A couple owns a life insurance policy, including a Children's Term rider. Their son is reaching the maximum age of dependent coverage, so he will have to convert to permanent insurance shortly. Which of the following will he need to provide for proof of insurability?

a) His parents' federal income tax receipts.
b) Medical exam and parents' medical history.
c) Proof of insurability is not required.
d) Medical exam.

#106. A provision of an insurance policy precluding the insured from collecting twice for the same loss is known as

a) Consent to settle loss.
b) Right of salvage.
c) Appraisal.
d) Subrogation.

#107. Which is true regarding the acquisition of underwriting sources?

a) Acquiring information from outside sources is illegal to decide an applicant's insurability
b) The applicant must be informed of the sources contacted and how the information is collected
c) The insurance provider does not need to notify the applicant of how the information is gathered—informing only of the source is sufficient
d) The insurance provider only needs to notify the applicant of how the information is being gathered—the sources need not be disclosed

#108. The coverage offered by a disability income policy that does not pay benefits for losses occurring as the result of the insured's employment is called

a) Occupational coverage.
b) Workers compensation.
c) Nonoccupational coverage.
d) Unemployment coverage.

#109. Which of the following entities is capable of legally binding coverage?

a) Insurer
b) The insured
c) Federal Insurance Board
d) Agent

#110. An insured purchased a life insurance policy in 2000 and died in 2007. At that time, the insurer discovered that the insured had misstated information on the application. What can they do?

a) Refuse to pay the death benefit due to the misstatement on the application
b) Pay a reduced death benefit
c) File a lawsuit for the right not to pay the death benefit
d) Pay the death benefit

Your exam is divided into multiple parts. You will now be presented with questions about Texas Insurance Laws.

#111. A producer receives an Emergency Cease and Desist Order for habitually misrepresenting her insurance policies. The producer knows she did not commit the stated violations and wants to contest the charges in a court hearing. Which of the following is true?

a) The judge will decide when the hearing will be held
b) The hearing can be set for any time within the next year unless both parties agree to a later date
c) The hearing date must be set for exactly ten days after the request is made
d) The hearing must be held within 30 days after the date the Commissioner receives the request for a hearing

#112. All advertisements are the responsibility of the

a) Department of Insurance.
b) Insurer.
c) Soliciting agent.
d) Advertising agency.

#113. An agent offers his client free tickets to a concert in exchange for purchasing an insurance policy. The agent is guilty of

a) Twisting.
b) Controlled business.
c) Rebating.
d) Coercion.

#114. Insurance providers are allowed to disclose the HIV-related test result to all of the following EXCEPT

a) Another insurance provider.
b) The insured's doctor.
c) A reinsurer participating in the underwriting process.
d) The Texas Department of Health.

#115. Where in the LTC policy must the insurance provider state the renewal provision?

a) In the policy appendix
b) Anywhere the insurer deems appropriate
c) On the first page
d) In the Provisions and Exclusions section

#116. Under a life insurance policy, upon the submission of a death claim, when must the insurance provider pay the policy benefit?

a) Immediately after receiving written proof of loss
b) On the anniversary of the policy
c) Within 30 days
d) Within 60 days

#117. Which individual will be eligible for health insurance coverage through the Marketplace?

a) A permanent resident lawfully present in the U.S.
b) Someone who has Medicare coverage
c) A U.S. citizen who is incarcerated
d) A U.S. citizen living abroad

#118. Using words or symbols similar to what entity is prohibited in life insurance advertisements?

a) Federal government
b) Insurer
c) Department of Insurance
d) Stock

#119. Which of the following is NOT a possible penalty for violating the Insurance Code?

a) An administrative penalty
b) Payment of restitution
c) A cease and desist order
d) A fine of up to $100,000

#120. Which of the following is a percentage of the cost of care or a specific dollar amount the member must pay?

a) Prepayment
b) Contractual cost
c) Copayment
d) Cost share

#121. An insured bought an insurance policy five years ago. Last year, he received a dividend check from the insurer that was not taxable. This year, he did not receive a check from the insurer. From what type of company did the insured buy the policy?

a) Reciprocal
b) Nonprofit service organization
c) Stock
d) Mutual

#122. A producer explains the details of a life insurance policy to a client; however, the producer does not realize that the state has recently rewritten two provisions. The producer inadvertently misrepresents the policy, making it more attractive than it is. What best describes this situation?

a) Deceptive claim settlement practice
b) There is no misconduct
c) Fraud
d) Misrepresentation

#123. Which of the following factors will cause issue age policy premiums to increase?

a) Increased benefits
b) Increased deductible
c) Inflation
d) Age

#124. Who can receive dividends from a mutual insurer?

a) Subscribers
b) Stockholders
c) Agents
d) Policy owners

#125. Which of the following individuals would be required to have a license as an insurance producer?

a) A director at an insurance company who performs executive, administrative, and managerial duties
b) A salaried employee who advertises and solicits insurance business
c) An individual whose activities are limited to producing insurance advertisements
d) A full-time salaried employee who provides information for group insurance

#126. In Health Maintenance Organizations, a Primary Care Physician is known as a

a) Subscriber.
b) Gatekeeper.
c) Preferred provider.
d) Producer.

#127. Which of the following is a type of insurance policy that is typically used in credit life insurance?

a) Increasing term
b) Whole life
c) Equity-indexed life
d) Decreasing term

#128. An advertisement is required to represent which of the following accurately?

a) The insurance company's assets
b) The insurance company's corporate structure
c) The insurance company's financial standing
d) All of the above

#129. What unfair trade practice involves circulating deceptive sales material to the public?

a) Defamation
b) Coercion
c) Misrepresentation
d) False advertising

#130. Which of these will NOT be considered unfair discrimination by insurance providers?

a) Assigning applicants different risk classifications based on gender identity
b) Discriminating in benefits and coverages based on the insured's lifestyle and habits
c) Charging applicants different premium rates based on their ethnicity despite having similar health histories
d) Canceling individual coverage based on the marital status of the insured

#131. According to the provisions included in the Patient Protection and Affordable Care Act, all of the following are required preventive care services EXCEPT

a) Cervical cancer examinations for all women beginning at age 40.
b) Diet counseling for adults.
c) Well-woman visits and counseling.
d) Screenings for behavioral disorders and autism in children.

#132. Which of the following documents must be given to the applicant or policy owner when replacing a policy?

a) Policy illustrations
b) Notice Regarding Replacement
c) Disclosure Authorization Form
d) Buyer's Guide and Policy Summary

#133. All of the following statements about the continuing education requirement in the state of Texas are true EXCEPT

a) All licensed agents must comply by January 1st of even-numbered years.
b) It does not permit excess credit hours to be carried over to the next reporting period.
c) Hours can be completed using independent self-study courses or classroom study.
d) It requires completing 24 hours of approved training every two years.

#134. All of the following are requirements for a person to be licensed, EXCEPT

a) Pass the licensing exam.
b) Pay the appropriate fees.
c) Provide a financial statement.
d) Be at least 18 years old.

#135. The Insurance Commissioner can examine the affairs of any insurance provider as often as necessary but not less frequently than once every

a) Year.
b) Two years.
c) Three years.
d) Five years.

#136. What is the primary difference between a stock company and a mutual company?

a) The types of whole life policies offered
b) Ownership
c) The death benefit amount
d) The number of producers

#137. Which provision states the insurer's right to change premium amounts?

a) Insurance provider's Rights
b) Coverage Limitations
c) Continuation Provision
d) Premium Provision

#138. All of the following must be included in the HMO's application for a certificate of authority EXCEPT

a) Financial records of the organization applying.
b) Records of previous insurers.
c) A map of the geographic area to be served.
d) A schedule of charges for the first 12 months.

#139. Under the state nonforfeiture law for life insurance policies, insurance companies must offer at least one of the following nonforfeiture options EXCEPT

a) Shortened benefit period.
b) Reduction of premium.
c) Reduced paid-up.
d) Extended-term.

#140. Health Maintenance Organizations that have a contract with outside physicians to deliver health care services to their subscribers pay those providers on a

a) Fee-for-service basis.
b) Usual, reasonable, or customary basis.
c) Capitation basis.
d) Medicare allowable basis.

#141. The Commissioner of Insurance issues a Cease and Desist Order to a producer. How many days after the order was issued does the producer have to contest the charges in court?

a) 10 days
b) 30 days
c) 60 days
d) 90 days

#142. Which of the following best describes an insurance company that has been formed under the laws of Texas?

a) Alien
b) Foreign
c) Domestic
d) Sovereign

#143. If an insurer offers Medicare supplement policies, it is required to offer which of the following plans?

a) A-N
b) A
c) A and B
d) A-J

#144. How long is a newborn covered without notification to the insurance provider?

a) From the time labor has begun—the insurance provider must be notified within 31 days
b) From the moment of birth—the insurance provider must be notified within 90 days
c) A newborn is not covered without notifying the insurance provider
d) From the moment of birth—the insurance provider must be notified within 31 days

#145. An applicant correctly notifies their insurer of a claim, but the insurer waits extremely long to process it. Which of the following terms best describes the insurer's behavior?

a) Misrepresentation
b) Fraud
c) Unfair claims settlement practice
d) There is nothing wrong with this incident—insurers do not have a stated deadline to process a claim

Practice Exam 1 Answers

#1. **c) The insurance company**

Fixed annuities guarantee a minimum interest amount to be credited to the purchase payment. Income payments never vary from one payment to the next. The insurance company can afford to make guarantees because the money of a fixed annuity is deposited in the insurer's general account, which is part of its investment portfolio. The insurer makes conservative investments to ensure a guaranteed rate to the annuity owners. (p. 22)

#2. **d) The length of time during which accumulated money is converted into income payments**

The annuity period is when accumulated money is converted into an income stream. (p. 21)

#3. **b) Reduced paid-up**

The reduced paid-up nonforfeiture option delivers protection until the insured reaches age 100. The face amount is reduced to what the cash value would buy. (p. 38)

#4. **d) Monthly.**

If a claim involves disability income benefits, the policy requires that those benefits are paid not less frequently than monthly. In other situations, the insurer can specify the period of 45 or 60 days to pay claims. (p. 89)

#5. **d) Equity-indexed annuities seek higher returns**

Equity-indexed annuities are not securities. They invest aggressively to aim for higher returns. The Equity-Indexed Annuity has a guaranteed minimum interest rate like a fixed annuity. The current interest rate that is credited is often tied to a familiar index such as the S&P 500. (pp. 22-23)

#6. **c) Group coverage must be extended for recently terminated employees up to a certain period of time at the former employee's expense.**

COBRA mandates employers with 20 or more employees to continue group medical insurance for terminated workers and their dependents for up to 18 months to 36 months. The employee must pay up to 102% of the group coverage's premium. (pp. 80-81)

#7. **d) Adjust the benefit according to the reduced risk.**

The change of occupation provision allows the insurance provider to adjust benefits if the insured changes occupations. (pp. 89-90)

#8. **b) Refund the premiums paid.**

When the insured commits suicide within two years after the policy's effective date, the insurer's liability is limited to a refund of all premiums paid. (p. 34)

#9. **d) Reimbursement**

Traditionally, the insurance companies have provided the financing while the hospitals and doctors have provided the care. The HMO concept uniquely provides patient care and financing for its members. The HMO delivers benefits through services rather than reimbursement for these hospital or physician services. (pp. 69-70)

#10. **d) Material misrepresentation**

A material misrepresentation will determine whether or not a policy is issued. If the insured were truthful, it is likely that the insurance provider would not issue the policy. (p. 3)

#11. d) A policy owner who is not the insured

Third-party owner refers to a legal term used to identify an individual or entity that is not an insured under the contract but has a legally enforceable right. (p. 46)

#12. d) Applicant

Any changes made to the application have to be initialed by the applicant. (p. 62)

#13. a) A right to return the policy for a full refund of the premium

This provision allows the policy owner a specified number of days from receipt to review the policy and return it for a full refund of the premium if dissatisfied. This free-look period begins when the policy owner receives the policy, not when the insurance provider issues the policy. (p. 30)

#14. c) At least 20 employees.

Under the Consolidated Omnibus Budget Reconciliation Act of 1985 (COBRA), all employers with 20 or more employees must extend group health coverage to terminated employees and their families. (p. 80)

#15. d) The individual member

When a person becomes a member of the HMO, they select a primary care physician. Once chosen, the insurer will regularly compensate the primary care physician for providing care to that member. (p. 70)

#16. c) A longer elimination period means a lower cost of coverage

The elimination period is the number of days that must expire after the onset of an illness or an accident before benefits are payable. Longer elimination periods will result in a lower cost of coverage. (p. 91)

#17. b) Premium receipt.

When taking the initial premium, the producer should issue the applicant a premium receipt. (pp. 4-5)

#18. a) An index like the Standard & Poor's 500.

The minimum interest rate on an equity-indexed annuity is frequently tied to a familiar index like the Standard and Poor's (S&P) 500. (pp. 22-23)

#19. c) Time of Payment of Claims

The Time Payment of Claims provision stipulates that insurers will pay claims immediately upon receiving proof of loss, except for periodic payments, which are to be paid as stated in the policy. (p. 89)

#20. a) To deliver continuation of coverage for terminated employees

COBRA requires all employers with 20 or more employees to offer group health coverage to terminated employees and their families following a qualifying event. (pp. 80-81)

#21. c) Elimination period.

The elimination period is the time immediately after the start of a disability when benefits are not payable. This requirement eliminates filing many claims and reduces the cost of providing coverage. (p. 91)

#22. a) The beneficiary receives the full death benefit if it is determined that the prospective insured qualified for the policy

When the applicant dies the following day, the underwriting process will continue as though the applicant were still alive. If the insurance provider approves the coverage, the applicant's beneficiary will receive the policy's death benefit. (p. 5)

#23. **c) Insuring clause.**

The insuring clause is a provision found on the first page of the policy that states the coverage and when it applies. (p. 90)

#24. **d) Fixed period**

Under the fixed-period installments option, a specified period of years is chosen, and equal installments are paid to the recipient. The payments continue for the specified period even if the recipient dies. (p. 41)

#25. **d) The insured can renew the policy for another ten years but at a higher premium rate**

Guaranteed renewable and convertible policies can be renewed, without evidence of insurability, for another similar term or can be converted to permanent insurance without evidence of insurability. (p. 14)

#26. **c) To let the consumer compare the costs of different policies**

The buyer's guide presents generic information about life insurance policies and lets the consumer compare the costs of different policies. The policy summary includes information about the policy and the insurer's information. (p. 9)

#27. **d) Annuitization period**

The annuitization period (annuity period) is when accumulated money is converted into an income stream. (p. 21)

#28. **b) Buyer's Guide**

The buyer's guide is a consumer publication that presents life insurance in general terms to assist applicants in making decisions. It is a generic guide that does not describe the specific policy of the insurance provider but instead explains life insurance in a way that the average consumer can comprehend. (p. 9)

#29. **a) The owner needs to be the party to receive benefits.**

The annuity owner and the annuitant do not need to be the same person. (p. 21)

#30. **b) Ask the applicant to sign a statement of good health**

When the premium is not received until the policy is delivered, the producer must collect a statement of good health confirming that the insured's health status has not changed since the policy was approved. (p. 9)

#31. **a) Elimination period.**

The elimination period is a waiting period imposed on the insured from the onset of disability until benefit payments begin. It is a deductible that is measured in days instead of dollars. (p. 91)

#32. **d) Policy summary**

A policy summary explains the features and elements of the specific policy to insureds. (p. 9)

#33. **d) 6 months**

Most insurance providers apply a 6-month waiting period from starting a disability until the first premium is waived. (p. 35)

#34. **d) Pay the claim.**

The accident occurred during the grace period. Consequently, the insurance company will pay the claim. (p. 88)

#35. **d) It can only be changed with the written consent of that beneficiary**

Once an irrevocable beneficiary is listed on the policy, their written consent is required to change this designation. (p. 31)

#36. **a) Income.**

Income is not a loss covered under a typical Accidental Death & Dismemberment (AD&D) policy. AD&D coverage provides a lump-sum benefit payment if the insured dies from an accident or in the event of losing particular body parts resulting from an accident. (pp. 76-77)

#37. **c) Equity-Indexed Annuity.**

The interest rates of Equity-Indexed Annuities are tied to the performance of the Standard and Poor's 500 Index. (pp. 22-23)

#38. **c) Waiver of Premium rider.**

The waiver of premium rider causes the insurance provider to waive future premiums when a disease or accident causes a disability lasting at least six months. (p. 91)

#39. **c) Neither approved the application nor issued the policy**

When the agent takes the application and issues a conditional receipt, the insurance provider still needs to approve the application and issue the policy. (p. 5)

#40. **c) It is fully funded by Social Security taxes (FICA).**

Medicare Part B is funded by monthly premiums and the federal government's general revenues. (pp. 101-103)

#41. **b) Modified endowment contract.**

Insurance policies that develop cash value faster than a seven-pay whole life contract are known as Modified Endowment Contracts. (p. 56)

#42. **c) The insurance provider can increase the policy premium on an individual basis**

A guaranteed renewable provision has the same features as a noncancelable provision, except that the insurance provider can increase the premium on the policy anniversary date. The premiums cannot be increased on an individual policy, only on a class basis. (pp. 94-95)

#43. **c) Joint Life**

A Joint Life policy insuring two lives would be the most affordable. The premiums are based on an average age, and the insurer pays a death benefit only at the first death. (p. 20)

#44. **b) PPO**

PPOs contract on a fee-for-service basis. (pp. 70-71)

#45. **c) Survivorship life**

Survivorship life is also known as a last survivor or second-to-die policy. It is the same as joint life in insuring two or more individuals for a premium based on a joint age. (p. 20)

#46. **a) A clear statement that identifies the insured and the nature of the claim.**

The Notice of Claim provision stipulates that the first notice of injury or sickness covered under an accident and health policy must contain a clear statement that identifies the insured and the nature of the claim. (pp. 88-89)

#47. **d) The death benefit would be smaller.**

When an insured withdraws a portion of the death benefit through this rider, the benefit payable at death is reduced by that amount, plus the amount of lost earnings by the insurer in interest income. (p. 37)

#48. a) At the time of application.

At the time of application, an agent must notify an applicant that the insurer might request a credit report. (pp. 6-7)

#49. a) The insured can carry over the amount of this year's expenses to next year, which will help meet next year's deductible

A carry-over provision in a health insurance policy allows the insured to carry over this year's expenses to meet next year's deductible. (p. 92)

#50. d) A standard risk is representative of the majority of people.

Standard risks are typical of most people of their age and with similar lifestyles. These people are the average risk. (p. 8)

#51. b) An insured is diagnosed with a terminal illness and needs help paying for medical treatment

Accelerated benefits are paid when insureds suffer financial hardship due to severe illness. Benefits are not taxable. (p. 55)

#52. d) $120 a day

Most long-term care policies will pay the benefit amount in a specific fixed dollar amount per day, irrespective of the actual cost of care. (p. 77)

#53. c) Term

Children's term riders offer term insurance with coverage expiring when the minor turns a certain age. (pp. 35-36)

#54. c) Joint and survivor.

A joint and survivor settlement option pays while either beneficiary is still alive. (p. 41)

#55. c) Free Look Period

The Free Look provision allows a policy owner ten days after the policy is delivered to decide whether or not they want to keep the policy. When the policy owner decides to return the policy within this period, they receive a full refund of all premiums paid. (pp. 30, 90)

#56. a) Stop-loss limit

A stop-loss limit is a specific dollar amount beyond which the insured is no longer required to participate in the sharing of expenses. (p. 91)

#57. b) The insured.

Payments for loss of life benefits are made to the designated beneficiary. If no beneficiary was named, payment proceeds are paid to the deceased insured's estate. Claims other than death benefits are paid to the insured or their estate unless otherwise assigned by the insured. (pp. 89, 114)

#58. c) 90 days.

Most policies will pay the accidental death benefit provided that the death resulted from the accident and occurred within 90 days. (p. 36)

#59. d) To reduce the risk of financial loss because of the death of a key employee

Businesses can suffer a financial loss because of the premature death of a key employee with specialized skills, knowledge, or business contacts. A company can reduce the risk of such a loss using key person insurance. (p. 53)

#60. a) The plan is funded by permanent insurance only.

Employer-paid premiums fund key person insurance. (p. 53)

#61. b) 10 days

The grace period is seven days if premiums are paid weekly, ten days if paid monthly, and 31 days for all other modes. (p. 88)

#62. b) To purchase a smaller amount of insurance than the original policy.

The dividends are used to buy a single premium policy in addition to the face amount of the permanent policy. (p. 40)

#63. d) The Medical Information Bureau

Medical exams provide information on an applicant's current health. An agent's report and inspection report provide an applicant's personal information. Only the Medical Information Bureau (MIB) will provide information about an applicant's medical history. (p. 7)

#64. a) Signed waiver of premium.

Upon policy delivery, the producer is not required to obtain a signed waiver of premium. (p. 9)

#65. c) Insuring clause

The insuring clause specifies the party to be covered by the policy and the beneficiary who will receive the policy proceeds if the insured dies. The policy proceeds are paid to the insured's estate if no beneficiary is named. (p. 30)

#66. d) Collect payment at the time of delivery

The agent must deliver the policy to the insured and collect any premium due at delivery. (p. 9)

#67. c) Attained age.

The premium charged for the increase will be based on the insured's attained age. (pp. 36-37)

#68. b) Insurer

If an insurer requests a medical exam, the insurer is responsible for the exam's costs. (p. 7)

#69. d) A policy summary

A policy summary typically includes all the listed information and must be delivered along with a new policy. (p. 9)

#70. a) It is lowered to the amount the cash value would purchase as a single premium

When a reduced paid-up nonforfeiture option is chosen, the face amount is lowered to the amount of what the cash value would purchase as a single premium. (p. 38)

#71. a) Unlimited

Under a policy's Physical Exam and Autopsy provision, an insurance provider can have the insured examined unlimited times at its own expense while a claim is pending. (p. 89)

#72. a) All plans

Core benefits are included in all Medicare supplement plans. (pp. 105-106)

#73. c) The cash value available to the policy owner

Liquidity in life insurance refers to the availability of cash to the insured. Specific life insurance policies offer cash values that can be borrowed anytime and used for immediate needs. (p. 53)

#74. c) For 31 days.

Under the conversion privilege, an employee has 31 days to convert to an individual policy. (p. 48)

#75. **d) Reinstatement provision**

Policy owners can reinstate a lapsed policy within three years by paying back premiums with interest and proving proof of insurability. (p. 33)

#76. **c) Application**

An individual can apply to a provider for insurance, which requests that the insurer review the information and issue an insurance contract. (pp. 3-5)

#77. **d) Promising to pay as per the contract terms**

The consideration clause requires the insurance provider to promise to pay per the contract's terms. (pp. 30, 90)

#78. **c) The policy will end when the cash value is reduced to nothing.**

This option, typically chosen at the time of application, allows the premium to be paid automatically from the contract's guaranteed cash value in case of a possible policy lapse. Once the cash value is exhausted, however, the policy will terminate. (pp. 33-34)

#79. **c) Decreases**

Because the insurance provider would have the premium to invest for a whole year, they would decrease the premium. (p. 32)

#80. **d) Standard**

Standard, substandard, and preferred are the three rating classifications that signify the risk level of insureds. (p. 8)

#81. **c) Extended-Term.**

The Extended-Term nonforfeiture option has the same face amount as the original policy but for a shorter period. (pp. 38-39)

#82. **d) Immediate**

With an immediate annuity, distribution starts within one year of purchase. (p. 23)

#83. **b) Need**

With some federal funding, Medicaid is a program managed by the state to provide medical services for those in need. (pp. 107-108)

#84. **b) Life income with period certain**

Life income with period certain guarantees payments for life and specifies a guaranteed period of continued payments. If the recipient dies during this period, payments will continue to a designated beneficiary for the remaining time. (p. 41)

#85. **c) Its goal is to direct patients to providers that offer discount services.**

Insureds are given care by providers who have agreed to discount their charges. (pp. 68-69)

#86. **b) Viator**

Viator refers to the owner of a life insurance policy who enters into or seeks to enter into a viatical settlement agreement. (p. 46)

#87. **b) Relief for a major caregiver**

Respite care intends to offer relief to the family caregiver. It can include a service such as someone coming to the home while the caregiver takes a nap or goes out for a while. Adult daycare centers also offer this type of relief for the caregiver. (p. 79)

#88. **d) Pay the policy proceeds only if it would have issued the policy.**

The conditional receipt states that coverage will be effective either on the application date or the date of the medical examination, whichever occurs last, provided the applicant is insurable as a standard risk and the policy is issued as applied. (pp. 5, 62)

#89. **b) When the agent delivers the policy, receives the initial premium, and the applicant provides a Statement of Good Health**

The agent must collect the premium during policy delivery when the initial premium is not paid with the application. The applicant will likely need to complete a Statement of Good Health. (p. 9)

#90. **c) Copayment is a set dollar amount.**

With copayment and coinsurance provisions, the insured shares a portion of the service cost with the insurance company. Unlike coinsurance, a copayment has a fixed dollar amount the insured must pay each time certain medical services are used. (p. 91)

#91. **c) Attending Physician's Statement**

An Attending Physician's Statement (APS) is the best way for an underwriter to assess an insured's medical history. The report contains past diagnoses, treatments, length of recovery time, and prognoses. (pp. 7, 21)

#92. **c) Paid-up option**

With the paid-up option, an insured can use accumulated dividends to pay the policy earlier than planned. (p. 40)

#93. **d) Coinsurance.**

The larger the percentage of shared expenses the insured pays, the lower the required premium. (p. 91)

#94. **c) FINRA.**

Variable annuities are considered securities. An individual must be registered with FINRA (formerly NASD) and hold a securities license and a life agent's license to sell variable annuities. (pp. 18-19, 22)

#95. **c) It allows the insured to return the policy if dissatisfied for any reason within ten days for a full refund of premiums**

The free look is a mandatory provision found in all life and health policies that allows the insured to return the policy within a specified number of days and receive a full refund of the premium if dissatisfied with the policy for any reason. (pp. 30, 90)

#96. **c) Face amount**

Decreasing term insurance features a level premium and a death benefit that will decrease each year over the life of the policy term. (p. 15)

#97. **b) Death benefits are only paid if death occurs within 24 hours of an accident.**

Under an Accidental Death and Dismemberment policy, the death benefit is paid if the accidental death occurs within 90 days of the accident, not 24 hours. (pp. 36, 77)

#98. **c) Lower.**

Survivorship Life is similar to joint life in that it insures two or more individuals for a premium based on a joint age. The primary difference is that survivorship life will pay on the last death rather than upon the first death. Because the death benefit is not paid until the last death, the joint life expectancy is extended, resulting in a lower premium than what is usually charged for joint life. (p. 20)

#99. **d) Principal sum**

The principal sum is paid for accidental death. In cases of accidental dismemberment or loss of sight, the policy will pay a percentage of that principal sum, often referred to as the capital sum. (p. 74)

#100. **c) Attending physician**

Home health care is care given in one's home. It could include occasional visits to the individual's home by registered nurses, licensed vocational nurses, licensed practical nurses, or community-based organizations like hospice. (p. 78)

#101. **c) Is defined as the premium payment frequency and amount.**

The mode refers to the frequency of the policy owner's premium payment: monthly, quarterly, semiannually, or annually. The premium amount will change accordingly. (p. 32)

#102. **d) The old policy should remain in force until the new policy is issued**

The agent must ensure that the current policy is not canceled before the new policy is issued. (pp. 64, 147-148)

#103. **a) This is a form of insurance that covers part-time employees**

Partial disability covers full-time working insureds. (pp. 115-116)

#104. **c) The loan balance will be deducted from the death benefit**

If the insured does not repay the loan and interest and the insured dies, it will be deducted from the death benefit. (p. 31)

#105. **c) Proof of insurability is not required.**

Under a Children's Term rider, children reaching the maximum age stated in the policy can convert their coverage to a new policy without providing proof of insurability. (p. 33)

#106. **d) Subrogation.**

Subrogation precludes the insured from collecting twice for the same loss. (p. 117)

#107. **b) The applicant must be informed of the sources contacted and how the information is collected**

An insurer must inform the applicant of all sources that will be contacted in determining the applicant's insurability, in addition to how the insurer will gather the information. (pp. 5-8)

#108. **c) Nonoccupational coverage.**

Most group disability income is nonoccupational coverage, only covering insureds off the job. (p. 115)

#109. **a) Insurer**

An insurance provider is capable of legally binding coverage. Agents cannot bind coverage. (p. 62)

#110. **d) Pay the death benefit**

The incontestability clause prevents insurers from denying a claim because of statements in an application after the policy has been in force for two years, even based on concealment of a material fact or a material misstatement of facts. (p. 33)

#111. **d) The hearing must be held within 30 days after the date the Commissioner receives the request for a hearing**

The Commissioner must hold the hearing within 30 days after receiving the request for a hearing. (p. 124)

#112. **b) Insurer.**

The insurance provider who markets their policies is responsible for these advertisements, regardless of who created, wrote, presented, or distributed them. (p. 142)

#113. **c) Rebating.**

When agents give or promise anything of value not stated in the policy, they are guilty of rebating. (p. 133)

#114. **a) Another insurance provider.**

Insurance providers are not allowed to disclose the HIV-related test result to another insurance provider. (p. 152)

#115. **c) On the first page**

A renewal provision must appear on the first page of the long-term care policy. (p. 153)

#116. **d) Within 60 days**

The insurance provider must pay death claims within 60 days upon receipt of written proof of death. (p. 136)

#117. **a) A permanent resident lawfully present in the U.S.**

A permanent resident of the U.S. is eligible for health insurance on the Marketplace. (p. 155)

#118. **a) Federal government**

Life insurance advertisements are prohibited from using words or symbols associated with the federal government. (p. 142)

#119. **d) A fine of up to $100,000**

In addition to revoking or suspending a license, the Commissioner can issue a cease and desist order, order the payment of an administrative penalty, and order the licensee to make restitution. The penalty for a violation cannot exceed $25,000. (p. 125)

#120. **c) Copayment**

A copayment is a percentage of the cost of care or a specific dollar amount the member must pay. For instance, the member might pay $5 or $10 for each office visit. (p. 162)

#121. **d) Mutual**

After paying claims and other operating expenses, unpaid funds are returned to the policy owners as dividends. If all funds are paid out, dividends are not distributed. (p. 123)

#122. **b) There is no misconduct**

Although the producer misrepresented the policy to a client, to be charged with conducting a deceptive claim settlement, the producer had to misrepresent the policy knowingly. (p. 132)

#123. **a) Increased benefits**

An increase in benefits will cause issue age policy premiums to increase. (p. 153)

#124. **d) Policy owners**

A mutual insurer has no stock and is owned by the policy owners. Because they may receive a dividend (not guaranteed), such policies are known as participating policies. Dividends received by a mutual insurer's policy owners are not taxable. (p. 123)

#125. **b) A salaried employee who advertises and solicits insurance business**

An individual does not require an insurance producer license if they only advertise without an intent to solicit insurance. However, once solicitation occurs, a license is required. (p. 128)

#126. **b) Gatekeeper.**

A subscriber in an HMO plan chooses or is given a primary care physician. That subscriber's health care is directed through that physician regarding treatment and whether or not the subscriber should be referred to a specialist for treating specific medically necessary procedures. (p. 162)

#127. **d) Decreasing term**

Credit insurance is a type of coverage written to insure the debtor's life and pay off the loan balance in the event of the debtor's death. It is typically written as decreasing term insurance. (p. 147)

#128. **d) All of the above**

An advertisement cannot contain misleading or untrue statements regarding the insurer's corporate structure, assets, financial standing, age, or position in the insurance business. (pp. 132-133, 142-143)

#129. **d) False advertising**

This practice is deceptive, false, or misleading advertising. (pp. 132-133)

#130. **b) Discriminating in benefits and coverages based on the insured's lifestyle and habits**

Discriminating against individuals of the same class with equal life expectancies or because of ethnic group, race, or nationality would be unfair discrimination. Discriminating against the insured's lifestyle and habits (such as dangerous hobbies or smoking) is acceptable. (p. 133)

#131. **a) Cervical cancer examinations for all women beginning at age 40.**

Cervical cancer exams as a preventive service will only be available for women at a higher risk. Answers B, C, and D are required preventive care services. (pp. 157-158)

#132. **b) Notice Regarding Replacement**

During policy replacement, the replacing agent must present a Notice Regarding Replacement to the applicant, which the applicant and the agent must sign. (p. 147)

#133. **a) All licensed agents must comply by January 1st of even-numbered years.**

Unless otherwise exempt, licensees must complete 24 hours of continuing education each renewal period before the license expiration date. (pp. 129-130)

#134. **c) Provide a financial statement.**

An applicant must be at least 18, pass the state license exam (within the past 12 months), pay the appropriate fees, and provide an application before a license can be issued. A financial statement of the individual is not required to be licensed. (pp. 126-127)

#135. **d) Five years.**

The insurance commissioner must examine each insurance provider at least once every five years. (p. 124)

#136. **b) Ownership**

Policy owners own mutual companies, while stockholders own stock companies. (p. 123)

#137. **c) Continuation Provision**

The Renewal Provision, also known as a Continuation Provision, must be included on the first page of a Medicare supplement policy. This provision specifies the right of the insurance provider to alter premium amounts. (p. 153)

#138. **b) Records of previous insurers.**

Also included is a list of the names, addresses, and official positions of those responsible for the applicant's affairs; a copy of the evidence of coverage forms to be issued to enrollees; a description of the quality assurance program, including peer review; a description of complaint procedures to be used; and any information required by the Commissioner. (p. 163)

#139. **b) Reduction of premium.**

Reduction of premium is a dividend option (it is not a nonforfeiture option). The other answers are the required nonforfeiture options in life insurance policies issued in Texas. (pp. 148-149)

#140. **c) Capitation basis.**

HMOs usually pay the provider a fixed amount per subscriber in exchange for the agreed-upon medical services, called a capitation basis. (p. 164)

#141. **c) 60 days**

The individual charged can request a hearing to contest or review the charges. They must make a written request within 60 days of receiving the emergency cease and desist order. (p. 124)

#142. **c) Domestic**

A company is considered a domestic company when conducting business within the state in which it is incorporated. (p. 122)

#143. **b) A**

An insurer must provide each applicant a policy form offering the basic core benefits (Plan A) if it will deliver any Medicare supplement policies. An insurer does not have to issue all or any of the supplement plans B through N. (p. 153)

#144. **d) From the moment of birth—the insurance provider must be notified within 31 days**

A newborn is covered without notification to the insurance provider from birth. The insured must notify the insurance provider within 31 days of delivery. (p. 152)

#145. **c) Unfair claims settlement practice**

When an insurance provider frequently or knowingly commits an act that deceives or neglects an insured, it is an unfair claims settlement practice. In this example, there is no reason why the insurance company was justified in waiting to process the claim. (p. 136)

PRACTICE EXAM:

2

Your preparation is paying off

You are about to take a second Texas Life, Accident, and Health practice exam. This exam consists of *145 questions (130 scoreable questions plus 15 pretest questions)* and is *2 hours and 30 minutes* long. It is better to wait until you can fully devote your attention to completing it in the allotted time if you do not have enough time to complete this exam right now.

Any skipped questions will be graded as incorrect. The following chart breaks down the number of questions in each chapter and by topic.

General Knowledge *(100 scoreable questions plus 10 pretest questions)*	# of Questions
Completing the Application, Underwriting, and Delivering the Policy	12
Types of Life Policies	15
Life Policy Riders, Provisions, Options, and Exclusions	15
Taxes, Retirement, and Other Insurance Concepts	8
Field Underwriting Procedures	8
Types of Health Policies	16
Health Policy Provisions, Clauses, and Riders	15
Social Insurance	6
Other Insurance Concepts	5
Texas State Law *(30 scoreable questions plus 5 pretest questions)*	
Texas Statutes and Rules Common to Life and Health Insurance	14
Texas Statutes and Rules Pertinent to Life Insurance Only	6
Texas Statutes and Rules Pertinent to Accident and Health Insurance Only	7
Texas Statutes and Rules Pertinent to Health Maintenance Organizations (HMOs)	3

Raw scores will be converted to scaled scores that range from 0 to 100. The scaled score you receive is neither the number of correctly answered questions nor the percentage of questions correctly answered. A passing score is 70. Any score below 70 demonstrates how close you came to passing. The exam score is not based on each portion separately but on each exam as a whole.

Your exam is divided into multiple parts. You will now be presented with the General Knowledge portion.

#1. Which of these individuals is eligible for a Health Savings Account (HSA)?

a) Marley is insured by a High Deductible Health Plan (HDHP)
b) Dallas is 68 years old
c) Skyler is a dependent on her parent's tax returns
d) Tatum is insured by a Low Deductible Health Plan (LDHP)

#2. The cost for an autopsy covered under the physical exam and autopsy provision is paid by

a) The state's autopsy fund.
b) The health insurance policy's limits of coverage.
c) The estate of the insured.
d) The insurance provider.

#3. In life insurance, the waiting period on a Waiver of Premium rider is

a) 30 days.
b) 3 months.
c) 5 months.
d) 6 months.

#4. The two components of a universal policy are

a) Mortality cost and interest.
b) Separate account and policy loans.
c) Insurance and cash account.
d) Insurance and investments.

#5. An insurance provider receives a report regarding a potential insured about the potential insured's habits, hobbies, and financial status. What type of report is that?

a) Agent's Report
b) Underwriter's Report
c) Inspection Report
d) Medical Information Bureau's report

#6. What is the purpose of an agent providing a conditional receipt to an applicant?

a) It intends to provide coverage on a date earlier than the date on which the policy is issued
b) It makes a guarantee to an applicant that the insurance policy will be issued in the amount applied for through the application
c) It serves as proof of the agent determining that the applicant is fully insurable for coverage by the insurer
d) The agent provides it only to applicants who prepay all premiums in advance of the policy issue

#7. Under a disability policy, a small business owner is an insured that funds a buy-sell agreement. If the owner becomes disabled or dies, which of the following would the policy provide?

a) Cash to the owner's business partner to achieve a buyout
b) The rent money for the building
c) The business manager's salary
d) Disability insurance for the owner

#8. What is a key feature of a dental expense insurance plan that is NOT usually found in a medical expense insurance plan?

a) A low monthly premium
b) Low-cost deductibles
c) Diagnostic and preventive care
d) A broad coverage area

#9. A heart surgeon has an accident and develops tremors in his right arm. Which definition of total disability will cover him for all losses under a disability income policy?

a) Own occupation—more restrictive than other definitions
b) Any occupation—less restrictive than other definitions
c) Any occupation—more restrictive than other definitions
d) Own occupation—less restrictive than other definitions

#10. All of the following are true about the cancellation of an individual insurance policy under the rights of renewability rider for cancelable policies EXCEPT

a) The insurance provider must provide the insured with a written cancellation notice.
b) Claims incurred before cancellation must be honored.
c) An insurance provider can cancel the policy at any time.
d) The insurance provider retains unearned premiums.

#11. Which of the following named beneficiaries would NOT be able to receive the death benefit directly from the insurance provider in the event of the insured's death?

a) A business partner of the insured
b) The deceased insured's wife
c) The former wife of the deceased insured
d) A minor son of the insured

#12. An insured has undergone multiple hospitalizations and surgeries for an illness during the summer. His insurance provider no longer bills him for medical expenses. What term best describes the condition he has met?

a) Out-of-Pocket Limit
b) Maximum Loss Threshold
c) Maximum Loss
d) Stop-Loss Limit

#13. In a business life insurance policy, the premiums paid by the employer are

a) Tax-deductible by the employee.
b) Always taxable to the employee.
c) Never taxable to the employee.
d) Tax-deductible by the employer.

#14. Concerning a decreasing term policy, all of the following are true EXCEPT

a) The payable premium amount steadily decreases throughout the contract
b) It has a lower premium than level term
c) The contract only pays in the event of death during the term, and there is no cash value
d) The face amount steadily decreases throughout the contract

#15. A husband and wife incur medical expenses credited to a single major medical insurance deductible. Which type of policy do they have?

a) Combined
b) Joint
c) Mutual
d) Family

#16. Which of the following is NOT a term for the period when the beneficiary or the annuitant receives income?

a) Liquidation period
b) Depreciation period
c) Annuitization period
d) Pay-out period

#17. Which entity has the authority to revise or make changes to an insurance policy?

a) Department of Insurance
b) Broker
c) Producer
d) Insurer's executive officer

#18. Which type of policy can be changed from one that does not build up cash value to the one that does?

a) Decreasing Term Policy
b) Whole Life Policy
c) Convertible Term Policy
d) Renewable Term Policy

#19. A general disability policy owner is injured during a war, rendering her disabled. What will be the extent of benefits that she will receive?

a) 100%
b) 50%
c) 25%
d) 0%

#20. Which disability policy provision describes conditions, such as total and permanent blindness or dismemberment, that automatically qualify the insured for full disability benefits?

a) Residual disability
b) Presumptive disability
c) Dismemberment disability
d) Partial disability

#21. The life income joint and survivor settlement option guarantees

a) Income for two or more recipients until their death.
b) Payment of interest on death proceeds.
c) Payout of the full death benefit.
d) Equal payments to all recipients.

#22. When is the earliest a policy can go into effect?

a) When the first premium is paid and the policy is delivered
b) When the insurance provider approves the application
c) After the underwriter reviews the policy
d) When the application is signed and a check is provided to the agent

#23. Which of the following is NOT a dividend option?

a) Fixed-premium installments
b) Accumulated at interest
c) Reduction of premium
d) Paid-up additions

#24. Concerning the free-look provision, the insurer

a) Is required to issue a free policy for 30/31 days.
b) Is required to issue a free policy for ten days.
c) Is required to allow the policy owner to return the policy for a full refund.
d) Cannot charge a premium after ten days.

#25. Rob has an individual major medical policy that requires a coinsurance payment. Rob rarely visits his physician and wants to pay the lowest premium possible. Which coinsurance would be best for Rob?

a) 90/10
b) 50/50
c) 75/25
d) 80/20

#26. Regarding variable annuities, which of the following is CORRECT?

a) A person selling variable annuities must only have a life agent's license
b) The annuitant assumes all the risk on the investment
c) The funds are invested in the insurer's general account
d) The insurer guarantees a minimum interest rate

#27. The insurance provider makes a last-minute change before a customer's agent delivers their policy. The agent informs the customer of this change, and it is accepted. What must the agent do next?

a) The agent should ask the customer to sign a statement acknowledging that they know about the change
b) Nothing—the agent is not legally required to do anything else
c) The agent must notify the beneficiary of the change to the policy
d) If the change affects the premium, the agent must have the customer sign a statement acknowledging the change

#28. What term describes the total amount payable per point in a relative value system of determining coverage for a given procedure?

a) Practical value
b) Conversion factor
c) Relative value
d) Translation factor

#29. Which of the following includes information regarding an individual's credit, reputation, character, and habits?

a) Consumer History
b) Insurability Report
c) Agent's Report
d) Consumer Report

#30. Which of the following is INCORRECT regarding Medicaid?

a) It provides medical services to low-income individuals who cannot provide for themselves
b) It pays for outpatient care, hospital care, and laboratory and X-ray services
c) The federal government pays about 56 cents for every Medicaid dollar
d) It is a program solely administered by the federal government

#31. What kind of life insurance policy requires an insured only to pay premiums for a specific number of years until the policy is paid up?

a) Graded Premium Life
b) Limited-Pay Life
c) Variable Life
d) Adjustable Life

#32. How many pints of blood will a Medicare supplement's core benefits cover?

a) None; Medicare pays for it all
b) Everything after the first 3 pints
c) 1 pint
d) The first 3 pints

#33. All of the following statements about equity index annuities are correct EXCEPT

a) They invest more aggressively to aim for higher returns.
b) The annuitant receives a fixed return.
c) They have a guaranteed minimum interest rate.
d) The interest rate is tied to an index like the Standard & Poor's 500.

#34. Which provision would prevent an insurer from paying a claim to somebody other than the policy owner?

a) Entire Contract Clause
b) Proof of Loss
c) Payment of Claims
d) Change of beneficiary

#35. Which of the following is another term for an annuity's accumulation period?

a) Premium period
b) Liquidation period
c) Annuity period
d) Pay-in period

#36. If only one party to an insurance contract makes a legally enforceable promise, what type of contract is it?

a) Unilateral
b) Adhesion
c) Conditional
d) A legal but unethical contract

#37. The equity in an equity index annuity is linked to

a) The annuitant's stock portfolio.
b) The insurer's general account investments.
c) An index like the Standard & Poor's (S&P) 500.
d) The returns from the insurer's separate account.

#38. When a life insurance policy was issued, the policy owner specified a primary and a contingent beneficiary. A few years later, both the insured and the primary beneficiary died in the same auto accident, and it was impossible to resolve who was the first to die. Which entity would receive the death benefit proceeds?

a) The insured's contingent beneficiary
b) The insurance company
c) The insured's estate
d) The primary beneficiary's estate

#39. Which of the following statements regarding Medicare is NOT correct?

a) Medicare Part B provides physician services
b) Medicare Advantage has to be provided through HMOs
c) Medicare Advantage can include prescription drug coverage at no cost
d) Medicare Part A provides hospital care

#40. Under a group life plan, which insured employees can convert to individual insurance of the same coverage after the plan is terminated?

a) Employees who have no history of claims
b) Employees who have been insured under the group life plan for at least five years
c) Employees who have worked in the insurance company for at least three years
d) Employees who have dependents

#41. Which of the following must a producer receive to sell variable life insurance policies?

a) Certificate of Authority
b) SEC registration
c) FINRA registration
d) Variable products license

#42. Whose responsibility is it to ensure that all of the questions on an application have been answered?

a) The beneficiary
b) The agent
c) The insurer
d) The applicant

#43. What license or licenses are needed to sell variable annuities?

a) No license is required
b) Both a life insurance license and a securities license
c) Only a life insurance license
d) Only a securities license

#44. An insured owns a $50,000 whole life policy. At age 46, the insured cancels their policy and exercises the extended-term option for its cash value, currently $20,000. What is the face amount of the new term policy?

a) $20,000
b) $25,000
c) $50,000
d) The insurance provider will determine the face amount

#45. The policy owner pays for her life insurance annually. Until now, she has received a nontaxable dividend check every year. She has decided to use the dividends to help pay her next premium. Which of the following options would allow her to do this?

a) Paid-up addition
b) Accumulation at interest
c) Cash option
d) Reduction of premium

#46. In medical expense insurance policies, which of the following is NOT an exclusion?

a) Military duty
b) Self-inflicted injuries
c) Routine dental care
d) Coverage for dependents

#47. Which of the following terms best describes the concept that the insured pays a small premium for a large amount of risk on the insurance provider's part?

a) Warranty
b) Aleatory
c) Adhesion
d) Subrogation

#48. An agent is ready to deliver a policy to an applicant but has not received payment. Upon delivery, the agent collects the applicant's premium payment, answers any questions, and then leaves. What did the agent forget to do?

a) Collect a late payment fee
b) Ask the applicant to sign a statement of good health
c) Offer the applicant a secondary policy
d) Ask the applicant to sign a statement confirming policy delivery

#49. Alison is buying a permanent life insurance policy with a face value of $25,000. While this is all the insurance she can afford now, Alison wants to ensure that additional coverage will be available in the future. Which of the following options should be found in the policy?

a) Nonforfeiture options
b) Guaranteed insurability option
c) Dividend options
d) Guaranteed renewable option

#50. Upon the insured's death, methods used to pay the death benefits to a beneficiary are called

a) Settlement options.
b) Designation options.
c) Beneficiary provisions.
d) Death benefit options.

#51. Representations are oral or written statements made by the applicant that are

a) Guaranteed to be true.
b) Found to be false after additional investigation.
c) Immaterial to the acceptability of the insurance contract.
d) Considered to be true to the best of the applicant's knowledge.

#52. Which type of hospital policy pays a specified amount every day that the insured is in a hospital?

a) Surgical
b) Blanket
c) Medigap
d) Indemnity

#53. A rider attached to a life insurance policy providing coverage for the insured's family members is called the

a) Other insured rider.
b) Change of insured rider.
c) Juvenile rider.
d) Payor rider.

#54. When added to a permanent life insurance policy, which rider provides an amount of insurance for all family members?

a) Spouse rider
b) Children's rider
c) Additional insured rider
d) Family term rider

#55. A guaranteed renewable disability insurance policy

a) Is renewable at the insured's discretion to a specified age.
b) Is renewable at the insurance provider's option up to the specified age of the insured.
c) Is guaranteed to have a level premium for the duration of the policy.
d) Cannot be canceled by the insured before age 65.

#56. All of the following are true about insurance policy loans, EXCEPT

a) The policy will terminate if the loan plus interest equals or exceeds the policy's cash value.
b) Policy owners can borrow up to the full amount of their whole life policy's cash value.
c) Policy loans can be made on policies that do not accumulate cash value.
d) The outstanding loan and interest amount will be subtracted from the policy proceeds when the insured dies.

#57. A person is insured under her employer's Group Disability Income policy. The insured suffered an accident while on vacation that left her unable to work for four months. Which would be true if the disability income policy pays the benefit?

a) Benefits from employer contributions are fully taxable as income to the employee
b) The insured must wait two additional months to receive the benefits
c) For the business, payments are not considered tax-deductible as a business expense
d) The insured can deduct medical expense benefits from their income tax

#58. In a replacement situation, all of the following have to be considered EXCEPT

a) Assets.
b) Benefits.
c) Limitations.
d) Exclusions.

#59. An insured wants to name his wife as the beneficiary of his health policy. He also wishes to retain all of the rights of ownership. What beneficiary designation should the insured give to his wife?

a) Revocable
b) Primary
c) Contingent
d) Irrevocable

#60. An insured is involved in an auto accident. Besides general, less severe injuries, the insured permanently loses the use of their leg and is entirely blind. The blindness improves one month later. To what extent will the insured receive Presumptive Disability benefits?

a) Full benefits until the blindness lifts
b) No benefits
c) Full benefits
d) Partial benefits

#61. The provision in a health insurance policy that ensures that the insurance company cannot refer to any document that is not found in the contract is the

a) Incontestability clause.
b) Legal actions clause.
c) Entire contract clause.
d) Time limit on certain defenses clause.

#62. Which of the following can be paid for by key person insurance policies?

a) Costs of training a replacement
b) Loss of personal income
c) Workers compensation
d) Hospital bills of the key employee

#63. An applicant signs an application for a $75,000 life insurance policy, pays the initial premium, and is given a conditional receipt. If the applicant is killed in a car accident the next day,

a) The insurer could reject the application because an ongoing medical problem did not cause the insured's death.
b) The beneficiary would receive the $75,000 death benefit if it was determined that the insured qualified for the policy.
c) The premium would be returned to the insured's estate since the policy was not issued.
d) The insurer could reject the death claim because the underwriting process was never completed.

#64. Before insurers can cover a loss, what is the initial period stated in a disability income policy that must pass after the policy is in force?

a) Contestable period
b) Elimination period
c) Grace period
d) Probationary period

#65. According to the Entire Contract provision, a policy must contain

a) A declarations page that includes a summary of insureds.
b) A buyer's guide to life insurance.
c) A listing of the insured's former insurance provider(s) for incontestability provisions.
d) A copy of the insurance application.

#66. The relation of earnings to insurance provision allows the insurance company to limit the insured's benefits to their average income over the last

a) 6 months.
b) 12 months.
c) 18 months.
d) 24 months.

#67. An insured provided their insurance company with a notice of claim but has yet to receive any claims forms from the insurer. The insured submits proof of loss and describes the extent of the loss in a hand-written letter to the insurance company. Which of the following would be true?

a) The claim most likely will not be paid since the insured still needs to submit the official claims form
b) The insurance company will be fined for not providing the claims forms
c) The insured must submit proof of loss to the Department of Insurance
d) The insured is compliant with the policy requirements regarding claims

#68. When a beneficiary receives payments consisting of principal and interest, which portions of the payments are taxable as income?

a) Interest only
b) Both principal and interest
c) Neither principal nor interest
d) Principal only

#69. Which of the following is also called a second-to-die policy?

a) Juvenile life
b) Joint life
c) Survivorship life
d) Family income

#70. Since an insurance policy is a legal contract, it must adhere to the state laws that govern contracts, requiring all of the following elements EXCEPT

a) Legal purpose.
b) Offer and acceptance.
c) Conditions.
d) Consideration.

#71. Which of the following is true concerning optional benefits with long-term care policies?

a) They are available for an added premium
b) Only standard benefits are available with long-term care policies
c) They are offered at no additional cost to the insured
d) They are included in every policy

#72. A partnership buy-sell agreement where all partners buy insurance on the life of each of the other partners is called a

a) Key person plan.
b) Split-dollar plan.
c) Stock redemption plan.
d) Cross-purchase plan.

#73. Which of the following does the Insuring Clause NOT specify?

 a) A list of available doctors
 b) Covered perils
 c) The insurance company
 d) The name of the insured

#74. The primary reason to obtain disability income insurance is to

 a) Reimburse medical expenses and a loss of income resulting from accidents at work.
 b) Reimburse lost income while in the hospital.
 c) Reimburse a family's loss of income because of the insured's death.
 d) Replace income lost because of a disability.

#75. Health Savings Accounts (HSAs) are designed to

 a) Insure against catastrophic losses.
 b) Provide duplicate coverage for health care costs.
 c) Help people save for qualified health expenses.
 d) Increase individual interest income.

#76. Which of the following explains the right of the policy owner to choose options, change beneficiaries, and receive the proceeds of a policy?

 a) Assignment Rights
 b) Owner's Rights
 c) The Entire Contract Provision
 d) The Consideration Clause

#77. The two types of assignments are

 a) Complete and partial.
 b) Complete and proportionate.
 c) Absolute and collateral.
 d) Absolute and partial.

#78. When Steve purchased his health policy, he was a roofer. He has since changed occupations and now manages a bookstore. Upon notifying the insurance provider of his change of occupation, the insurer should

 a) Adjust the benefit commensurate with the decreased risk.
 b) Increase the benefit.
 c) Return any unearned premium.
 d) Consider decreasing the premium.

#79. All of the following are Nonforfeiture options EXCEPT

 a) Extended-term
 b) Reduced paid-up
 c) Interest only
 d) Cash surrender

#80. Which of the following is an example of a limited-pay life policy?

 a) Level Term Life
 b) Straight Life
 c) Life Paid-up at Age 65
 d) Renewable Term to Age 70

#81. An insurance provider is attempting to determine an applicant's insurability and decides to obtain medical information from several different sources. Which entity is required to be notified of the investigation?

 a) The applicant
 b) The Commissioner of Insurance
 c) The medical examiner
 d) The State Department of Insurance

#82. The policy provision that prevents the insured from bringing any legal action against the insurer for at least 60 days after proof of loss is known as

 a) Proof of loss.
 b) Legal actions.
 c) Time limit on certain defenses.
 d) Payment of claims.

#83. While a claim is pending, an insurer can require that

a) An independent examination should be performed as often as reasonably required.
b) The insured will be examined only within the first 30 days.
c) The insured will be examined only once each year.
d) An independent examination only once every 45 days.

#84. Which of the following is NOT an example of insurable interest?

a) Employer in an employee
b) Child in a parent
c) Debtor in a creditor
d) Business partners in each other

#85. Which of the following policy components includes the insurer's promise to pay?

a) Entire contract provision
b) Insuring clause
c) Premium mode
d) Consideration clause

#86. Which statement correctly describes group disability income insurance?

a) In long-term plans, monthly benefits are limited to 75% of the insured's income.
b) Employees do not have any participation requirements.
c) Short-term plans deliver benefits for up to one year.
d) The insured's income determines the extent of benefits.

#87. At what point would a misrepresentation on an insurance application be considered fraud?

a) Any misrepresentation is considered fraud
b) If it is intentional and material
c) Never—statements made by the applicant are only representations
d) When the application is incomplete

#88. Can a person who belongs to a Point-Of-Service plan use an out-of-network physician?

a) No
b) Yes, but they have to use the POS physician first
c) Yes, but they have to use the HMO physician first
d) Yes, and they have to use any preferred physician, even if not part of the HMO

#89. The purpose of managed care health insurance plans is

a) To provide for the continuation of coverage when an employee leaves the plan.
b) To give the insured an unlimited choice of providers.
c) To coordinate benefits.
d) To control health insurance claims expenses.

#90. What is the advantage of reinstating a lapsed policy instead of applying for a new one?

a) The cash values have gained interest while the policy lapsed
b) The original age is used to determine the premium
c) Proof of insurability is not required
d) The face amount can be increased

#91. Which of the following products has a securities license requirement?

a) Variable annuity
b) Fixed annuity
c) Equity-Indexed annuity
d) Deferred annuity

#92. Which of the following provisions is a requirement in health insurance policies?

a) Intoxicants and narcotics
b) Physical examination and autopsy
c) Free-look
d) Unpaid premiums

#93. Under the mandatory uniform Notice of Claim provision, the first notice of sickness or injury covered under an accident and health policy has to include

a) An estimate of the total medical and hospital costs for the loss.
b) A complete physician's statement.
c) An adequately clear statement to identify the insured and the nature of the claim.
d) A statement from the insured's employer stating that the insured could not work.

#94. The life settlement broker represents whom in a life settlement contract?

a) The owner
b) The insurer
c) The beneficiary
d) The life settlement intermediary

#95. Under the uniform required provisions, proof of loss under a health insurance policy typically should be filed within

a) 90 days of a loss.
b) 20 days of a loss.
c) 30 days of a loss.
d) 60 days of a loss.

#96. What is the best way to change an application?

a) Draw a line through the previous answer and insert the correct one.
b) Start over with a new application
c) Erase the incorrect answer and replace it with the new answer
d) White out the previous answer

#97. An agent collected the entire premium with the life insurance application, and the policy was issued two weeks later. When does the policy's coverage take effect?

a) As of the first of the month after the policy is issued
b) As of the policy issue date
c) As of the application date
d) As of the policy delivery date

#98. Level term insurance provides a level premium and a level death benefit during the policy term. If the policy renews after a specified period, the policy premium will be

a) Determined by the insured's health.
b) Based on the insured's issue age.
c) Discounted.
d) Adjusted to the insured's age at the time of renewal.

#99. Group health insurance is characterized by all of the following EXCEPT

a) A master contract.
b) Lower administrative costs.
c) Conversion privilege.
d) Adverse selection.

#100. Under a disability income insurance policy, if the insured changes to a more hazardous occupation after the policy has been issued and a claim is filed, the insurer should do which of the following?

a) Cancel the policy
b) Increase the premium
c) Exclude coverage for an on-the-job injury
d) Adjust the benefit commensurate with the increased risk

#101. The type of dental plan that is incorporated into a major medical expense plan is a

a) Stand-alone dental plan.
b) Blanket dental plan.
c) Integrated dental plan.
d) Supplemental dental plan.

#102. The corridor deductible extrapolates its name from the fact that it is employed between the basic coverage and the

a) Comprehensive expense coverage.
b) Interval expense coverage.
c) Limited coverage.
d) Major medical coverage.

#103. Group life insurance is a single policy that offers coverage to group members. Which of the following statements regarding group life is CORRECT?

a) Coverage cannot be converted when a person leaves the group
b) Premiums are calculated by age, occupation, and individual underwriting
c) Full (100%) participation of members is required in noncontributory plans
d) Every member covered receives a policy

#104. What type of policy allows the insurer to cancel a policy at any time?

a) Cancelable
b) Renewable
c) Guaranteed renewable
d) Noncancelable

#105. An insured is covered under two group health plans—her own and her spouse's—and suffered a loss of $2,000. After the insured paid $500 in coinsurance and deductibles, the primary insurance provider covered $1,500 of medical expenses. What amount, if any, would be paid by the secondary insurance provider?

a) $1,000
b) $2,000
c) $500
d) $1,500

#106. An insurance policy that only requires a premium payment at its inception protects the entire life of the insured and matures when the insured reaches age 100 is called

a) A Modified Endowment Contract (MEC).
b) Level term life.
c) Graded premium whole life.
d) Single premium whole life.

#107. All of the following are true of an owner of an annuity EXCEPT

a) The owner has to be the party to receive benefits.
b) The owner pays the annuity's premiums.
c) The owner has the right to designate the beneficiary.
d) The owner is the party who can surrender the annuity.

#108. In a life insurance policy, why would it be advantageous to designate a contingent (or secondary) beneficiary

a) It determines who receives policy benefits if the primary beneficiary dies
b) It allows creditors to receive payment from the proceeds
c) It ensures that the policy proceeds will be split between the primary and contingent beneficiaries
d) It requires an individual who is not the primary beneficiary to handle the estate

#109. Most policies will pay the accidental death benefits provided that the death is caused by the accident and takes place within

a) 30 days.
b) 60 days.
c) 90 days.
d) 120 days.

#110. An insured bought a disability income policy that has a 10-year benefit period. The policy specified a 20-day probationary period for illness. When the insured is admitted to the hospital with an illness two weeks after the policy issue date, how much will the policy pay?

a) The policy will pay until the insured's release from the hospital
b) Nothing—illnesses are not covered during the contract's first 20 days
c) The insured will receive a return of the premium
d) The policy will pay up to ten years of benefits

Your exam is divided into multiple parts. You will now be presented with questions about Texas Insurance Laws.

#111. Which of the following is TRUE regarding credit life insurance?

a) The creditor is the policy owner
b) The debtor is the annuitant
c) The creditor is the insured
d) The debtor is the policy beneficiary

#112. Which of the following would be required to obtain a Certificate of Authority?

a) Subscribers
b) The HMO
c) Agents
d) Enrollees

#113. A banker is about to close on a customer's loan. The bank is prepared to approve the loan, but only if the customer buys a life insurance policy from the bank in the loan amount. This scenario is an example of

a) Loading.
b) Defamation.
c) Twisting.
d) Coercion.

#114. What is the minimum renewability standard for a long-term care policy issued in Texas?

a) Permanent
b) Conditionally renewable
c) Guaranteed renewable
d) Cancelable

#115. Under the ACA, health insurance can no longer be underwritten based on which of the following factors?

a) The applicant's health condition
b) The applicant's family composition
c) The applicant's age
d) The applicant's tobacco use

#116. An insurance provider publishes intimidating brochures that portray their competition as professionally and financially unstable. Which of the following best describes this insurance provider's act?

a) Legal, as long as the information can be verified
b) Illegal until the Guaranty Association provides an endorsement
c) Legal, as long as the other insurance providers are paid royalties for using their names
d) Illegal under any circumstance

#117. The owner of a small cafe submits a claim to his insurance provider after a loss caused by a fire. The insurer's investigation identifies a police report that shows the fire may have been of a suspicious origin. Which of the following can the insurance provider do?

a) Immediately deny the claim
b) Delay an acceptance or rejection decision
c) Decrease the claim amount
d) Ignore the claim

#118. Which individual can legally receive a commission from selling life insurance policies?

a) An employee of a life insurance company who is not licensed
b) A life and health insurance counselor
c) A licensed life insurance agent
d) A licensed insurance consultant

#119. In Texas, how is the Commissioner of Insurance put into office?

a) Appointed by the Governor for a 2-year term
b) Appointed by the Governor for a 4-year term
c) Appointed by the Senate for a 2-year term
d) Through an election—at the same election when other state officials are chosen

#120. Under a life insurance policy, when must the insurance provider pay the death benefit proceeds after a death claim is submitted?

a) Immediately after receiving written proof of loss
b) Within 30 days
c) Within 60 days
d) On the following anniversary of the policy

#121. Unless the individual in violation requests a hearing, the emergency cease and desist order is final after how many days from the date it is received?

a) 30 days
b) 31 days
c) 60 days
d) 61 days

#122. During a sales presentation, an agent intentionally makes a statement that could mislead the insurance applicant. This scenario describes

a) Twisting.
b) Coercion.
c) Misrepresentation.
d) Defamation.

#123. An insured in a group policy misstated their age on the insurance application. Because of this, the insurance company will most likely

a) Impose a fine on the insured.
b) Issue an amended policy.
c) Adjust the premium.
d) Cancel the coverage.

#124. A temporary license holder can receive a commission from the sale of a policy made to all of the following individuals EXCEPT

a) An accountant at a competing insurance company.
b) The license holder's family doctor.
c) The license holder's sister-in-law.
d) The license holder's spouse's best friend.

#125. How many essential benefits exist in every health care plan under the Affordable Care Act (ACA)?

a) 5
b) 10
c) 12
d) 15

#126. An agent or producer whose license has been revoked cannot receive another license in Texas for

a) Two years.
b) Five years.
c) Six months.
d) One year.

#127. Which of the following terms describes making false statements about the financial condition of any insurance provider to injure any individual engaged in the insurance business?

a) Undercutting
b) Twisting
c) Slandering
d) Defamation

#128. Most Health Maintenance Organizations operate through what type of system?

a) A group enrollment system, either as a member of an association or at their place of employment
b) An individual fee-for-service system
c) Individual subscribers
d) A group formed to obtain HMO coverage

#129. All of the following are unfair claims settlement practices EXCEPT

a) Failure to adopt and implement reasonable standards for settling claims.
b) Failure to acknowledge relevant communication regarding a claim.
c) Proposing negotiations to settle the claim.
d) Refusal to pay claims without a proper investigation.

#130. Under which circumstance will a nonresident license automatically be suspended, canceled, or revoked?

a) If the licensee resides in Texas for more than 180 days in a calendar year
b) If the licensee's home state suspends, cancels, or revokes the licensee's resident license
c) If the licensee resides in their home state for less than 180 days in a calendar year
d) If the Commissioner of Insurance from the licensee's home state issues a cease and desist order to the licensee

#131. An applicant for a license must include information about their place of business for a minimum of

a) Six months.
b) Three months.
c) Five years.
d) Three years.

#132. To be eligible for tax credits under the Affordable Care Act, individuals must have income at what percent of the Federal Poverty Level?

a) Between 100% and 400%
b) Higher than 300%
c) Less than 10%
d) Between 10% and 100%

#133. Which entity is not required to obtain a Certificate of Authority?

a) Subscribers
b) The HMO
c) Agents
d) Enrollees

#134. In credit life insurance, which of the following would be the beneficiary?

a) Insured
b) Company
c) Borrower
d) Creditor

#135. A producer holds an insurance license in Kansas and wants to conduct insurance business in Texas. The agent became licensed before written exams were required. Consequently, the producer still has not passed any exam. Which of the following is true?

a) The written exam requirement is waived if the producer has practiced for more than 30 years
b) The written exam requirement will be waived
c) The producer must take either the Kansas or Texas written exam
d) The producer must take a special transition class and pass a short exam administered at the end

#136. Which of the following is NOT required to be specified in the outline of coverage included in long-term care policies?

a) Basic information regarding the insurance provider
b) Basic information about supplementary policies
c) The policy number
d) The right to return the policy for a full refund

#137. A man with a $1 million life insurance policy died. When filing the claim, his wife and children were surprised to learn that no beneficiary was named on the policy. What happens to the death benefit?

a) The insurance provider retains the benefit
b) It goes to the insured's estate
c) It is divided among his children
d) It is given to his wife

#138. An insurance company incorporated in which location would be considered a foreign insurer in Washington, D.C.?

a) Mexico
b) Canada
c) Washington, D.C.
d) Maryland

#139. An HMO subscriber no longer meets plan eligibility requirements. When can the insurance provider cancel coverage?

a) No sooner than after 15 days
b) No sooner than after 30 days
c) Never; coverage is noncancelable
d) Immediately

#140. In Texas, the state's continuing education (CE) requirement

a) Consists of completing 24 hours of CE every two years.
b) Must be completed by all licensed agents (resident and nonresident).
c) Must not be extended or waived under any circumstances.
d) Only applies to life, accident, health, and annuity licensees.

#141. How many days after the date of issuance to an applicant is a temporary license valid?

a) 30 days
b) 60 days
c) 90 days
d) 180 days

#142. The Small Employer classification refers to any person or firm that employed how many employees during the preceding year?

a) No more than 10
b) Between 1 and 25
c) At least 2 and not more than 50
d) At least 10 and not more than 100

#143. Within how many days must an insured inform the insurance provider of a child's birth and pay any required fees?

a) 180 days
b) 31 days
c) 60 days
d) 90 days

#144. What is the primary purpose of the Texas Life and Health Insurance Guaranty Association?

a) To help protect policy owners and beneficiaries against financial loss as a result of the insolvency of an insurer
b) To encourage life insurance providers to write substandard business
c) To allow agents to continue to solicit insurance, even if the insurer they represent is financially impaired
d) To protect the reputation of the Department of Insurance if they issue a Certificate of Authority to an insurer that becomes insolvent

#145. A producer discovers his newest client was the result of a referral. To show his gratitude to the referring customer, the agent could

a) Offer the customer money for every referral they bring in.
b) Thank the customer.
c) Return the customer's first premium of a new policy.
d) Send the customer a gift as a token of appreciation.

Practice Exam 2 Answers

#1. a) Marley is insured by a High Deductible Health Plan (HDHP)

To qualify for a Health Savings Account (HSA), a High Deductible Health Plan must cover an individual who cannot have coverage under other health insurance except for accident, specific injury, disability, vision care, dental care, or long-term care. Also, the person must not be eligible for Medicare and cannot be claimed as a dependent on anyone else's tax return. (pp. 72-73)

#2. d) The insurance provider.

Where not forbidden by state law, the insurance provider, at its own expense, can cause an autopsy to be performed on a deceased insured. (p. 89)

#3. d) 6 months.

Most insurance providers impose a 6-month waiting period from the time of disability until they waive the first premium. (p. 35)

#4. c) Insurance and cash account.

A universal policy has two components: insurance and a cash account. (pp. 17-19)

#5. c) Inspection Report

Inspection reports cover financial and moral information about a potential insured, typically supplied by credit agencies and private investigators. Insurance providers that use inspection reports are subject to the rules outlined in the FCRA. (p. 6)

#6. d) The agent provides it only to applicants who prepay all premiums in advance of the policy issue

A conditional receipt is the most common type and is provided when the applicant turns in a prepaid application. (pp. 5, 62, 88)

#7. a) Cash to the owner's business partner to achieve a buyout

If an owner becomes disabled or dies, the disability policy under the buy-sell agreement would provide enough cash to achieve a buyout of the company. (p. 76)

#8. c) Diagnostic and preventive care

Diagnostic and preventive care are features of dental insurance plans usually not found in medical expense insurance plans (teeth cleaning, fluoride treatment, etc.). (p. 82)

#9. d) Own occupation—less restrictive than other definitions

In theory, the heart surgeon could find other work. However, because his disability income policy specifies that he is covered for his own occupation, he would be wholly covered. (pp. 115-116)

#10. d) The insurance provider retains unearned premiums.

Under this rider, the insurer can cancel the policy at any time or the end of the policy period. Unearned premiums are returned to the policy owner on a pro-rata basis. (p. 94)

#11. d) A minor son of the insured

Insurance providers must pass death benefits to a minor beneficiary through a guardian or trustee. (p. 32)

#12. d) Stop-Loss Limit

A stop-loss limit is a specific dollar amount beyond which the insured no longer has to participate in the sharing of expenses. (p. 91)

#13. **d) Tax-deductible by the employer.**

Whenever the policy is for the employee's benefit (executive bonus), the premiums that an employer pays for life insurance on an employee are tax-deductible to the employer as a business expense. (p. 54)

#14. **a) The payable premium amount steadily decreases throughout the contract**

Decreasing term policies have a level premium and a death benefit that decreases yearly over the policy term. (p. 15)

#15. **d) Family**

In a family deductible, expenses for two or more members of a policy owner's family can meet a standard deductible in a given year, regardless of the expenses incurred by other family members. (pp. 91-92)

#16. **b) Depreciation period**

In the annuitization period, accumulated money is converted into an income stream. It is also called the liquidation, annuity, or pay-out period. (p. 21)

#17. **d) Insurer's executive officer**

Only the insurer's executive officer, not an agent, has the authority to make any changes to the policy. The insurer must have the insured's written consent to the change. (p. 88)

#18. **c) Convertible Term Policy**

A convertible term policy includes a provision that allows the policy owner to convert to permanent insurance. (p. 15)

#19. **d) 0%**

General disability policies exclude military service, war, overseas residence, intentionally self-inflicted injuries, or injuries suffered while committing or attempting to commit a felony. (p. 75)

#20. **b) Presumptive disability**

Presumptive disability is a provision in most disability income policies that defines the conditions that will automatically qualify the insured for full disability benefits. (pp. 74-75)

#21. **a) Income for two or more recipients until their death.**

The Life Income Joint and Survivor option guarantees an income for two or more individuals for their entire lives. Most contracts state that the surviving individual will receive a reduced payment after the other dies. There is no guarantee that all life insurance proceeds will be paid to the recipients. (p. 41)

#22. **d) When the application is signed and a check is provided to the agent**

The policy's effective date can be as early as the application date if the applicant submits the premium along with the application and the policy is issued as applied. (p. 9)

#23. **a) Fixed-premium installments**

Accumulation at interest, reduction of premiums, and paid-up additions are the options for policy owners when taking their dividends. (pp. 39-40)

#24. **c) Is required to allow the policy owner to return the policy for a full refund.**

This provision allows the policy owner a certain number of days from receipt to review the policy and return it for a full premium refund if dissatisfied. This free-look period begins when the policy owner receives the policy, not when the insurance provider issues the policy. (pp. 30, 90)

#25. **a) 90/10**

A larger percentage paid by the insured results in a lower required premium. (p. 91)

#26. b) The annuitant assumes all the risk on the investment

Because the annuitant's payments into the variable annuity are invested in the insurer's separate account, the annuitant assumes the investment risk. (p. 22)

#27. a) The agent should ask the customer to sign a statement acknowledging that they know about the change

The agent must explain the changes whenever an insurance provider revises a policy. The insured must sign a statement acknowledging the explanation. (p. 64)

#28. b) Conversion factor

The assigned points (relative value) of 200 are multiplied by a conversion factor, representing the total amount payable per point to determine the amount for a given procedure. (p. 69)

#29. d) Consumer Report

Consumer reports include information about a consumer's credit, character, reputation, and habits collected from employment records, credit reports, and other sources. (pp. 6-7)

#30. d) It is a program solely administered by the federal government

Medicaid is an assistance program for individuals with insufficient income or resources to pay for health care. States administer the program that both federal and state funds finance. (pp. 107-108)

#31. b) Limited-Pay Life

In a limited-pay policy, the premiums for coverage will be completely paid up well before age 100, typically after a certain number of years. (p. 16)

#32. d) The first 3 pints

Medicare supplemental policies cover the coinsurance cost and deductibles for Parts A and B. Since Medicare will not cover the first 3 pints of blood, a Medicare supplement plan will pay for that. This benefit is considered a core benefit. (p. 105)

#33. b) The annuitant receives a fixed return.

Equity-indexed annuities include a guaranteed minimum interest rate. While they are aggressive, the annuitant will not have to worry about receiving less than what the minimum interest rate would yield. (p. 19)

#34. c) Payment of Claims

The Payment of Claims provision specifies that issuers must pay the claims to the policy owner unless the death proceeds have to be paid to a beneficiary. (p. 89)

#35. d) Pay-in period

The accumulation period is also called the pay-in period. It is when the annuitant makes premium payments into an annuity. (p. 21)

#36. a) Unilateral

Only one party to the contract is legally bound to do anything in a unilateral contract. (p. 3)

#37. c) An index like the Standard & Poor's (S&P) 500.

Equity-indexed annuities are not securities; they invest aggressively to aim for higher returns. An equity-indexed annuity has a guaranteed minimum interest rate similar to a fixed annuity. The current interest rate that is credited is often tied to an index such as the S&P 500. (pp. 22-23)

#38. **a) The insured's contingent beneficiary**

The Uniform Simultaneous Death Law assumes that the beneficiary dies first in a common disaster. Proceeds are paid to the contingent beneficiary or the insured's estate if no beneficiary is designated. (p. 32)

#39. **b) Medicare Advantage has to be provided through HMOs**

Medicare Part A provides hospital care. Medicare Part B provides doctors and physician services. Medicare Advantage (Part C) offers expanded benefits for a fee through private health insurance programs like HMOs and PPOs. (pp. 98-105)

#40. **b) Employees who have been insured under the group life plan for at least five years**

If the master contract is terminated, each person on the plan for at least five years can convert to individual insurance of the same type of coverage. (p. 48)

#41. **c) FINRA registration**

Agents selling variable life products must be registered with FINRA. They must also be licensed within the state to sell life insurance. SEC registration is for securities, not agents. (pp. 18-19)

#42. **b) The agent**

The agent must ensure that the application is properly signed and that every question is answered correctly. (p. 62)

#43. **b) Both a life insurance license and a securities license**

Producers must have both a life insurance license and a securities license to sell variable annuities. (p. 19)

#44. **c) $50,000**

The face amount of the term policy would be the same as the face amount provided under the whole life policy. (pp. 38-39)

#45. **d) Reduction of premium**

The Reduction of Premium option lets the policyholder apply a policy's dividends toward the following year's premium. (p. 39)

#46. **d) Coverage for dependents**

A medical expense insurance policy excludes self-inflicted injuries, military duty, and routine dental care. (p. 92)

#47. **b) Aleatory**

An insurance contract is aleatory in that it requires a small amount of premium in exchange for a significant risk. (pp. 2-3)

#48. **b) Ask the applicant to sign a statement of good health**

When the premium is not submitted until the policy is delivered, the agent must receive a statement of good health, which acknowledges that the insured's health status has not changed since the policy was approved. (p. 9)

#49. **b) Guaranteed insurability option**

Under the guaranteed insurability option, the insured can purchase additional insurance amounts at specific times without proving insurability. (pp. 36-37)

#50. **a) Settlement options.**

Upon the insured's death, settlement options are methods to pay death benefits to a beneficiary. (pp. 40-42)

#51. **d) Considered to be true to the best of the applicant's knowledge.**

Representations are an applicant's statements that they believe to be true. (p. 3)

#52. **d) Indemnity**

A Hospital Indemnity policy pays a fixed amount for every day the insured is hospitalized, unrelated to medical expenses. (p. 81)

#53. **a) Other insured rider.**

The other insured rider helps provide insurance for more than one family member of the insured. This rider typically offers term insurance with the right to convert to permanent insurance. (p. 35)

#54. **d) Family term rider**

A family term rider is a single rider that provides coverage for every family member. (p. 36)

#55. **a) Is renewable at the insured's discretion to a specified age.**

Guaranteed renewable means the insured can keep the policy until a specific age. However, while the insurance provider cannot increase the rates individually, they can raise them by class. (pp. 94-95)

#56. **c) Policy loans can be made on policies that do not accumulate cash value.**

The policy loan option is only contained in policies that have cash value. (p. 33)

#57. **a) Benefits from employer contributions are fully taxable as income to the employee**

In a plan entirely funded by the employer, the employee's income benefits are included in their gross income and taxed as ordinary income. (p. 76)

#58. **a) Assets.**

In a replacement situation, the producer must compare the benefits, limitations, and exclusions in the current and proposed replacement policies. (p. 64)

#59. **a) Revocable**

If his wife is named the revocable beneficiary, the insured would be the policy owner and could change the contract. His wife would receive any death benefits. (p. 31)

#60. **b) No benefits**

Presumptive Disability plans provide full benefits for specified conditions. These policies usually require the loss of use of at least two limbs, total and permanent blindness, or loss of hearing or speech. Benefits are paid, even if the insured is capable of working. (pp. 74-75)

#61. **c) Entire contract clause.**

The entire contract clause is a mandatory provision that is required by law. (p. 88)

#62. **a) Costs of training a replacement**

A key person insurance policy will pay for replacing the employee and running the business. (pp. 53, 76)

#63. **b) The beneficiary would receive the $75,000 death benefit if it was determined that the insured qualified for the policy.**

When an applicant pays the initial premium, coverage becomes effective on the condition that the applicant is deemed insurable on the application date or the medical exam date if required. (p. 5)

#64. **d) Probationary period**

The probationary period is when a policy is in force before the insurer covers claims resulting from an illness. (pp. 74, 90-91)

#65. d) A copy of the insurance application.

The entire contract provision states that the policy, application copy, and any amendments or riders make up the entire contract. (pp. 30, 88)

#66. d) 24 months.

The relation of earnings to insurance provision permits the insurer to limit the insured's benefits to their average income over the last 24 months. (p. 90)

#67. d) The insured is compliant with the policy requirements regarding claims

When claims forms are not furnished to the insured, the claimant is considered to have complied with the policy requirements if they submit written proof of the occurrence to the insurance provider. (pp. 88-89)

#68. a) Interest only

Only the interest is taxable as income if a beneficiary receives payments that include both principal and interest portions. (p. 55)

#69. c) Survivorship life

Survivorship life, also called a second-to-die or last survivor policy, is similar to joint life in that it insures two or more individuals for a premium based on a joint age. (p. 20)

#70. c) Conditions.

Conditions are part of the policy structure. Legal purpose, offer and acceptance, and consideration are essential parts of a contract. (p. 2)

#71. a) They are available for an added premium

Optional benefits, like guarantee of insurability and return of premium, are available with long-term care policies for an additional premium. (p. 77)

#72. d) Cross-purchase plan.

In a cross-purchase plan, every partner involved buys insurance on the life of each of the other partners. With a cross-purchase plan, every partner is the owner, premium payer, and beneficiary of the life insurance on the lives of the other partners. The amount of the life insurance is equal to each partner's share of the purchase price of the deceased partner's business interest. (pp. 53-54, 118)

#73. a) A list of available doctors

The insuring clause specifies the insurance company, the insured, what kind of losses are covered, and how much the insurer would compensate for the losses. (pp. 30, 90)

#74. d) Replace income lost because of a disability.

Disability income insurance intends to replace income lost because the insured is disabled. (pp. 35, 74-76)

#75. c) Help people save for qualified health expenses.

HSAs help people save for qualified out-of-pocket healthcare expenses like a High Deductible Health Plan (HDHP) deductible. (pp. 72-73)

#76. b) Owner's Rights

Policy owners can learn about their ownership rights by referring to the policy. (pp. 30, 114)

#77. c) Absolute and collateral.

An absolute assignment involves transferring all ownership rights to another person or entity. Collateral assignment involves transferring partial rights to another individual to secure a loan or other transaction. (p. 31)

#78. d) Consider decreasing the premium.

Changing to a less hazardous occupation qualifies Steve for a lower premium rate. (pp. 8, 34)

#79. c) Interest only

Nonforfeiture values include extended-term, reduced paid-up, and cash surrender. Interest only is a settlement option. (p. 38)

#80. c) Life Paid-up at Age 65

Limited-Pay Whole Life policies are all paid when the insured turns 65. (p. 16)

#81. a) The applicant

By law, an insurance provider must notify the applicant of all sources it will contact to determine the applicant's insurability and how the insurer will gather the information. (pp. 7-8)

#82. b) Legal actions.

This mandatory provision requires that legal action to collect benefits can be started 60 days after proof of loss is submitted to the insurance company, giving the insurer time to evaluate the claim. (p. 89)

#83. a) An independent examination should be performed as often as reasonably required.

While a claim is pending, an insurer can require an independent examination as often as reasonably required. (p. 89)

#84. c) Debtor in a creditor

The three recognized areas in which insurable interest exists include a policy owner insuring their own life, a family member (spouse or relative), or the life of a key employee, business partner, or someone who has a financial obligation to them. A debtor does not have an insurable interest in the creditor. (p. 5)

#85. b) Insuring clause

The insuring clause contains the insurance company's promise to pay. (pp. 30, 90)

#86. d) The insured's income determines the extent of benefits.

Group plans generally specify the benefits based on a percentage of the worker's income. Group long-term plans provide monthly benefits typically limited to 60% of the worker's income. (p. 76)

#87. b) If it is intentional and material

A misrepresentation is a fraud if it is intentional and material. Fraud would be considered grounds for voiding the contract. (p. 3)

#88. d) Yes, and they have to use any preferred physician, even if not part of the HMO

In a Point-Of-Service (POS) plan, individuals can visit an in-network provider at their discretion. They are free to do so if they decide to use an out-of-network physician. (p. 71)

#89. d) To control health insurance claims expenses.

Managed care is a system of providing health care and health care services. It is defined by arrangements with selected providers, ongoing quality control programs, utilization reviews, and financial incentives for members to use procedures and providers covered by the plan. (p. 116)

#90. b) The original age is used to determine the premium

The reinstatement provision allows the policy owner to put a lapsed policy back in force, subject to proving continued insurability. If the policy owner reinstates it, the policy is restored to its original status. (pp. 33, 88)

#91. **a) Variable annuity**

A variable annuity is a security regulated by the Securities Exchange Commission (SEC) and state insurance regulations. Consequently, an individual must hold a securities license and a life agent's license to sell variable annuities. (p. 22)

#92. **b) Physical examination and autopsy**

Physical examination and autopsy are mandatory provisions required by law. (p. 89)

#93. **c) An adequately clear statement to identify the insured and the nature of the claim.**

Under this provision, each policy must include a statement identifying the insured and the nature of the claim. (pp. 88-89)

#94. **a) The owner**

A Life Settlement Broker is an individual who, for payment, solicits, negotiates, or offers to negotiate life settlement contracts. Life settlement brokers only represent the policy owners. (p. 47)

#95. **a) 90 days of a loss.**

Under these provisions, the insured should file proof of loss under a health insurance policy within 90 days of a loss. (p. 89)

#96. **b) Start over with a new application**

The best way to correct an application is to start with a new one. (p. 62)

#97. **c) As of the application date**

If the applicant turned in the premium with the application and the policy was issued as requested, the effective date of the policy's coverage would typically coincide with the date of application. (pp. 4-5)

#98. **d) Adjusted to the insured's age at the time of renewal.**

When a level term product is renewed at the end of the period, the premium will be based on the insured's attained age. (p. 14)

#99. **d) Adverse selection.**

When an insurance provider issues a group health insurance policy, they must cover everyone in the group under the master contract. The group underwriting process is designed to avoid adverse selection. (pp. 79-80)

#100. **d) Adjust the benefit commensurate with the increased risk**

An insurance provider must consider the insured's hazardous occupation when determining a policy's premium rating. (pp. 34, 89-90)

#101. **c) Integrated dental plan.**

When dental coverage is offered under a major medical plan's benefits, the dental coverage and medical coverage are integrated plans. Any deductible amount can be satisfied by either dental or medical expenses. (p. 82)

#102. **d) Major medical coverage.**

The corridor deductible extrapolates its name from the fact that it is applied between the basic coverage and the major medical coverage. (p. 69)

#103. **c) Full (100%) participation of members is required in noncontributory plans**

Under a noncontributory plan, an insurance provider will require 100% of eligible employees to enroll. Every employee must be included if the employer pays all of the premiums. (p. 48)

#104. **a) Cancelable**

A cancelable policy can be canceled any time with written notice from the insurance provider. The insurance provider must refund any unearned premium and continue to honor any claims submitted before the cancellation date. (p. 94)

#105. **c) $500**

Once the primary insurer has paid the full benefit, the secondary insurer will cover what the primary insurer will not pay, such as deductibles and coinsurance. (p. 115)

#106. **d) Single premium whole life.**

Single premium whole life requires the entire premium to be paid in a single lump-sum payment at the policy's inception. (p. 16)

#107. **a) The owner has to be the party to receive benefits.**

The owner is the individual who buys the contract and has all the rights, like naming the beneficiary and surrendering the annuity. The owner does not have to be the person who receives the benefits; it could be the annuitant or the beneficiary. (p. 21)

#108. **a) It determines who receives policy benefits if the primary beneficiary dies**

Naming a contingent beneficiary ensures that a beneficiary will receive policy proceeds if the primary beneficiary dies before the insured. (p. 31)

#109. **c) 90 days.**

Most policies will pay the accidental death benefit as long as the death resulted from the accident and takes place within 90 days. (p. 36)

#110. **b) Nothing—illnesses are not covered during the contract's first 20 days**

Under some disability income policies, a probationary period is another waiting period imposed in addition to the elimination period. Loss resulting from illness is not covered if it occurs during the probationary period. (p. 74)

#111. **a) The creditor is the policy owner**

In credit life insurance, the creditor is the policy owner and beneficiary, while the debtor is the insured. (p. 147)

#112. **b) The HMO**

A certificate of authority from the Commissioner is required to establish or operate a Health Maintenance Organization. (p. 163)

#113. **d) Coercion.**

This scenario is an example of the illegal practice known as coercion, which requires the applicant to purchase insurance from a specific insurance company as a loan condition. (p. 133)

#114. **c) Guaranteed renewable**

All long-term care policies or certificates issued in Texas must be guaranteed renewable or noncancelable. (p. 153)

#115. **a) The applicant's health condition**

When health insurers set their premium rates, they can only base them on four standards: geographic rating area, family composition, age, and tobacco use. (p. 155)

#116. **d) Illegal under any circumstance**

When an insurance company criticizes the financial standing of another insurer to injure that insurer, it has committed an illegal trade practice called defamation. (p. 133)

#117. **b) Delay an acceptance or rejection decision**

Insurance providers can delay an acceptance or rejection decision for 30 days if arson is suspected. (p. 136)

#118. **c) A licensed life insurance agent**

A person or corporation that is not a licensed insurance agent cannot accept commissions or other valuable considerations. Agents have to be licensed in the line of insurance being sold to receive commissions. (pp. 134-135)

#119. **a) Appointed by the Governor for a 2-year term**

The Governor appoints the Commissioner of Insurance for two years as established by the Insurance Code. (p. 123)

#120. **c) Within 60 days**

Upon receipt of written proof of death and confirming the claimant's right to the proceeds, the insurance provider must pay death claims within 60 days. (p. 136)

#121. **d) 61 days**

Unless the individual in violation requests a hearing, the emergency cease and desist order is final 61 days from the date it is received. (p. 124)

#122. **c) Misrepresentation.**

It is illegal to publish, issue, or circulate any illustration or sales material that is misleading, false, or deceptive regarding the policy benefits or terms, the payment of dividends, etc. (p. 132)

#123. **c) Adjust the premium.**

In group insurance, if the insured participant misstates their age, the insurer will adjust the premium and the benefit to the correct age. (p. 146)

#124. **c) The license holder's sister-in-law.**

A temporary license holder's sale to a family member or an individual with whom the temporary license holder has a business or employment relationship will not pay a commission. (p. 134)

#125. **b) 10**

Under the ACA, there are ten essential benefits. (p. 157)

#126. **b) Five years.**

If an individual's license has been revoked, they cannot receive another license in Texas for five years. (p. 131)

#127. **d) Defamation**

Defamation refers to making false statements intending to injure any individual engaged in the insurance business. (p. 133)

#128. **a) A group enrollment system, either as a member of an association or at their place of employment**

Most HMOs operate almost exclusively through a group enrollment system, where every member pays a fixed monthly premium, whether or not they use the services of the HMO that month. (p. 162)

#129. **c) Proposing negotiations to settle the claim.**

Negotiations between insurers, policy owners, and insureds may come into play when settling a claim. (p. 135)

#130. **b) If the licensee's home state suspends, cancels, or revokes the licensee's resident license**

The Department of Insurance will automatically suspend, cancel, or revoke a nonresident license if the licensee's home state suspends, cancels, or revokes the licensee's resident license. (p. 127)

#131. c) Five years.

An application must include the applicant's full name, age, residence, occupation, and place of business for the previous five years. Applicants must also state whether they have ever held a license, had it revoked, or been refused a license. (p. 126)

#132. a) Between 100% and 400%

Citizens and legal residents with incomes between 100% and 400% of the Federal Poverty Level (FPL) are eligible for the tax credits under the ACA. (p. 156)

#133. b) The HMO

A certificate of authority is required to establish or operate a Health Maintenance Organization. (p. 163)

#134. d) Creditor

In credit life insurance, the creditor is the policy owner and beneficiary. (p. 147)

#135. b) The written exam requirement will be waived

When a currently licensed foreign producer obtains an insurance license before written exams are required, the Commissioner waives the written exam. (p. 125)

#136. b) Basic information about supplementary policies

The outline of coverage must follow the standard format included in the insurance regulations. It must provide information regarding the insurance company, the policy number, and essential features, as well as explain the right to return the policy for a refund. (p. 153)

#137. b) It goes to the insured's estate

An insurer will pay the death benefit to the insured's estate if no beneficiary is named in the policy. (pp. 31, 114)

#138. d) Maryland

A foreign insurance provider is an insurance company incorporated in another state or territorial possession. Mexico and Canada are foreign nations, so their insurance providers will be considered alien insurers. An insurance company incorporated and operating in Washington, D.C., would be considered domestic. (p. 122)

#139. d) Immediately

HMO coverage can be canceled for failure to meet eligibility requirements. Insurers may immediately cancel coverage. (pp. 163-164)

#140. a) Consists of completing 24 hours of CE every two years.

An agent's license must be renewed every two years on their birthday in either even or odd-numbered years, depending on the license issue date. Agents must complete 24 hours of CE each renewal period unless exempt. (p. 129)

#141. d) 180 days

The Commissioner has the authority to issue a temporary agent's license to an applicant being considered for appointment as an agent by an insurer, another agent, or health maintenance organization (HMO) without requiring a written examination. The temporary license remains valid for 180 days after the date of issuance. (p. 127)

#142. **c) At least 2 and not more than 50**

Small employer refers to any person, firm, partnership, corporation, or association that employed at least 2, but at most 50 eligible employees during the previous calendar year. (p. 154)

#143. **b) 31 days**

An insured must inform the insurance provider of a child's birth and pay any required fees within 31 days. (p. 152)

#144. **a) To help protect policy owners and beneficiaries against financial loss as a result of the insolvency of an insurer**

The Texas Life and Health Insurance Guaranty Association will protect policy owners and beneficiaries against losses from the insolvency of an insurer. (p. 136)

#145. **b) Thank the customer.**

Unless the customer is also an insurance producer or was formerly a producer, it is illegal for the producer to pay or offer to pay for referrals. (p. 133)

FINAL EXAM

This last test will ensure you are ready to pass the licensing exam

You are about to take a Texas Life, Accident, and Health final practice exam. This exam consists of *145 questions (130 scoreable questions plus 15 pretest questions)* and is *2 hours and 30 minutes* long. It is better to wait until you can fully devote your attention to completing it in the allotted time if you do not have enough time to complete this exam right now.

Scoring well on the Final Exam will boost confidence and ensure you possess the knowledge necessary to perform well on the test.

Any skipped questions will be graded as incorrect. The following chart breaks down the number of questions in each chapter and by topic.

General Knowledge (100 scoreable questions plus 10 pretest questions)	# of Questions
Completing the Application, Underwriting, and Delivering the Policy	12
Types of Life Policies	15
Life Policy Riders, Provisions, Options, and Exclusions	15
Taxes, Retirement, and Other Insurance Concepts	8
Field Underwriting Procedures	8
Types of Health Policies	16
Health Policy Provisions, Clauses, and Riders	15
Social Insurance	6
Other Insurance Concepts	5
Texas State Law (30 scoreable questions plus 5 pretest questions)	
Texas Statutes and Rules Common to Life and Health Insurance	14
Texas Statutes and Rules Pertinent to Life Insurance Only	6
Texas Statutes and Rules Pertinent to Accident and Health Insurance Only	7
Texas Statutes and Rules Pertinent to Health Maintenance Organizations (HMOs)	3

Raw scores will be converted to scaled scores that range from 0 to 100. The scaled score you receive is neither the number of correctly answered questions nor the percentage of questions correctly answered. A passing score is 70. Any score below 70 demonstrates how close you came to passing. The exam score is not based on each portion separately but on each exam as a whole.

Your exam is divided into multiple parts. You will now be presented with the General Knowledge portion.

#1. If the benefits of a basic medical insurance plan are exhausted, what type of plan will begin covering those losses?

a) Social security
b) Supplementary major medical
c) Supplementary basic medical
d) None—once benefits are exhausted for a given benefit period, the insurance provider is responsible for covering the remainder of the expenses

#2. When an insured reinstated their major medical policy, they were involved in an accident that required hospitalization. Upon reinstatement of the policy, when would this accident be covered?

a) After 10 days
b) After 31 days
c) It would not be covered
d) Immediately

#3. What is the primary purpose of the Coordination of Benefits provision in group insurance?

a) Encourage hospitals to keep their charges reasonable
b) Prevent over-insurance
c) Prevent lawsuits between insurance providers involved in the claim
d) Ensure the payment of claims by every policy in effect at the time of the claim

#4. Under the Payment of Claims provision, to whom will the insured's benefits be paid if the insured is deceased?

a) The insured's estate, even if a beneficiary is alive
b) The insured's beneficiary's first choice
c) To any remaining debtors the insured owes
d) The insured's primary beneficiary

#5. In an HMO, what is the purpose of the gatekeeper?

a) Ensuring that patients do not go to physicians outside of the HMO's area
b) Establishing strong preventive care
c) Ensuring that services are properly prepaid
d) Controlling costs

#6. A coffee shop owner has a business overhead expense policy that will pay a maximum monthly benefit of $2,500. Her actual monthly expenses are $3,000. If the owner becomes disabled, the monthly benefit payable under her policy will be

a) $2,100.
b) $2,500.
c) $3,000.
d) $2,000.

#7. Life insurance creates an immediate estate. Which of the following statements best explains this?

a) The death benefit will always be paid to the insured's estate
b) The face value of the policy is payable to the beneficiary upon the insured's death
c) The policy has cash values and nonforfeiture values
d) The policy generates immediate cash value

#8. An Equity-Indexed Annuity will grow based upon

a) Performance in a separate account.
b) Current interest rates.
c) An interest rate determined by the banking system.
d) Performance of a recognized index.

#9. For a contract to be enforceable by law, the purpose of the contract must be

a) Legal and not against public policy.
b) For financial gain.
c) For the benefit of the general public.
d) Of pure intent.

#10. How long would the grace period be under a policy if the insured pays a monthly health insurance premium?

a) 7 days
b) 10 days
c) 14 days
d) 25 days

#11. Which of the following dividend options is used when the owner of a participating whole life policy uses the dividend to provide more life insurance coverage?

a) Paid-up additions
b) Reduce the premium
c) Fixed amount
d) Reduced paid-up

#12. In the application process, what is the purpose of the Agent's Report?

a) To provide disclosure to the applicant
b) To give additional information about the applicant to the underwriters
c) To explain policy features and benefits to the applicant
d) To deliver medical information about the applicant to the underwriters

#13. Which entity can include optional provisions in a health insurance policy?

a) The state
b) The policyholder
c) The federal government
d) The insurance provider

#14. The reduction of premium option uses the dividend to reduce

a) This year's premium.
b) The previous year's premium.
c) The premium on any other policy owned by the policy owner.
d) Next year's premium.

#15. What is the purpose of a buy-sell agreement?

a) To help the business meet overhead expenses in case of the owner's death
b) To reimburse the business in case of a key employee's death
c) To protect business employees against loss of income because of the owner's death
d) To allow the business buyout in case of the owner's death

#16. In a health insurance policy, what is the purpose of the impairment rider?

a) To cover impairments that otherwise could not be covered
b) To provide disability coverage
c) To identify pre-existing conditions
d) To exclude coverage for a specific impairment

#17. What is the meaning behind a contract of adhesion?

a) Since the insured does not take part in preparing the contract, any ambiguities would be resolved in the insured's favor
b) The contract holder has the ultimate power of promise
c) The insurance provider can go to another for representation
d) It ensures that the insured does not receive more than the value of the loss

#18. Regarding the definition of total disability, which of the following statements is INCORRECT?

a) Total disability can be the inability to perform the duties of one's own occupation
b) Total disability is the inability to perform partial duties of any occupation for which an individual is suited because of education, training, or experience
c) Disability is defined differently under certain disability income policies
d) Total disability can be the inability to perform any occupation for which an individual is reasonably suited because of experience, training, or education

#19. Variable insurance and variable annuities are regulated by

a) SEC, FINRA, and Departments of Insurance.
b) Departments of Insurance only.
c) NAIC.
d) SEC and FINRA only.

#20. An agent delivers a life insurance policy. She explained a policy change and asked the applicant to sign a statement acknowledging that she described the changes. The agent confirms that the premium has yet to be paid and needs to be paid before the policy goes into effect. She collects a Statement of Good Health, relinquishes the policy, and leaves. What did she do wrong

a) She left the policy with the insured without collecting the premium.
b) She should have created a new policy instead of changing the old one.
c) She didn't need to collect a statement of good health.
d) Nothing.

#21. The Uniform Provision Law that prevents an insurance provider from altering its agreement with a policyholder by referring to documents or other items not found in the policy is called the

a) Legal Action Provision.
b) Grace Period Provision.
c) Reinstatement Provision.
d) Entire Contract Provision.

#22. An underwriter is reviewing an applicant with an extensive medical history. Which of the following would provide the underwriter with a better understanding of the applicant's treatments for the various illnesses?

a) MIB Report
b) Policy application
c) Medical exam
d) Attending Physician's Statement

#23. The stop-loss feature on a major medical policy intends to

a) Establish the number of claims filed on a policy in a calendar year.
b) Establish a maximum out-of-pocket cost that an insured must pay for medical expenses in a calendar year.
c) Establish a maximum out-of-pocket cost that an insured must pay for medical expenses for the policy's life.
d) Discourage an insured from making unnecessary visits to the doctor's office.

#24. What does it mean when insurance contracts are unilateral?

a) The insured is required to make a promise to pay the premium
b) Each party to the contract exchanges something of value
c) A promise is made only at the time of policy application
d) Only one party makes a promise

#25. Which of the following is NOT true concerning a noncancelable policy?

a) The guarantee to renew coverage typically only applies until the insured turns age 65
b) The insured has the unilateral right to renew the policy for the contract's life and can discontinue paying premiums to cancel it
c) The insurer can increase the premium above what is stated in the policy if the claims experience is greater than expected
d) The insurer cannot cancel the policy

#26. According to the Common Disaster clause, which of the following will be assumed if the insured and primary beneficiary die in the same accident, and it cannot be determined who died first?

a) The primary beneficiary's estate and the contingent beneficiary split benefits equally
b) The insured died before the primary beneficiary
c) The primary beneficiary died before the insured
d) The deaths occurred at the same time

#27. Which of the following best describes a Major Medical Expense Policy?

a) It delivers coverage to an insured who is confined to a hospital with a daily benefit amount and a specified benefit period

b) It delivers catastrophic medical coverage beyond basic benefits on a usual, customary, and reasonable basis

c) It delivers surgical coverage to an insured with a schedule indicating charges for each procedure

d) It delivers coverage for in-hospital doctor visits that are nonsurgical

#28. A dentist has been off work for four months because of a disability. His dental assistant's salary would be paid by

a) Business Overhead Insurance.

b) Disability Income.

c) Key Employee Disability.

d) Partnership Disability.

#29. Jacki reviews an agreement on the first page of her policy, which contains a list of losses that her insurance provider will cover. What is the name of this agreement?

a) Statement of Loss Coverage

b) Consideration Clause

c) Insuring Clause

d) Coverage Provisions

#30. Which of the following premium modes would result in the lowest overall premium?

a) Quarterly

b) Semi-annual

c) Monthly

d) Annual

#31. Which federal act defines rules regarding protected health information?

a) HIPAA

b) ACA

c) ERISA

d) COBRA

#32. The guaranteed purchase option is also known as the

a) Multiple indemnity rider.

b) Impairment rider.

c) Evidence of insurability rider.

d) Future increase option.

#33. To buy insurance, the policy owner must face the prospect of losing money or something of value in the event of loss. What is this concept called?

a) Insurable interest

b) Indemnity

c) Exposure

d) Pure loss

#34. At what point is an automatic premium loan generated?

a) Upon the insured's death

b) Once the policy is delivered

c) Upon the surrender of the policy

d) Following the grace period

#35. A whole life policy that will generate immediate cash value is a

a) Variable life policy.

b) Limited-pay policy.

c) Single premium policy.

d) Continuous premium policy.

#36. Which of the following statements about the Medical Information Bureau is correct?

a) Medical Information Bureau report information is available to all physicians

b) The Medical Information Bureau assists underwriters in evaluating and classifying risks

c) The Medical Information Bureau report must be attached to every life insurance policy issued

d) Every life insurance applicant receives a copy of the life insurance medical exam findings

#37. An insured was diagnosed two years ago with kidney cancer. He was treated with surgeries and chemotherapy and is now in remission. He also has a 30-year smoking history. The insured is now healthy enough to work and has recently secured a full-time job. Which describes the health insurance that he will most likely receive?

a) He would be accepted under an insurance policy if a rider excluding cancer-related conditions is attached.
b) He would be covered under his employer's group health insurance plan without higher premiums.
c) He would be covered under his employer's group health insurance plan. However, he would pay higher premiums than the other employees.
d) He would be denied coverage because of the risk his prior medical history poses.

#38. Policy loan requests, except for loan requests for payment of past-due premiums, can be deferred for a period of up to

a) 30 days.
b) 90 days.
c) 6 months.
d) 9 months.

#39. Which of the following is NOT an indicator of a competent party?

a) Mental proficiency
b) Comprehension of contract
c) Business profession
d) Legal age

#40. A viatical settlement is a transaction outside the life insurance provider where the owner sells the life insurance policy for which of the following?

a) A percentage of the policy's face amount
b) More than the face value
c) A predetermined multiple of the premium
d) The policy's face amount

#41. An annuity owner receives the same guaranteed payment each month. What type of annuity is it?

a) Fixed
b) Immediate
c) Guaranteed
d) Single

#42. An insurance policy is required to have all of the following to be valid EXCEPT

a) Countersignature.
b) Acceptance.
c) Consideration.
d) Offer.

#43. The corridor deductible applies between

a) Basic and major medical coverage.
b) Limited and comprehensive.
c) Minor and major coverage.
d) Primary and secondary coverage.

#44. When dealing with life settlements, the term "owner" refers to the

a) Owner of the original life policy.
b) Owner of the insurance company.
c) Life settlement broker.
d) Life settlement provider.

#45. Jake's retirement plan meets all federal requirements and entitles him to certain tax benefits as the plan owner. What term best describes Jake's retirement plan?

a) Unqualified
b) Variable
c) Deferred
d) Qualified

#46. All of the following are required to sign a health insurance application EXCEPT the

a) Producer.
b) Insurer.
c) Proposed insured.
d) Applicant.

#47. An insured has an individual disability income policy with a 30-day elimination period. She becomes disabled on June 1st for 15 days. When will she collect on her disability income payments?

a) She will not collect anything
b) She will collect 15 days of payment after 30 days
c) She will begin collecting on the 15th day
d) She will begin collecting on June 1st

#48. Regarding an Ordinary (Straight) Life policy, all of these statements are true EXCEPT

a) It does not have a guaranteed death benefit.
b) It is funded by a level premium.
c) It builds cash value.
d) If the insured reaches age 100, the policy matures, and the face amount is paid to the insured.

#49. Which of the following is the general enrollment period for Medicare Part B?

a) March 1st through March 31st every year
b) January 1st through March 31st every year
c) March 1st through May 31st every year
d) January 1st through January 31st every year

#50. Which provision can be added to a permanent life insurance policy, at no cost, to ensure that the policy will not lapse if there is cash value?

a) Past Due Premium option
b) Application to Reduce Premium option
c) Automatic Premium Loan option
d) Mode of Premium option

#51. An insured and his spouse recently had a child. Which of the following riders would let the couple insure their child at a specified amount for a limited time?

a) Payor rider
b) Guaranteed insurability rider
c) Spouse term rider
d) Children's term rider

#52. An insurer is trying to determine an applicant's insurability and decides to obtain medical information from several different sources. Which of the following has to be notified of the investigation?

a) The Medical Information Bureau
b) The State Department of Insurance
c) The medical examiner
d) The applicant

#53. Which of the following is INCORRECT regarding an insurance policy's consideration clause?

a) The insurance provider's consideration consists of delivering coverage
b) The insured's consideration consists of giving information on the application and agreeing to pay the premium
c) Consideration must be equal on the part of both the insurance provider and the insured
d) Consideration refers to the exchange of values

#54. What is the purpose of a policy's benefit schedule?

a) To provide the average charges for procedures
b) To include the dates for the payment of benefits
c) To list the insured's copayments and deductibles
d) To state what and how much is covered in the plan

#55. When filling out an insurance application, the applicant needs to correct a mistake. How can the applicant fix the error if a new application is unavailable?

a) White out the incorrect answer and write the new one over it
b) Cross out the incorrect answer, write the correct one beside it, and add their initials next to the new answer
c) Either white out the answer or cross it out and write the new answer beside it
d) Nothing—a fresh application has to be obtained

#56. When a whole life policy is surrendered for a reduced paid-up policy, the new policy's cash value will

a) Remain the same.
b) Decrease over time.
c) Reduce to the pre-surrender value.
d) Continue to increase.

#57. Under the mandatory uniform provision of Proof of Loss, the claimant must submit proof of loss within what period after the loss?

a) 60 days
b) 90 days
c) 2 years
d) 30 days

#58. Medicare is a health insurance program for all the following EXCEPT

a) Individuals with permanent kidney failure.
b) Individuals who have been on Social Security Disability for two years.
c) Individuals with low assets and low income.
d) Individuals 65 or over.

#59. Which of the following forms of care include daily nursing and rehabilitative care that individuals can only receive from medical personnel under the direction of a physician?

a) Assisted living
b) Skilled care
c) Intermediate care
d) Custodial care

#60. An applicant gives his agent a completed application and the initial premium. What can the agent issue him that acknowledges the initial premium payment?

a) Conditional Receipt
b) Provisional Receipt
c) Advanced Premium Receipt
d) Premium Receipt

#61. Who is the individual upon whose life the annuity income amount is calculated?

a) Owner
b) Insured
c) Annuitant
d) Beneficiary

#62. All of the following could qualify as a group to obtain group health insurance EXCEPT

a) A multiple employer trust.
b) A small employer with 14 employees.
c) An association of 35 people.
d) A labor union.

#63. The amount and the frequency of the premium payment are known as

a) Net premium.
b) Level premium.
c) Plan mode.
d) Premium mode.

#64. Ellen is covered under a health plan provided by her employer. Her benefits administrator said that her insurance would pay most of the covered expenses if she saw a provider on her plan's list. If Ellen decided to be treated by a provider not on the list, her portion of the bill would be more significant. Ellen is covered under a/an

a) Limited health plan.
b) Preferred Provider plan.
c) Coordinated plan.
d) HMO group plan.

#65. Which statement is TRUE regarding an Agent's Report during the application process?

a) It becomes a part of the entire contract after the policy is issued
b) It is a required element of the contract
c) It provides the agent's observations about the proposed insured
d) It is only used when the initial premium is not collected with the application

#66. HMO members pay a small fee when they see their primary care physician. This fee is called a

a) Stop-loss.
b) Copay.
c) Coinsurance.
d) Deductible.

#67. Regarding the premium in a 10-year level premium policy, which of the following is TRUE?

a) The premium will remain the same at renewal.
b) The premium will decrease at the end of the term.
c) The premium will be level for the first few years of the policy but will increase by the 10th year.
d) The premium will remain level for ten years.

#68. Which of the following statements is NOT true regarding health insurance policy provisions?

a) Insurance providers can add provisions that do not conflict with uniform standards
b) All additional provisions written by insurance providers are cataloged by their respective states
c) All individual policies include Universal Mandatory Provisions
d) Insurance providers can only offer optional provisions allowed by the state where the policy is delivered

#69. What is the purpose of key person insurance?

a) To provide retirement benefits to key employees
b) To provide senior managers with the ability to purchase shares in the business
c) To cover decreased business revenues as a result of a key employee's death
d) To provide key employees with life insurance coverage

#70. Which of the following can a life insurance policy provide?

a) Survivor protection
b) Protection against outliving one's assets
c) Creation of a future liability
d) Liquidation of one's estate

#71. If an annuitant dies during the accumulation period and there is a beneficiary named in the annuity, the insurer would pay annuity benefits to the

a) Named beneficiary.
b) Annuitant's estate.
c) Next of kin.
d) Insurance company.

#72. A Major Medical Expense policy would exclude coverage for all of the following treatments EXCEPT

a) Dental care.
b) Cosmetic surgery.
c) Drug addiction.
d) Eye refractions.

#73. According to the Time Limit on Certain Defenses provision, statements or misstatements made in the application at the time of issue cannot be used to deny a claim after the policy has been effective for a minimum of how many years?

a) One year
b) Two years
c) Three years
d) Five years

#74. Who must ensure that every question is answered and all necessary signatures are collected on the application?

a) The agent
b) The applicant
c) The insurer
d) The underwriter

#75. When the policy is issued, what happens to the copy of the application for health insurance?

a) It is returned to the insured
b) It becomes part of the entire contract
c) It is filed with the Department of Insurance
d) It is discarded

#76. Which is true when comparing a Joint Life Policy to two individual life policies of the same amount on the same insureds?

a) Joint Life has a lower premium than the total of the two individual policies
b) Joint Life has a premium identical to the sum of the two individual policies
c) The Joint Life premium can only be paid monthly
d) Joint Life has a higher premium than the total of the two individual policies

#77. In an insurance contract, what is the consideration on the insurer's part?

a) Decreasing premium amounts
b) Paying the premium
c) Underwriting
d) Paying a claim

#78. Answers to questions in an insurance application are called representations and, as such, they are

a) Absolutely true.
b) Not true.
c) Warranties.
d) Believed to be true to the best of the applicant's knowledge.

#79. Due to an injury, an insured has been unable to work for eight months. When her life insurance premium came due, she could not pay, yet the policy remained in force. The policy includes

a) Nonforfeiture options.
b) A waiver of premium rider.
c) Guaranteed insurability benefits.
d) A facility of payment clause.

#80. Under a major medical policy, policy owners have the right to do what if they do NOT receive the necessary claim forms within 15 days of their notice to the insurance provider of a covered loss?

a) Demand full payment immediately for the claim
b) Speak with a claims adjuster or another representative from the insurance provider
c) Submit the description in their own words on a plain sheet of paper
d) Be reimbursed for any deductible or copayment on the claim

#81. What guarantees that the information in the insurance contract is accurate?

a) A binder
b) A warranty
c) A representation
d) Utmost good faith

#82. The Guaranteed Insurability Rider allows policy owners to buy additional amounts of life insurance without proof of insurability at all of the following EXCEPT

a) The birth of a child.
b) Marriage.
c) The purchase of a new home.
d) Approximately every three years between the ages of 25 and 40.

#83. Which of the following statements is INCORRECT?

a) The physical exam and autopsy provision gives the insurance provider the right to examine the insured as often as may be reasonably necessary while a claim is pending
b) The insurance provider also has the right to conduct an autopsy if not forbidden by state law
c) The insurance provider does not have the right to conduct an autopsy
d) The physical exam and autopsy provision gives the insurance provider the right to examine the insured at its own expense

#84. Which of the following is NOT usually an excluded cause of disability in an individual disability income policy?

a) War
b) Complications from pregnancy
c) Injury resulting from illegal activity
d) Suicide

#85. A person buys a life insurance policy and lists his parents as the beneficiaries. He can change beneficiaries at any time. What type of beneficiary designation does the policy have?

a) Irrevocable
b) Contingent
c) Primary
d) Revocable

#86. In an individual health insurance policy, all of the following are excluded from coverage EXCEPT

a) Purely cosmetic surgery.
b) Treatment received in a government hospital.
c) Mental illness.
d) Experimental procedures.

#87. Which of the following is the primary source of information that an insurance provider uses to evaluate an insured's risk for life insurance?

a) Insurance application
b) Risk analysis
c) The law of large numbers
d) Agent's Report

#88. In a noncontributory group policy

a) 100% of eligible employees have to participate.
b) 75% of all employees have to elect to join the plan.
c) 100% of employees have to be allowed to participate.
d) 75% of eligible employees have to elect to join the plan.

#89. When a business wants to ensure it can cover losses due to the disability of its top employee, the company should get which type of insurance?

a) Key person disability income
b) Group health insurance policy
c) Health Savings Account (HSA)
d) Business overhead expense

#90. Medicare Part A services do NOT include which of the following?

a) Private Duty Nursing
b) Post hospital Skilled Nursing Facility Care
c) Hospitalization
d) Hospice Care

#91. Whose responsibility is it to ensure that the application for health insurance is accurate and complete?

a) The agent's
b) The policy owner's
c) The underwriter's
d) The applicant's

#92. Dividends received on participating life insurance policies are

a) Not taxable because they are a return of unused premiums.
b) Taxable because they are a return on your investment.
c) Not taxable because they are a return on your investment.
d) Taxable because they are a return of unused premiums.

#93. Which of the following would NOT trigger the payment of Accelerated Death Benefits?

a) Being permanently disabled
b) Terminal illness
c) Requiring an organ transplant for the insured to survive
d) Being permanently institutionalized

#94. An employee that becomes ineligible for group coverage due to termination of employment or a change in status must exercise an extension of benefits under COBRA

a) Within 10 days.
b) Within 60 days.
c) Within 30 days.
d) Before termination is complete.

#95. When an insured is unsatisfied with an issued policy, they may return it to the insurance company and receive a refund of the entire premium paid at which of the following times?

a) Within ten days of when the insurance company received the first premium
b) Within ten days of when the policy was delivered
c) Before any claim has been filed on the policy
d) Within ten days of when the policy was issued

#96. When can HIV-related test results be provided to the MIB?

a) When given authorization by the patient
b) Only when the test results are negative
c) Only if the person is not identified
d) Under any circumstance

#97. Which of the following is an acceptable reason for an insurance company to contest the payment of a claim based on statements in the application?

a) The insured died too soon after applying for the policy
b) The insurance company has already paid out the expected benefit amount for the year
c) The application contains a correction
d) The application contains material misstatements

#98. The insured must surrender the right to sue a negligent third party to the insurance provider upon payment of a loss. This insurance concept is known as

a) Insurable interest.
b) Entirety.
c) Subrogation.
d) Indemnity.

#99. An adjustable life policy can assume the form of

a) Only term insurance.
b) Only permanent insurance.
c) Either term insurance or permanent insurance.
d) Neither term insurance nor permanent insurance.

#100. When an insured's membership in a group is terminated, the insured can convert to

a) Term with proof of insurability.
b) Whole life without proof of insurability.
c) Whole life with proof of insurability.
d) Term without proof of insurability.

#101. Under the mandatory uniform Notice of Claim provision, policy owners must submit written notice of a claim to the insurance provider within what time parameters?

a) Within 10 days
b) Within 20 days
c) Within 30 days
d) Within 60 days

#102. The manner and frequency that the policy owner pays the premium is known as the

a) Premium mode.
b) Grace period.
c) Premium clause.
d) Premium consideration.

#103. What is the difference between a 20-pay whole life policy and a straight life policy?

a) Premium payment period
b) The benefit settlement option
c) The face amount and cash value
d) Policy maturity date

#104. Which of the following services will NOT be provided by an HMO?

a) Emergency care
b) Inpatient hospital care outside the HMO's service area
c) Unlimited coverage for drug rehabilitation treatment
d) Treatment for mental disorders

#105. Which act was introduced to lower the cost of health care by utilizing preventive care?

a) Medical Freedom Act
b) HIPAA
c) HMO Act of 1973
d) Employee Retirement Income Security Act (ERISA)

#106. A husband and wife incur costs attributed to a single major medical insurance deductible. In their policy, which type of deductible do they have?

a) Per occurrence
b) Family
c) Flat
d) Annual

#107. Which of the following terms defines when an annuitant makes payments into the annuity?

a) Loading period
b) Accumulation period
c) Premium building period
d) Annuity period

#108. Which of these can be described as a flexible premium adjustable life policy?

a) Whole Life
b) Term Life
c) Credit Life
d) Universal Life

#109. In a whole life policy, cash value guarantees are called

a) Dividends.
b) Nonforfeiture values.
c) Living Benefits.
d) Cash Loans.

#110. What is the automatic option when a whole life policy is surrendered for its nonforfeiture value?

a) Reduced paid-up
b) Extended-term
c) Paid-up additions
d) Cash surrender value

Your exam is divided into multiple parts. You will now be presented with questions about Texas Insurance Laws.

#111. The Commissioner can issue a temporary agent's license to applicants under consideration for appointment as an agent by an insurer, another agent, or a Health Maintenance Organization (HMO)

a) Without a written examination.
b) With a written examination.
c) Without completing the required training.
d) With a recommendation letter from the insurer, agent, or HMO considering the appointment of a temporary license applicant.

#112. Long-term care policies issued in Texas must be

a) Cancelable.
b) Guaranteed renewable.
c) Nonrenewable.
d) Conditionally renewable.

#113. When an agent suspects a fraudulent insurance act has been committed in Texas, whom should the agent inform first and foremost?

a) The agent's insurance provider
b) The Insurance Fraud Unit of the Texas Department of Insurance
c) The defrauded insureds
d) The state police department

#114. Which of the following statements is CORRECT?

a) Advertisements can imply false statements as long as they do not guarantee false statements
b) Solicitation of insurance cannot be associated with the federal government
c) An advertisement can mislead the public about corporate structure as long as it is not guaranteed
d) Advertisements can use terms that the general public may not understand

#115. Two individuals of the same age, health status, and life expectancy apply for individual insurance coverage. When the same insurer issues the policies, the premium rates differ based on the insured's race. What practice does this describe?

a) Defamation
b) Negligent underwriting
c) Misrepresentation
d) Unfair discrimination

#116. Which statement is an accurate description of dividends from a life insurance policy?

a) They are not taxable and are not guaranteed
b) They are paid as a return of premium to policy owners by stock insurers
c) They are guaranteed to be paid and taxable as income
d) They are likely to be larger in nonparticipating policies

#117. What provision helps ensure that the insured is protected in the event of an unintentional lapse in the policy?

a) Lapse protection
b) Continuity
c) Free look
d) Grace period

#118. Which best describes the unfair trade practice of rebating?

a) Making statements that misrepresent an insurance policy to induce an insured to replace the policy
b) Charging premium amounts over and above the amount specified in the policy
c) Making false statements maliciously critical and intended to injure another individual in the insurance business
d) Offering an inducement of something of value not stated in the policy

#119. The death proceeds for life insurance policies must be paid to the claimant within what period after receiving proof of the insured's death?

a) 10 days
b) 30 days
c) 60 days
d) 6 months

#120. What type of health insurance plan offers broad medical expense coverage without requiring insureds to satisfy a deductible?

a) Blanket
b) Comprehensive
c) Indemnity
d) Major medical

#121. A temporary license in Texas is valid for

a) 60 days.
b) 90 days.
c) 120 days.
d) 180 days.

#122. Which of the following is INCORRECT?

a) Testimonials used in advertisements may or may not apply to the advertised policy
b) Testimonials used in advertisements have to be genuine
c) Advertisements cannot imply that the applicant's health will not be considered in issuing the policy unless true
d) Advertisements may not imply special treatment beyond policy terms

#123. An insurance provider who conducts insurance in Texas but whose articles of incorporation are registered in Canada is considered what type of insurer?

a) Foreign
b) Alien
c) Unauthorized
d) Surplus lines

#124. Under a Health Maintenance Organization, child immunization costs cannot be charged for children under what minimum age?

a) Three
b) Six
c) Seven
d) Ten

#125. The sharing of commissions is legal if

a) The other party is an insurance company.
b) The other party is licensed for the same lines of insurance as the agent sharing the commission.
c) The other party has permission from the agent's client.
d) The other party has a valid insurance license.

#126. What is NOT a requirement on a Medicare supplement policy's first page?

a) Continuation Provision
b) The company's rights to change premiums
c) Premium rates
d) Renewal Provision

#127. An illustration used during the sale of a life insurance policy has to include a label stating

a) Life insurance illustration.
b) Guaranteed items.
c) Subject to change.
d) Representation of insurance.

#128. A Medicare supplement plan must have at least one of the following renewal provisions?

a) Guaranteed renewable
b) Conditionally renewable
c) Nonrenewable
d) Noncancelable

#129. Which of the following is true regarding the ACA health care tax credit?

a) Tax credits are sent to the taxpayer to lower monthly insurance premiums
b) Individuals receiving Medicaid are not eligible
c) Tax credits are based upon a taxpayer's or family's expected annual medical expenses
d) Every wage earner who buys health care insurance is eligible for the tax credit

#130. A Texas resident agent looking to sell insurance to clients in another state needs

a) A Certificate of Authority in that state.
b) A nonresident license in that state.
c) A foreign agent's license in that state.
d) A resident license in that state.

#131. HMOs attempt to identify medical problems by

a) Early detection through regular checkups.
b) Providing reduced health services to all U.S. citizens.
c) Limit the number of physician choices.
d) Providing health services close to home.

#132. How many hours of continuing education must resident agents complete every two years?

a) 10
b) 20
c) 24
d) 40

#133. A newborn child will automatically be covered under a parent's health insurance plan for how many days?

a) 60 days
b) 180 days
c) 364 days
d) 31 days

#134. Which is true regarding policy conversion from group to individual coverage?

a) Conversion needs to occur within 31 days
b) The amount of individual coverage has to be greater than in the group policy
c) Benefits will be forfeited if the insured dies during the conversion period
d) The insurance provider must require evidence of insurability

#135. When differentiating mutual insurers from stock insurers, which statement is true?

a) Stock insurers issue nonparticipating policies and are owned by the shareholders
b) Stock dividends are tax-free, while policy dividends are taxable
c) Nonparticipating policies can pay dividends to the policy owners
d) Mutual insurers issue participating policies and are owned by the shareholders

#136. An insurance company owned by its policy owners is called a

a) Mutual insurer.
b) Fraternal insurer.
c) Stock insurer.
d) Reciprocal insurer.

#137. Which of the following is the distinguishing characteristic of the interest-adjusted net cost method?

a) Comparing interest rates at a specified point in time
b) Buying equity-indexed life insurance
c) Keeping yearly premiums and dividends level
d) Considering the time value of money in comparing life insurance costs

#138. In Texas, for an employer to obtain group health coverage for small employers, what percentage of employees must be covered by the plan?

a) 25%
b) 50%
c) 75%
d) 100%

#139. Which of the following entities is considered the principal?

a) The insurance provider issuing a policy
b) The agent or producer soliciting the policy
c) The director of the insurance company
d) The head of the Department of Insurance

#140. Insurance providers cannot conduct insurance business in Texas without a

a) Certificate of Insurance.
b) Letter of Clearance.
c) Certificate of Authority.
d) Broker's license.

#141. In individual health insurance coverage, the insurance provider must cover a newborn from birth, and if additional premium payment is required, how many days should be allowed for payment?

a) Within 15 working days
b) Within 31 days of birth
c) Within a reasonable time
d) Within 10 calendar days

#142. Which of the following is true regarding drug and alcohol addiction treatment coverage in group health insurance policies issued in Texas?

a) Benefits provided must be the same as those for any other physical illness
b) Coverage cannot be less than for any other physical illness
c) Coverage is optional and can be offered at the insurance provider's discretion
d) Coverage is not available

#143. Concerning a network-model HMO, which of the following is true?

a) It is the same as a group-model HMO
b) It contracts with one exclusive group of physicians to cover all medical services
c) All patients are treated on a fee-for-service basis
d) It contracts with independent groups of physicians to provide medical services to subscribers

#144. An insurer that operates for one or more charitable, religious, educational, social, or benevolent purposes for the benefit of its members is known as a

a) Fraternal insurer.
b) Mutual insurer.
c) Reciprocal insurer.
d) Stock insurer.

#145. Which of the following best describes a rebate?

a) An agent selling insurance primarily to himself, his family, and his friends
b) An agent returning part of her commissions to her client as an inducement to buy
c) An agent misrepresenting policy provisions or coverages at issue
d) An agent requiring an insured to purchase insurance from her as a condition of a loan

Final Exam Answers

#1. b) Supplementary major medical

Supplementary Major Medical policies complement the coverage payable under a basic medical expense policy. After the basic policy pays for services, the supplemental major medical policy will cover costs not paid for by the basic policy and costs exceeding the maximum. The supplemental policy will provide coverage if the time limit is used up in the basic policy. (p. 69)

#2. d) Immediately

The Reinstatement provision allows a lapsed policy for nonpayment of premiums to be reinstated (put back in force). A reinstated policy covers accidents immediately; however, there is a 10-day waiting period for coverage of any sickness. (p. 88)

#3. b) Prevent over-insurance

The Coordination of Benefits (COB) provision minimizes or prevents over-insurance. Typically, under the COB provision, one insurance policy is primary, and the other is secondary. The primary policy pays first. Once the primary policy has paid its full benefit, the insured will submit the claim to the secondary or excess insurer for additional payable benefits. (p. 115)

#4. d) The insured's primary beneficiary

The Payment of Claims provision specifies to whom claims an insurer will make payments. While alive, all benefits are payable to the insured. If the insured dies, death benefits are paid to the beneficiary. (p. 89)

#5. d) Controlling costs

Initially, the member picks a primary care physician (PCP) or gatekeeper. Whenever a member needs the attention of a specialist, the primary care physician has to refer the member. This process helps keep the member away from higher-priced specialists unless seeing one is essential. (p. 70)

#6. b) $2,500.

Business overhead expense insurance reimburses the insured for the covered expenses incurred or the maximum specified in the policy, whichever is less. (p. 75)

#7. b) The face value of the policy is payable to the beneficiary upon the insured's death

Unlike a traditional estate, where the value of personal wealth is typically built up over time, a life insurance policy's face value is available immediately in one lump sum upon the insured's death. (p. 53)

#8. d) Performance of a recognized index.

An Equity-Indexed Annuity grows based upon a specific recognized index such as the Dow Jones or the S&P 500. (pp. 22-23)

#9. a) Legal and not against public policy.

Contracts must be legal and not against public policy to be enforceable by law. (p. 2)

#10. b) 10 days

A policy's grace period must be at least ten days if premiums are paid monthly. (p. 88)

#11. a) Paid-up additions

Paid-up additions are dividends used to provide more life insurance coverage. (p. 40)

#12. b) To give additional information about the applicant to the underwriters

The agent uses the Agent's Report to discuss their observations regarding the proposed insured. Since the agent is considered an essential source of information available to the underwriter, the agent must provide all pertinent facts about the applicant truthfully and honestly. (pp. 4, 6)

#13. d) The insurance provider

The insurance provider can include optional provisions in the health insurance policy. Insurance providers can use additional provisions that do not conflict with the uniform provisions if they receive approval from the state where the policy is delivered. (p. 90)

#14. d) Next year's premium.

With the reduction of premium option, the insurance provider uses the dividend to reduce the following year's premium. (p. 40)

#15. d) To allow the business buyout in case of the owner's death

Buy-sell agreements establish someone else's intent to buy out the business upon the insured's death and set a purchase price on a business. (p. 76)

#16. d) To exclude coverage for a specific impairment

The impairment rider can be attached to a policy to eliminate coverage for a defined condition. (p. 93)

#17. a) Since the insured does not take part in preparing the contract, any ambiguities would be resolved in the insured's favor

A contract of adhesion is drafted by one of the parties to the contract (the insurer). It is either accepted or rejected by the other party (the insured). Insurance policies are offered on a "take it or leave it" basis. (p. 2)

#18. b) Total disability is the inability to perform partial duties of any occupation for which an individual is suited because of education, training, or experience

Total disability is defined differently under various disability income policies. Some policies use a fairly strict definition, like the "any occupation" definition, similar to Social Security. Other insurance companies have adopted a more liberal definition. (p. 115)

#19. a) SEC, FINRA, and Departments of Insurance.

The Securities and Exchange Commission (SEC) and the Financial Industry Regulatory Authority (FINRA) regulate variable insurance products at the federal level. At the state level, variable products are regulated by the Department of Insurance. (pp. 18-19)

#20. a) She left the policy with the insured without collecting the premium.

A policy goes into effect once the premium has been paid. Since the agent did not collect the premium with the app, she must obtain a Statement of Good Health from the applicant when delivering the policy. In this scenario, the agent should have collected the policy premium when leaving the policy with the insured. (p. 9)

#21. d) Entire Contract Provision.

A copy of the application becomes a part of the entire contract. Items not specified in the application are not a part of the contract. (pp. 30, 88)

#22. **d) Attending Physician's Statement**

An Attending Physician's Statement (APS) is the best way for an underwriter to evaluate an insured's medical history. The report includes past diagnoses, treatments, length of recovery time, and prognoses. (pp. 7, 63)

#23. **b) Establish a maximum out-of-pocket cost that an insured must pay for medical expenses in a calendar year.**

A stop-loss feature is a provision that gives financial security to the insured. It limits the maximum amount paid in co-payments and deductibles during a calendar year. (p. 91)

#24. **d) Only one party makes a promise**

Only one party to the contract is legally bound to do anything in a unilateral contract. The insured makes no lawfully binding promises. However, an insurance provider must legally pay losses covered by a policy in force. (p. 3)

#25. **c) The insurer can increase the premium above what is stated in the policy if the claims experience is greater than expected**

The insurer cannot cancel a noncancelable policy or increase the premium beyond what is specified in the policy. The insured has the unilateral right to renew the policy for the contract's life. However, the insured can cancel the policy anytime by discontinuing premium payments. (p. 94)

#26. **c) The primary beneficiary died before the insured**

According to the Common Disaster clause, if it cannot be determined who died first, it will be assumed the primary beneficiary died first. Consequently, the proceeds go to the contingent beneficiary. (p. 32)

#27. **b) It delivers catastrophic medical coverage beyond basic benefits on a usual, customary, and reasonable basis**

Major Medical Expense Policies provide a broad range of coverage under one policy instead of the limited coverage available under the Basic Medical Expense Policies. It provides catastrophic medical coverage beyond basic benefits on a usual, customary, and reasonable basis. (p. 69)

#28. **a) Business Overhead Insurance.**

Business overhead insurance will pay for the ongoing business expenses of a self-employed person, like rent or salaries, while the self-employed person is disabled. (p. 75)

#29. **c) Insuring Clause**

The Insuring Clause lists the insured, the insurance provider, what kind of losses are covered, and how much the insurer would compensate for the losses. (pp. 30, 90)

#30. **d) Annual**

Paying the premium once a year would be the least expensive payment mode because of fewer billing and loading charges. (p. 32)

#31. **a) HIPAA**

Under HIPAA's Privacy Rule, protected information includes all identifiable health information transmitted or held by a covered entity or its business associate in any format or media, whether oral, paper, or electronic. This information is known as protected health information (PHI). (pp. 8, 63)

#32. **d) Future increase option.**

The guaranteed purchase option is also known as the future increase option and will let the insured buy additional amounts of disability income coverage without evidence of insurability. (p. 94)

#33. **a) Insurable interest**

Insurable interest is a financial interest in the life of another individual or a possibility of losing something of value if the insured dies. (p. 5)

#34. **d) Following the grace period**

Automatic premium loans are designed to automatically take a portion of the policy's cash value to pay the premium, thereby preventing the policy from lapsing. Automatic premium loans are initiated after the grace period has ended. (p. 33)

#35. **c) Single premium policy.**

Whole life policies that generate immediate cash value are single premium policies. (p. 16)

#36. **b) The Medical Information Bureau assists underwriters in evaluating and classifying risks**

The Medical Information Bureau is a source of underwriting information focusing on the applicant's medical history. Member insurance companies support the Bureau. (p. 7)

#37. **b) He would be covered under his employer's group health insurance plan without higher premiums.**

Because the insured was hired for a full-time job, he would be eligible for his employer's group health insurance plan. (pp. 79-80)

#38. **c) 6 months.**

While the insurance provider can defer requests for other loans for up to six months, loan requests for payment of due premiums must be honored immediately. (p. 33)

#39. **c) Business profession**

Competent parties to a contract must be of legal age, clearly understand the contract, be mentally competent, and not be under the influence of alcohol or drugs. (p. 2)

#40. **a) A percentage of the policy's face amount**

A viator typically receives a percentage of the policy's face value from the person who buys the policy. The new policy owner maintains the premium payments and will eventually collect the full death benefit. (p. 46)

#41. **a) Fixed**

Fixed annuities offer payments that do not vary from one payment to the next. (p. 22)

#42. **a) Countersignature.**

Insurance contracts are legally binding, and they all contain four essential elements. Countersignature is not a necessary part of a contract. (p. 2)

#43. **a) Basic and major medical coverage.**

The corridor deductible is applied between the basic and major medical policies. (p. 69)

#44. **a) Owner of the original life policy.**

In a life settlement, the term owner refers to the life insurance policy owner who seeks to enter into a life settlement contract. (pp. 8-9, 46-47)

#45. **d) Qualified**

The owner of a qualified retirement plan is entitled to tax benefits. For a retirement plan to be qualified, it must meet specific federal requirements. (pp. 48-49)

#46. **b) Insurer.**

Health insurance applications require the signatures of the proposed insured, the policy owner (if different than the insured), and the producer or agent. (p. 62)

#47. **a) She will not collect anything**

In this scenario, the insured did not satisfy the elimination period and will not collect anything. (p. 74)

#48. **a) It does not have a guaranteed death benefit.**

Ordinary (Straight) Life is a basic policy that charges a level annual premium for the insured's lifetime and provides a guaranteed, level death benefit. (p. 16)

#49. **b) January 1st through March 31st every year**

The general enrollment period for Medicare Part B is January 1st through March 31st. (p. 101)

#50. **c) Automatic Premium Loan option**

When the premium is not paid and the policy reaches the end of the grace period, with the automatic premium loan option, the insurer can borrow the premium from the cash value as a loan to prevent the policy from lapsing. (p. 33)

#51. **d) Children's term rider**

The children's term rider lets children be added to the insured's coverage for a specified amount for a limited time. (p. 35)

#52. **d) The applicant**

It is required by law that an insurance provider informs the applicant of all sources that will be contacted to determine the applicant's insurability and how the insurer will gather the information. (p. 63)

#53. **c) Consideration must be equal on the part of both the insurance provider and the insured**

Consideration is a prerequisite to a valid contract but does not necessarily have to be equal. (pp. 2, 30)

#54. **d) To state what and how much is covered in the plan**

Some medical expense insurance plans include a benefit schedule, explicitly stating what is covered in the plan and how much. (p. 93)

#55. **b) Cross out the incorrect answer, write the correct one beside it, and add their initials next to the new answer**

There are two ways to correct a mistake on an application. The first and best option is to start over with a new application. If that is not practical, draw a line through the wrong answer and enter the correct one. The applicant must initial the right answer. (p. 62)

#56. **d) Continue to increase.**

The new policy continues to build its cash value and will remain effective until maturity or the insured's death. (p. 38)

#57. **b) 90 days**

Policy owners must file a proof of loss within 90 days of loss. In cases of continuing loss, within 90 days after the end of a period for which the insurance provider is liable. (p. 89)

#58. **c) Individuals with low assets and low income.**

Medicare is a federal program for individuals over 65, on Social Security for two years, and individuals with permanent kidney failure. (p. 98)

#59. b) Skilled care

Skilled nursing care is daily nursing and rehabilitative care that can only be delivered by medical personnel under the direction of a physician. Skilled care is almost always delivered in an institutional setting. (p. 78)

#60. a) Conditional Receipt

The most common receipt is a conditional receipt, only used when the applicant turns in a prepaid application. (pp. 5, 62, 88)

#61. c) Annuitant

The annuitant is the individual whose life the annuity income amount is calculated. (p. 21)

#62. c) An association of 35 people.

Group insurance can be issued to the employer, employee, or groups formed for a purpose other than obtaining insurance. Associations must have at least 100 members. (pp. 79, 154)

#63. d) Premium mode.

Premium payment mode refers to the frequency at which the policy owner pays the premium. (p. 32)

#64. b) Preferred Provider plan.

Under a preferred provider plan, the insurance company has contracted with specific providers to deliver services at a certain rate. When an insured chooses treatment from another provider who does not have a contract with the insured, the coinsurance rate could be decreased, with the insured paying a higher percentage of the charges. (pp. 70-71)

#65. c) It provides the agent's observations about the proposed insured

The Agent's Report provides the agent's observations regarding the proposed insured. Although it is a part of the application process, the Agent's Report does not become a part of the entire contract. (pp. 4, 6)

#66. b) Copay.

A copayment or copay is a specific dollar amount or percentage of the cost of care that the member must pay. For example, the HMO member may have to pay $5 or $10 for each office visit. (p. 70)

#67. d) The premium will remain level for ten years.

Level premium term insurance provides a level premium and a level death benefit during the policy term. When the policy renews at the end of a certain period, the premium will be adjusted to the insured's age at renewal. (p. 14)

#68. b) All additional provisions written by insurance providers are cataloged by their respective states

Every health insurance policy must include Uniform Mandatory Provisions. These specific provisions are required to be in every health insurance contract. Insurers can add provisions that do not conflict with the uniform provisions if approved by the state where the policy is delivered. These additional provisions are not cataloged. (p. 90)

#69. c) To cover decreased business revenues as a result of a key employee's death

The business is indemnified for the loss of earnings that the key employee would have been responsible for until the company hires and trains a replacement. (p. 53)

#70. **a) Survivor protection**

Life insurance can provide the necessary funds for survivors to maintain their lifestyle if the insured dies. This concept is known as survivor protection. (p. 52)

#71. **a) Named beneficiary.**

When an annuitant dies during the accumulation period, the insurer will pay annuity benefits to the named beneficiary, provided a beneficiary is named in the annuity. (p. 21)

#72. **c) Drug addiction.**

Treatment for alcohol and drug addiction is delivered on a limited basis. (pp. 70, 92)

#73. **b) Two years**

The Time Limit on Certain Defenses provision is similar to the Incontestability provision in life insurance policies. No statement or misstatement (except for any fraudulent misstatements) made on the application at the time of issue can be used to deny a claim after the policy has been effective for two years. (p. 89)

#74. **a) The agent**

The agent must ensure that every question is answered and all required signatures are collected on the application. (p. 62)

#75. **b) It becomes part of the entire contract**

If the policy is issued, a copy of the application is stapled to the back of the policy. It becomes a part of the entire contract. (p. 62)

#76. **a) Joint Life has a lower premium than the total of the two individual policies**

A Joint Life policy has a lower premium than the total premium of two individual life policies of the same amount on the same insureds. (p. 20)

#77. **d) Paying a claim**

The binding force in any contract is called consideration. The insured's consideration is the payment of premiums and the health representations in the application. The insurance provider's consideration is the promise to pay in the event of a loss. (pp. 2, 30, 90)

#78. **d) Believed to be true to the best of the applicant's knowledge.**

Representations are statements an insurance applicant believes to be true to their knowledge. (p. 3)

#79. **b) A waiver of premium rider.**

The Waiver of Premium rider causes the insurance provider to waive future premiums if the premium payer is disabled for six months or more. (pp. 35, 91)

#80. **c) Submit the description in their own words on a plain sheet of paper**

Insureds can submit the description in their own words on plain paper if a proper form is not provided. This mandatory provision is in every individual health insurance policy. (p. 89)

#81. **b) A warranty**

Warranties are considered something guaranteed to be true or a statement of fact. A breach of warranty is considered grounds for voiding the policy. (p. 3)

#82. **c) The purchase of a new home.**

Guaranteed Insurability Riders allow policy owners to buy additional insurance without providing proof of insurability at marriage, a child's birth, and approximately every three years between the ages of 25 and 40. (p. 36)

#83. **c) The insurance provider does not have the right to conduct an autopsy**

The insurance provider usually has the right to conduct an autopsy if state law does not allow it. (p. 89)

#84. **b) Complications from pregnancy**

Usually, disability income policies do not cover losses caused by military service, war, overseas residence, intentionally self-inflicted injuries, or injuries suffered while committing or attempting to commit a felony. (p. 75)

#85. **d) Revocable**

Policy owners can change a revocable beneficiary at any time. (p. 31)

#86. **c) Mental illness.**

The lifetime benefit for major medical coverage typically limits the amount payable for mental or emotional disorders. The benefit is commonly a separate lifetime benefit, and there usually is a limit on the number of outpatient visits per year. (p. 92)

#87. **a) Insurance application**

The insurance application is the primary source of information that an insurance company uses to evaluate an insured's risk for life insurance. (p. 3)

#88. **a) 100% of eligible employees have to participate.**

In a noncontributory group policy, 100% of eligible employees must participate in the group plan. (p. 48)

#89. **a) Key person disability income**

Key person disability income covers losses resulting from the disability of its top employee. (p. 76)

#90. **a) Private Duty Nursing**

Medicare Part A services do not include private duty nursing. (pp. 99-101)

#91. **a) The agent's**

It is the agent's responsibility to ensure that the application for health insurance is accurate and complete. (p. 4)

#92. **a) Not taxable because they are a return of unused premiums.**

Dividends received on participating life insurance policies are not taxable because they are a return of unused premiums. (p. 54)

#93. **a) Being permanently disabled**

Being permanently disabled would not trigger the payment of accelerated death benefits. (pp. 34-35)

#94. **b) Within 60 days.**

The free look period starts when the policy is delivered. It is commonly ten days from the policy's delivery date but can vary for different policies. Most states mandate this provision for individual policies. (pp. 80-81)

#95. **b) Within ten days of when the policy was delivered**

The free look period starts when the policy is delivered. It is commonly ten days from the date the policy is delivered but can vary for different policies. Most states mandate this provision for individual policies. (p. 90)

#96. **c) Only if the person is not identified**

Insurers are required to maintain strict confidentiality regarding HIV-related test results or diagnoses. The MIB cannot receive test results if the individual is identified. (p. 63)

#97. d) The application contains material misstatements

An insurer can contest the payment of a claim based on a material misstatement of facts or concealment of a material fact within the first two years after the policy became effective. (p. 33)

#98. c) Subrogation.

Claims should be paid only once and by the liable party. The insurance provider pays the policy and has the right to try to be repaid by the party who made the loss occur. (p. 117)

#99. c) Either term insurance or permanent insurance.

Adjustable life was created to offer the policy owner the best of both worlds (term and permanent coverage). An adjustable life policy can take the form of either term insurance or permanent insurance. (p. 17)

#100. b) Whole life without proof of insurability.

When an employer terminates a member's membership in a group, they can convert to whole life insurance without providing proof of insurability. (p. 48)

#101. b) Within 20 days

This mandatory provision requires the insured to provide the insurer or its agent with a written notice of a claim as soon as possible or within 20 days of the loss. (p. 88)

#102. a) Premium mode.

The premium mode is the manner and frequency of the policy owner's premium payments. (p. 32)

#103. a) Premium payment period

Just like straight life, a limited-pay whole life policy endows for the face amount if the insured lives to age 100. In 20-pay whole life, coverage is completely paid for in 20 years. (p. 16)

#104. c) Unlimited coverage for drug rehabilitation treatment

Emergency care must be provided for the member in or out of the HMO's service area. The HMO also includes inpatient hospital care, in or out of the service area. The services can be limited when treating mental, emotional, or nervous disorders, including drug or alcohol rehabilitation or treatment. (p. 70)

#105. c) HMO Act of 1973

The main goal of the HMO Act of 1973 was to lower the cost of health care by utilizing preventive care. (p. 69)

#106. b) Family

With a family deductible, expenses for two or more family members can satisfy a standard deductible in a given year, irrespective of the costs incurred by other family members. (p. 92)

#107. b) Accumulation period

The accumulation period is a term that denotes the time during which the owner makes premium payments, which then earn tax-deferred interest. (p. 21)

#108. d) Universal Life

The generic name of Flexible Premium Adjustable Life is Universal Life. The policy owner can increase the premium amount going into the policy and later decrease it again. (pp. 17-18)

#109. **b) Nonforfeiture values.**

Because a permanent life insurance policy has cash value, specific guarantees are built into the policy that the policyholder cannot forfeit. These guarantees are known as nonforfeiture values and are required by state law to be part of the policy. Insurers must provide a table showing the nonforfeiture values in the policy for a minimum of 20 years. (p. 16)

#110. **b) Extended-term**

Under the extended-term option, the insurance provider uses the policy's cash value to convert to term insurance for the exact face amount as the previous permanent policy. (pp. 38-39)

#111. **a) Without a written examination.**

The Commissioner can issue a temporary agent's license to an applicant under consideration for appointment as an agent by another agent, an insurer, or a health maintenance organization (HMO) without a written examination. (p. 127)

#112. **b) Guaranteed renewable.**

All long-term care policies or certificates issued in Texas must be guaranteed renewable or noncancelable. (p. 153)

#113. **b) The Insurance Fraud Unit of the Texas Department of Insurance**

When a person suspects a fraudulent insurance act has been committed, they must report the information in writing to the Department's Insurance Fraud Unit within 30 days. (p. 134)

#114. **b) Solicitation of insurance cannot be associated with the federal government**

Insurers cannot use any combination of words or symbols similar to those of state or federal government agencies if they may imply that the advertisement is associated with a government agency. (p. 142)

#115. **d) Unfair discrimination**

Discrimination regarding rates, premiums, or policy benefits for individuals within the same class or with the same life expectancy is illegal. (p. 133)

#116. **a) They are not taxable and are not guaranteed**

Dividends are a return of excess premiums. They are not taxable and are not guaranteed. (p. 123)

#117. **d) Grace period**

The grace period protects the policy owner against an unintentional policy lapse. If the insured dies during this period, the death benefit is payable; however, the unpaid premium will be subtracted from the death benefit. (p. 145)

#118. **d) Offering an inducement of something of value not stated in the policy**

Rebating is offering anything of value not stated in the policy as an inducement to buy insurance. (p. 133)

#119. **c) 60 days**

Upon receipt of written proof of death and the claimant's right to the proceeds, the insurer must pay death claims within 60 days after due proof of the insured's death. (p. 136)

#120. **c) Indemnity**

Indemnity health insurance plans, or first-dollar insurance, do not require insureds to meet a deductible before providing benefits. (p. 162)

#121. **d) 180 days.**

The Commissioner can issue a temporary agent license in Texas for 180 days. (p. 127)

#122. **a) Testimonials used in advertisements may or may not apply to the advertised policy**

Testimonials must be genuine, accurately reproduced, and represent the author's opinion. If the individual is compensated, the testimonial must include "Paid Endorsement." (p. 142)

#123. **b) Alien**

An insurance company incorporated in a foreign country is considered an alien insurer. (p. 123)

#124. **b) Six**

Texas Health Maintenance Organizations cannot charge a fee for immunizing children from birth through age six. (p. 162)

#125. **b) The other party is licensed for the same lines of insurance as the agent sharing the commission.**

A licensed agent or insurer conducting business in Texas cannot pay commissions to a person or corporation unless they hold a valid agent's license for the same line of insurance. (pp. 134-135)

#126. **c) Premium rates**

Medicare supplement policies must include a continuation or renewal provision that is appropriately captioned and on the first page of the policy. They must also contain a provision allowing the insurance provider to change premiums and implement automatic renewal premium increases based on the policy owner's age (attained age policies). (p. 153)

#127. **a) Life insurance illustration.**

An illustration used in the sale of a life insurance policy has to include a label stating "life insurance illustration." (p. 143)

#128. **a) Guaranteed renewable**

Each Medicare supplement policy is required to be at least guaranteed renewable. (p. 153)

#129. **b) Individuals receiving Medicaid are not eligible**

Under ACA, states can extend Medicaid to individuals under 138% of the poverty level. People on public coverage programs like Medicaid are not eligible for the health care tax credit. (p. 156)

#130. **b) A nonresident license in that state.**

It is not illegal to sell insurance to customers in another state or commonwealth as long as an agent has a nonresident license in that state. Nonresident licenses are available without an exam since they are based on reciprocal agreements between states or commonwealths. (p. 127)

#131. **a) Early detection through regular checkups.**

Health Maintenance Organizations seek to identify medical issues by early detection through regular checkups. (p. 164)

#132. **c) 24**

Licensees must complete 24 hours of continuing education (CE) every two years, including at least three hours of ethics. (p. 129)

#133. **d) 31 days**

A newborn is covered without notification to the insurance provider from birth. The insured has to notify the insurance provider within 31 days of delivery. (p. 152)

#134. **a) Conversion needs to occur within 31 days**

Those covered under a group policy for at least five years must apply for an individual policy and pay the first premium to the insurance provider within 31 days after membership in a group plan terminates. (p. 146)

#135. **a) Stock insurers issue nonparticipating policies and are owned by the shareholders**

Stock companies owned by shareholders generally issue nonparticipating policies. Policy owners do not share in losses or profits. (p. 123)

#136. **a) Mutual insurer.**

Mutual companies issue participating policies and are owned by the policy owners. (p. 123)

#137. **d) Considering the time value of money in comparing life insurance costs**

The interest-adjusted net cost method considers the time value of money when comparing life insurance costs by applying an interest adjustment to yearly premiums and dividends. Interest is considered for every year that premiums and dividends are figured. (pp. 143-144)

#138. **c) 75%**

Coverage under a small employer group plan is available if 75% of the eligible employees elect to be covered. (p. 154)

#139. **a) The insurance provider issuing a policy**

The insurance provider issuing a policy is considered the principal. (p. 122)

#140. **c) Certificate of Authority.**

Except for surplus lines insurers, insurers must acquire a Certificate of Authority from the Department of Insurance to transact insurance in this state. (p. 123)

#141. **b) Within 31 days of birth**

The insured must notify the insurance provider of a newborn child and make any additional payments within 31 days. (p. 152)

#142. **a) Benefits provided must be the same as those for any other physical illness**

Regarding coverage for drug and alcohol addiction treatment in group health insurance policies issued in Texas, the benefits provided have to be the same as for any other physical illness. (p. 152)

#143. **d) It contracts with independent groups of physicians to provide medical services to subscribers**

A network-model HMO has contracts with two or more independent groups of physicians to deliver medical services to its subscribers. (p. 162)

#144. **a) Fraternal insurer.**

A fraternal benefit society is required to operate for the benefit of its members and their beneficiaries. (p. 123)

#145. **b) An agent returning part of her commission to her client as an inducement to buy**

Returning part of a commission to a client as an inducement to buy is considered rebating. Controlled business involves selling insurance primarily to oneself, their family, and friends. Misrepresenting policy provisions or coverages at issue is an unfair claims practice. Requiring an insured to buy insurance as a loan condition is coercion. (p. 133)

INDEX

A NOTE FROM LELAND

What did you think of *Texas Life and Health Insurance License Exam Prep*?

First of all, thank you for purchasing this study guide. I know you could have picked any resource to help prepare for your Life and Health exam, but you chose this book, and I am incredibly grateful.

I hope the book added value to your studies and gave you the confidence to pass the exam on your first attempt. If you feel this book adequately prepared you and helped you pass the exam, I'd like to hear from you. I hope you can take some time to post a review on Amazon and include a screenshot of your passing score. Your feedback and support will help this author improve this book and his writing craft for future projects.

Thank you again, and I wish you all the best in your future success!

Leland Chant

Made in the USA
Coppell, TX
31 January 2025

45231022R00164